Praise for *Twelve Stones*

Wherever your spiritual journey takes you, it is not complete until you read *Twelve Stones*, a most unorthodox journey to faith. Barbara Carole creates drama and immediacy in telling this very personal story about tough times, triumph and the discovery of new dimensions. It is the story of a truly unstoppable woman. I love the *Twelve Stones* message!

Cynthia Kersey
Author of *Unstoppable!* a *Publisher's Weekly* bestseller

David had five stones to get Goliath, Joshua had twelve stones to show the saving power of God, and now you will know why and how you can use them to create miracles in your own life. Happy reading!

Mark Victor Hansen
Co-author of *Chicken Soup for the Soul*

Barbara Carole's gripping account, *Twelve Stones*, reads like a self-performed open-heart surgery. For me, it resembles a candidly frank, modern version of Augustine's *Confessions*, in the feminine gender. This is one of those rare books that, once read, lingers in memory until it has been thoroughly pondered.

Don Richardson
Author of *Peace Child, Lords of the Earth* and *Eternity in Their Hearts*

Twelve Stones takes you on a mesmerizing journey, stopping at points of call that may be romantic, tragic, even funny—but each giving insight into the heart of meaning itself. Whatever your spiritual path may be, ultimately this immensely readable book proves that each individual life matters.

Kim Pearson
Author of *Making History: How to Remember, Record, Interpret and Share the Events of Your Life*

Twelve Stones

A MEMOIR

Twelve Stones

NOTES *on a* MIRACULOUS JOURNEY

Barbara Carole

Regal

From Gospel Light
Ventura, California, U.S.A.

Published by Regal
From Gospel Light
Ventura, California, U.S.A.
www.regalbooks.com
Printed in the U.S.A.

Library of Congress Cataloging-in-Publication Data
Carole, Barbara.
Twelve stones : notes on a miraculous journey / Barbara Carole.
p. cm.
ISBN 978-0-8307-4606-4 (hard cover)
1. Carole, Barbara. 2. Christian biography. I. Title.
BR1725.C243A3 2008
277.3'082092—dc22
[B]
2008025134

1 2 3 4 5 6 7 8 9 10 / 15 14 13 12 11 10 09

Rights for publishing this book outside the U.S.A. or in non-English languages
are administered by Gospel Light Worldwide, an international not-for-profit ministry.
For additional information, please visit www.glww.org, email info@glww.org, or write
to Gospel Light Worldwide, 1957 Eastman Avenue, Ventura, CA 93003, U.S.A.

*And Joshua set up at Gilgal the twelve stones they had taken
out of the Jordan. He said to the Israelites, "In the future when
your descendants ask their fathers, 'What do these stones mean?'
tell them, 'Israel crossed the Jordan on dry ground.' For the Lord
your God dried up the Jordan before you until you had crossed
over. The Lord your God did to the Jordan just what he had done
to the Red Sea when he dried it up before us until we had crossed
over. He did this so that all the peoples of the earth might know
that the hand of the Lord is powerful and so that you might always fear the Lord your God."*

JOSHUA 4:20-24

*The God who did miracles to lead His people
to the Promised Land did no less for me.
This book is my altar of twelve stones.
I write to remember and to honor what God has done.*

*The story told to you in this book is true. I write, not as a spinner
of tales, but as one driven to share the greatness of God's love.
The characters, places and incidents recounted are not
products of the author's imagination (of which I have very little),
but they bear a striking resemblance to those in my life,
because they are real. However, names of the characters have been
changed to protect the privacy of the not-so-innocent.
And to protect me from their wrath!*

Contents

Prologue

O my soul, it is not only after the future thou must aspire; thou must aspire to see the glory of thy past. Thou must find the glory of that way by which thy God has led thee, and be able even of thy sorrow to say, "This was the gate of heaven!"

GEORGE MATHESON (1842–1906)

"What's a nice Jewish girl like you doing in a place like this?" My pastor smiled as he asked the question in preparation for my baptism. I had heard that question dozens of times from less friendly quarters: "How could someone like you become a Christian?" or "How can an intelligent woman believe such nonsense?"

I looked out over the pews. How, in just a few minutes, could I convey to these smiling parishioners the immensity of what had brought me to my knees? They could probably never understand how uncomfortable it was for a Jew to be confronted with Christianity.

My mind flashed back, remembering . . .

To be Jewish and believe in Jesus was unacceptable. Impossible. It meant giving up who I was. I *liked* being Jewish. I had no desire to give up my rich heritage, my culture. "Jewish" was our peculiar sense of humor, our love of music and dance, our holiday foods and candlelight rituals. It was the soothing sound of my grandparents' Yiddish around a Passover table and the expressive affection of relatives. A Jewish household was warmth . . . comfort.

The kind people in this church probably didn't know that in the Jewish community, the word "Christianity" is synonymous with hatred and persecution. The very name of "Jesus" stirs terror in the Jewish heart. Genetic fear cries out, "Remember the Inquisition . . . the pogroms. Remember all that was done to us *in the name of Christ*." So whatever spiritual paths and teachings I had explored, I'd have never—*never!*—imagined accepting Christianity.

Even the concept of a fatherly God seemed to be a fairy tale for the feeble-minded and the weak at heart. Intelligent, thinking people understood that humans invented God to escape the brutal reality of life. One had to be courageous and self-sufficient—tough enough to deal with life on its own terms.

That was my state of mind when I left the university at the age of 18 to explore foreign lands and seek like-minded people who asked penetrating questions. At 20, I married Stephen, an artist who shared the intensity of my quest and who was equally exhilarated by the thrill of the unpredictable.

Stephen. His name opens a floodgate of memories. Together we worshiped at the altar of art and romance, striving to recreate the essence of existence and make every moment a masterpiece. We greeted each new day with energy—writing and painting in the hidden garrets of Paris, in the Roman ruins of south-central France, in Moroccan villages and in the sunlight of southern California. We embraced the drama of life, danced to its music and inhaled deeply the fragrance of its flowers. Stephen and I thought we had all the answers, and we gloried in our brilliance.

We were wrong. In my ill-fated marriage, and the relationships that followed, I was always attracted to the wrong kind of love. Conventional marriage held no appeal for me. I turned away repeatedly from opportunities to marry a "good, solid man," the kind my mother recommended. I was drawn instead to those who offered artistic and intellectual adventure but who were incapable, ultimately, of wholesome love. This is not a modern issue; the Bible is full of stories about calamitous affairs, such as Samson's intoxication for Delilah, or David's for Bathsheba. Much like an addiction to alcohol or drugs, the need for passion can be a form of bondage. In the wrong situation, it can be positively satanic.

That bondage brought me to a low, low point, one that is painful even to recall. But in that low place was a remarkable discovery that compulsions can be turned off, as one shuts down an electrical current with the instant flick of a switch. In my life, that switch was the Holy Spirit of God.

Facing the waiting parishioners, I cleared my throat and tried to explain. "I've wrestled against God for many years. So if God wanted me—and for reasons I'll never understand, He did—He had to work miracles." (I did not use the term lightly: God worked breathtaking "miracles" to turn me from a life that was . . . well, somewhat unorthodox.)

"In my fortieth year, having experienced a series of traumatic losses, it became important to find out who—and *if*—God was. I needed to know. 'God,' I said, feeling very awkward, 'if You exist, show Yourself. Provide a signpost I cannot mistake, a sign pointing my way to You. If there is no sign, I won't be surprised. But if that sign appears, I will follow where You guide.' I prayed for the sign, more as a spiritual exercise than an expectation, on several occasions.

"One early Saturday morning in spring, I was hiking in a nearby canyon with my friend Susan. Nothing strange about that. We'd been hiking that same canyon every Saturday for years; I still do. But I had no idea, on that particular day, that I was traveling the road to Damascus.

"As we climbed the hill, Susan pointed, startled, at an animal in our path. It was a goat, a black one. We climbed higher, and there before us was another goat, a white one. Then another. When we reached the crest and looked down over the other side of the hill, we saw a whole herd of goats—hundreds of them!

"Susan and I looked at one another. *Goats?* Out here in the canyon? All the times we'd walked out here, there'd never been any goats.

"We started toward the grazing animals, then stopped when we saw the goatherd. Who has seen a goatherd lately? What was a goatherd supposed to look like? Well, this fellow seemed to have stepped off the pages of a nineteenth-century storybook. He wore a wide-brimmed straw hat and carried a staff with a crook on the end. Under his arm was a big Bible. No kidding—a Bible. Susan is a secular intellectual individual, and not given to 'visions.' But she was there, and she saw him too.

" 'Susan, we've got to talk to this guy and see what he's about,' I said. We took the path toward him and, after a polite exchange of greetings, asked about the herd. The goatherd seemed pleased to have our company and talk. He explained the differences between grazing goats and milking goats and how you train the dogs. We must have been chatting about half an hour when I couldn't resist asking, 'Why do you carry that Bible with you?'

"He smiled and opened it. Words spilled out of his mouth—something about Isaiah, prophecies . . . I don't remember what he said. I didn't understand it. He could have been speaking Swahili for all I knew. And yet I couldn't stop listening. He quoted Scripture passages on and on like he'd never stop. Something about the sound of the words had me spellbound.

"Susan tugged on my arm. 'C'mon, let's get out of here.' But I couldn't tear myself away. He kept discoursing about his God, and the Bible, and all these things I didn't understand. Susan kept urging me to leave. Our morning was warming into noon. In deference to my friend, I told the goatherd, 'I'm sorry, we have to go. Thank you for telling me all this.' All what? What had he been talking about, and what did it mean?

"The goatherd looked intently and steadily at me with sun-blazing blue eyes. Then, though his words were spoken softly, I felt as if he'd dropped a bomb. Unblinking, kind of half smiling, he said, 'I had to come. I had to tell you. You prayed for it.' "

I'd have been glad to dismiss the goatherd as an apparition or hallucination, but he was all too real. He launched me on a journey—not a journey I would have chosen, and not even one I liked, but one that eventually brought me to my knees before almighty God.

It took a long time, and many more miracles, to overcome the rebellion of my reason and the roots of my Jewish heritage. Still, it caused me to wonder: Is this what happens when you pray? Goatherds appear in broad daylight and talk gibberish? Was he really a goatherd? Some say he was possibly an angel. *What might happen,* I wondered, *if I were to pray* again?

Stranger on the Earth

You do not belong to the world.

JOHN 15:19

I am a stranger on earth.

PSALM 119:19

. . . as aliens and strangers in the world . . .

1 PETER 2:11

My name, "Barbara," comes from a Greek word meaning "stranger" or "foreigner." Could my parents have foreseen that I was born on the wrong planet, among people I'll never understand? No place is home. I often wonder how I got here in the first place. And why.

I have a younger sister to fight with; my parents have each other. They are two wonderful people but, alas, of very different temperaments. Mom rises early at dawn; Dad stays up through the night. Mom is, shall we say, "relaxed" about her housekeeping; Dad is orderly. Mom is spontaneous and impulsive; Dad examines every angle, every contingency, before taking a step. Sometimes he's so careful that he doesn't take the step. But my parents do share strong ethical values, like honesty and kindness. They are good people—just not good for each other.

I don't have many friends. I'm too plump, too shy, my hair and clothes aren't right. We are the only Jewish family in an Italian Catholic neighborhood. The kids on the street call me "Christ-killer."

I am five years old and it is bedtime. Mom says not to wait up for Daddy. "He'll be home too late—not until ten or eleven." But I always wait.

My room is dark. From my bed I watch stripes of light slide across the wall when a car goes by on the street below. The headlight swooshes through venetian blinds from the window to the door. I wait. Swoosh. Many silent moments later: swoosh. At last, the click of the front door. He's home! Soon I'll hear his step in the hall. He'll stop at my room and open the door a crack.

"You awake, little girl?"

"Yes, Daddy."

He sits on the edge of my bed. "Scooch over."

Sometimes, when he comes home from work, Daddy tells stories about people in countries far away. Fascinating countries. One day, when I grow up, I'm going to see them.

"Where shall we go tonight, Daddy?"

"How 'bout Paris? Today's the fourteenth of July and people are dancing in the streets."

"How come?"

"Well, once there was a queen of France. Her name was Marie Antoinette. This queen was very spoiled; she couldn't understand what it meant to be poor. And her people were starving. Her counselor, falling to his knees, pleaded with her to do something about it. 'Please, Your Majesty,' he wailed, 'the people have not even *bread*!'

"But Marie Antoinette didn't understand the urgency. 'No bread?' she murmured, trying to decide between ruby earrings or the sapphire. 'Well then, let them eat cake.' At that, mobs of hungry, angry people stormed the palace, and the French Revolution began."

I love my daddy's stories. And I like to look at him, too, 'cause Daddy's handsome. He has beautiful dark eyes with thick lashes, black wavy hair and, of course, the mustache. I've never seen Daddy without a mustache; it's part of him.

Sometimes we talk about being Jewish. I tell him that kids in the neighborhood make fun of me. They hate me because I killed Jesus. "I didn't kill Jesus, Daddy, did I?"

"No, of course not." He strokes my hair. "They don't know what they're talking about."

"But the Church told them!"

"Just because it's the Church doesn't mean it's right. Remember that. You should question everything . . . everyone. Always seek truth for yourself." Daddy says be proud of being Jewish. He never lets me attend school on Yom Kippur or Rosh Hashanah.

"I can't get a gold star for attendance, 'cause you make me miss three days every year," I complain.

"Jews have worn gold stars that got them killed," he replies. "If you go to school on the high holy days, people will think you're ashamed of being

Jewish. Be proud of your people, not the silly star."

Daddy tells me stories about what happened in Germany, and it's like I'm there. "Even schoolteachers had to follow the Nazi program," he says. "Students spied on their parents. Can you imagine? They listened for whispered conversations and reported anything said at home that might be anti-Hitler. The kids who brought in reports were rewarded. Then their parents disappeared."

I try to imagine it.

"And Jewish kids had a hard time getting through the streets to school without getting hit by rocks. Often the doors to their homes were battered down as they slept, and they were ripped away into the night with their families, taking nothing, not even precious photos."

"Where did they go?"

"They were taken to railroad depots and shoved into cattle cars, squashed tightly against one another with no room to sit or lie down. Of course there were no toilets, and they had to relieve themselves standing where they were. They traveled many days in the freezing cold. Some were old. Some were pregnant. Some had back problems. Some lived through the journey to experience the camps; others didn't."

I am on the cattle car with them and I cannot breathe for the stench and the squeezing of cold, damp bodies on all sides of me.

"As the people arrived, Nazi soldiers separated the families. Young, sick and old people to the left; the strong ones who could work to the right."

"What happened to the people on the left line, Daddy? And the right line? Where did they go?"

"The left line went to 'shower rooms.' The soldiers ordered them to take showers and clean up, but they were led instead to chambers where they were again packed in tightly. Then gas pellets leaked poison through the venting system and put them to sleep.

"The 'lucky' ones on the right went into dormitories where cold wind whipped through broken slats. They slept . . ." (*Did they ever really sleep?* I wonder) " . . . without blankets, three to four on a frozen wooden slab.

"When dawn came, at about four o'clock in the morning, they had to stand, naked, in the snow for hours and hours during roll call. Anyone who complained of pain or fell down was shot instantly, right where they stood, between the others."

"Was it the same for the women?"

"The same and worse." Daddy looks away. For a minute I'm not sure he'll continue. Then he says, kind of whispering, "Doctors did medical experiments on the women with no anesthetic. They did it for 'science' they said, but I think they destroyed the insides of Jewish women so they couldn't have babies and propagate the race."

I stare, saucer-eyed, unable to comprehend such suffering. Daddy looks troubled. "Maybe I shouldn't be telling you this. But it is important to know what happened and pass it on. People must never forget."

I live the stories Daddy tells: the long death marches on torn feet, the work camps and whips, the factories where they'd make soap and lamp shades from the skins of our sisters and brothers. I see myself rushing down a manhole in the street, hiding with other Jews—three men, a woman, and an infant—in a sewer pipe, while Nazis tromp overhead. We hold our breath and dare not move a muscle. But suddenly, the baby starts to cry. We look at one another, certain this is our last moment before a horrible death. Frantic, the woman puts her hand over the baby's mouth. Silence. The troops eventually pass. Slowly, slowly, we let out our breath. We still don't dare move until sunlight gives way to dark. The baby is quiet. Unnaturally quiet. She is dead. Her mother's eyes roll up to heaven and her face contorts in a silent scream. She collapses.

I dream of the camps. Sometimes I am running away, terrified, through the woods. I hear the soldiers and barking dogs close behind.

As long as Daddy is here, I am okay. "Anxiety is a waste of your best energy," he always says. "The very thing you worry about can turn out to be the most exciting thing that ever happens to you. Be open to it."

Daddy has strong feelings about ethics, values and kindness; he hates cruelty. When kids in school make fun of someone handicapped, or act mean to an animal, he steps in and tells them that it's wrong. Daddy is tender with all God's creatures.

"Did God make us, Daddy? Do we believe in God? The boy across the street says if we don't believe in God, we'll go to hell."

"Right," Daddy says. "The Church controls people by scaring them. But you ask if there's a God?" He pauses a long while. "Look at a flower. Or the ecosystem of a lake. Most of all, look at our human bodies. Is there anything so marvelous? So complex? See how it is put together with such delicate intricacy?" He looks off into space. "It didn't come about by chance. I'm an engineer. I know *design* when I see it." Daddy is convinced our world was created by an intelligence so vast it brought the whole universe into being. At the same time, focused on infinitesimal details, the Intelligence created a unique design for every snowflake that falls, so tiny you need a microscope to see it.

Daddy reveres the natural world. On summer vacations in the country, we go together on long walks along the lakes and forests and waterfalls he loves so much.

Some nights, Daddy plays his ukulele or the accordion my uncle sent us when he was a soldier in Germany. Daddy can play almost anything. If he hears the music in his head, he can make it come out on an instrument. He says it's a gift from his mother who is a pianist. Other nights, he reads Shakespeare to me. He acts out all the parts and we have our own private theater.

Daddy shares lots of things with me, even about his job and the projects he's working on. "Maybe I'll grow up and be an engineer like you, Daddy. Can I invent things, too?"

"Not too many women are engineers, Cookie, but don't let that stop you. Reach for the moon. You can do anything you set your mind to."

"Did you reach for the moon, Daddy?"

He shrugs. "I had to quit college and go to work. We were in the Great Depression then. Nobody could get jobs, even if they had degrees. So college seemed useless. Instead, I got a job fixing radios."

Mom says Daddy is brilliant. "Jordan didn't get past the first year of college, but he developed antiballistic early warning systems during the war. Later he pioneered the development of television, and core memory systems for early computers. Now he's designing equipment to take photos of the moon."

I'm proud of him too. When Daddy has an idea for something, he doesn't understand the word "can't." He has no patience for it. "Too many engineers have no imagination. They say, 'It can't be done; there's no formula for that.' I say to them, 'Then invent the darn formula! Make it happen.'"

When Daddy says "reach for the moon," he means it. If you can't reach it from a ladder, he expects you to invent something to get you there. In a quiet way the world will never hear about, I think Daddy touched the moon.

I'm alone at the table because Daddy isn't home from work. Mom says because he always comes so late, she has no help at home. She's tired. Her belly is big with a new baby. She says the baby's coming soon.

She has cooked dinner (squash, ugh!) and put the plate in front of me. I pick at it. Mom tells me to eat, but I can't swallow. It sticks in my throat. The food gets cold and Mom gets mad. She yells. The plate of squash slams into my face. Then she drags me, screaming, and blinded by the squash in my eyes, to the bathroom to wash the food off my face.

Days pass and no one says anything about the squash. I hide from her in a deep, unmoving sleep that is like the blessing of death. Mom is shaking me awake. "Get dressed. Hurry, we have to catch the train."

"Where are we going? Why is it still dark outside?"

"You'll see." She pulls clothes on me, takes me down the stairs to the street and walks quickly, so quickly I run to keep up, until we reach the train station.

"Where are we going, Mom?" I need to know. It scares me not to know.

"Hush, be good." Mom doesn't want to tell. The train arrives, its windows yellow with the light inside the cars. We find a seat, and it's strange to see it crowded. Other people travel around the city before sunrise too?

At last we get off, climb stairs to the street and walk four blocks to a big building. It's not a nice building. Inside, plaster walls are green on the bottom half, white on top. We sit for a long time on a hard wooden bench until our name is called. Mom stands and leads me toward the elevator.

"Here we go," she says, guiding me through the door. When it closes, I am on the inside next to a lady wearing white. I look around for my mom. She is still outside and we are moving up. "Mom!" I scream. "Mom! Where's my mom?"

The lady next to me says, "Don't worry. Come with me."

"But my mom . . . I can't go without . . ." Oh, suddenly I get it. Mom is getting rid of me because I didn't eat my squash. She left me! Left me! I scream hysterically. The lady in white leads me to a little room, removes my clothes and lays me on a narrow table with only a thin cotton covering. She wheels my table into another, larger room where there are men and women, also in white, and machines. They are going to grind me up and throw me away.

"Can't you get her to stop screaming?" one of the men asks, annoyed.

The lady tries to cover my nose and mouth with a big rubber mask. I fight her with all my strength. It's a struggle, but she overpowers me. A great blackness comes down on my face. My screams echo in the distance, from a tunnel. Why? Why is Mom throwing me away? I disappear into the blackness.

Now it is daylight and I hurt. I am propped up in a bed, and Mom is sitting alongside. "You must stop crying now," she begs. "The surgery can't heal with all this crying."

"What's that, 'surgery'?" I ask between sobs.

"They took your tonsils out. Apparently, that's why you haven't been able to eat. Bad tonsils. Here, look." She holds a dish of ice cream toward me. "You can have this."

"Can I come home?" Mom turns the question toward a man in white who is approaching my bed. "Not today," he says. "Her screaming caused complications. Perhaps on Friday."

Mom gathers up her coat and purse. I panic. "Are you leaving me here?"

"I'll be back tomorrow. Be a good girl and don't cry anymore. Promise?"

"Are you going to take me home, Mom? I'll eat all my food."

"Of course I'll take you home. As soon as Doctor says you can leave the hospital."

Doctor? I'm in a hospital? Why had no one told me? It would have been okay if I had known. Why didn't someone tell me?

❦   ❦   ❦

We have a new baby sister in our house now: Julia May. She cries a lot. Mom says she has a sick tummy. She's worried about the baby and very busy with her all the time.

One morning, Mom gets me dressed and takes me on a bus to a tall brick building. I don't like these surprise trips. I pull back at the entrance, afraid. "No, no! I don't want to go."

She pulls me, resisting, up a long metallic staircase to the second floor. "Why is it always so difficult? Can't you go nicely like the other children?" She leads me down the long hall to a great big room full of kids my age, and brings me, still crying, to a lady who is writing with chalk on a blackboard. The lady nods. Mom releases my hand, waves good-bye and walks out of the room. I lunge after her. "Mommy! Mommy, don't leave me!"

The lady holds me back until Mom disappears. "Come, join the others," she says. "We're going to play a game."

I don't want to play a game. I want to know why my mom left me. I'm scared. I sit in a corner and cry the entire day until Mom comes to take me home. The lady waves good-bye and smiles. "See you tomorrow."

"I don't like it here. I'm never coming back."

"Don't be silly," Mom says. "This is kindergarten. You'll be coming back every day. It seems nice enough. You'll get used to it."

Mom and Dad are excited. "We're going to move out of this tiny apartment, out of the Bronx, into a house of our own on Long Island. When we got married, during the Great Depression, we never dreamed we could ever buy a house!"

The house has an attic to hide in and a basement and a big green lawn. Mom's planting tulips, daffodils and dogwood trees. Dad's building a verandah at the side door and a porch in front. And in the basement, he's building a recreation room with pinewood walls. "You girls can play down here with your friends," he says. The television and his old piano are down there too. In the attic, he's constructing a second bath and two really big bedrooms with sloping ceilings and dormer windows—one for Julia and one for me. Yea! We won't have to share anymore. Each of us gets to decorate our room any way we want. I want mine yellow. It's my secret, sunny sanctuary.

There's a girl next door: Camilla. She's beautiful, with long dark hair and big dark eyes. I'm glad she wants to play with me, because she's nine, two years older. She has a handsome teenage brother. He doesn't notice me. Her family is Italian, like everyone on our street. I spend a lot of time in their house, because I love their food. Mrs. Bondatelli asks, "Don't they feed you at home?" as Camilla and I help de-vein the shrimp. Mr. Bondatelli teaches me to read the Italian newspaper and pronounce the words.

Camilla and I act out make-believe fantasies of queens and princesses in great palaces (she's always the queen; I'm the commoner). When we come back to real life, she tells me I will go to hell because I'm not Catholic.

"How do I get to be Catholic?"

"Learn the catechism, go to church and take confession. Here . . ." she shoves a little book into my hand. "Read this and I'll quiz you next week." I take it home, but the crucified Jesus is kind of gory.

Mom sees me curled up on the sofa, grimacing at the book. "What are you doing?"

"Becoming Catholic, so I won't go to hell."

"Oh." She shrugs. "It's okay. You'll get over it."

When I finish the catechism, I bring it back to Camilla. "I don't understand it."

"That doesn't matter. You just have to memorize it. Let's see if you can answer the questions." She hands me one of the weekly quizzes from her Catholic school class. Struggling, I answer enough of them to satisfy her. "Good. Now come to church with me on Sunday."

The church of Saint Bernadette is intimidating. The solemn, black-veiled nuns and the organ-filled Gothic architecture are imposing. I don't understand the Latin any more than I understand the Hebrew in our synagogue. People stare at me. *She's Jewish*, I bet they're thinking. *What's she doing here?*

"Let's go," I nudge Camilla after mass.

"Don't you feel washed and cleansed?"

"No."

"You will. After your confession, you'll see."

Saturday next, Camilla marches me back to church. She leaves me sitting in the pew while she goes into one of the wooden cabinets at the rear of the sanctuary. A half-dozen people are scattered here, kneeling, their heads bowed on clasped hands. Candles burn along the side walls. One or two women take a candle and hold it fervently near their heart. Am I supposed to take a candle too? No one speaks. Silence—a huge, monstrous silence—fills the vast high-arched sanctuary.

Camilla slips back into the pew and whispers, "Your turn. Remember how I told you."

I walk slowly toward the back and open the confessional door. It creaks, echoing around the stone arches of Saint Bernadette. I sit on the wooden bench and wait for the priest to come. *Where will he sit*, I wonder. *There's no room in here at all.* The opposite wall, about nine inches from my nose, has a small opening, barely enough for a bird to get through. No one comes. I continue to wait, silent and nervous.

"Well, child? Have you come to confess?"

"Yes," I whisper. "Where are you?"

"Here. On the other side of the wall."

"I can't see you."

"Of course. Begin your confession now, daughter."

"Father, forgive me for I have sinned—" I stop.

"Yes?"

"I can't see you."

"You're not supposed to see me, child. Confess your sins to God."

"Are you listening in?"

"Yes."

"Then I need to see you. I need to see who knows my sins."

"I am not important. It only matters that God hears your confession."

Aha! "I think you're right," I whisper back. "I'm going home now. I can talk to God there." I leave the confessional and the Catholic church.

They are at it again. My stomach knots with anxiety as I slip downstairs to escape the sound of my parents arguing. Mom's voice is loud and shrill. "Keep it down, Alice, you'll frighten the kids," Dad says.

I huddle near the furnace in the basement of our suburban home, a house like many others on the street, with neat lawns all in a row. The unknown years of my future stretch out before me, and I shiver. Will my life be like Mom's? Marriage and children bring her no fulfillment; she makes no bones about it. I always knew from day one that my arrival brought her no joy: only diapers to change, meals to fix, more chores. *What, then, awaits me?* I wonder. Am I to grow up, marry someone I'll never really know, have noisy, demanding children in a square salt-box house on a nondescript street, and go to PTA meetings? Am I eventually to wave farewell at my children's weddings, visit noisy, demanding grandchildren, and then lay down to die?

I want more. I know from Daddy's stories that there can be more. Huddled at the basement furnace, I make a vow. I will travel to all the faraway places Daddy tells me about and live as many different stories as I can fit into a lifetime. I can be an international newspaper reporter in a sophisticated city like New York. Or a teacher in a country town. Maybe a courtesan in a royal court . . . a painter in the south of France . . . a biologist in Africa, or a business executive in California—whatever it takes to make living an adventure. Because in my last moments, when my tired eyes close heavily, I never want to say, "I wish I had . . ." I want to smile and say, "It is well. For I have truly lived and loved."

Our attic is a wonderful place to be alone and secret. Today I find a blue book-let of handwritten poems buried in a trunk under old clothes. I bring it down-stairs to my mother. "What's this, Mom? Who wrote it?"

Mom blushes. "That's mine. It was a long time ago. Put it away."

I climb back up to the attic; but before I return the poems to the trunk, I read them. Mom wrote these lovely, romantic odes, the dreams of a young girl's heart. And they are beautiful. Why had she buried them?

"Your dad is a good writer too," Mom tells me at dinnertime. "The Depres-sion forced him toward more practical work, but he's always loved great litera-ture and poetry."

"Like the plays he reads to me at night? The Shakespeare?" She smiles.

I stop at the public library nearly every day after school to devour novels and biographies. I read walking, eating, on the bus, in the car, at home, at school re-cess. I always read. At bedtime, Dad pokes his head into my room. "Lights out!" he says. "You need your sleep. The book will still be there tomorrow." I turn off the lamp next to my bed, take a flashlight from the nightstand drawer, and pull thick covers over my head to hide the beam as I continue reading *Forever Amber* far into the night. Amber is magnificent. Daring, courageous and ingen-ious, she lives by her wits as a beggar on the streets, then finds her way to riches and love in the palace of a prince. Amber experiences all the adventure that life has to offer. I want nothing less.

"Don't let her come here," Mom says to Daddy. "I never want to see her face or hear her voice again, do you hear?"

"Alice, be reasonable, she's my mother, after all."

"And I'm your wife. She's been critical and belittling of me for 12 years now. Nothing I do is right. I can't bear it."

"And you shouldn't have to." Daddy sighs. "This'll be hard, but I'll tell her. From now on, I'll take the kids over there. It's best she not come here again."

Too bad. Julia and I like to ask Grandma Kate what will happen. Everyone in the Bronx does too. They come from far away, Daddy says, to have her read the tarot cards. "She's the best fortune-teller in the city."

"Do you believe in fortune-telling, Daddy?"

"I'm a scientist, so I don't believe in it. Except that I grew up with her, and I can't deny what I've seen over and over again."

"She can really do it, huh, Daddy?"

"She can really do it, honey. Every time."

My grandmother, the black-haired, dark-eyed, musical Katherine, was born in Romania, the issue of a love affair between a young Gypsy boy and an English girl. She was raised in England and emigrated from there to New York as a young woman, carrying with her the music and the mysterious psychic powers of her father's people. I wonder, *Do I have enough Gypsy blood in me to see the future too?*

Katherine married a quiet, simple man, a Russian tailor whom she completely overran. Daddy loved his father. I do too. Grandpa tells stories about ghosts he saw in swirling snowstorms in the dark Russian nights. Daddy says Grandma is vain and selfish. "We had so little money, but she spent it all and more on fine clothes, cars, furniture—things to impress people. She didn't care about anyone but herself. I wanted to go to college and become a professor. She made me quit school and go to work."

"Did she work too?"

"She played the piano for the silent movies."

"Did she teach you to play?"

"She tried. But to spite her, I refused to learn to read music. Silly, wasn't it? But to this day, I can't read music notes; I just play by ear."

I walk a mile or so to school each day and back, often imagining my movements watched by angels or beings in another realm. Everything I do is observed. Not judged, just observed. Do they follow me into the bathroom and watch me sleeping through the night? And if my life is being watched, is everyone else's watched too? Does everyone know about this, or am I the only one? And which of our lives, among all of us on Earth, do the angels choose to watch? If they choose mine, will it be interesting enough? Does it have a surprise ending, or does it just peter out?

I have weekly piano lessons. While the student before me struggles through his discordant effort on the keyboard, the ponderous old German piano teacher makes me wait on a sofa stacked with horror comic books. I hate them, they give me nightmares, but they are better than watching Herr Schlactner tear at his remaining white hairs and shout, "Ach! *Nein!* You moost leren. Wenn you do not leren besser, I hang you von your pants" (he points to ominous hooks hanging from the ceiling) "und feed you limburger cheese!" I look up. Are the hooks up there for plants? Or does he really hang his students? Remembering his collection of horror comics, I shudder.

For Daddy, the piano in his basement "rec" room provides cherished moments of relaxation. But I don't have Daddy's gift. I hate the lessons with Herr Schlactner. I practice while Daddy hammers and saws in the attic, two stories above. When I hit a wrong note, it is painful on the perfect pitch of his well-tuned ears. "That's a B *flat*, dadblastit!" he shouts down, "B flat, not A!"

Ballet lessons are more fun. I take a bus to the other side of town, get off in front of the cathedral, and walk four blocks to the studio. There, in my leotard and toe shoes, I am magically transformed. I close my eyes and lift off the ground, dancing, dancing right up a moonbeam to the heart of the white mystery that lights the nighttime sky.

Once a month, Mom gives me $50, in addition to my bus fare, to pay the ballet teacher. Each time, she says, "Don't lose this. It's a *lot* of money. Whatever you do, don't lose it. And be sure to bring home the receipt." Does she think I'm a baby or something? I'm nine years old. I can handle it.

Today we are working on fouetté pirouettes ("*fouetté*" means "whipped"). I'm the only one in my class who can't do them. I get up on point, my right toe touching my left knee, poised to whip out and spin me around. I never go around. I go down. It's humiliating. But last night I had the dream. My left leg stretched tight and held me solid over my point. The right leg extended, perfectly parallel to the floor, whipped around and carried me, floating, weightless, with it. Around and around. I flew on a cloud, an intoxicating wind holding me safely straight and erect. I'm not afraid now when it's my turn. The fouetté is in me; I can *feel* it. I *know* it, my body knows. I'm ready. Yes! My fouetté is second to none. It's the most wonderful day of my life.

At the end of class, I reach into my pocket to pay the teacher. No $50. I pull the pocket inside out. No $50. The other pocket. Also empty. Beads of sweat moisten my upper lip. It must have spilled on the bus when I took out the quarter.

"It's okay," my teacher says, "you can bring it next week." Is she kidding? There won't *be* a next week. I'm not sure *I'll* be next week, after I tell Mom I lost $50. On the walk to the bus stop, my stomach cramps with panic. The bus arrives. I think of facing Mom and can't get on. I turn away and face the cathedral there at the stop. One of the doors is open, like an arm reaching out to me.

Cool, dark and immense, the sanctuary is empty. No nuns here, no priests, no people to stare and wonder why a Jew dares enter. I kneel to pray in a pew. To whom? The angels who watch me? No, there seems to be an even greater Presence here, greater than my imagination, greater than the entire world. The Presence fills the silence, humbles me, and gives peace to my spirit.

I will go home now and tell Mom about the money. She'll scream and yell, of course, and I'll be scared like I always am when she's mad, but right now it's okay. Here in the cathedral, Mom's anger seems unimportant. In the pregnant silence, I come close to a world beyond the one we hear and see and touch, a realm of forces and mysteries we do not understand. Under the cool, vast cathedral arches, I brush close to the Presence that rules. Just like when I dance on moonbeams and reach the starlit sky, I get a glimpse.

It's my tenth birthday. Mom and Daddy have been shopping. There they are, pulling up in the car. Mom opens the door and a streak of golden puppy fur shoots past her, bounding toward me as I stand at the door. A piercing thrill sucks the breath out of me. Tears run down my cheeks. I have always wanted a puppy. Since I can remember, I've begged for a pup. Holding him, feeling his tongue spread wet joy all over my face, I am ecstatic.

Dad and my little sister are in love with him. Mom likes him too, though she won't admit it. But Tippy is mine—my inseparable best friend, the beat of my heart. Except when I go to school, the fox terrier mutt is never more than a few inches from my feet. Together—when I ride my bike, play, watch television, do homework or sleep—always together. We sit for hours and hours, hidden in our secret place behind the garage, and I tell Tippy all my private thoughts—things I would tell a best friend, if I had one. For as long as I talk, Tippy sits patiently, cocking his head, first to one side, then to the other, and occasionally, if what I say is interesting enough, lifting an ear.

In the summer, when we are on vacation in New Hampshire, Daddy, Julia and I take a rowboat out on the lake. Tippy prances back and forth on the dock, excited. The two of us get into the rocking boat and Dad holds up a finger. "Stay, Tippy. You wait here." The wagging tail droops instantly; the head and ears go down. The boat pulls away from the dock, taking us from Tippy on an unfamiliar, moving surface. He whines and yelps and runs frantically back and forth, seeking help as we draw farther away. He dips a paw into the water and pulls back, frightened. His yelping gets louder. We row farther and farther away. He can stand it no longer. Torn between his fear of the cold, strange water and his terror of losing us, Tippy circles around one last frantic time for help that isn't there, then throws himself off the dock in desperate pursuit.

"Daddy! He's going to drown!"

We turn back and row toward him as hard as we can. "He won't drown; dogs know how to swim," Daddy assures me. But I can't be calmed until we reach the paddling pup and drag him, drenched and soaking, into the boat.

Licking and nuzzling until he assures himself we are safe, Tippy showers us with a mighty doggy shake to unload the water from his fur.

"Okay!" I hug him, laughing, "I learned my lesson. We'll never leave you again, Tippy. Never!"

He's fond of rowboats now; he comes with us every time we go out.

I take a summer job on the assembly line of an electrical parts factory. You're supposed to be 16. I'm only 14, but they don't press the point. It's hard, sitting in the high wire chairs all day long, making the same single motion to twist the wire around the loop before sending it down the line. If you're too fast, people behind you get mad. If you're too slow, you block the people in front. You have to find the right rhythm. Even so, by the end of the day, my back has stabbing pains.

Most of the people are from Puerto Rico. They say I have to join their union, and I can tell it's best not to disagree. It's okay; I'm learning a lot of Spanish. And the lady who sits opposite me, across the table, is really nice. Velma's got cream-'n'-coffee skin and a velvety voice. She's a Jehovah's Witness, and she speaks softly to me, all day long, about God and the Bible. I don't believe what she says, but I like the way she tells it. It's the most important thing in the world to her and somehow, in her life, it's beautiful. I don't mind listening.

At high school, a lot of the kids come from heavy-drinking families. They hang out on street corners, holding their beer, and talk dirty. "Dirty" is how they understand sex and the female anatomy. My aunt Evelyn says I should enjoy my blossoming femininity, but I feel shame and awkwardness, because these are the boys I know, and this is how they see it.

Freddy is different. He lives in the neighborhood too, but he isn't part of that crowd. A husky five-foot-ten with light brown hair and green eyes on a full, almost round, face, Freddy looks clean and wholesome. Soft-spoken and gentle, he is older (19) and he works all day with his dad in construction. He has no interest in "hanging around."

When school lets out, his car is parked outside (he's the only one I know with a car). He leans across the seat to open the passenger door. "Hey, Barbara! Can I give you a ride home?"

I know what boys think when they get a girl in their car. I shake my head and walk away. The next day he is there again. And the day after. On the fourth day, he waits for me in the corridor as I come out of class. "Hey—" he protests, following me down the hall. "What are you afraid of? I'm just offering you a ride home. But if you give me a smile, there might be an ice cream soda in it for you too." An involuntary smile cracks my face.

He opens the car door. "What's your favorite flavor?"

Freddy courts me, protects me, and adores me. He creates a glass wall against the neighborhood environment and puts up a mirror in which I see myself differently. To Freddy, I am a precious flower to be held delicately, lest the petals fall; watered gently, kept in sunlight.

Freddy's mother is a devout Baptist. She goes to church three times a week, but she's not like Velma in the factory where I worked. She isn't loving and radiant, and she isn't pleased with Freddy's attachment to me. His father's eyes never leave the television set when we come in; he never says "hello" or "goodbye," and he doesn't seem to notice I am there.

Freddy is sweet. He talks about getting married when I'm old enough and when he can save enough money to get out from under his dad's heavy thumb. We kiss and sometimes pet a little and, as months go by, we go a little further. It never occurs to us there could be consequences. I'm devastated to discover that, at 15, I'm pregnant.

"Don't worry about it," Freddy assures me. "We'll get married now instead of later."

"But how—?" I have a hundred questions.

"We'll live at my parents' basement apartment until we can get our own place. Mom will help with the baby while you finish school." (Yeah, I can picture that!) "And we'll manage. It's not so bad. The baby might be kind of cute."

I have to tell Mom and Dad, of course. But it takes days to work up the courage, to find the right moment. I'm in the basement listening to Dad play the piano. He seems so happy when he plays. Here I come with a bulldozer to knock down his world. Tears drip down my cheeks as I sit behind him. Something makes him turn around. "Are you crying, honey?"

I shake my head.

"Hey . . . what's the matter? Is something wrong?"

"Daddy," I sob, "you're going to hate me!"

He gets off the piano stool to sit beside me. "How can I hate you? Did you do something terrible?"

"Yes. Daddy, I . . . I'm going to have a baby!"

He puts his arms around me. "Oh, honey, that's not a terrible thing. A baby is wonderful. Only—" the reality starts to hit him—"just not now . . . you're too young . . . oh, my God! Hmm, we'll figure something out. I've got to talk to your mother."

"No! Don't tell Mom. She'll be so mad."

"Nonsense. She's . . . she won't be too happy, though."

Daddy slowly climbs the stairs, thinking of what to say to Mom. I wait, every muscle in my body tensed to snapping. Then it comes. A wail. "*WHAT?!*" Then some words I can't make out. Lots of words.

"Alice, please. Calm down. This won't help."

More talk I can't make out. Then: "What did I do to deserve this?!" and more angry sounds. I don't dare leave the basement. I don't dare move. I hope they forget I am here.

Several days go by when, after dinner, the doorbell rings. Mom says, "Go to your room," and she opens the front door. I've never been sent to my room when company comes. Puzzled, I curl up at the head of the stairs where I can hear. What? *Am I imagining things?* Those are the voices of Freddy's mother and father! Our parents have never met; they don't even know each other's names. What in the world are they doing here?

Isolated phrases float up the stairs above the unintelligible murmur of their tight-lipped conversation. " . . . far too young . . ." "What kind of a life . . .?" "She's got to go to college, get an education . . ." " . . . arrangements . . ."

Whatever it is, they all seem to be in agreement. Then hurried good-byes, the front door opening, closing quickly, and silence.

Next Sunday afternoon, Mom asks me to get in the car with her. "We're going to see a doctor," she says.

Yes, I suppose pregnant girls have to see a doctor. We drive into the city, find the building—it's locked—and walk around to a rear entrance, which is open. The halls are dark and empty. We take the stairs to the third floor because the elevators aren't running, and knock at the office door. It is opened by the doctor himself. He leads me into an examining room.

"Won't be able to give you anesthetic," he mumbles, setting me up on the table, "takes too much time to get you awake and out of here afterward." I lie on the table, expecting an examination. Instead, the doctor rips the baby from the womb that nurtures and sustains its budding life. "Hmmm . . . a boy," he mutters distractedly. Frightened and confused, hot tears slide through my squeezed eyelids. A boy! My son . . . Michael.

A half-hour later, Mom and I are back in the car heading home. "You okay?" Mom looks at me anxiously. I am stunned, too dazed to answer. I'm still not sure what happened back there.

Once home, she puts me to bed and brings in tea. "I'll fix you something to eat," she offers. "What would you like?" I shake my head. Later that night the reality hits me, a torn-out emptiness that used to be a child inside me. I turn my face into the pillow and sob convulsively. For the next several days, I cry whenever I'm alone.

The subject is closed; no one mentions it again. Like it never happened. Only once, when Mom and I are washing dishes after dinner, I say, "He killed my baby." She pauses almost imperceptibly and continues drying, but she doesn't turn her eyes from the sink. "There was no baby," she answers. "It was only a fetus. Is your homework done?"

I know without a doubt that Mom and Dad did what they believe was best for me. They feel it's the only way I can get an education and live the kind of life they want for me. I trust, against my innermost conviction, that they are right. If only I didn't miss the baby so much. Maybe the longing for him will eventually go away?

Freddy and I are forbidden to see or contact one another, but he calls occasionally when our parents aren't home. "I won't let them keep us apart for long," he promises. "We'll get married, just as we planned."

I'm no longer sure. Something died when they took Michael. For me it isn't the same. And something else is becoming clear to me that I don't like. Why, I wonder, had no one asked *me* what I want? Where was *I* in all this? Where was Michael?

My parents have no religious convictions that cause them to doubt the rightness of what was done. But what stings painfully is that Freddy's piously devout, Bible-thumping Baptist mother had to know it was wrong. Why did she agree to it? I guess the social embarrassment and, worse, the thought of a Jewish daughter-in-law, are more important than the life of her grandson. Is that what her religion is all about?

We're moving again. Determined to get me into a better environment, Dad has found a job at RCA Laboratories in Princeton, New Jersey. Princeton! But it isn't just a new town Dad is looking for; it's a new life. "You'll meet college-minded kids in this school, friends who want to build a future."

This time, Dad isn't buying a house; he's designing one. He brings his blueprints home at night, spreads them on the floor and shows us. "See, the front door will be here. As you come into the flagstone entry," he points at a square on the blueprints, "you'll see the glass living room wall . . . here . . . looking out on the trees. Up here . . . that's a balcony . . . looks over the living and dining room. Of course they'll have high ceilings."

To Mom it's just blue lines, numbers, arrows. "I can't see it, Jordan, but I'm sure it'll be beautiful."

I lie down on my stomach next to him on the floor. "I can see it, Dad." I see the lines growing from a concept into living spaces, colors, textures of wood and stone.

"There's my room!" Dad and I pore over the blueprints and share the dream as the house takes shape. He goes to the house every night after work to see that it gets done right. "They're only putting two nails in the studs," he says. "They'll have to redo all of them."

When the walls are up and the windows in, we spend hours choosing wallpaper, paint colors, carpet samples, drapery textures. I don't know if Dad did it on purpose, but creating our new home is the first thing to make me feel good since my baby. Not that a house can replace a child, but the process of seeing it grow—it's good for me.

The day comes when Dad, bursting with excitement, says our new home is ready. Before driving to the house, though, he gives us a tour of the town. Princeton, with all its splendid tradition, is as pretty as a picture postcard come to life.

We drive off the main road onto a winding lane. On our left are fields of wild flowers. On the right, spacious houses with rambling lawns, flowerbeds and trees between them. Hidden behind the houses and the trees—oh, it's beautiful!—a large lake. I'll learn to ice skate next winter. I'll skate all the way to where it eventually narrows at the stone bridge that crosses to the university campus. I imagine afternoons on the shore of that lake, where I will sit with Tippy, write my poems, keep my diary and, in the spring, watch the rowing crews float by, training with their rhythmic shouts.

"There's our house!" I shout. Recognizing it from Dad's drawings, I almost leap out of the car before it pulls into the circular driveway and stops. Here it stands, risen from the blue lines to become a three-dimensional reality, a monument to Daddy's genius and elegant vision.

"Wo-o-w." I let out a long breath. Standing in the hall, I face sliding glass doors and picture windows opening to the wooded yard that is ours, all ours. "This is fantastic, Dad!"

Our neighbors are upscale professionals in the sciences and halls of academia. At the high school, kids are clean-cut, wholesome, focused and preparing seriously for college.

One of my new friends is Ele (pronounced Aiy-le) from Germany. Ele is high-spirited and tall, with short, spunky blonde hair. Her father, a renowned professor, was invited to teach for a year at the Institute for Advanced Studies. His daughter, not surprisingly, is well read, full of ideas, fluent in the classical languages, and as expressive in English and French as her native German.

I drive to her small white house behind the Institute. There we have our secret garden lit by colorful Japanese lanterns she strings along the clothesline. In the garden, Mahler and Mozart drown out chirping cicadas and crickets. Ele reads aloud the poems of Göethe and talks about Germany, where one day she and I will rent a castle in the Black Forest.

Ele opens up a world of music and literature so magical to me that, having now seen it, I'll never be the same. I feel like Dorothy in the Emerald City of Oz. Glimpses I had in earlier years of an eternal Presence are forgotten now. Ele's is a world of well-honed minds, human achievement, and glorification of the arts—not art as God's gift to us, but as the ultimate accomplishment of mankind. Nonsense like faith or prayer might be all right for the blue-collar Italian community of my childhood; clearly, it doesn't belong here.

Spring blooms into summer, and the autumn day when we will part for our respective colleges is upon us. For now, we still have the night and the colorful Japanese lanterns. "Come!" Ele reaches down to pull me up from the grass. "Let's go back to the swinging vine bridge over the stream."

We follow the forest trail, holding hands, in order not to lose one another in the dark, black night. The path continues for almost a mile, but in the blackness it feels much, much farther. Things we wouldn't notice in the light of day become major challenges now: the rise and fall of the ground; the branches and twigs underfoot; the sounds, smells, and soft leafy things (we hope they are leafy things) brushing across our faces. As we walk, we trap fireflies in a jar with a perforated lid. We must save the candles for when we get to the river's edge.

"Here we are. Hey! What's this?" Ele lights a candle. Its flame reveals a small abandoned rowboat bobbing at the grassy bank. It has no oars, only handmade paddles. Without hesitation we jump in and untie the rope. "This is neat. Let's go!"

"Sh-h-h-h . . ." The silence of the stream, the black candlelit night, and the dark imposing shadows of the great trees forbid the sound of our voices. We fasten a candle on each end of the boat. It glides, smooth and silent, downstream. Branches hang over the water as we slip by; insects sing nocturnal choruses and the water is warm on our hands.

There is no moon, only the light from our candles. One of them burns behind Ele's head so that her expression is obscured in black silhouette. Her hair absorbs and reflects the light so that it's brighter even than the flame itself. I can only see—and will never forget the sight—a halo of brilliant, white-blonde shining hair, the only light in a dark boat on a dark river in a dark night around a dark face.

This night, magic and alive with fireflies, is time stolen from another world, a farewell gift for parting friends. I fear I may never see Ele again, this girl who widens my horizons, who makes me see the mythology of God and the glory of humankind. Ele. A daring imp, a bit of a rascal with round blue eyes and full lips smiling with a twist in one corner, like a boy's. Silent before the candle, she will always be gliding, gliding over a stream that continues on and on, a stream whose end I may never see.

Princeton in 1958 is an ivy-covered town, dominated by the prestigious univer-sity full of bright, ambitious young men. Dating is new and exciting. Henry, a medical student who will join his dad's practice when he graduates, takes me to the Princeton-Yale and other football games, and to parties at his elegant supper club on campus. Henry is polished, practical and status conscious.

The other student that I see is Edward, who is from a Philadelphia main-line family. A philosophy major, Edward admires Jean-Paul Sartre, so I call him "J.P." We share poetry readings, coffee houses, chess and existential dialogues.

Edward takes me to a play at the university's Murray Dodge Theatre. When the curtain comes down, he takes me backstage to meet the cast. Enthralled, I commit my evenings and weekends to working with the stage crew on new productions.

Freddy drives from Long Island to see me as often as possible, before he is drafted into the army. I promise to write, and I do—for a while. But there is no innocence now to the love we once had; the foundation of our future is a small grave. My new friends, future-oriented, intent on making a difference in the world, are more exciting. Freddy can't compete.

I send a "Dear John" letter to his Army camp, and Freddy does not write to me again. I regret the pain my letter has undoubtedly caused, and I fervently hope he marries someone wonderful, someone as loving and caring as he is. He deserves no less.

Sometimes Edward and Henry take me to classes with them in Princeton's venerable lecture halls. At first it feels intimidating, but I quickly find myself stimulated by this level of teaching. I attend every day—especially Edward's lit-erature classes—and spend many hours at the campus library researching a pa-per for my high-school class on how Socialist thinking affected the plays of George Bernard Shaw.

While I am happily buried in the Princeton University library stacks, Mom hears a knock on our front door at home.

"Truant officer, Ma'am. Is your daughter home?"

"Here? Of course not, she's in school."

"No, Ma'am, she isn't. She hasn't been in school for almost three weeks now."

Mom is strangely tense at dinner. "So, where do you go every day?" she asks abruptly.

I look up, startled. "Me?"

"Yes, you. Where do you go when you leave here in the morning?"

My dad, puzzled, stares at the two of us.

"To school, of course."

"Don't lie to me! I know you're not in school. The truant officer was here today."

"They still have those?" I ask.

"Just tell me where you go!"

I put down my fork, resigned. The wonderful academic adventure is over. "I do go to school," I say evenly. "Just not the one you think. I go to classes at the university. A history class and a class on European literature. I'm writing a paper for my English class in the library. Our high school library doesn't have the books I need."

"How do you get in?" Mom asks. "They let anyone walk into their classes? A girl, no less?"

"Henry and Edward take me as their guest. That's allowed. The professors have gotten used to seeing me. No one says anything."

Mom gives Dad a desperate "do something" look.

"Barbara," Dad scratches his cheek, "it's okay to attend lectures at the university. But only if you keep up with your schoolwork and your grades. Understood?"

"Deal. Thanks, Dad!" I return to school and restrict my Princeton literary pursuits to after hours.

Mom sees the future looking bright with two of Princeton's finest, Henry and Edward, on our doorstep every weekend. Henry will not only be a successful doctor; he'll be a successful *Jewish* doctor. Her maternal heart beats fast at the thought of it. "You can love a rich man, too, you know. There are worse places to live than New Rochelle."

"Mom!"

"Well? Did he ask you?"

"Yes," I admit, "he asked."

"And? *And?*"

I hesitate, and then tell the truth. "Mom, I don't like it when he kisses me."

"Don't like it?"

"I mean, I like kissing, but I don't like when *he* kisses me."

"Oh." Her face drops. Then, shaking off her disappointment, she says with determination, "Well, that settles it. You can't marry a man if you don't like his kisses."

So! She understands. She surprises me on that one. Does that mean she likes Daddy's kisses?

Edward, Mom thinks, is an interesting prospect too. He isn't Jewish, of course, too bad, but he's got money, more money than we can dream about. But Edward can't break away from his life. Despite his philosophical searching, his contempt for the coming-out parties and the prejudices of his family's elite traditional ways, Edward will graduate, turn his back on the Jewish girl he wants, and return home to marry a pretty debutante whose family is accepted in mainline circles.

I don't give it a lot of thought. Edward is fun, easy to be with. At times we surprise one another with moments of closeness. But it's play, not love. Like toddlers in a sandbox, we come together, share our toys, touch one another to discover, and go our separate ways.

Jeannie grabs my arm after class: "Can you get your dad's car tonight?"

"Probably. Why?"

"My parents have a summer house on the lake at Keen, New Hampshire. Wanna go?"

"With your family?"

"No!" Jeannie giggles. "Just me and you."

I hesitate. Senior-year exams are coming up this week.

"We'll miss the finals."

Jeannie presses her lips together and raises an eyebrow. "So what!"

"Okay."

I leave a note and take the car after Mom and Dad are in bed. We head north, driving through the night until we reach the small country town. Jeannie shows me how to get in through the broken latch on a rear bedroom window. Tired, we crawl into unmade beds and sleep.

A brilliant sun wakes us to the beauty of a sparkling lake in the pine forest. It's like being freed from a cage. Shouting for joy, we plunge, laughing, into the water. It's wonderful. Toward noon, we drive into town to stock up on groceries, books, and bug repellent so we can stay awhile. "Let other fools sweat the finals," Jeannie throws her hands up to the sky, "we are in paradise."

On the fifth day, we are racing down a hill. But my head goes down faster than my feet and I roll, head over heels, down, down until I bump to a stop on a pile of rocks at the bottom. I lie there screaming hysterically. "Looks like you broke your toe," Jeannie says, trying to calm me. I don't care about the broken toe; what has me screaming is the realization I had landed in a nest of snake eggs. "It's swelling badly," Jeannie insists, "you need a doctor."

Reluctantly, I agree to return home.

Once the toe is tended, Mom is concerned about the exams I missed. "How will you graduate?" She pleads with the principal to let me make up the exams. I don't know what she said, but I guess Mom is a pretty good negotiator because, to my dismay, they allow it.

"Why are you making such a big deal about graduation and admission to the university, Mom? I just want to get a job, so what's the point?"

"It's very important to us, and especially to your grandparents," Mom explains. "Grandpa and Grandma were farmers in Russia. There was no money; they had to grow the food they ate. But the ghetto was overrun with brutal

Cossacks who massacred, raped and pillaged them. So Grandma and Grandpa worked underground to support a revolution and depose the barbaric Czar Nicolas II. I bet you don't think of your Grandma and Grandpa as political rebels, do you?"

I shake my head. "Not hardly."

"Yes, well, their lives in the Jewish ghetto were seriously endangered. They escaped and came to this country with nothing but the clothes they wore and the brass samovar Grandma clutched under her arm. Oh, and something else: a passion to educate their children to be more than peasants on the land.

"Single-minded about her goals, Grandma worked as a seamstress in the sweat shops by day and took piece goods home to work on through the night. She had to be up all night anyway to keep the rats off her babies' beds—that is, mine and your uncle's. Grandma sewed, shooed rats away from us kids, and saved her pennies. Grandpa ran the grocery store. When your uncle and I graduated high school, it was the major triumph of their lives. For them, it was the miracle of America.

"Eventually, when I married your father, you came along—the first grandchild! From that day, Grandma and Grandpa saved every penny they could put aside to see you through the university."

I know how frugally Grandpa and Grandma live. I often spend summers in their small Harlem apartment. Since childhood, I loved making tea in the brass samovar Grandma carried to America. You could turn the spigot and water ran out.

In their neighborhood, ours were the only white faces, but I don't think Grandpa or Grandma ever noticed. "People are people," Grandpa would shrug. Wrapped in his sweater, he read the Yiddish newspaper through wire-rim glasses. "It's not what kind of skin they have; it's what's in their hearts you have to look for." He sipped his tea from a glass.

I had summer playmates in their neighborhood. I especially liked "Dandy," the little girl who lived down the hall. Dandy and I were sitting on the stoop one morning, watching people pass by on the street.

"Hey, Dandy, what color is that lady's dress?"

"Red, silly! You know that."

"But how do I know what's 'red' to you is the same as what's 'red' to me?"

"It's red," Dandy insisted. "Red is red."

"But your eyes are looking out of black skin and mine are looking out of white skin. How do we know colors look the same to both of us?" It was perturbing to imagine that the same object might appear different to her. Dandy had finally appreciated the seriousness of my question. She was devising tests we might run to verify that what one saw the other saw too.

Just then Dandy's mom came out of their apartment and watched us, engrossed in our query. She turned sharply toward my grandmother's door and knocked.

"Good morning, Maven," Grandma said with her thick old-world accent.

"Rosie, we got to do something about the girls. They spendin' much too much time together."

"Too much time for what, Maven?"

"It ain't natural. They come from different worlds and it cain't lead to no good."

"Maven, please don't tell Dandy they can't play. They're good friends. You and me, we're good friends. What's the harm?"

"I just don't want Dandy gettin' no ideas about things she ain't never goin' to have. I don't wanna see her hurtin'."

"Let them be, Maven. They won't hurt each other. Unless we teach them how."

Grandpa always took me to the store so I could "help" him. He let me take his customers' money and ring up the cash register. He taught me how to count change too, and my arithmetic skills got pretty sharp at the age of five or six. When the customers didn't have money, I had to keep an account of how much they owed in his little blue book with the column lines.

"What if they don't pay you, Grandpa?"

"Lots of times they can't. Lots of times."

"So what then?"

His shoulders did a that's-life kind of shrug. "Folks got to eat."

Grandpa's store was the social crossroads of Harlem. His customers, mostly women, came from all over the neighborhood, and not just for food. Once the items were crossed off their grocery lists, they lingered to talk, to find out what was happening behind closed doors down the hall and across the street, to complain about their kids, their in-laws and, most of all, their husbands. What stories for me to hear! Sometimes the voices got very loud and excited. But when Grandpa spoke, his soft whispery voice would put a hush over everyone. He was the peacemaker. The marriage counselor. The gentle, loving spirit that could calm an angry heart.

Grandpa and Grandma never taught me anything about God; they had no knowledge of such things. But they knew plenty about family and love, honesty, integrity and kindness. These lessons they drove home.

"For 17 years," Mom says, interrupting my memories, "Grandpa and Grandma saved money with a vision burning in their hearts. 'A college graduate! Barbara will be the family's first college graduate.' And now that you're of an age to enroll, Grandpa took his bag of pennies, nickels and dimes to a bank and exchanged it for 15 one-hundred-dollar bills. Oh, you should've seen how proud he was, handing them to me."

"'This is for Barbara at the university.' (You could tell, when he said 'university,' it had a capital U.) 'It's for her education.'

"Of course I didn't tell them that $1,500 will barely get you through the first year," Mom says, "but I'll be darned if I let your truancy prevent you from passing your exams and graduating."

At the University of Wisconsin, I start freshman year living in a dormitory. My roommate, Martha, a blonde, blue-eyed native of Wisconsin ("Wi-*skan*-san" she says), is not friendly to an immigrant from New York. She's talking on the telephone when I return from classes. Her back is to the door, and she does not see me enter. "No, Dad," she is saying, "no, I don't see any horns. I tell you she doesn't have horns, but I'm absolutely sure. She *told* me, that's how I know. She's a Jew. I'm rooming with a Jew!"

I cough discreetly, to let her know I'm there. "Got to go, Dad. Love you. I'll call tomorrow."

I'm stunned. My parents told me there were people like this, but honestly, I didn't believe it. Martha arranges a transfer to another room.

On campus, I am drawn to a circle of poets, social idealists, and artists. They remind me of Ele's world. We are the 60s generation and—as Dad always said—we accept nothing without questioning. We are outraged at the ethics of the business world; we doubt the viability of marriage; we question the wisdom of traditional family life. "A certificate doesn't make a relationship," we protest. "We're looking for love, not empty marriages. We want art, not material security. We strive for integrity, not status." We are dedicated to realizing our full potential. Unfortunately for some in our group, that quest leads to mind-altering hallucinogens and "pot."

I don't live in the dorm anymore. I share an apartment with three girls, two my age and Carol who is older, a medical student. Life in that apartment is chaotic and messy. Carol can get all kinds of "uppers" and "bennies," and I use them on one occasion, when I need to stay up four, five days in a row, without sleeping, to study for exams. I see blades of grass from the inside out, a green so intense it blows your circuits. Light—sparkling, reflecting on moving lake water—pierces my eyes like firecrackers. Magnificent. Memorable. But I don't want to do it ever again.

By day we study hard. At night, I join my friends in coffee houses to discuss philosophy and aesthetics, picking colored wax drippings from Chianti bottles that serve as candleholders. We probe the mysteries of life and demand answers.

Tippy's been with me from childhood to my late teens. He's a faithful and devoted doggy friend. More faithful, alas, than we are to him.

Dad takes a job in the South Pacific Kwajalein Islands. He calls to let me know that they are moving, and they have to find another home for Tippy. "They don't allow us to transport pets," he says. I can hear in his voice how sad he is.

"You *can't* leave him behind!" I wail.

"And you can't take him to the dormitory at the university, either." Dad says. "I've located a farm where the people seem nice. They have other dogs there, too, and Tippy can run free in the country. He'll be happy there."

I fly the thousand miles home from Madison to say good-bye to Tippy. The four of us drive with him to the farm and meet his new owners. Julia and I are crying when the car pulls to a stop. Tippy leaps out, running and barking with joy for not being on a leash. Fifteen minutes later, when we return to the car, he jumps back in with us, ready to go home.

We have to take him out. He looks puzzled when the rest of us pile in and he is told to stay. The motor starts up. Tippy is still outside, pulling hard against the farmer's firm hold on his collar. He whines. My sister and I are sobbing. The car pulls away and Tippy howls desperately. I watch him, through streaming tears, from the rear window. He is still howling as we draw farther and farther away, front legs pawing the air, trying to get free and come after us. If my heart isn't literally broken into jagged fragments, I can't explain the searing pain throughout my chest and guts.

I first meet Stephen as a freshman on the university campus. He is at the center of a crowd, leading a folk-singing fest with his guitar. Tall and slim, with curling brown hair and intense, questioning brown eyes, his features might almost be too delicate but for the rugged, square jaw that imprints manliness to his face. What attracts me, though, is how he moves. Like an athlete: graceful, strong, sure. He seems to take control.

I catch his eye and we talk briefly, then he turns away. We run into one another here and there that first year, but he's always with taller, thinner, blonder women. Oh, well.

For now, I'm seeing an Egyptian student, the son of a high government official. Farid teaches me a lot about Palestinian-Israeli relations from the other side. My parents are not totally comfortable with this friendship with an Arab.

It comes to an end when Stephen finally asks me out. Stephen is a sculptor, a fine arts major. Our first date reveals a kindred affinity for art, political activism, and a quest for truth. I like his insatiable curiosity and his energy.

But emotionally he is unstable, and our romance is rocky. We break up after six months.

A friend, Nancy, tries to distract me from my disappointment. "Come to a party with me Saturday," she coaxes. "I want you to meet Ralph. He's a prince. A once-in-a-lifetime opportunity. I've told him about you."

I am reluctant. I show up wearing a dowdy dress, no makeup, and a frown. Ralph is tall, with black hair, and obviously intelligent and not at all bad to look at. He brings me a glass of wine and tries hard to get a conversation going. I'm not very helpful.

"Ralph comes from a wealthy, aristocratic family in Austria," Nancy whispers. "Be a little nicer to him. Smile, at least." But I miss Stephen, and I can't encourage Ralph.

Nancy tries again. She introduces me to Phillip, a medical student and a Wisconsin native. I remember seeing Phillip out at the lake. He had a build you can't help noticing. "He won't call *me*," I tell Nancy, "his girlfriend is beautiful!"

"They broke up. And you're pretty too," Nancy says.

I shake my head, "No. No, I'm not." I'd never been told I was pretty. My sister was "the pretty one"; I was "bright." Surely a man as attractive as Phillip won't want me.

"Well, Phillip seems to think you're pretty. And Ralph did. A lot of people do. Go out with him, you ninny."

Across a heavy wooden table in the pub, Phillip holds a tall glass of foamy beer. He has a seductive smile. We've spent several evenings together now talking about our plans after school, about his favorite football team, my favorite writers, and things happening in the world.

He leans back on the bench. "Ever see ice fishermen?" I shake my head. "C'mon. I'll show you."

He takes my mittened hand and leads me carefully over a snow bank onto the frozen lake. Silent steps, gliding with my arm in his, snow falling softly on our hair. Further and further from the shore toward the center of the hard, shining lake, toward death in chilling darkness, or life in Phillip's warmth. It is a moonlit poem in black and white and shimmering silver. A night I will remember.

Phillip calls regularly now. "Bet you don't know what a great cook I am. You haven't lived until you try my apricot chicken and rice."

Dinner is almost ready when I arrive. He has set a small table in the living room and made it really nice with a tablecloth and candles. "Be right back," he says, dashing into the kitchen to pull the chicken from the oven. Waiting, looking around at the neat but stark apartment that needs a woman's touch, I know that Phillip is a fine man. I also know that before the night is over, I will feel those tan, muscular arms around me. Excitement wells up—and so does the urge to flee.

"Almost there!" Dishes rattle in the kitchen.

Phillip is almost too good to be true. Men like him don't happen to girls like me.

I quietly pick up my coat and slip out the door into the crisp, black, icy night. I don't know what drives me away, why I can't sink into the safety and security of love and marriage with a man like Phillip.

I run home, hoping Stephen will call again soon.

It is the middle of my sophomore year, and Stephen still hasn't called. I don't want to remain on campus anymore. When my parents send money for tuition fees, I find a travel agent and buy passage on a boat to France. Hopefully, Dad won't mind. This is my chance to see if his stories tell it like it is.

A week on the *Paquebôt Île Saint-Louis* is my first experience with luxury. There are sumptuous dinners in elegant dining rooms and dancing into the night. Games on the deck in the afternoon sun, leisurely strolls watching waves in moonlight, and glances exchanged with gentlemen I will never see again.

Our ship lands late in Le Havre. I haven't converted my American dollars to francs, and the banks are closed. Hungry and tired, I huddle on a step in the shelter of a doorway. That's where I sleep, on the doorstep, until the banks open in the morning. There I discover the French make pretty money—colorful reproductions of classical art. I trade art for breakfast and buy a ticket for a train to Paris.

In Paris, I enroll at the school of the Alliance Française to learn French, and then write my parents to let them know where I am. A note comes back. Just two lines from Mom: "*We hope you like it there. As far as we're concerned, you bought a one-way ticket.*" I guess she's pretty mad.

I have been in this hateful hotel room for three weeks now. Dingy flowers on the wallpaper close in on me. I reach for the telephone on the wobbly round table next to my bed, and then pull my hand back. What number can I call? I don't know anyone here.

I wander streets alive with people taking after-dinner strolls. Café terraces buzz with conversation. Paris is colorful and wonderful. But it's lonely. It's my nineteenth birthday, and I have no one to share it with. The Seine flows quietly, reflecting lights from lanterns on the quay. Am I the only one in this entire city who is alone? Turning from the river, I head across a cobblestone plaza to a crowded café in Saint Germain and slip behind a small table. The coffee is great. At least that. I can pretend the foaming milk on top is whipped cream. There should be whipped cream on a birthday.

"Sorry to intrude, *Mademoiselle*." A man approaches my table. "Is this chair taken?" I shake my head, expecting him to remove it. Instead he sits with me.

"Bernard," he says, extending his hand to mine.

"Barbara."

"Bar-bar-a, Bar-bar-a. It is the name of a beautiful poem by Jacques Prévert. You know it?" He doesn't wait to find out. Melodic verses roll off his tongue about a rainy night during the war when a soldier finds a mysterious woman named Barbara.

"That's not me."

"Of course not. You were just a baby during the war, *non*? So, Ba-a-r-bar-a-a" (he rolls out the syllables) "what are you doing here tonight?"

"It's my birthday." I didn't want to say that. How do such stupid things escape my lips?

"Perfect!" Bernard claps his hands in delight. "We shall make a party!"

A man and a woman enter the café. They look around, searching for someone, then head for our table. "There you are, Bernard! We were afraid you'd gone without us."

"Ah, no." Bernard shakes first the man's hand, then hers. "I was detained by this delightful young lady. Anne . . . Jean-Pierre, this is" (a slight pause for dramatic effect) "Ba-a-r-b-a-r-r-a." There, he's doing it again, rolling out the syllables like that.

"Bar-r-bar-r-r-a," Anne and her brother, Jean-Pierre, say in unison. Now they, too, recite the poem of Jacques Prévert. How did I get so lucky as to have this name?

"So," says Bernard, rising from his chair, "we go now." I lift my hand to wave good-bye. He takes it and pulls me from the chair. "Come," he says. "The others are waiting."

"What others?"

"Our party. It is your birthday, *n'est-ce pas*?" I hesitate; they are strangers, after all. But curiosity wins over prudence. Bernard drives us to an apartment building in the artistic Montparnasse section, leads us up the stairs, and opens a door without knocking. There really is a party. People, music, champagne. Anne introduces me around the room ("*cette petite américaine*" she calls me). I exhaust my limited vocabulary on polite exchanges and am about to drown in a sea of francophonic tonalities when Jean-Pierre appears, takes my arm, and leads me to a quiet corner.

"You have known Bernard a long time?" he asks.

"Yes. About four hours now."

Jean-Pierre laughs. "Good. I was afraid there might be something more."

"Afraid? Would I be in some danger?"

"Oh, no. It's just that . . . well, if I may be frank, I would like to see some more of you. Unfortunately, I am leaving Paris."

"Well then, call me when you return."

"I will . . . unless you consent to come with me. In that case, I shall fetch you at 7:30 in the morning."

"Why would I do that?"

"Because . . ." he searches for something persuasive. "Because you are here to learn all there is to know about France, and because I am going to my family farm in the mountains of Dijon, which is an extremely interesting region. And because . . ." (he does have a beguiling smile) "you will never find a more devoted guide. Besides, I shall miss you terribly if you don't come."

I am packed by dawn, glad for an opportunity to escape this miserable hotel room and the noisy occupants next door. At 7:30, standing at the curb with my suitcase, the cool, baby-fresh air of morning feels like a good way to start a new adventure. A blue convertible pulls up. Blond curls, blue eyes smiling, Jean-Pierre waves, and I climb in. "Ready for breakfast?"

Face to face across the small round table, I become uncomfortably aware that Jean-Pierre's expectations for this trip may differ somewhat from mine. I have been afraid to sleep with any man ever since the abor—since they took Michael. I have to set things straight.

"Jean-Pierre . . ." His smile is as fresh as the morning sun. "I . . . I'm very happy to be traveling with you, but—"

"I am happy, too." He takes my hand.

"But I don't want there to be any misunderstanding between us. About our friendship on the trip, I mean." He stares blankly. Am I able to get this across with my limited French? "I mean . . . I want us to have fun, but not . . ." Oh, just say it! "We can't make love, okay?"

"How do we know until we try?"

"We aren't going to try. Please."

He lifts his coffee cup in a toast. "Whatever you say, Ba-a-r-b-a-a-r-r-r-a. I live to please you."

Jean-Pierre doesn't speak a word of English. Heading east through the countryside toward the mountains of Dijon, he chatters cheerfully, and I struggle to get the gist of it. He's a soldier in the French army, on leave because of an injury to his leg. "They gave me 10 months to heal, but I'm fine now. And there are still two months before I must return to duty. So we'll have a good time, no?"

"Two months off, with nothing to do?"

"I have much to do. I am teaching French to a beautiful American. I will introduce her to the culture of my country."

It is late when we approach the farm, its old stones faintly visible in moonlight. We are tired. The house is cold and dark, the cupboards empty but for the provisions we bring with us from the market. "I'll put on a fire and make the beds. We'll take care of the rest in the morning." He knows his way around in the dim light. "This was my room as a child. Tonight it is yours." He spreads the sheets and lays the blanket. I shiver in the cold, dark house. Was this a good idea, coming here with him? He is a stranger, really.

Morning dawns and sunlight brings cheer to the old stone house. I follow the sound of clinking dishes and the scent of rich brewing coffee down the stairs to the kitchen. Jean-Pierre has the table set on a sunny terrace.

"*Bonjour, chérie!* Look what I have prepared for you. Wait until you see the farm. We have mountains to climb and places to go."

"It's lovely! Uh . . ." I haven't been able to find the toilet since I got up and I am embarrassed to ask. He sees me looking around. "Out there." He points beyond the trees to the barn.

Jean-Pierre knows the terrain of his region, its history, its people, and he is proud to share it. We speak French from the time I open my eyes until they shut, my jaw muscles aching and exhausted by night. But Jean-Pierre teaches me well and I am learning fast. He corrects every error, every grammatical syntax, every word I mispronounce. Even when he flirts and I put him off, or in rare moments when I am angry, if I don't express myself in a fluent, colloquial French, he corrects me. That makes me laugh.

Days become weeks. The French comes easier and, as the muscles grow accustomed to the French sounds and shapes of words, my jaw doesn't hurt as much.

We have fallen into a pattern of enjoying ourselves immensely by day and arguing at night. Jean-Pierre says it's foolish not to share a bed and make love, but I hold my ground. Actually, he is adorable, and I'd really like to, but my fear is too great. We share affection and attraction, but maintain an existential difference on what to do about it.

After eight beautiful weeks on the Dijonnaise farm, I return to Paris with an accomplished fluency. Jean-Pierre returns to military service.

Money is running out. I've been working part-time as a proofreader and editor at the *Paris Review* magazine office, but it doesn't pay enough to live. I now take work as a translator at a news agency. They pay four centimes (roughly two-thirds of a penny) per word, and it goes slowly because I still have to look up many words in the dictionary; but the work makes me even more proficient in French. Simultaneous verbal translation for meetings and conferences pay more, but it's harder. My first assignment is a meeting between agents of the agricultural departments of France and Canada. I panic. I don't know the specialized terminology for agriculture. Then I have an idea. I ask the French-speaking agent to begin. This way, I can hear the vocabulary and use the same words when it's time to translate for the English-speaking party. It works, but simultaneous translation is a killer. I sweat it every time.

At the student restaurant, I get a five-course meal for thirty-five cents. It's called, pretentiously, *Le Foyer des Artistes et Intellectuels*. Tonight I sit across from a redheaded American, Hank, who talks about driving to Turkey in his VW bug. He's looking for a driving companion to share expenses. "I'll go." The words shoot out before I can think it through.

Hank and I drive through France, Switzerland, Italy, Yugoslavia, Bulgaria, Romania, Greece and Turkey. At each destination, we share the least expensive room we can find. This is strictly a business arrangement; Hank finds me as uninteresting as I find him. In the morning, he goes his own way. "Me, I'm out to hit the tourist spots," he says. "The stuff you like is too artsy."

On the road, between cities, our meals consist of bread, cheese and Valencia oranges, washed down with a local red wine. We sleep in the car and argue about who gets the back seat and who will struggle with the gearshift between the seats in front.

Tonight we're driving through Yugoslavian fields. It's so dark we literally can't distinguish the road from the grass on both sides. The map is useless; we're totally lost. Hank says let's stay where we are until daybreak. It's my turn for the back seat. I curl up, cramped, cold and uncomfortable until sleep mercifully blots out the dampness penetrating my bones.

I awaken before dawn, my body bent and frozen, and turn a stiffened neck toward the window. Maybe I'm not awake at all; maybe this is a surrealistic, monochromatic dream. Everything I can see—sky, grassy fields—everything is painted in shades of soft aqua, turquoise, sage; our little green car is surrounded by a tall, dense forest of green-blue lollipops. I don't know how else to describe it. As far as I can see to the left, the right, behind and ahead, they stand like soldiers: thousands and thousands of tall, straight rods with perfectly round tops silhouetted against the predawn light.

"Hank, do you see what I see? Am I hallucinating?" He shrugs (that's how he deals with not having an answer) and gets the car back to the road. Ten minutes later he swears. "We're running out of gas."

"So let's get some," I say.

"Sure. Right. In the middle of a Yugoslavian nowhere, we'll just stop for gas."

"Ask him." I point to a very old man sitting on the stone steps of a farmhouse. "He looks like he'd know the area."

"You ask him," Hank growls. "My Serbo-Croation is a bit rusty."

"Sir," I call, stepping out of the car. "Do you speak French or English? We are running out of gas." The old man squints to have a better look at me. He doesn't move. Doesn't speak. Just keeps squinting.

"Sir? *Monsieur* . . .?" Hank snickers behind me. Slowly, oh so slowly, the old man leans forward and starts to stand. He totters.

"Here, let me help you." I run toward him.

"Naw." He holds out his hand, palm forward to keep me back. "I'm fine."

"Why, you speak English!" Even more astonishing, he has no accent.

"Yu-u-p. Spent 46 years in San Francisco. Came home to die."

Hank isn't snickering anymore.

"So you run outta gas, huh?" The old man tells us where we can buy some. We chat for a while about San Francisco and what he missed in Yugoslavia, and his family. I tell him about the field we slept in last night. "Have you seen it? It's beautiful."

"Seen lots of 'em. It's an onion field. Onion fields look like that."

Right. What does a girl from New York know about onion fields?

I love talking to the old gent. I'd stay all day, but Hank is getting impatient.

"Good-bye, sir. Thanks for your time. I wish you many years to enjoy your homecoming."

"Not too many, I hope." He waves. "It's time. I'm ready."

Weeks later we return to Paris. Several letters from Stephen wait for me at American Express. My heart leaps as I tear open the envelopes. He wants me to come back. I pack and prepare to leave without a second thought.

Back on campus, I take a part-time job and make up the lost semester in two summer sessions. Stephen and I are reunited and doing fine now. Stephen is finishing his bachelor's degree in art, while I focus on history, classical dance, and literature. Our life is good together; it is rich with sculpture, poetry, political action, and late-night philosophic discussions with friends.

Among the artists who share his painting studio, Stephen tells me about a girl from Kansas. "Her name's Lorna. You should meet her. I know the two of you will hit it off."

It isn't all smooth, at first. Lorna and I meet like two planets of energy colliding, grating and, eventually, melting into a new, blended entity. There's an otherworldliness about Lorna that takes some getting used to, that I eventually learn to take seriously.

Lorna's large, deep-set eyes are pale green-blue. Her mouth is like a soft pink flower. When she's thinking hard about something, she cocks her head to the right and her left hand twiddles strands of long honey-colored hair. A gentle Kansas twang belies her striking intelligence and depth of perception. Often, her sentences begin with, "The thang of it is . . ."

With Lorna, I can penetrate to levels of exploration I've never reached before. She opens doors to unseen worlds. Together we journey on a quest for spiritual truths, a road we might, it appears, share for life.

One Flesh

"For this reason a man will leave his father and mother and be united to his wife, and the two will become one flesh." This is a profound mystery.

EPHESIANS 5:31-32

It won't be a wedding actually, just a small party. And because my family and Stephen's live so far away, none of them will be there. My parents are concerned about Stephen's unstable background. "He's never experienced anything resembling 'normal' in the way of family life," Mom says.

"I don't care, Mom. I'm not marrying for a home with a white picket fence and children. I am creating a union with a soul mate, a fellow seeker."

Mom just shakes her head. She doesn't understand. Stephen and I are on a journey to discover what life is really about, why we are here, and how we can live with meaning. Our parents don't have answers for us; we have to find our own.

Stephen's mother is a beautiful and enormously talented pianist. But as a young mother, she was also emotional and alcoholic and unable to manage a child. So, as a toddler, Stephen was passed from one foster home to another, until his father retrieved him several years later.

His father! An activist in the Communist party, Pete had married 11 women (Stephen's mother was number 2). I met most of them at a Thanksgiving dinner in New York last year, when 8 of the 11 wives sat around the table. Why did they all come? Maybe they gathered to give thanks that they weren't married to Pete anymore, and to see who now is.

At the table, too, was Stephen's eldest brother, Lee. A wealthy bachelor, Lee is a cynical woman-hater. He lives a cultured, but self-indulgent, life. When he realized Stephen was serious about marrying me, he lectured him about the dangers of trusting a woman. And he threatened to cut off his financial support for school if I were to get pregnant. If that happens before we get our degrees, he said, we must have an abortion. I dislike him intensely.

Missing from that table was Stephen's middle brother, Hal. They don't talk much about him.

People say you marry a family, not just an individual. I don't believe it. Stephen and I do everything together; we think and move and breathe as one. We are going to redefine marriage.

The night before our wedding, I am awakened by a dream. It has clarity and precision, and images as distinct as those we see awake. In the dream, I am running across the state of Wisconsin, trying to escape a fearsome person pursuing me. The cold, icy wind causes me to wrap a heavy winter coat tightly around me. Across the brilliant blue ocean stretched out before me, the states between Wisconsin and Mexico appear as flat, sand-island stepping stones, recognizable by their shapes. I step forward onto Illinois and start running southwest. Missouri . . . it isn't quite so cold here, I let my coat fall loose . . . Oklahoma . . . Texas . . . Now it's very warm. The coat falls into the water. A warm breeze caresses my cool skin and causes my thin, light-blue cotton dress to flow. The dress, splashed by the waves, sticks close to me, close and wet, a protective embrace. Mexico calls out to me. Leaping through the warm spray from one state to the next, my body resonates to the playful dance between the wind and sea.

Texas . . . Mexico. I am in a sea-blue lagoon. Children splash in the water. Their mothers wash clothes nearby, chatting in the musical tones of their tropic tongue. Friendly people, warm, colorful. People with whom it would be safe to stay.

The dark face of one of these strong, stocky earth mothers suddenly sharpens in fear. "*Cuidado!*" she shouts ("Watch out!") and the warning is clearly for me. "*Cuidado!*" I turn and find a revolver pointing at my abdomen. Click. The assassin cocks the gun. Who could possibly want to shoot me? Looking up to my assassin's face, I see it is Stephen. His eyes bore into me with a piercing look of hatred: stone cold, immovable.

Whew! I think, when I wake up in the morning. Silly dreams.

We are married in a rabbi's study with two friends present as witnesses. Afterwards, in our apartment, there are 20, maybe 30 other friends waiting with pizza and champagne to celebrate with us. That's it. That's the wedding. After dinner, we climb into the car my father gave us and drive off for a honeymoon summer in Mexico.

The dingy little apartment we rent in Mexico City has a garden on the roof where Stephen paints. I model for him, muscles aching as I try not to move.

He leans back from the canvas, tall and lean, his brown hair glinting gold in the bright sun. He holds one brush with his teeth; the other moves swiftly across the canvas in simple lines taking shape as me.

We explore every street, every dark corner of Mexico City. It becomes part of who we are together, a shared adventure, a stone in the foundation of our marriage. Mexico would be beautiful, in its way, except for the pervasive poverty and the smells.

We leave the city after several weeks and drive south to the silver artisans in Taxco, and then head west toward Guadalajara and the coast. Eventually, we find a sleepy little fishing village called Puerta Vallarta. No one had ever heard of Puerta Vallarta, until a year ago, when Elizabeth Taylor's film *The Night of the Iguana* was shot on location here. Now the town has electricity. The artisans and shops on the main street, along the ocean shore, are charming. Behind this street are hillside houses and scenic wild country, but you need horses to get there.

Our small hotel, outside the central part of town, is isolated on the beach of *Los Muertos* (the Dead Ones). Facing the sea on stilts, our room is surrounded by banana and coconut trees. There are no other guests. Carlos, the owner, is a once-handsome Spanish Civil War veteran. He cooks fish over a fire on the beach for our dinner and tells stories of the war. A small, furry animal, attracted by the smell of fish, wanders near our fire, apparently too hungry to be afraid.

"Ooh, what's that?"

"A *téjon*," Carlos says. "It's very much like a raccoon but for the long pointy nose and the ringed tail. They are very intelligent, like monkeys. This one's a baby," he observes, scooping it up. "Must be orphaned."

The animal lets me stroke him and draws closer. "Oh, he's cute! Let's keep him." Stephen nods. "We'll call him 'Taco.'" Taco climbs all over us and plays like a child, although he's shy when others are around. We'll take him back with us to the States.

It's hard to see the brutal poverty, untreated disease, and resignation that rule life in rural Mexico. A nice lady across the road makes our breakfast. She lives in a fly-infested single room with a dirt floor, raising her children and chickens together. On moonlit evenings, people bathe at the river inlet. Their bodies are shiny silhouettes in full moonlight, effervescent with tiny bubbles of splashing foam.

Gold-pink rays of the rising sun color rhythmic waves that roll in to wet my feet. Everything is splendid, except for the violence in my gut. We've been careful about not drinking untreated water or eating anything that isn't cooked or peeled. But when brushing my teeth, I absentmindedly rinse with tap water and, although I spit it out, it is too late. I am violently ill. The local doctor shrugs. "*Touristas*," he says. "All the *gringos* get it."

Touristas keeps me up throughout the night. A reflection of myself in the water reveals how much weight I've lost. I look skeletal. Each time my reflection in the water forms, a wave washes it away. I don't like that. It makes the insubstantiality of my life too real.

When I feel stronger, we go to the market in town. Today, an older woman with bold jewelry and blondish-red hair approaches us at the tortilla stand. "I haven't seen you before," she says. "I know everybody in this village."

We introduce ourselves and tell her Stephen is a sculptor.

"Aha!" she responds. "You want to meet artists, poets, writers? You come to my house up there." She points toward the hills. "Just ask for Doña Elena. Everyone knows where it is. Come tonight."

Without hesitation, Stephen accepts. "Thank you, we'll be there."

"How is it we find artists and writers everywhere we go?" I laugh. "Surely there are housewives, secretaries, insurance salesmen, and people mending fences. Why don't they show up in our world?"

That night, we climb the path through town, past the ancient church and up into the hills. Higher and higher, we look back at the red-tiled roofs below, the flower-smothered balconies, and bright-colored stone paving. The streets conspire to create a picture of gaiety. But walking through them, we hear the cries, smell the odors, feel the destitution.

"Are you okay?" Stephen is concerned each time I need to pause on the climbing path. "Can you make it up to Elena's house?"

"I'm fine." I am unwilling to share my growing agony.

At Elena's house, I rest and the pain recedes. Stephen meets Claudio, a painter and surrealist poet. Kindred spirits, it looks like they will see each other on the beach or in town almost every day.

Along the shore behind our hotel, waves grow higher and clouds gather. One of the furious coastal storms is upon us, the kind that pass as quickly as they begin. Returning quickly to our room, I cannot climb more than half of the flight of steps before I have to sit and rest. This is happening more and more often.

Stephen returns from a walk with Claudio and takes me in his arms. "I like this marriage business," he says, nuzzling my neck. "I don't care what anyone says, it's not the same as living together."

"Yes," I agree. "There's wholeness to it. We aren't just lovers; we are a family."

"Good thing," he chuckles. "If we were just lovers, this honeymoon would be the end of the affair!"

I'm glad he can laugh at it, because I spend my nights sitting on the john, with a pail in front of me, doubled over in pain. Hardly the romance newlyweds anticipate. "If this doesn't break us, we have a pretty good chance of making it."

"We'll make it," he promises. "You and I will break the curse of my family. For us, it's 'til death do us part.'"

"The way I feel now," I moan, "that could be tomorrow."

Summer passes quickly. It's time to return to campus for our senior year. We pack Taco into an open cage on the back seat and drive through California to visit my uncle and aunt in Los Angeles. Stephen hasn't met them yet.

My aunt's face registers shock. "What on earth has happened to you?" she gasps. "So pale, so thin—"

"I have a little stomach trouble. Are you going to invite us in?"

"Just long enough to call a doctor."

Dr. Townsend advises us to get to a hospital immediately. "Your amoebic dysentery may be turning into hepatitis."

"We have no insurance," Stephen says. "Our medical is covered by the university hospital in Madison."

"Well, then, young man, you get your bride into the car and start driving right now. Don't stop until you reach Wisconsin. Do I make myself clear?"

I crawl into the back seat with a pillow, too weak to protest the aborted visit with my cousins. Stephen drives two days and two nights, with Taco's cage on the front seat, next to him. He hardly stops to sleep until we reach the hospital. Just in time, they tell us. After a week of tests and medications, they let me go home. It is more than a year until I fully regain my strength.

It is a classic old house, with our apartment downstairs and another upstairs. I am busy fixing it up to make it pretty. Taco amuses us. The mischievous little beast gets into everything, and his intelligence is amazing. We love him. Stephen and I have just a year to complete our bachelors degrees and prepare for graduate school—he in fine arts, and I in comparative literature.

My husband's warmth draws people to him. He doesn't hesitate to talk with strangers and invite them home. People—artists, mostly—gather at our house for late-night discussions. We probe the meaning of art, music and morality. Energetic, propelled by philosophic ideals, we and our friends believe we are invincible. We can reform society, reform the entire world maybe.

"Are people the same in other countries as in America?" Stephen wonders. "Do others live the shallow, hypocritical lives that we do here? Or have they discovered deeper levels of living?"

"I don't know; I never lived anywhere else."

"Maybe it's time we do," Stephen says.

Often, when discussing the problems in our American social institutions, we muse about an ideal culture. We promise one another that if, after traveling to other countries, we don't find it, we'll create a perfect community of our own. We spend many long nights defining the ground rules of our new society.

"We're not the first," our friend Harold says. "Communal experiments, like the Oneida community, all began with honest intentions and principles of brotherhood. But they all failed."

Why? I wonder. If people strive to serve one another, and sublimate individual gain for the collective good, if the common goal is to destroy selfishness and petty rivalry, and everyone agrees, why have so many communes failed? Idealists started the Russian Revolution, envisioning an unselfish social structure, and look what a monstrosity it became. The Chinese did the same, but their world today is cold and cruel. Our own country, founded on noble concepts of democracy, today is driven by power and greed. Even Israeli kibbutzim, probably the most successful of the communal experiments, fail to satisfy profound and basic needs. Children don't want to be raised by a community; they want their own mommy and daddy.

"Y'know, Stephen," I muse, "I'm beginning to wonder if there is something inherently wrong with human beings. Think about it. Every attempt to live with pure justice and noble principles has failed. It starts out right, then what happens? People start fighting, quarreling, disputing interpretations and positioning for power. Factions form, and you have groups jockeying for control. Bingo! You're back to politics."

"So you're saying even when the system's good, something's inherently wrong with *people*?"

"Maybe. I think people want to be good. They want desperately to be good. But they can't."

"Whoa!" Stephen is alarmed. "You're talking like the folks who believe in original sin."

"Sounds awful, doesn't it? But what if it's true?"

Being happy and maintaining a loving relationship is easy. Neither Stephen nor I come from an Ozzie-'n'-Harriet kind of home, and we don't know anyone who does. As far as we're concerned it's a fairy-tale concept. It doesn't exist. We have no models for raising children. We've never known parents whose lives and activities revolve around their kids. We think we'd like to have children, but it's an abstract idea. We don't really know what we'd do with them. For now we're content to journey side by side on the seeker's trail. We have found no God worthy of worship, no social structure that calls to us, no family that generates joy. There are only two things we believe in: the sacredness of art, and our self-determined commitment to one another.

We met Gary Haynes just a few months ago, when he came to Madison as a professor of Anthropology. He's become a close friend and spends a lot of time in our home. Gary wants to get married, he says, but his wife has to be Catholic and share his philosophic outlook.

Aha! Thérèse flashes through my mind. She and I had shared a room at "The French House" on campus. Thérèse was one of the French nationals who helped the rest of us perfect our language skills. She returned home to Paris last year.

"Gary, I know the woman for you. I'm not kidding, she's perfect. She's Catholic, she wants kids, she's your age, and her favorite philosopher is Teilhard de Chardin. Her thoughts and emotions run deep, and she's a loyal friend. Look, here's a photo of her."

It's not a great photo, but it's all I have. Gary smiles. "I'll call her."

"There's just one hitch," I tell him. "She's in France."

"Oh. Then I can write."

Gary writes. Thérèse responds. He writes again, sending 14 pages; 18 pages come back. Letters fly over the Atlantic—volumes, tomes, outpourings of their deepest thoughts, dreams, memories of the past, and hopes for their future.

In my world literature class, we study medieval spiritual giants like Saint Augustine and Saint Teresa of Ávila. We also read sections of the Bible. This isn't my first exposure to the Bible; I've tried a couple of times to read it but always got bogged down in the "begats" and gave up. I'm bogged down again.

Two nuns in the class invite me to their bungalow for lunch and try to help me through it. But Scripture has no meaning for me. Still, I'm curious about how the nuns live and what they believe.

"Why doesn't the Church allow contraception?" I ask. "I understand about abortion; you don't want to end a life, but why not contraceptives, when no life exists?"

They look at one another, unsure. Sister Anne ventures, "Perhaps it's because of sex." I squint, perplexed. "Perhaps, if a couple isn't afraid of getting pregnant, they'd make love all the time. It would get out of hand."

I burst out laughing. "Forgive me, Sister, but I wish it were so! If there were more sex, maybe there'd be fewer quarrels!" Blushes color the sisters' cheeks inside the black-and-white veils. "It isn't the fear of pregnancy that keeps sex in check," I tell them. "Marriage itself takes care of that." Now they look puzzled. "In marriage, romance fades into routine, familiarity, exhaustion from chores and children," I explain. "In that context, one has to work hard to keep romance alive."

So far, Stephen and I have managed to avoid the deadly trap of routine, the nine-to-five job, and kids. I smile, content. "But not us! We're still in love; we always will be."

We have our masters' degrees now. Time to face adulthood. Most of our friends find jobs. Buy homes. Have kids. We're not ready. I am awarded a Fulbright Scholarship to write a book about the existentialists Camus and Dostoevsky. Stephen wants to study engraving in the Paris studio of a famous European printmaker, Stanley William Hayter. We pack up our apartment and find a home for Taco. We're going to live with artists and writers in France.

House hunting in a foreign city, with unfamiliar customs, is hard. Thank heaven we can stay at Thérèse's apartment while searching for one of our own.

We are drawn to Saint Germain, where writers and artists have always gathered in its famous cafés to discourse and argue, and probably always will. There is a quaint, very charming, but tiny, apartment, right in the heart of Saint Germain, owned by a Russian count. We long to take it, but it is way beyond our means. Instead, we rent a larger, less charming, and much less expensive place near the flea market at Clignancourt.

We are packing to move when Thérèse receives another letter from Gary.

"He's coming!" she cries. "Here!"

"Great. It'll be fun to see him."

"To ask me to marry him, he says. Oh! And look—a copy of his request for leave of absence." Thérèse holds the paper in front of my eyes.

"To woo a wife . . ." it says. "Thérèse! How wonderful! Will you say yes?" Her deepening color is my answer.

Two weeks later, we prepare a special lunch for Gary's arrival. His plane is due in an hour. Thérèse has changed her outfit three times. She's dropping things—the knife she's cutting tomatoes with, an egg that splatters on the floor. I'd better get her out to meet that plane. "You'll be late, hurry. I can finish lunch and set the table."

"I can't," she stammers. "You go. You get him."

"Thérèse! He's not coming all this way to see *me*. He'll be very disappointed if you aren't there."

She fusses nervously with her hair. "It is such a peculiar moment. We have shared so much in our letters, but—"

"But?"

Her hands fly out. "We've never met! We're complete strangers. What if . . . oh, Lord, what if we don't like one another? I'm not pretty . . . what if—?"

I yank the apron off her. "Go! He's wild about you. Go."

They return to the apartment two hours later, smiling, holding hands. We welcome Gary, and I pull Thérèse into the kitchen. "What happened?"

"He knew me immediately. When he came from the gate, I reached out to shake his hand. But he took both my hands, pulled me into a hug, and whispered, 'Hello, Princess.' That's what he calls me in his letters. At that moment, it was like we'd been together forever."

"Hah! And you might well be."

That evening, we visit the home of Thérèse's parents so Gary can meet the family. He speaks formally to her father of his intentions, receives the go-ahead, and Thérèse announces the engagement after dinner.

Her mother is ecstatic. "We owe this all to you, Barbara; how can I ever thank you?" (Why do older people cry when they're happy?) "Gary is wonderful. I'm so happy. But, of course, Thérèse will now be living in America." Her voice drops. "It's a long way off."

"But Gary promised—"

"Yes, he's thoughtful. He says he'll bring her home every summer. And he means to do it. But, Barbara, a professor does not earn much money. They'll come next summer, and maybe the one after that. But it will get difficult. Especially when there are children. No, my dear, I am a realist. But it does not matter. He is such a good man. We are grateful, deeply grateful."

Gary's leave is short. If they are to have a honeymoon, they must marry quickly. Thérèse gives notice at her school and prepares rapidly for her new life. There is first the civil wedding at City Hall, then a Catholic wedding at the church. Ooof! It's over. They're off.

But the wedding lingers with me. What made it so different from my own? The white dress? The crowd of people? The elegant food? No, it was her *family*. That's it. We had no family at our wedding. I never thought it mattered. Until today. I didn't realize how marriage affects a whole family. It's not just a union of two individuals; this event affected her sisters, brother, aunts, parents and her whole community. It *matters* to them. Funny, I never thought of that before. I didn't see my marriage as expanding my family, melding it into another's. I saw it as a personal event affecting only Stephen and me. When Thérèse insisted they be married in a church, I agreed, "Yes, it's prettier, warmer than a civil ceremony." But I see now that it's more. For them, for her family, the wedding is a holy sacrament.

I am torn. Part of me longs to feel that too. The other part, the rational part, asks, "Isn't *love* a sacrament? Why do we need the Church to make it so?"

Paris is a daily adventure. The ancient cobblestone streets and old stones link us to the parade of centuries, and the architectural aesthetics of even ordinary buildings heighten our senses. Plumbing in our modest little apartment is old-fashioned, and we don't have the comforts we take for granted in America, but life is bathed in the excitement of discovery.

Stephen is one of very few accepted as an apprentice at Hayter's studio, the *Atelier 17*. There he meets artists from around the world, including Kaiko Moti and Krishna Reddy, who have developed groundbreaking techniques for twentieth-century printmaking. Stephen works under their tutelage.

At the end of the day, I meet Stephen at the studio on the rue Daguerre, the street with its wonderful open markets, blocks and blocks of fresh, colorful vegetables, fruits and flowers. Also on that street are some of the best Vietnamese and North African restaurants, where we often eat with artists from the studio. We are a boisterous, rowdy bunch, gorging ourselves on couscous and camaraderie.

I found a job teaching at the American School, but when France now decides to pull out of NATO, it pulls the job out from under me. That leaves $570 a month from my Fulbright scholarship and Stephen's stipend to cover rent, food, metro passes, my ballet lessons and Stephen's art supplies. Museums and movies cost almost nothing, especially for students and old people. We buy fish and vegetables for pennies, and there are lots of restaurants where we get a full hot meal for less than 10 francs ($2). Money isn't an issue. We manage.

My Fulbright scholarship requires that I write a comparative study of the authors Camus and Dostoevsky. Albert Camus was a twentieth-century French atheist; the other a nineteenth-century Russian Orthodox Christian believer. The commonality between these two giants, their pursuit of ultimate reality, is the thread that connects me intimately with both of them. After my morning ballet class, I spend afternoons at France's great national library, the Bibliothèque Nationale, to do my research.

Today, the hushed, imposing chamber of the vast reading room, the long tables with rows of green-glass-shaded lamps, and the high-ceilinged stone-and-marble arches feel oppressive. I close my books and step outside to the surrounding sunlit gardens. Aaah. The scent of flowers—their gay, primary colors, and the blueness of the sky awaken my senses.

For one brief, blessed moment, I am granted an intense awareness of the Creator's Presence. I can't say who or what the Creator is, but the Presence is overwhelming. I stand frozen, fearing that any movement might break the fragile brilliance of the connection. God is . . . touching me. I hold my breath, attempting to prolong the moment. But it slips away to leave me weak and wondering.

I meet Stephen in front of the Louvre. We take a pleasant stroll through the elaborate gardens of the Tuilleries towards the *Marais*, the Jewish quarter where French Jews maintain old-world ways. "Stephen—" I want to share how God—or whatever it was—touched me on a sunbeam breaking through the trees of the library gardens. But something is lost in the telling.

One of Paris' magical bridges takes us over the gently flowing waters of the Seine to the elegant Ile Saint Louis. A second bridge brings us to the Left Bank, where colorful cobbled streets of the Latin Quarter lead to our favorite bookstore.

Shakespeare & Co., a bookstore selling English-language books, faces Notre Dame Cathedral on the riverbank. Formerly the site of Sylvia Beach's haven for starving writers, it is now owned by George Whitman, grandnephew to the poet Walt Whitman. He carries on the Beach tradition. Amongst the packed and crowded bookshelves is a stone wishing well in the center of the floor, surrounded by tattered sofas and armchairs. Expatriates and students and would-be writers read, undisturbed, or share books with a stranger. When destitute poets and writers haven't got money for a hotel, George gives them beds upstairs amongst more packed and crowded bookshelves.

George, presiding over this little kingdom with his dog sleeping at his feet, also publishes *The Paris Magazine*, a repository of letters, fiction and essays by contemporary literary dignitaries. I'm flattered that he takes an interest in my stories.

Tonight, when we return to our apartment, I curl into an armchair to read George's latest issue. Dazzled by the great word crafters, I pore over articles and short stories contributed by Lawrence Durrell, Allen Ginsberg, Jean-Paul Sartre, Marguerite Duras and . . . Barbara Ilaynia. *Oh, my gosh.* "Stephen!" I run into our bedroom, which is also his sculpting studio. "Stephen, look! Can you believe this? George has published one of my stories!"

Stephen lifts the mask off his face, shuts down the acetylene torch, and peers at the page I wave wildly under his nose. Taking the magazine from my shaking hand, he looks at my story and flips through the issue, grinning. "Well, honey, you're in good company. Right up there where you belong."

It is our second winter in France, and the metro is on strike. "Have to walk to the library," I grumble, bundling up with a coat and sweater. I set out toward the river. Usually I love this walk; it is magnificent. But today I keep my head down against the cold, and see only my worn shoes. Wish I had warm boots.

At the entrance to our metro station people are going down the stairs to enter. Had they been *clochards* (homeless people), I wouldn't wonder; it's warmer down there. But these are ordinary business people. I stop a woman and ask. "The metro *is* on strike, isn't it?"

"Yes." She continues toward the stairs.

"Then why—?"

"It's on strike; it's not stopped. They run every four minutes instead of every two. It's a little more crowded, that's all."

"So what's the point?"

"Come. You'll see." I follow her into the station. Everything appears normal until we arrive at the train platform. There is no ticket-taker guarding the entrance. The trains run, and the people ride—for free. I chuckle. They won't have to strike very long before the City is on its knees.

The French have a unique and humane approach to strikes. Two months ago, there was a gas strike. Gas was shut off during business hours only, so factories, offices and commerce came to a grinding halt. But it was turned back on from noon to two, when families unite for lunch, and again when they come home for the evening. French strikers hit businesses, not people.

Our apartment, on the north side of Paris, near Montparnasse, has no central heat, and the two small space heaters are useless. We eat breakfast wearing scarves and gloves. We type wearing scarves and gloves. In the kitchen, we turn all the gas burners on full blast before getting into the narrow shower stall, between the window and the stove. Getting out of bed these cold mornings is hard. Slipping in between the icy sheets at night is just as bad. "You go first," Stephen always says.

"No way!" I protest. "You get in and warm it up for me."

Tonight, to escape the frigid apartment, we venture out to eat dinner at a cozy little restaurant in the neighborhood. We huddle close against the wind-driven snow. In the darkness of night, white specks fly across the glow of street lamps. At the end of the narrow cobblestone street, a red-gold light in the restaurant window reflects warmth, friendly company and hot, tasty food. We quicken our steps.

"*Bonsoir, Monsieurdame*" comes the singsong greeting. "Sit near the fire and have a hot grog. You are brave to come tonight."

"We'd be braver still to stay home," I mutter.

Country stew, piled high and utterly satisfying, is followed by salad, a cheese tray, fruit, dessert and coffee. We are fortified for the trek back. Waving goodnight, we open the door, and the warm cocoon is shattered by an icy blast.

Walking as quickly as the deepening snow allows, we pass a parked Audi with its interior lights on. A young couple sits inside reading a map with a flashlight. Seeing us approach, the woman calls out with a strong German accent.

"*S'il vous plaît!*" Longing to escape the cold night, we hesitate to stop, but she calls again. "Can you tell us the best route out of Paris toward Madrid?"

We stop. "Let's see your map." It's colder every minute. "Listen," Stephen tells them, "we live only a block away. Come up to our place for some hot tea. We'll mark the route for you."

The spiced tea warms our insides. The man, Sergio, says it was hard to find work in his native Spain, so he went to Germany where the economy was better. There he met Ingrid, a schoolteacher. Ingrid's family doesn't approve of her romance with a laborer. Sergio is now bringing her home to meet his family in Madrid, where they'll be married. We talk until it is very late. Stephen suggests they stay the night and get an early start in the morning.

They look at one another with obvious relief. "*Gracias*, you are very kind." Another glance between them, and Ingrid nods almost imperceptibly. "Say, why don't you come with us?" Sergio urges. "You can spend the winter in the south, where it is warm. We can take you as far as my home in Madrid. My parents will insist that you stay for the wedding, as their guests. Then you can continue south to Torremolinas. My country is beautiful. Why remain here in the cold?"

"Just like that?" I laugh. "Just leave?"

"Why not?" Stephen asks. "What's to stop us?"

Why not, indeed? We've never seen Spain.

In the morning, I serve breakfast American style (eggs, toast and coffee) and we pile into the Audi. Once past the city gates and through the suburbs, the drive across central and western France is lovely. We chat cheerfully in broken Spanish.

It's late when we reach the border. "Sergio, let me take the wheel for a while," Stephen suggests. "We won't be in Madrid until tomorrow evening—you need a break."

"No, no, I'm fine. Really. I don't like anyone to drive my new car."

We stop at a roadside restaurant for dinner and continue on into the night. Stephen repeats his offer to drive so Sergio can sleep, but Sergio becomes irritated. I nudge Stephen. "Let him be, he's stubborn." We settle into the back seat and fall asleep.

A shrill scream pierces our restless nap. Waking to a blinding brightness, it takes a moment to realize we are on a short, narrow bridge, colliding with a huge transport truck. The headlights of that truck, not four feet from my nose, have just come through our windshield with the deafening crash of splintering glass and metal. Struck, as with a jackhammer, we jolt to a sudden halt. The back of the front seat squashes against my knees. "Stephen, are you all right?" A stream of blood trickles down the side of his face. Oh, God! "Stephen! Sergio! Ingrid! Someone, help!" It is still and quiet. Am I the only one alive? Stephen stirs and moans. "Honey, are you okay? Talk to me, please." He moans again. "I'm fine . . . fine. Just my glasses broke . . . cut my face . . . what about you?"

"I'm fine." We try to see what is happening with Sergio and Ingrid, but the front seat pins us back. Sirens. Voices. Police pulling out the broken windows, reaching for Sergio's inert body. Ingrid sobbing.

The police place Sergio on a stretcher and into a waiting ambulance. Then they use crowbars to pry the doors open for the rest of us. The car looks like an accordion. Sergio's new car that he wouldn't let anyone else drive.

The truck driver who hit us is beside himself. "Never, in all my years on the road—*Dios mio*, I might have killed them!" He runs back and forth between his truck and our car. The sight of the crumpled car and our possible injuries generate his mounting hysteria.

They guide the three of us into the police car and ask questions in Spanish we can't answer. We follow the ambulance taking Sergio to the hospital. A doctor tells us he's all right. Just knocked unconscious and cut badly on his forearm. But when he finds out what happened to his car, he wishes he were dead.

The police release us and we take a bus the rest of the way to Madrid, arriving at the ancient wooden door of Sergio's family home close to midnight. Exhausted, our nerves shattered, it is difficult to be socially graceful. The story comes tumbling out.

"*Madre de Dios*! You must eat and rest now." Sergio's mother hurries into the kitchen to reheat the special dinner she had prepared for a much earlier arrival. His younger brothers and sister hang on every word.

"Come, come to the table!" Mama proudly serves her squid in black-ink sauce. "Special for my Sergio. It's his favorite. You know this?"

"No, we've never tasted it before." The squid looks like it's still swimming in the black gook. Keep smiling, I tell myself. These people have eaten it before and they didn't die. Stephen shoots me a desperate look. I smile sweetly, encouraging him to be polite. We eat. Actually, it isn't bad.

After dinner, we clear the table. Then Sergio's father wants to show us photographs in the living room. Exhausted, and wanting only to collapse into a soft bed, we sit dutifully on the sofa. Suddenly Stephen nudges me. "Do you see that?"

"What?"

"That!" I follow his eyes. A framed photograph sits on top of the television. It is a portrait of Adolf Hitler, with a small swastika flag on one side and the flag of Spain on the other. *Keep calm,* I think. *It can't be what it looks like. Maybe it's a relative who just looks like Hitler.*

"Who is that, Señor Bañuelos?"

"A great, great leader." He takes the photo in his hands. "We had hoped he'd lead *España.* You don't know of Adolf Hitler in America? He is a model for our youth."

We are frozen. Obviously, they don't know we are Jews. What to say? These people are our hosts. We just ate at their table and will be sleeping in their home. They seem kind and generous. And they idolize a genocidal murderer of Jews.

"It's very late," I stutter, "and we are shaken from the accident. Perhaps we could go to bed?"

But there is no sleep for us. It's unthinkable to go unconscious under such a roof. "What if they find out we're Jewish?" I whisper to Stephen. "Will we swim in black ink sauce on the table tomorrow night?"

These are hospitable, churchgoing people whose kids take Communion and cross themselves before statues of the saints. How does it all go together? The more I see of Christianity, the more it frightens me. "Let's get out of here," I beg Stephen. "Let's leave!"

"It's three o'clock in the morning. Without a car, where can we go? We have to wait until morning, when the buses run."

Sergio is disappointed. "No breakfast? We thought you'd stay a few days; there's a lot to see here in Madrid." His parents appear bewildered as we grab our bags and run into the street.

A bus takes us south to the seaside town of Torremolinas. There, along the oceanfront, three boys race their motorcycles. We ask if they'll rent one to us. Three dollars a day? Okay.

We float on the motorcycle along the ocean shore, lie on the sand to read, and buy a paper cup full of *calamares* to nibble as we walk the ancient, narrow streets. After the shock of the accident and the fascist family fiasco, it is calming to be by ourselves, just Stephen and me.

Stephen and I are in tune; we think and move as one. "I'm the luckiest guy in the world," he says, hugging me. His love is the source of my beauty, my strength; it is the wellspring of my joy. Without Stephen, there is no meaning to life. There are just Hitlers and scary people and a dangerous world. Near his energy, his exuberance, I am safe.

Following the warmth of the sun further south, we spend several days in Gibraltar, a friendly place where monkeys roam the streets. Then we ferry across the Straits to Morocco, and board a creaky old bus. The driver stops, after several hours, in a small village and opens the door.

"This is Chefchaouen. End of the line."

We step onto the rocky dirt road. The bus pulls away, covering us with clouds of hot dust. People stare at the strange Westerners. Half a dozen young boys clamor around us, begging, some offering to be our "guide." We brush them away.

One boy, dark and very handsome, stands on the periphery observing us. His black eyes flash with intelligence. "*Vous cherchez un hôtel?*"

Startled by his good French, Stephen answers. "*Non, merci*, we aren't staying. We'll be hitching a ride out."

"No cars pass through this road," the boy says. Stephen and I exchange a glance that says, *Sure, he wants us to stay so he can get his commission on a hotel.*

"I see one coming now." Stephen stands at the edge of the road and sticks up his thumb. The boy shakes his head. "That one will turn right at the third house."

The car slows, the driver stares curiously at Stephen, passes, then turns right at the third house. We wait 40 minutes until another car appears. Stephen jumps up to hitch again. The boy shakes his head at our refusal to accept what he says. "That one will turn before he gets to us. It's the builder."

The car turns before it gets to us. After the fourth car, Stephen gives in. "Okay, take us to the hotel. But we don't need a 'guide'; we can manage on our own." The boy shrugs and leads the way.

"What's your name?"

"Ahmed."

Ahmed leads us to a primitive blue building. It looks like all the other stucco houses; how would anyone know it's a hotel? The owner answers the door and takes us to the third floor. It's very quiet. There doesn't seem to be anyone else in the place. The corridors are balconies overlooking the town and the mosque. Our room is large enough to hold a small bed and table with a washbasin. The bathroom is across the hall.

"I hope you will be comfortable," Ahmed says and leaves. He doesn't hold out his hand or wait for a tip.

An aroma wafting up the stairs from the kitchen below tells us that dinner is ready. Khalil, the hotel owner, is also the chef. He has made chicken stew, rich with vegetables and hot spices, perhaps the tastiest we've ever had. Pleased that we like it so much, Khalil invites us the next day to watch him prepare the meal in the kitchen. I spend many evenings in Khalil's kitchen, and learn Moroccan secrets of spicing food.

Ahmed returns every morning and becomes a part of our life. I want to remember him in his childhood vitality: Ahmed leading us to the mosque; Ahmed playing like a child in the sheep pens; Ahmed giggling in grassy meadows, while Stephen sketches him in charcoal, begging him to sit still; Ahmed warning merchants in the market, "These are my friends; treat them well." It is amazing how love grows between people who live in worlds so different they are incomprehensible to one another. The culture is foreign. The human boy is not.

I look around the market, curious. "There are no women here! Don't they like to shop, to see their friends and neighbors?"

"Our women stay home. They aren't for the world to see. Men go to market." On the streets, women are covered in black shrouds. Ahmed says we are not to be deceived by the covering. "Moroccan women, like women everywhere, use cosmetics and fix their hair. They use henna to make it red." *What for*, I wonder, *if they can't be seen?*

Our friendship with Ahmed grows, and he invites us to his home. His father, a severe, old-looking man with a white beard, greets us with formal reserve. Stephen asks permission to take a photo of him, together with his son "for a memento we can keep." The old man's mouth opens in horror. His hands fly to his face.

"He doesn't allow graven images," Ahmed explains. "Evil spirits can get into us through these images."

We apologize. Ahmed's father leads us stiffly into the dank receiving room of his house, and then disappears. The room is empty but for the shelf carved into the stucco wall, covered with a blue cushion. We wait 20 minutes, in silence, until he returns with a tray of hot, sweet tea. "My mother made the tea, but she can't meet you. My father will serve it." Ahmed translates our appreciation for his father's hospitality, and we try to communicate our fondness for his son. But conversation is stilted, and I'm glad when the visit is over.

Little girls skip and play in the streets. "Until what age can they go about like that in skirts and blouses, their hair flying free?" I ask, thinking of the black-shrouded women and Ahmed's mother hidden from her guests behind thick, silencing walls.

"Until the first sign of womanhood. After that, they remain with their family."

"They never visit? Don't have friends?"

"Oh, yes. There are pathways between the courtyards of our houses. They know how to get from one to another without exposing themselves on the streets."

I could have been born here, I think with dread, *buried alive like my Arab sisters.* The heavy oppression of their existence behind the veil, the walls, their submission as chattel, weighs with intense discomfort on my heart. I can't stay long in this land, I tell myself. I can't breathe.

At the outskirts of the village, a different tribe of people herd sheep and goats on the hillside. High on the impossibly steep, sliver-narrow footpaths, they prod heavily laden donkeys with merciless sticks. One slip and they'd have a rapid end, hundreds of feet below in the ravine. It seems a harsh life on the mountainside. But their woven robes have many colors and their women's faces are bare.

"Berbers," Ahmed explains. "They aren't like us. They roam the mountains and live in tents with their animals. Their ways are ancient."

Ancient? I blink. *And Ahmed's people are space age?* Observing these tough-skinned people, I see humor, warmth, and affection toward their playful, healthy-looking children. Though Ahmed sneers at their "backward" ways, they appear happier, more light-hearted than their grim Arab neighbors. If I had to live here, I'd run away to a Berber village.

Today, we wander about without Ahmed, and stop at a café for tea. I follow several steps behind Stephen. Something wet and slimy hits my leg. Then my arm. I don't realize what's happening at first, but after a few seconds I let out a cry. Stephen whirls around. "They're spitting on me! These horrible people are spitting on me!" I back out and run, afraid they will stone me next.

Safely back at the hotel, I shrink into a corner with my books. Stephen and Khalil are engrossed in their daily game of chess. Later, when Ahmed arrives, we tell him what happened. I start to shake again.

"I'm so sorry; I should have told you the cafés are for men only. It's unholy for a woman to enter, even a Westerner."

I suppress my outrage until I am alone with Stephen. "Unholy! Christian, Muslim, whatever, 'holiness' seems to be an excuse for cruelty and killing. The more I see of religion, the more I despise it."

"Me too. What people do in the name of holiness! Torture during the Inquisition. Stoning women for exposing a bit of ankle. Slaughtering children to blot out the shame of an illegitimate birth. What, besides human cruelty, can possibly be 'unholy'?"

I read to Stephen what I wrote today in my journal:

The shapeless, formless fear I've known since birth envelopes me here in this Muslim land, like a suffocating black shroud. I don't understand the ways of these people, how they think or feel. Far, far beyond the barrier of language, social and religious responses I cannot understand separate me from the swarming crowds of humans with whom I cannot relate. This is separateness more frightening than isolation.

December passes. Then January, February, March. Spring is warming Paris; we can return. Ahmed, sitting on the floor of our hotel terrace, is sad to see us go.

"No more than we are to leave you. You've become a little brother to us." I hug him tightly, reluctant to release him to the oppressive ways of his people. Will this precious child grow up to squint suspiciously at strangers? To beat his wife and kneel, face to the ground, in terror before a God of punishment? What will he do with his joy, his sparkling laughter and quick intelligence? I long to whisk him away.

"Ahmed," Stephen places his hand on the boy's shoulder, "I told you when we met we wouldn't pay you to be a guide. But you've been wonderful, and we'd really like to leave something for you."

"No." Ahmed raises his long-fingered, dark hand in protest. "I need nothing."

"Please. Isn't there anything you'd like?"

After hesitating a few seconds, Ahmed utters, "There is something . . ."

"Tell us."

"My younger sister. She gets cold in winter. If she had something warm—stockings, gloves, perhaps a scarf?"

Good heavens, they are so poor they cannot dress against the winter! How could I have been so unaware? I thought his father had been cold; had he simply been embarrassed, offering his poverty to "rich" Westerners? We never imagined ourselves as rich. We are students. We hitchhike because we can't pay for train tickets. But of course we're rich. And stupid. And unobservant. I'm deeply shamed.

"Ahmed," I whisper, "nothing for *you*?"

A proud shake of his head says he won't hear of it. That firm gesture humbles me. In this delightful boy I see holiness. If there were a God, He would love Ahmed, the child He made so beautiful.

Eager for the familiarity of modern life in Paris, we are unexpectedly disoriented upon our return. It feels like a time warp. Which is real: jet planes and computers, or sheep on rocky mountain paths?

"Morocco seems 'primitive,' as in 'long ago,' but it's *now*," Stephen says. "And Paris is now too. Maybe our linear concept of time is wrong."

Hmmm. Stephen may be on to something. In the great cosmic realm, maybe there is no "then" and "now." Maybe it's all one, all occupying a single space-time. Stephen and I fall silent, facing something greater than finite minds can fathom.

I pack a box of woolens for Ahmed's sister, and some things for him too. I tuck in a letter. Will it arrive? Will we ever hear from Ahmed again? Communication from one geographic area to another is easy. But can it flow from one reality to another, across realms of "now" and "then," both of which live but never touch?

Nina is an artist in the studio where Stephen works. She is leaving Paris for a year and says we can live in her studio rent-free. It is a 600-year-old storefront, behind the military museum at *Les Invalides*. Sight unseen, Stephen accepts the offer; it seems too good a deal to pass up.

Stephen inserts the key in the lock and the door swings open. My heart sinks to my toes in despair. Never, ever, have I seen such filth and clutter. From the front room, we can hardly squeeze through a clearance path into the kitchen. Paintings are piled high on the floor and counters. The smell of grease pervades everything. There is no place to sit. No table to work on. Barely room to stand. In the center of the room is an ancient wood-burning stove beside a little pile of chopped wood.

"That's our heat." Puffy clouds surround Stephen's words in the chilly air.

We climb a very narrow, precarious staircase to the loft, just large enough to fit an old lumpy mattress on the floor. That's our bedroom. "Well!" Stephen's white breath comes out in a whoosh. "They say a mattress on a hard surface is good for your back."

"Yeah. Makes it easier for the rats to get you too. Where's the bathroom?"

Down the creaky, rickety stairs, out the back door and across a grimy, unkempt courtyard, is a small outhouse. "This'll be great when we have to get up in the middle of the night," Stephen moans, "especially now that it's winter. Guess we'll keep a flashlight next to the bed."

Our apartment at Clignancourt is already rented, so we can't go back. How stupid to have taken this place without seeing it first! "Keep a stiff upper lip, sweetheart," Stephen says, lifting my chin with his finger and kissing the tip of my nose with cold lips. Unable to speak, I walk sideways past the wood stove toward the kitchen, careful not to brush against the drawing table or debris laden with grease and dust, afraid to breathe in and contaminate my body. Oh, Lord. Is this where our flight from materialistic suburbia has brought us?

"We can't live in this filth," I moan. We spend the next two weeks scraping grease off the kitchen surfaces. It is the impossibility of *The Myth of Sisyphus*; we haven't made a dent. And how do we clean the rest of the place if we can't throw out Nina's stuff? She left no room for us—Stephen, me, and the rats. Yes, rats. At night, if we get up to go to the outhouse, they scuttle away in the unexpected beam of the flashlight. I screamed the first time I saw them. Now I lie awake on the mattress, listening to their scurrying feet, afraid to fall asleep. When I do, I dream of being chewed by the rats.

I can't work here, can't sleep, can't eat. The clutter, the smell of grease, the ugliness clog my brain, and I inhale nausea with every breath. I carry my research to the library; I write in cafés—anywhere but in "that place" where I am claustrophobic, losing weight, and depressed.

Stephen scouts around for another place to live and discovers *La Cité des Arts*. "It's amazing," he says. "It has soundproofed studios for musicians, bright skylit apartments for painters, and high-ceilinged studios with air vents for sculptors. Best of all, it's subsidized by the government, so the rent is very low. But don't get your hopes up. I have to submit a portfolio and application. Only a few are selected as residents—when there's a vacancy."

Stephen has a beautiful portfolio, but so do many other applicants. It is another three months in our rat hole before a letter of acceptance arrives. We pack and move in an hour.

La Cité des Arts is a different world. Adjacent to the bright entrance lobby of polished wood and stone, a gallery exhibits sculptures and paintings made by the residents. A steel-and-rosewood staircase leads to the library and conference rooms on the lower level. Our studio, clean and bright, has a 20-foot ceiling, a tiny but modern kitchen, a sitting-room loft, miniature bedroom and small bath. Everything is immaculate and shiny. I shout and leap and dance and throw my hands in the air. "Yes! Yes! Yes!"

Even the location is perfect. On one side is the colorful Jewish quarter, *le Marais*, and on the other is the *Île Saint Louis* with Nôtre Dame cathedral and the Latin Quarter a few minutes' walk away. In the friendly atmosphere of the *Cité* it is easy to meet painters, musicians and writers from all over Europe, India, Africa . . . They tell us about life in their various countries and have an infinite curiosity about the USA. Stéfan, a Parisian pianist and composer, is the one most special to us.

"Will you let me sit in your studio while you practice?" I ask.

"Why would you put yourself through such torture?"

"Some day people will pay a fortune to hear your music. I want to listen while it is still affordable!" In his studio often, I try to penetrate the enigma of his gift, his ability to create this glorious music. If I can understand that, maybe I can grasp the concept of creation itself. And glimpse the mystery of its source.

Sitting at the dinner table with Thérèse's family, we are again struck by their joy in having her back for the summer. Just like at her wedding, the tightness of their family bond strikes a chord in us. For the first time since we are married, Stephen and I feel we want to settle down. We want to grow roots and see branches sprout, branches solid in their tie to the earth and reaching up to the heights of eternity.

Walking home, Stephen turns me toward him, and takes my hands. "I want to make a baby. A family. What do you say?"

"How about lots of babies? Five? Six?"

"Yes! All we can have!"

"Kids are a lot of work, you know."

"Nonsense. It'll be fun."

"Yes," I tell him, "we'll have children, you and I, we'll make a family. Our children will marry and have children. And we'll gather 'round a table of love like at Thérèse's parents' house."

We walk on, Stephen pressing my arm against his side. We approach the door to our studio and stop dead in our tracks. A tall, lanky man, his head dropped between his knees, sits on our doorstep.

"A vagrant?"

Stephen squints. "No. Oh, my gosh, it's . . . it's Hal!"

Hal? The middle brother who's been missing all these years? The man waiting at our door looks up and stands. He resembles Stephen.

"Hal, what the—?"

"Hey, man, how ya doin'?" Hal shuffles awkwardly. They don't embrace.

"Uh, come in, come in. How'd you find us?"

Hal just shrugs.

"You hungry?"

"You can say that again." Hal is obviously exhausted. His clothes are ragged and there are large holes in his shoes. He *walked*, he says, 800 or 900 kilometers, all the way from Marseilles in the south. Hal says he escaped from the French Foreign Legion.

"You're crazy, man. Nobody escapes from the French Foreign Legion."

"*I* did. What you got to eat?"

Two weeks later, we wake up and find Hal gone. He disappears as unexpectedly as he arrived. No note. No address. He has no money, nor had he asked for any, so we don't know where he'll go. "No use worrying," Stephen says. "When Hal wants us to know where he is, he'll contact us."

"What a strange family you married into," Mom says when I call and tell her about Hal's visit. "His father had 11 wives, his mother married 4 times . . . Brothers come and go and disappear . . ." For just a fleeting second, a shadow passes with a cold chill over my heart. I brush it away. "Heck, Mom, I didn't marry his family; I married Stephen. We'll create our own family. It'll be different."

She sighs. "I hope so."

Great timing! Lorna and her husband are passing through Paris on their way to the University of Pau, in the Pyrenees Mountains, where he will teach for a year. They arrive on the very day Stephen's first exhibit of etchings will open at *Shakespeare & Co.* What an event to share with them! For us, this exhibit represents our first hope for a brighter future. Financially, that is. *If people just see his work,* I think, *it'll open up new opportunities. We'll be able to afford the baby and . . . the baby. Why has nothing happened yet?*

Arriving at the bookstore, we are surprised to see lights and crowds of people. Something's going on. Where are the usual scruffy student travelers? This is a well-dressed, upscale looking crowd. "Wow! So many people to see my show!" Stephen holds the door open for us. Entering, I look around, eager to see his work displayed.

There is art on the walls, lots of it, but it is not Stephen's. Bewildered, we work our way through the crowd, looking for even one recognizable etching. Stephen locates the owner. "What's going on, George? Where's my exhibit?"

"I'm sorry, Stephen," George Whitman waves his arm helplessly. "You see—"

"Don't worry about it, George, I'll explain," a confident voice interrupts. A light-skinned black man, slim and handsome, stretches out his hand to shake Stephen's. "I'm sure you don't mind, my friend. We had to borrow your space for the evening. Everything will be back in place tomorrow morning, I promise."

"Who are you?" Stephen glares.

"Please . . ." George tries to calm Stephen. He whispers, "This gentleman is one of our major supporters. I couldn't refuse him. I'm sorry."

The dark man has a disarming smile. "My name is Yves Monaud, and I am a great admirer of your work. Unfortunately, there is an art dealer of international renown who is here for today only. I had no other opportunity to present this work. Perhaps, before the evening is over, I might be able to show him some of yours, as well."

Stephen bites his lip, restraining his response. Monaud, ignoring Stephen's anger, shepherds him around the room and introduces him to visitors in the gallery. I hope Stephen takes advantage of the occasion. This could turn out to be a break.

When the reception ends, at 11:30, Monaud approaches us. "I'm going to a party," he says. "You have been so gracious about my interruption of your exhibit. Will you come as my guests?" We look at one another and shrug. Lorna and Steward had left to catch the red-eye an hour ago. Why not?

Monaud drives up to an elegant apartment residence on the right bank. "Who's house is this?" Stephen asks.

"The granddaughter of . . ." Yves names the founder of a famous modern art museum in New York. The high, ornate front door is unlocked. When Yves opens it, we're a little overwhelmed by loud rock music, the heavy-sweet odor of marijuana, and a din of voices. "Throw your coats in there," someone says, pointing to a dark room on our left. My eyes focus in the dark room and I see people rolling around on the bed atop the coats in the shadows. I turn away, bewildered and embarrassed, still clutching my coat.

In the living room, a blond man in a short kimono sits spread-legged on a stool and reads poetry in a strong, rich voice. He is tall and thin, with sculpted features. He is also stark naked beneath the kimono. A hot flush covers my face. I'd better find Stephen and tell him we have to get out of here. But Stephen is talking with Yves about people they met at the exhibit. I hesitate. Maybe we are fortunate to have met Yves; maybe we shouldn't rush off too quickly. Say, what's that in Stephen's hand? Oh, no! He raises a marijuana cigarette to his lips and inhales deeply.

I'm about to say something sharp when, still addressing Stephen, Yves puts his arm around my shoulder. "You are indeed a lucky man. I hope you know it."

"Of course I know." Stephen smiles at me.

"Good. But should you ever forget, she is entitled to have an affair. And if she does, it must be with *me*."

I pull away from Yves. "You are audacious."

"And you are beautiful," he replies.

Dawn sheds a frail light on Paris when I drag Stephen away from the party, still in full swing. The metro has long stopped running. We walk across the city to our studio at the *Cité des Arts*, breathing deeply to fill our lungs with fresh air, cleaning out the marijuana stench and the surrealism of the past few hours. Stephen puts his arm around me and pulls me close. "Monaud knows a good thing when he sees it. I better make sure you feel appreciated." I don't answer. "What's the matter, sweetheart?"

"What's with the weed? You looked like you were blending in perfectly with that disgusting crowd!" Seeing him suck in that grass made me sick. Marijuana had been popular when we were at the university, but we always stayed away from it. It had been a relief, when we got to France, not to see it around. Until tonight, that is. *Chez les artistes.*

"I was just curious to try once—"

"Once, right. That's how it starts. Once."

"You're right, it was stupid. I promise, sweetheart, that'll never happen again."

"I sure hope not. Y'know, Stephen, we gave up jobs and stability to dedicate ourselves to art. We always said 'art is an end to itself.' But what is the means to that end? Look at the party we just left! Those people are artists and writers, some of them pretty famous. And they make me sick!" I throw up my hands. "Is this what we worship?"

"Sweetheart, not all artists are like that, and you know it. We aren't like that. And yes, our life *is* meaningful. Because we have each other. Remember that."

He's right. So what's the discomfort within me? Maybe it's big-city life. "It might be nice to live in a small village where life is simpler."

"Everybody knows your business in a small town," Stephen warns.

"So? What've we got to hide?"

"Small-town folk can be narrow-minded. It might be hard to find people who share our values."

"Like people at that party, *they* share our values, right?" I stop walking and make him listen. "Exactly what values do we want to share, Stephen?"

"Honey, we've discussed this a hundred times. Above all, the pursuit of truth, even when it defies convention. Love and kindness toward others. Honesty. You really think you'll find it in a small town?"

"I don't know. Maybe."

"Well, at the studio the other day, I heard that Caroline DeVoile—you know her? She's a potter. Anyway, she lives in Alba, a village near Montélimar, and I heard she wants someone to build a kiln for her. I didn't pay much attention at the time."

"Montélimar? That's south-central France. Could be nice."

We continue walking, silent, wrapped in our separate thoughts. What's missing that art and Paris and Stephen can't give me? Must be the frustration of not being able to make a baby. It's been a year now. Every time I see a child, I feel empty. If I believed in God, I'd think I'm being punished for Michael . . . for the baby I didn't have.

"Oh, look!" We stop short. A tiny, newly hatched sparrow lies injured on the sidewalk. Stephen bends down. "Looks like a cat might have gotten it. The wing is broken and bleeding. He picks up the bird ever so gently and carries it in his pocket to keep it warm. Immediately, the anger I'd felt toward Stephen at the party dissipates. The gentle man who loves little creatures, this is the Stephen I love.

Back in our studio, we crush seed from the bird feeder, mix it with warm water, and feed the little sparrow with an eyedropper. Stephen fixes a tiny splint for its wing and we hope for the best.

The wing heals and the bird grows strong. Every time we go home, afraid we might crush it underfoot, we call out, *"Ou es tu?"* ("Where are you?") At the sound of our voices, the sparrow hops from her hiding place, up to one of our shoulders, where she remains as we walk around the house. That's become her name: "Ouestu" (pronounced "oo-way-tiu"). Lately, we've taken to walking the streets and visiting friends with her. She never leaves our shoulders. Sometimes it's messy, so we put a handkerchief under her. Who would imagine a wild sparrow to be so trusting?

Ouestu has been with us five weeks and never tries to fly. I take her out to the yard behind our studio, place her on the ground, and start flapping my arms. "Like this," I tell her. She looks up at me. I flap again. She flutters to my shoulder. No progress. I set her on the ground again and enter the house. She waits for me to come back. Watching from the window, I see two sparrows fly down to her from nearby trees. Within minutes, they teach her to flap her wings and she soars up with them, up past the trees and into the sky.

It's good, I think. *A bird should know how to fly. She's with her own now.* But tears slide down my cheek. Ouestu has shown us how a little creature overcomes fear and instinct to love and bond and trust. No words. No promises. We have simply become a part of one another. In the process of caring for her, a precious tenderness had grown. That tenderness, I realize, is even more important than art or adventure. I will miss her.

Stephen returns at five o'clock as usual, calling as he enters, "Ouestu?" I am about to explain to him that she isn't here anymore when Ouestu flies in through the door and lands on his shoulder. I'm astounded. We feed her with the eyedropper.

"Are you going to let her out again today?" Stephen asks in the morning.

"Birds gotta fly," I say, resigned. I take Ouestu out to the yard, leave her, and return to the studio. Her bird friends swoop down to collect her and off they go. Five o'clock that afternoon she returns and taps on the window. It becomes a routine. She flies off with her friends to freedom and the open sky each morning. Amazingly, she returns, promptly at five o'clock, to what is now her home.

Fall turns into winter. A gusty wind blows. Ouestu is due home and the door is wide open. Swooping down right on time, she aims for the opening but, caught in the heavy gust, she crashes against the adjacent window. Stunned, Ouestu falls to the ground. We rush to pick her up. She is breathing, but her entire left side is crushed. Weeping, we wrap her in a blanket and call a vet. She is dead before dawn.

Stephen agrees to build a kiln for Caroline DeVoile, the potter in Alba. She offers to have us stay at her house.

The tiny village is perfect. Exactly what I've fantasized. Life is reduced to the exquisite simplicity of food, shelter, water . . . and our work. Stephen sculpts. I write poems. I fill the pages of my journal and make good progress on my Fulbright study.

Every morning when I walk, I feel a deep attachment to the narrow cobble passages. My hands brush the thick stone walls, loving the rough texture and the warmth. Centuries of time pass from the stones into my hands, ages of human living travel from my hands into my blood. Timeless. I am a woman in no time, a woman, as those before, tasting the joy of life.

Within these ancient walls, little shops with no signs are hidden. You just have to know which doorway to step down into for the cheeses or the meats. We get to know the merchants and neighbors quickly. Above all, Louis and Ngoc Huyen.

Both had been pharmacy students in Paris, where they fell in love and married. After graduating, however, they could not find work. Desperate, they left Paris and came with their infant daughters to raise sheep on Louis's family farm in Alba. Ngoc carries bitter memories of her shattered homeland in Vietnam. Frustrated about her wasted training and education, about the career she had planned in Paris, she resents motherhood in a primitive village and, sometimes, takes it out on her little girls. But our presence cheers her and, almost every day, we are with them in their tiny two-room stone house.

Patrice and Fanny frequently join us. Native to the area, and lacking the sophistication of Louis and Ngoc, they are easygoing and laugh easily, especially when we try to speak the colorful slang of their region.

We three couples bond instantly and become a community unto ourselves. The utter simplicity of our lives, shared so completely among the six of us, brings the peace and joy I haven't found in a complex city. Here, I do not feel alone. I want to stay forever with the sheep and goats and our friends in Alba.

Caroline's ancient stone house has been gutted and remodeled. Inside, despite the rustic furnishings, it is bright and sunny with white stucco walls and all the modern conveniences. Caroline, however, is not easy to live with. Our presence seems to be an intrusion, a constant irritant. We'd love to get a place of our own if we just had the money.

"I have an idea," Patrice says. "I'm not sure you'll like it, but my cousin has a shell near the river—"

"Oh, Patrice, not the shell!" Fanny protests.

"Come on, I'll show you." Patrice leads us toward the river. "It's one of the original Roman ruins. It has great historical value, but . . . well, there it is!"

"It looks like all the other stone houses. Like Caroline's," I observe.

"On the outside," Fanny says. "But that's all there is to it. It's a shell. There's nothing inside."

"Nothing?"

"See for yourself."

Inside are two empty spaces with raw stone floors, separated by a wall. In one space is a huge fireplace and hearth. Holes in the walls, if they had glass, might have been windows. There is no furniture. No stove. No bathroom or sinks or water or electricity. Just stone walls and floors and, oh yes, a rafted ceiling.

"It's summer," Patrice shrugs apologetically. "You won't need heat."

After Nina's filthy studio in Paris, we can live anywhere. At least this is clean, in a raw, natural sort of way.

"We'd need a bed, a table and two chairs. Also some cooking pots and kettles. How do we wash ourselves and our clothes?"

"The river." Patrice points outside. "And we've got extra kitchen things we can bring over."

"If you buy the wood," says Fanny, "I bet Louis will make the table and chairs. He's good."

"Stephen?"

"It's up to you, honey. We can stay with Caroline, or . . . this."

"What will your cousin charge us to stay here?"

"Oh, you don't have to pay. He isn't doing anything with it."

We move our few things in. Patrice and Fanny show us how to cook over a roaring fire and where Stephen can draw water from the river. We store it in large pitchers for drinking and washing. But I'm not comfortable without a bathroom.

"There's a cave below," Stephen ponders, one hand on his hip, the other cupping his forehead. "Can we build a latrine in there?" Patrice and Stephen take a flashlight to scout the cave. "It'll work," Stephen says when they return. "But it'll stink to heaven."

"Don't you Americans know anything?" Patrice teases. "Put lye in the hole. There won't be any smell." We're skeptical, but Stephen digs a deep hole and fills it with lye. Then, with help from Louis, he builds a wooden bench with a hole in the seat over it. They sand it smooth, and it's pretty comfortable. Patrice is right; lye works.

Without electricity, our days begin at dawn and end at dusk. When the sun rises, bright and yellow on the stone houses of our village, we boil water for coffee and coat fresh, crisp bread with creamy butter. I wash laundry by hand in the cold river. "But the big sheets don't get really clean," I complain to Fanny.

"*Ma petite américaine*, without her electrical appliances," she laughs. "Just boil them in the big kettle over the fire and add soap suds to the water. They'll be clean."

Tonight I complete another chapter for my Fulbright project by the light of a Coleman lantern. Tired, I pick up the light, follow my elongated shadow into the bedroom and pull back the covers. Oh! I let out a piercing scream. A huge, furry tarantula scampers from the dark space beneath my pillow. Stephen scoops it up and throws it outdoors.

"Aghhhh! I almost sat on it! Oh, God, are there others under the blanket?"

"No, honey, no others. Calm down."

"How do you know? You don't. You're just saying that. You don't know. I don't want to go down to the john in the dark; I don't want to sleep with tarantulas." Stephen checks thoroughly under the pillows and sheets to assure me there are no other uninvited guests. He holds me. "Do you want to go back to Paris?" he asks. "I'm sure I can get my job back at Hayter's studio."

Leave Alba? That's a jarring thought. Here, we are surrounded by people who care. If we get a sore throat, they bring hearty homemade soup. If we have a problem, they work it through with us.

"No. We belong here. We'll just be careful about the bugs."

"Good." Stephen is relieved. "Because I feel that way, too. Maybe, when I finish Caroline's kiln, I can find other work."

It's been two-and-a-half years since I've seen my parents. I miss them. I'd like to fly home, but it costs too much. "Go," Stephen urges, "it's important."

Los Angeles is light years away from Alba. The plane lands amidst immaculate avenues dotted with palm trees and swimming pools. Faucets make hot and cold water flow. Electric lights, gas stoves, television. I'll never take them for granted again.

I spend three weeks in my parents' home. Stephen sends letters daily, long narratives detailing the lives of our friends and neighbors in Alba. He rigged up a new system to draw water through pipes from the river to the house, he says, so he doesn't have to lug the heavy bucket four times a day.

He writes humorous stories and anecdotes: tender, passionate declarations of love. Wonderful, priceless, memorable letters! Every day. I clutch them to me and vow I'll save these letters until my death.

It is so good to be with Mom and Dad again, but Stephen and our little village are home to me now. Stephen borrows a neighbor's car to pick me up at the bus station in Montélimar, and we spend the afternoon in ardent reunion.

Around four o'clock, Patrice knocks at our door. "Come over tonight for dinner. Fanny's cooking up a storm to welcome you back. Louis and Ngoc will be there too."

Their house is warm and fragrant with the spice bouquet of Fanny's hearty stew. Patrice is as proud of her cooking as he is of his farm. "C'mere," he says, taking a large lantern from the shelf, "I'll show you something.

We follow the beam of light through a moist grassy field to the barn. Inside, hay covers the floor and is piled against the stone walls. It is all gold in the lantern's soft rays. There is a rustling sound, a gentle bleating, and a dozen young goats surround us. They nuzzle up to us, their soft noses on our hands. Some stand on their hind legs and rest their front hooves on our chests. I return their embrace. "I had no idea goats were so sweet!"

"*Mais si*," Patrice smiles. "Goats and lambs make good pets. The kids love to bring them in the house, and sleep with them."

It is a surrealistic moment. The gentle animals, entrancing in the hazy golden light and straw-clover scent, embody Alba's sweet simplicity. I kneel in the hay, petting the happy little goats, until Patrice begs me to get back to Fanny's kitchen.

"Silly, isn't it?" I tell Stephen in English, so the others don't understand. "This moment, this sweet, fragrant moment in an unknown village so small it is only found on local maps will be marked on my heart forever. Something about the goats is . . . I don't know . . . *important*. Someday I hope to know why."

Stephen completes the building of Caroline's kiln. Having no experience with herding sheep, he can't find any more work in the area. Broken-hearted, we realize we must leave Alba.

Back in Paris, Stephen tries to distract me from my despondency. "Hey, Paris is not a bad place to celebrate your twenty-fourth birthday. Where would you like to go?"

"Le Coupôle for dinner."

Le Coupôle is a large, elegant café in Montparnasse, a favorite of affluent artists, writers and actors. We've been there many times, usually to meet friends, but we have never allowed ourselves more than a *café crème*.

We dress in our finest, board the metro, and emerge in front of the bright café, glowing with shiny brass fixtures and dark polished wood. In the restaurant section, the city's best-dressed chat casually at tables set with white cloths.

We enter the café section. No white cloth on our table; it has a marble top. The waiter brings a menu. I gasp. Prices on the café side are a fraction of those in the restaurant, but still far beyond our reach! Stephen doesn't say a word. I study the menu a long moment, and then suggest the onion soup.

"They're famous for their onion soup. I've been thinking about it all afternoon. Thick and rich, with all the bubbling hot cheese on top, the melted croutons—would you like to share an onion soup with me?"

He grins. "Sounds great. *Une soupe à l'onion*," he tells the waiter, "*et deux cuillières.*"

"*Oui, Monsieur*, two spoons. And something to follow, *Monsieur*?"

"We'll see."

Waiting for the soup, Stephen nods toward a huge obese gentleman in a tuxedo at a nearby table. A cloth napkin, tucked in his collar, drapes across his expansive chest. He eats alone, concentrating intensely as his waiter places before him one elaborate course after another.

I ask who that is when our steaming soup arrives. "That is Monsieur Le Chatonnais, Madame. He is here every evening, our most valued client."

"Alone? Every night?"

"Every night. I have never known him to be absent."

Wealthy and alone. Sad. We are poor, Stephen and I; even the single bowl of onion soup is more than we can afford, but at least it's shared. And in Alba, being poor didn't mean anything; everyone reached out a hand to help the next. I miss Alba. I'd give up the polished wood and brass glamour of Le Coupôle in a minute to be back in Fanny's kitchen on the farm.

The soup is good, though. We savor each spoonful of the tasty cheese-topped broth, trying to make it last.

A dark, attractive man on the restaurant side catches my eye and recognizes us. He lays his white cloth napkin on the table, crosses into the café and approaches. It is Yves Monaud. He smiles, claps Stephen on the shoulder while shaking his hand and leans down to me for the customary *bise*, a quick kiss on both cheeks. But his lips brush my skin and linger.

"What brings you here tonight?"

"Barbara had a longing for onion soup."

"Ah yes, the best onion soup in Paris. And what have you ordered next?"

"Actually," I cut in, "I'm rather full."

Yves places his business card on the table and leans over for another *bise* before leaving. "Call me," he says to both of us, but looking only at me. "I'd love to visit with you soon." He crosses back to the elegant dining room with white linen cloths. "Enjoy your onion soup."

My dissertation is going well; the scholarship committee is pleased with the progress. In Hayter's studio, Stephen finds the artistic stimulation he needs to grow. Some of his colleagues, like ourselves, explore spiritual teachings. "Come with us! We go every Thursday to hear Krishnamurti lecture."

"Who's that?"

"You don't know him? Ah, Krishnamurti is a renowned sage and author from India. Come see for yourselves."

We sit in a circle on the floor around Krishnamurti. His words fall like sparkling jewels, illuminating glimpses into eternal truths. His voice is gentle, unhurried and seems to come from the depths of the universal soul.

"Fascinating, isn't he?"

"He is," I admit, "but we would never be doing this in Alba. We didn't seek the meaning of life in Alba. We just lived it, and lived it fully."

Stephen says I'm romanticizing. "We didn't hang up our brains in Alba, did we? We still have much to learn about unifying with cosmic truth."

"One cannot approach truth by any religion or any belief system whatsoever," Krishnamurti teaches. "You cannot achieve transformation through an organization or group. Only the ever-deepening awareness of your own mind . . ."

We return every week, seeking infinite comprehension. Krishnamurti rejects all religions because, he says, "religion, nationality and tradition separate us from the rest of mankind, and separation breeds violence. The key for unlocking the treasure of the human mind is meditation. Meditation is a well of inexhaustible water."

Inexhaustible water. Those words echo vaguely in my memory. Oh, yes, sophomore year, the course on "The Bible as Literature." Jesus talked with a woman drawing water from the well and said . . . what was it?

> Everyone who drinks water from this well will be thirsty again, but whoever drinks the water I give him will never thirst. Indeed, the water I give will become . . . a spring of water welling up to eternal life (John 4:13-14).

So who's got the lock on inexhaustible water? Krishnamurti's meditation? Or Jesus? And who, if anyone, will bring peace to Earth? Krishnamurti says nothing will end violence and suffering—no political system, no religion, no philosophy. Only a transformation of the human psyche.

"If only a dozen people are transformed," Krishnamurti tells us, "it will change the world." One dozen. Jesus transformed a dozen disciples. Historically, we have to admit Jesus had a major impact on the world.

Alba comes to mind again. Jesus spent His whole life in a little village like that. It's where He lived and taught. They called Him "the Shepherd." I bet He'd have loved the baby goats of Alba.

Three years and still no baby. A battery of tests at a fertility clinic and . . . nothing. The tests continue. A compulsion to conceive destroys the spontaneity of our love. It's not fair; lots of our friends get pregnant just thinking about it. One couple gloated just the other night, "*Il y a encore un petit polichinelle dans le tiroir.*" I translated for Stephen: "There's still another little puppet in the drawer." Their second baby is on the way.

I'm convinced the ache of emptiness is punishment for the baby I let go when I was 15. For that untimely, unnatural intrusion into my womb, I pay the price of childlessness. It haunts me. Michael would have been ten this month. Michael, my son . . .

Walking toward the metro at Saint Michel, Stephen and I pass a shoe store on the boulevard. In the window is an attractive pair of high, black leather boots. It's so cold; how I'd love to wrap them around my legs.

"How much are they?" Stephen draws me toward the window casing.

"Oh, 200 francs! Forget it."

"You can use a pair of boots."

"We can use the $40 for rent and food. Come on, we'll be late." I tug on his sleeve. We take the metro to the city limits at Neuilly, then walk almost two miles to the fertility clinic. Normally it's a pleasant stroll through the affluent suburb. Today we freeze in the brutal cold. I put one hand in Stephen's pocket, the other in my own. But there are no pockets for my feet. After about a mile on the icy pavement, I can walk no more and sit, overcome by pain, on the curb. Stephen takes off my shoes and rubs my toes until some feeling returns. That's worse than the numbness; now I feel the sting. He puts his gloves on my feet and wraps them in his long scarf. I sit that way for a few minutes, then try to walk again, but can't for very long. There are no cafés out here, no bus stops or stores where we can thaw out. Stephen tells me to sit again on the curb. He rewraps the gloves and scarf on my feet. "Wait here; don't move 'til I get back."

I lean against a telephone pole and eventually fall asleep. By my watch, it is an hour and a half when Stephen's rapid steps awaken me. "How're you doing? How're the feet?" He drops a box on the street next to me.

"Okay, I suppose. I don't feel them much."

"Try these." Opening the box, he pulls out two tall leather boots with a furry lining. He runs the zippers down and slips them onto my legs.

"Ahhh." So good, so warm. "But $40!"

"Yeah, well, I'm partial to wives with feet. Let's see if these will get us to the clinic."

I love the boots. I love Stephen for getting them. I will never, ever, part with them, even if we end up living in the Sahara Desert.

Mom and Dad have just gone through a divorce. Mom looks lost and frightened. She doesn't say so, of course. She says, "I'm fine, just fine," but she's come to Europe to visit with my sister, Julia, and me. Julia's husband is stationed at the army base in Stuttgart, Germany, and they have an eight-month-old baby. Mom's first grandchild and my very own little niece!

We go to see them together. Mom says she's here because she misses the baby, but I can tell she's also here because she needs to be with us. Silently, without burdening anyone, she is going through her private hell. What a terrible thing a divorce must be. Stephen and I are so fortunate not to have to know.

Our last trip to the medical clinic may have done it for us. I'm two weeks late! If it's true I've conceived, the frozen feet will have been well worth it. I'm bursting to tell Mom; this would really cheer her up. I'm sure there's a baby inside me; everything in my body says it's true, but I'll wait to see the doctor before I say anything, even to Stephen.

Ten agonizing days before an envelope arrives from the clinic. I tear it open, eager to announce my secret. Yes! It is comfirmed!

Two weeks later, I feel a tearing cramp and something wet. Oh, no! I rush into the bathroom, bleeding profusely. Not wanting to alarm Mom, I say I'll be back shortly. I run to the street and hail a cab. It's an enormous extravagance, but I've got to save this pregnancy.

After his examination, the doctor shakes his head. "I'm sorry; there's nothing we can do."

The baby—like my little bird, Ouestu—is gone.

Stephen rushes home early from the studio. "Sweetheart, Barbara, it'll be all right. We'll have others, I promise you."

"I wanted this one!"

"I know, honey, I did too." He holds me tight and rocks me.

"I'm being punished for Michael," I moan.

"Honey, that's silly. Who's punishing you?"

He's right: who, indeed? In moments of pain and weakness, even intelligent people imagine there's a God of justice. Silly, isn't it? Still, the thought keeps running over and over in my mind: I'm being punished for Michael. I'm being punished for Michael. I sob.

"We'll be okay, sweetie, there will be babies; I promise. In the meantime, we have each other, right? We have each other, and that's something no one can take away."

Departed Full and Brought Back Empty

. . . the Almighty has made my life very bitter. I went away full,
but the LORD has brought me back empty . . . The LORD has afflicted me;
the Almighty has brought misfortune upon me.

RUTH 1:20-21

My Fulbright scholarship is coming to an end; our savings are depleted. We've looked for work; but without a permit, the French do not hire foreigners. I suggest Stephen consider teaching at a university.

"I don't want to teach, I want to sculpt."

"Be practical, Stephen. In the States, the closest thing to a subsidy for artists is the university. It's the only way you can earn a living, get medical and other benefits, and still have time to work. They even provide a studio and equipment!"

We send letters—hundreds of letters—to colleges in every American city, except New York and Los Angeles. New York is too big and crowded and gray. Los Angeles . . . well, it's probably irrational, but I think of Los Angeles as the center of the drug culture, the cutting edge of weirdsville. I can live just about anywhere else.

We search the mail eagerly every day. Nothing. A month passes. Nothing. Two more months pass. It's discouraging.

I'm making rabbit stew for dinner—an inexpensive Italian recipe we love—to cheer us up. Ah, there he is, and smiling.

"Smells good! Hope you made a lot."

"Hi! What kept you so late?"

"I saw a man sketching in the Luxemburg Gardens. Not the usual touristy stuff, this guy's work was *good*. So I stopped to talk with him. Turns out he's

American. A professor. Brought his wife and baby to Paris for spring vacation. I invited them for dinner. Is it okay?"

"Sure."

Jess and Rita Carlitza arrive with their baby girl by the time the stew is ready. They are fun, and our conversation is animated. Jess teaches in the art department at the University of Southern California, and he is enormously impressed with Stephen's work.

"There's an opening on our faculty—I'd love to see you fill it, Stephen. Have you got photos I can take back with me?"

In just six weeks, a letter from Jess says, "Come."

"Los Angeles," I groan. I had told Stephen I'd follow him anywhere but there! "Whoever writes the script for our lives didn't check this out with me first." I try to treat it lightheartedly, as we prepare for the big move, but there's a cold block of premonition in the pit of my gut. I feel vulnerable before a nameless threat.

We change planes in New York. It's a good opportunity to visit Dad's mother, Katherine. Grandma hasn't seen me in 16 years. She prepares the rich and tasty chicken soup I loved as a child, and plays the piano for us. She hasn't lost her touch! Stephen opens his sketchbook and begins to draw her at the keyboard. She stops playing with a shriek. "No! Don't draw me with glasses on!" Stephen apologizes. She continues playing—without glasses—so he can draw.

After her concert, she offers to read the tarot cards for us. "She's very good," I explain to Stephen. "People come from all over the Bronx to have her read. I don't think she's ever been wrong."

"Great," Stephen settles back. "Might as well know what's in store for us. Any kids?"

Grandma Kate spreads the cards on the kitchen table. "Hmm." She stares at them, silent, for a long moment. "There are two men in your future, Barbara," she says slowly. "One is fair, blond. The other has dark . . . no, black, hair."

"What about Stephen? He has light brown hair."

"I am not reading his cards right now, I am reading yours."

"But, Grandma, I'm married to Stephen, remember? There aren't going to be any fair or dark men. *This* is my man!"

"I only know what I see here," she apologizes. "Sorry."

Stephen teaches etching and engraving at USC, in the heart of downtown Los Angeles. I am fortunate to find a position at the opposite end of town, the west side, in the UCLA French department. One of their faculty unexpectedly submitted her resignation; there is an immediate vacancy. My interview with Mademoiselle Hachelle, entirely in French, of course, convinces her I'm fluent. She hands me the textbook she has written. "You will start with two classes of French I and one of French II."

It's a challenge. My experience with French is mostly conversation and reading. Now I have to learn grammatical structure and writing skills. It will be good for me. There's a nice balance to life here at the university. I teach French in the morning and continue with ballet, three afternoons a week in the dance department.

My ballet teacher and his wife, soon leaving to dance on a year-long tour in Asia, offer to rent their colorful little house in West Hollywood to us while they are gone. Still hoping for a baby, we think the yellow sunroom, facing the garden, would make a great nursery. We arrange for fertility tests at the university clinic.

Grandma Rose (Mom's mom) died some years ago, while I was still in college. Grandpa Ari, lost without her, has been living with my aunt and uncle here in Los Angeles. But he's sick now. Very sick. Mom says he'd been hanging on with all his might until Stephen and I got home from Europe. "He didn't want to die without seeing you again. You're the apple of his eye."

Stephen and I visit him in the hospital every day. You should see the look on his face when we tell him Stephen and I are teaching. He and Grandma came to this country driven by a vision of having their children educated. When their grandchildren graduated from college and continued for advanced degrees, it was more than they could have dreamed. Now my husband and I are faculty members at two major universities. Grandpa summons all his waning energy to sit up against his pillow.

"Professors," he says and bows his head. It sounds reverent. "Professors . . ." He lies back and closes his eyes, reaching for my hand. "One more thing, and I will die a happy man."

"What's that, Grandpa?"

"Sometime you'll make a family? Little ones?"

I exhale a wistful sigh. He has no idea of the difficulty we have conceiving. "Yes, Grandpa, I think so." His eyes sparkle with hope. I raise my eyebrows teasingly. "Maybe even before the end of the year!"

I shouldn't have said that. But it makes him so happy, I can hardly regret it. A few days later, Grandpa slips away.

Stephen's mother calls from Texas. "Darlings," Lonnie drawls. "I'm thrilled y'all're back home again. Can't *wait* to see you! As soon as you settle in, I'll make a trip out there. Don't know how I'll find the money—gigs have been slow this year, but don't you worry, we're doing just fine. Anyway, I'll get out there if I have to crawl."

Lonnie is a gifted musician. Playing piano is as natural to her as breathing. I've seen her practice with a novel propped up where music should be. She can play the heart out of a piece and move you to tears. Unfortunately, Lonnie never made her mark in the concert halls. She got into a hard-living drinking crowd and became a dance hall, nightclub player instead. Now she's remarried and living in San Antonio with her fourth husband (who was also her second, before Stephen's father). He plays saxophone. "We'd love to see you, Lonnie. Come as soon as you can."

"Oh, sweetie, y'all call me 'Mom,' y'hear? Now listen up, you two, and promise me you'll call Mike Careno. I told him you would. He and Nadine are dying to see you."

"Who's Mike Careno?" I whisper to Stephen, but Lonnie hears. "You don't mean to say you haven't met them!"

"Mom," Stephen cuts in, "we're just getting settled in California. *I* haven't met them either."

"But you know who they are! Haven't you told Barbara?" Without taking a breath, she rushes on. "Mike's daddy, Victor Careno, is an actor. He's had small parts in hundreds of films. Trust me, when you see his face, you'll know it."

"You're losing me, Lonnie," I interrupt. "Why are we supposed to call this 'Mike' guy?"

"Oh, how silly. I do ramble on, don't I? Victor was my lover for seven years, honey. Mike was just a teenager then. But his daddy and I were supposed to get married. So you see, Mike is almost my son."

"So what happened? Why didn't you get married?"

"Because I met Ed Ilaynia, Stephen's daddy. Of course, he wasn't Stephen's daddy at the time; Stephen wasn't born yet. But I met Ed at a party one night, and that was it! Love at first sight. Don't you laugh, now, it's true. Love at first sight. He asked me to marry him that very same night, and we ran off to Las Vegas."

"The same night?" I couldn't believe it!

"That's right, honey!" She laughs. "I suppose you think it was a bit hasty?"

"What about poor Victor?"

"Yes, well . . . he didn't know what hit him, he said. Never did get over it. But he married a nice gal some time later, and we all stayed friends. Victor and I are still good friends. So you see, darlin', it's like family. They'd be very upset if y'all don't call."

"We'll call, Mom," Stephen utters weakly and hangs up.

I can't hold back my laughter. "What a character!"

"Wish you married into a more conventional family? Your mother sure does."

"Of course not." I put my arms around his neck. "Conventional is boring. *You* are never boring. Now call Mike who's almost your brother, 'cause his father is almost your mother's—" Stephen throws a pillow at me and dials the number.

Mike and Nadine invite us to their house in Hollywood. They have five grown kids, 19 to 27 (the three boys are Mike's and the girls are Nadine's from previous marriages). Mike is a big, tall man, gray-haired and very handsome. Nadine is short, roly-poly, and silver-haired too. They are screenwriters. At one time they had numerous film and television credits, but they were blackballed in Hollywood during the McCarthy era because of their liberal views. With only an occasional script these days, they live modestly.

Mike, a great storyteller, brings back the McCarthy era vividly. Painful memories, not only of losing their livelihood but also of friends they loved who turned their backs on them. It was a time when people—even famous people— lived in fear.

They can't believe how I got my job at UCLA. "You made a call and that was it?" Mike's eldest son is incredulous.

"Someone was leaving. They had to fill the spot."

He shakes his head. "That's not how it's done at universities. People apply months, years, in advance. There are procedures, waiting lists. I've never heard of such a thing." In my ignorance, it hadn't occurred to me there was anything unusual about it.

"If we believed in God," Stephen laughs, "I'd say Someone is watching out for us."

The home of Mike and Nadine is a comfortable retreat for their kids, who visit often, and for us.

They introduce us to the Ouija board, a game that becomes a frequent favorite. I am not comfortable with it, but I say nothing, because I can't explain why. It is just a feeling. Tonight, we have "contacted" someone who claims to be the illegitimate son of an English king. None of us recognize his name, not even Mike's son who was a European history major. Nadine looks it up in the encyclopedia, and sure enough, the child, secreted away, lived a short life but did actually exist.

A silent chill falls over our group. The Ouija board, like ghost stories, is just supposed to be for fun. It isn't real, is it?

"Let's not fool around with this anymore, okay?" I suggest. "We don't know what we're playing with."

Mike is rummaging through his messy desk, looking for a book Stephen wants to borrow. He stops suddenly and smiles at me strangely. "You have a little secret, don't you?"

"What on earth are you talking about?"

"You're pregnant, aren't you?"

My eyes widen with astonishment. "Why would you say something like that?"

"I know a pregnant woman when I see one. The way your eyes shine, your skin glows." He stops when tears spring to my eyes. "You mean you don't know?"

"If this is a joke, it's a cruel one."

He puts his hands on my shoulders. "No, honey. I didn't mean it as a joke."

"If I were pregnant, I'd know, wouldn't I?"

"Sorry, I thought you did," Mike said, still convinced.

Thursday morning I have an appointment to get my teeth cleaned. The dentist picks and probes. "Hmmm," he says in a cheerful, teasing voice. "Looks like someone's expecting, huh?" I sit bolt upright in the chair. "From the look of your gums, I'd say there's a fair probability you might be pregnant. Am I right?"

That does it. I head straight to the clinic for a test and sure enough . . . !

Stephen is ecstatic. "This is just the first one," he says, "there'll be lots more."

"Okay," I agree. "We can start a farm."

After four years of futile effort, tests, more tests, clinical procedures, losses, I can hardly trust my happiness. But the doctor assures us this baby is strong and healthy.

I love being pregnant! We read books and study pictures showing the stages of a baby developing. We play classical music and speak in loving tones to the baby to get him used to the world he's coming into. Stephen puts his ear to my tummy, hoping to hear something that would reveal the mystery of what is going on in there. I can't wait to wear maternity clothes.

Months pass, but I don't show. I don't feel anything kick. I start to worry.

"Everything looks just fine," the doctor says at my next monthly exam.

"I had a horrible dream that I was giving birth to a fish." My voice shakes. "Maybe the baby has no arms or legs."

The doctor laughs. "Nonsense. You have a fine baby growing in there. Be grateful. If he's calm and quiet inside, he'll be calm and quiet when he's here too."

In the sixth month, my waist thickens. Not enough for a maternity dress, just enough to look like I'm gaining weight. In the seventh month, a student approaches me after class one afternoon. "*Madame*," he falters. "I, uh . . . well, we drew straws, and I lost, and I have to ask—"

"What is it, Todd?"

"The class is making bets," he blurts out. "Are you going to have a baby?"

I raise my eyebrows. "Which side did you bet on, Todd?"

Through his black skin, he blushes. "Tell you what," I say. "If everyone in the class gets a B or better on next week's exam, I'll let you know. If not, you'll all have to wait and see." Poor Todd. He was embarrassed to have to ask. Now he has to face the kids and say he still doesn't know.

I continue my daily ballet classes. My muscles are tight and my skin is firm. When my belly gets bigger, I wear Stephen's T-shirts over my leotard, but I don't stop dancing. I'm sure Ariel likes the music too.

Oh, yes, his name is Ariel. After my grandpa. I don't like it when people say "the baby" or "it." "It" is Ariel. A little person. "But what if it's a girl?" everybody protests. "What will you call her?" I haven't any idea. Because it isn't a girl; it's Ariel.

Having washed the cloth diapers my sister gave to me, I'm hanging them in the sun when the first labor pain arrives. Stephen wants to rush off to the hospital, but there's plenty of time. Why waste this lovely day inside a hospital? I'd rather wait in the garden until the water breaks. Even when we eventually get to the hospital, nothing much is happening. The contractions are still far apart. We play chess to while the time away.

"You're supposed to teach this afternoon. Go," I tell Stephen. "There's nothing you can do here. I'll try to sleep until you get back." Reluctantly, he leaves. Naturally (it's Murphy's, or somebody's, law) the baby comes before Stephen returns. Yes, it *is* a boy; it's Ariel. I am woozy, euphoric.

My dad is here, waiting with me for Stephen. His hand brushes the damp hair from my face. "Hi, sweetheart, how do you feel?"

"Strange, Daddy. Very strange." My voice sounds small and far away. "Like Moses when he came down from the mountain."

"How's that?"

"It's like I've seen God. I crossed the river of mystery to the unknowable, and I'm back again. I wish I could remember more."

When they take me to a room, Dad and Stephen leave, telling me to sleep. I can't. I long to hold my baby. "Where's my baby?" I ask the nurse.

"In the nursery, dear. We'll bring him to you in the morning."

"What time is it?"

"Eleven o'clock."

"I can't wait 'til morning. He needs to be with me now."

"I'll see what I can do."

I ask several times to have my baby brought in, and each time a nurse says, "Soon." Two hours pass. No sleep. No baby. I ring again. "Please bring my baby."

The nurse hands me some pamphlets published by the Catholic Church on motherhood and caring for a baby. "Perhaps this will help if you're restless," she says.

"I'm not restless; I am irritable. I need to see my baby. Please."

"This is not the scheduled visiting time."

"I don't care. My baby has just arrived in a foreign world. He feels lost and alone. I want him here with me." She does not respond and starts to leave the room. "Now," I insist. "If my baby isn't here in 10 minutes, I will scream at the top of my lungs and wake every patient on this ward."

She brings Ariel to me, wrapped in a blanket. Reaching for him, I gaze, for the first time, at his quiet, peaceful little face. It is a deep well of sagacity.

"Don't be discouraged if he cries and gets frustrated learning to suck," the nurse assures me. "Eventually he'll get it." She doesn't know my analytical son. When it doesn't work the first time, he stops, then tries again a different way, until he gets it right. I see no frustration; he seems to enjoy thinking it through. He is still so new, so fragile, physically, but his personality, his nature, is fully formed. I see it so clearly.

"Cute, isn't he?" the nurse says.

"Wise," I answer softly. "In this tiny person there is great wisdom. I have much to learn from this child."

Julia, bless her heart, comes to help for the first few days. I am so grateful, but I see her as through shadows. Nothing exists except this child, bonded to me, part of me, in a way no thing or person could ever be. We live, Ariel and I, in a euphoric little bubble. Our communication is a mystery, and it is complete. We live to feel one another's presence.

Every moment with this child carries the thrill of discovery. Love, of a kind unknown before, consumes me. Learning about him, I learn more about me too. This morning, for example, I read in a news magazine about a toddler in Vietnam. Snatched from his mother by the Vietcong, the little boy was returned to his village with his hands cut off. The photograph shows the mother lunging toward her child. My eyes are riveted on the picture. I feel *I* am that mother and the toddler is my Ari. Rage roars inside me, powerful and fierce. I race into the forest after the monster that did this to my child. I catch him. I tear him apart with my hands and a knife, ripping off his limbs, gouging out his eyes, cutting out his organs. It is horrible and gory, but I am aware only of the compelling urge to tear and hurt and destroy.

This can't be me. I abhor violence. But if someone were to harm this child of mine, I'd be capable of all of that and more. It's a part of me that didn't exist before. It's huge and strong and terrifying. But it's real. I will do anything—whatever is necessary—to protect and grow this precious being.

Stephen is a wonderful daddy. He loves bathing the baby, changing him, playing with him. We take Ariel everywhere we go—hiking, visiting, the movies.

We carry him on our backs or in a little portable bed. If he gets restless, I slip him under a big sweater and he nurses until he falls asleep.

We are happy. Stephen says we have all the riches the world can offer. Our life is blessed with the gentleness of peace, the comfort of contentment. For the first four months of Ariel's new life, I bask in boundless joy.

At the time of our return from France to the United States, in the late sixties, we discover that university campuses are drug-infested. These substances begin to intrude on our gentle world, as Stephen is drawn to experiment with marijuana and hallucinogens. To me they are evil, threatening, and unacceptable in our life. Stephen says they are harmless, that they might even help open his vision to new aesthetic dimensions. Eager to experience what they have to offer, he's appalled by my reaction.

A shadow dims the brightness of our little family's joy. Up until now, we have shared *everything*, Stephen and I. There has been no subject we couldn't dig into, no path we couldn't explore together. At first Stephen begged and cajoled me to try the marijuana and hallucinogens with him; now he shouts and demands. There are ugly arguments.

Once, to make peace, I try smoking marijuana with him and some of his friends in our living room. It burns my throat. I hate the bitter, unpleasant taste. Down the hall baby Ariel wakes and starts to cry. I need to go and see what's wrong, but my body will not rise from the chair. Must get up, baby's crying. I envision myself walking down the hall, poking my head into his room, and seeing that he's all right. But it isn't enough. I have to really go. I push and tug and feel myself straining to pull my weight, but I remain seated heavily in the chair. I'm frightened; no one is tending my baby. It seems like a long time, but at last, slogging through molasses, I struggle to break free of invisible chains holding me back and make my way to the nursery, to Ari's crib. On the white dresser, next to his bed, a lamp is lit with a frayed cord. Sparks shoot from the exposed wire, inches from Ari's bedclothes. Oh my God! Had I waited a few more moments . . . had he not cried to warn me . . . I can't bear to think. Baby, poor baby, your mama did such an irresponsible, stupid thing! For a puff of that vile stuff, I could have lost you.

"If that isn't the essence of evil," I tell Stephen, furious, "I don't know what is."

Something is happening to Stephen. I am living with the terrifying transformation of someone I know well into someone I don't. My affectionate, playful lover, the father of my child, is becoming a cold, cruel stranger I don't recognize. His eyes have become hard, round, burning coals. They don't look at things anymore; they bore into them.

When Gary and Thérèse come to visit, as they do each Christmas, Thérèse is aghast. "What happened to Stephen's eyes?"

I shake my head, indicating I have no idea. But at least now I know others see it too. I'm not imagining it. I beckon for them to follow me. In Stephen's studio, I pull out an engraving he has just finished. It's the image of an owl in delicate, muted shades. More like an oriental water-brush painting than an engraving, it's an extraordinary piece of work. Except that the piercing, evil look in the eyes of the bird is disquieting.

"Look at the title," I tell them.

" 'Self portrait,' " Thérèse whispers. "Positively unnerving."

"What within him created that?" Gary gasps.

"Satanic possession," Thérèse says, responding to her Catholic upbringing.

"The drugs," I answer, simultaneously. "Those hateful drugs."

Stephen hasn't come home after school. I wait, a nervous wreck, until almost midnight, and then call Jess and Rita to help me look for him. We drive first to the campus where everything is dark and locked up, then all over Los Angeles. Toward dawn, we find him, stoned—shouting, running naked through the Hollywood Hills.

"I'm okay," Stephen protests when we drag him into the car and cover him with a blanket. "Just a joint. I'm okay."

"Oh, sure," I mutter, "just a single joint." But it's true. Stephen's system can't tolerate any amount of alcohol or drugs. With just a beer or a few drags of marijuana, he is stoned out of his mind. Maybe it's because of his mother's alcoholism during her pregnancy. Who knows?

Stephen stays out night after night with his student buddies at their hallucinogenic parties. We fight frequently about it. "I'd invite you to come too," he says, sarcastically, "but you don't like my friends."

"I don't like drug parties."

"They're not drug parties. We're exploring important concepts. You want to see for yourself? Then come over after class tonight. Studio 4-B. We'll be there at 9:30."

I bundle up the baby, start the car, and drive downtown through a heavy rain. It's a cold night. I follow Stephen's directions carefully through the dark maze of the campus. Room 4-B. There it is. Only 9:15. I'll take the baby inside where it's warm and wait for Stephen's class to end. Holding Ari close, I run, huddled against the rain, to the metal door. It is locked. I bang on it. No response. Sheltering Ari inside my coat, I walk around to the side of the building where there's a window. Dark. Locked and dark. No one there. I don't get it; he said class ends at 9:30.

Back in the car we cruise around to see if we might have the wrong building, but a night guard assures me that is where the art classes are held. Ari and I wait in the car. Surely, if there were a change in plans, Stephen would come looking for us. We watch the dark, cold rain drip for 45 minutes. I start to cry. It's a cruel joke, dragging us out like this and disappearing with his students. I drive home slowly, crying all the way.

Things have deteriorated so badly it isn't a marriage anymore. Stephen's resentment, because I am not doing drugs with him, has solidified into chronic coldness. The stranger I live with is not the man I married.

It is lonely. It's scary. Tonight it's a bottomless despair. I consider swallowing a bottle of aspirin or cutting my wrists with a razor. The razor will hurt, but it's quicker and more sure. I look around the bathroom for the razor. Have done with it. If I can just stop crying and shaking. Want to do this clean and quick . . . what's that? Oh, the baby's crying. Concentrate; do it right. Just a minute, Ari, I'll be right there. Ari! Ari, oh my God!

I drop the razor, rush to his room and pick him up. "Don't cry, Baby, Mama's here. Mama's here." I am sobbing uncontrollably, hugging him tightly to my breast. "Oh, I'm sorry, darlin', so sorry. I wasn't thinking. No, no, I'll never leave you. Who would care for my baby if I leave?" I hold him in the rocking chair, back and forth, back and forth to the rhythm of my sobs. "Thank you, sweetheart, for calling me back. Mommy's stupid. Baby knows best. Mommy's here." We sit and rock . . . rock . . . rock . . .

The night slips away into dawn. I hear the front door open. Stephen enters, notices the light in the baby's room and sees us rocking in the chair. I raise my eyes to meet his and can't bear it. I look down again, hugging Ari close, taking comfort in the soothing, rhythmic motion. Stephen goes away, down the hall to our room and into bed. I want to leave him. I want to take my baby far away somewhere. But it was "until death do us part" and "for better or for worse." We'll have to work it through. Somehow.

Stephen discovers Scientology, his new spiritual path. "Read this!" he urges, handing me L. Ron Hubbard's book. "It's great stuff."

At least Scientology has got him away from the drugs; they don't tolerate that. And some of the philosophy makes sense to me, but it is just a repackaging of ancient Eastern philosophy and pop psychology. I find the organization distasteful, and I'm suspicious because of how much money new "recruits" must pay for courses and debriefings.

After a few weeks, Stephen doesn't speak like a normal person anymore; he sounds like a robot spouting formulated phrases. No matter what you say or how terribly upset you are, his response is always, "Thank you for sharing that." Or, "I hear you."

"I know you heard me," I say, exasperated. "Now can you please respond to me?"

"I get that you are upset."

For the second time since we've been partners in life, here is something we can't share. First the drugs, now Scientology. Stephen goes out most nights without me. I watch him shave and dress to look sharp for another evening at the Scientology "Celebrity Center," where musicians and actors gather and perform for one another. That's where he meets Karen, a well-known actress. They see a lot of each other and she calls the house, but he insists they are "just friends."

We've hit rock bottom. Desperate to save our marriage and the wholeness of our family, I suggest a psychotherapist. Stephen agrees to see him. John doesn't want to do one-on-one therapy with Stephen and me; he wants us to work in a group. I'm extremely uncomfortable with this. We're dealing with very private, personal matters. My life is falling apart. Our new baby needs a family—two parents—to grow up. It's hard enough to talk to a professional therapist about it, let alone a roomful of strangers. But I'll do anything. John's the doctor; he must know best.

This is 1968. Hostile therapy is the rage. When I share with the group what is happening in our marriage, they yell and call me names. If I express concern about Stephen using drugs, I am "controlling." If I hurt because of his rejection, I'm a "dependent fool."

"Stop worrying about the marriage!" they insist. "Work on yourself."

"But I care about my marriage. I want to save it!"

"No, you're avoiding working on yourself."

Stephen is fine with the group. He says exactly what they want to hear. Listening to him, you'd think everything was going well. What's his crazy wife so upset about? Stephen and I have lost our last vestige of communication. We are further estranged than I could ever imagine.

John decides now to separate us into different groups and have private weekly sessions with Stephen.

"Can I see you individually too?"

"No. Right now it's best that I spend time with Stephen. You continue in the group."

"I hate the group."

"All the more reason. Work through your feelings. And get your focus off Stephen. Learn more about yourself and how to live as a self-sufficient person."

"But he's my husband and the father of my child! We loved each other. I want to be like that again."

"It may never happen," John says with finality. "Deal with the reality. Take your baby, pack your bags, and head the Volkswagen van down an open highway into the next chapter of your life. Don't be afraid. Be open to a great adventure."

John is the therapist; I have to trust him. He sees all this objectively, which I can't. Why am I resisting him? Why don't I feel right about what he says?

I ask Stephen. "Do you have the same misgivings about John as I do?"

"Yeah."

"You do? But I thought you liked him!"

"I like him, but he's off base."

"Tell me why you say that." Stephen is very quiet. "Stephen?" Silence. "Stephen, please. I have to know. I'm putting my life, my baby's future into this man's hands, and I'm scared. What do you know?"

Stephen looks down at the floor. "He's been . . . sexual . . . with me."

The words bounce off my brain. They don't penetrate. I can't make sense of them. "You mean you're a homosexual?"

"No." It takes a long while for Stephen to make me understand, to tell me how John used his position to seduce him. "He said as an artist, I mustn't close myself off to any experience. I was terrified of homosexuals as a teenager. John said I had to confront that fear, enter into a homosexual encounter and overcome it. That's how it started."

Something snaps. My mind explodes. There is more here than I can process. If John and the others are right, it must be me who is crazy. I crumple on the floor in a heap. Oh God, I have a child to raise, and I am doubting my sanity, my ability to do it. I thought commitment to a marriage was right, to put all else aside and make it work. I thought both parents were supposed to raise their babies and make a home. Now a trusted psychotherapist is sexual with my husband and tells me to hit the road in a VW van. A group of my peers says I am sick and dependent because I care too much about our marriage. Is there no one on the face of the earth I can talk to? Anyone who can help?

In my dance class is a psychic, Louise. She says she can help find my true spiritual guide through this difficult time. I am desperate enough for anything at this point.

Louise and I sit cross-legged on the floor in her home, facing one another. I have given her a brief synopsis of what is troubling me. She takes both my hands in hers. "Close your eyes." Her voice is soft and sympathetic. Soothing. "I will lead you on a journey down through your consciousness," she explains, "and you will tell me exactly what you see. Okay?"

I nod and close my eyes. "We are going down, now," she whispers. "Down. Talk to me."

"We are wading in a rushing stream. We are sinking, sinking below the stream into the earth, down, down, to the core of the planet."

"Um hmmm," Louise acknowledges. I pass through many landscapes, and describe them. I see the face of a god in the sun; I cower beneath hostile stars; and I fall further down into dark caves, so far below the surface of the earth that Ari cannot come with me. Afraid to leave my baby, I am silent and shudder. "Continue," the psychic urges.

"There is a hag with a cauldron. I don't trust her; I hurry away. I meet a golden fish, a gentle, friendly fish. I like him. We play together and we are happy."

"Fish is your inner animal," Louise interjects. "He is your guide. Follow Fish."

"Uh oh. Stephen is approaching Fish and me. He wears a psychedelic shirt and shaggy beard. He steps viciously on Fish and squashes him. I try to save the sweet little fish and cuddle his bleeding body in my arms. But he dies." Hot tears splash on my hands. "I must go on alone. I am afraid."

Eventually, Louise brings me "back." We come up, up through the depths of the earth, up to the streambed where sunlight breaks through and up, at last, through the surface of the water. "You can open your eyes now."

"What am I to learn from this?" I ask the psychic. "Is it that I must go on alone?"

The last straw is the discovery of Stephen's affair with Ulna. Larry and Ulna are friends of ours, or at least I thought they were. She is tall, blonde, beautiful, and from Denmark. Stephen is attracted to tall, blonde women; I don't know why he married short, dark me. I react with hurt and anger and fury. Larry has no reaction.

"Don't you care? It is your wife, after all."

"Nah." Larry chuckles. "The truth is, I've become so bored with her, the idea that she's capable of *having* an affair makes her a bit more interesting."

Stephen is excited by the challenge of "transforming" this bland, impassive woman and sparking her passion. He initiates verbal marathons to probe beneath the lackluster surface and draw out something in the way of an opinion, a feeling. Her husband is amused. I am not. Stephen says he is helping them, but I'm unwilling to give my husband to the cause of improving their marriage.

This is the third venture where Stephen feels I oppose him. He wants my permission—my permission!—to work out one of his "hang-ups" (his fear of approaching beautiful women) by having sex with her.

"I don't see what all the fuss is about; I don't love her. I'm not sure I even like her, but I want to break through some of my barriers."

"Are you crazy, Stephen? I'm not your psychologist, I'm your wife!"

"Yes, you are. You're everything to me. My wife, lover, friend, companion in all I do. Why are you resisting me in this? Do you want me to see her behind your back? That's not the kind of relationship we want. Besides—" Stephen hesitates.

"What?"

"Larry, he's kind of interested in you."

"He what?!"

"Don't get huffy about it. He's attracted to your passion and intensity, your openness. It's precisely what he misses in Ulna."

"Just what do you expect me to do about that?"

"It's something we could explore together. Don't put a wedge between us, honey; it could be another experience for us to share."

"What I want to share with you is love. A family. A quest for spiritual and aesthetic values. This . . . you're as sick as they are. It's disgusting."

His resentment sharpens into expressions of cruelty. Systematically he destroys the positive things we built over the years, the sensitivity to one another's needs, the caring, the intimacy. Under the pretext of maintaining "honesty" between us, he tells me everything I desperately do not want to know about what "turns him on" about her. He verbalizes his fantasies, reveals details of their encounters and, when he wants to really hurt, he makes comparisons to hit my deepest vulnerabilities. Trustingly, we have revealed ourselves so completely that we have given to one another the power to annihilate. Stephen is using it. He's become a master of the art of psychological torture. I fear he wants to destroy me utterly.

I am a tourist in the land of insanity. I want to bang my head against the wall to block out the sound of his words. I sob for the disappearance of the man I once loved. We are past the point of no return. Even if Stephen tried to repair the damage, the very foundation of our love has been destroyed. Upon what would we build again?

The sun disappears early because it's winter. I return home from work with the baby, wondering what to do with the rest of my life. The house is dark. With the baby in my arms, I turn the key in the lock, slip in, and close the door behind me. Just as it clicks, there is the echo of another click. The back door in the kitchen?

"Stephen?" No answer. "Stephen! Is that you?" Nothing. I stand frozen still, holding the baby close to my pounding heart. Floorboards in the kitchen creak. "Stephen! If that's you, answer me! Don't play games, please." Total silence. Everything in the house, like me, is holding its breath. The floorboards creak again and the back door clicks shut.

Fumbling to get my key out of the lock, I slip out of the house, careful not to make a sound, and close the door behind me and Ari. Hoping we're not seen, I make our way to the car, place Ari in his seat, and back out quickly. My instincts shout, "Run!" I drive faster than I should onto the freeway toward my parents' house in Pasadena. Calm. I must calm down before we get there.

Late in the evening, Stephen calls. "What are you doing at your folks' house?"

"I was home earlier, about five o'clock, but something frightened me. Stephen, were you there?"

A low, deep-throated chuckle. A pause. Then, "You'll never know, will you?"

I do not return to the house again except once, to pack a few belongings. Property settlement is simple. "This is your favorite record; here, take it. I'll keep the books, since you don't read them anyway." There is no furniture (we rent the house furnished), no savings, stocks or bonds. Just lots of books, records, drawings, and some clothes.

Stephen weeps as I prepare to leave. At least there is that much of the man I had known left in him. Then, in a moment of flickering weakness, for the first time in months, we make love. It is a bittersweet farewell gesture.

There is no money for lawyers. One of the men in Stephen's therapy group, an attorney, says he'll handle the divorce for a few hundred dollars. Someone asks if it's a good idea to have one attorney representing both of us.

"Why not?" I ask. "There's nothing in dispute. I just want out."

"What about alimony or child support?"

"I'm sure he'll help with Ari. After all, it's his son too."

I'm heading down the highway in the VW van, Ariel in his car seat next to me. The road stretches before us into distant mountains of the unknown. I try to remember the man with whom I had fallen in love and united. Pain. There is only the searing, gripping pain with a burning paralysis in my gut. I mourn the death of a love, the destruction of a marriage, the tearing asunder of a union so complete.

Most of us take our marriage for granted. It's just there. It's comfortable. You do everything together—you don't even think about it. But the bond of marriage is powerful. Tear it apart and you realize how powerful it is. If the love is real, separation is unholy and unnatural. Like a medieval torture rack, it tears your body in two jagged pieces. Yes, something like that. Only worse.

A man will be united to his wife, and they will become one flesh.

One flesh. And the innocent fruit of that union, the fruit wherein his flesh and mine are one, is here on the seat beside me.

Stephen and Barbara are one no more. Stephen Ilaynia. Barbara Ilaynia. Two separate people. Two.

Having chosen him once, I wonder, *can I unchoose him now? Have I given so much of myself that I've become part of him whom I once chose, so that choice no longer exists?* Then to leave is to be reborn. But before rebirth is there not death? Must I die in some way, amputating half of my being to separate from him? In so doing, do I destroy us both?

"Good-bye," I whisper. "I will pray for you, if ever I learn how."

Streams in the Wasteland

See, I am doing a new thing! Now it springs up; do you not perceive it?
I am making a way in the desert and streams in the wasteland.

ISAIAH 43:19

I walk up and down the streets of Venice, a sunny beach town, with five-month-old Ari bouncing on my hip. I've been searching for an apartment, checking ads, making calls, and hearing "no" again and again because they don't accept children. It's discouraging. I stop to gaze at the ocean across the street; it is calm and vast and indifferent to my plight. Turning back to resume my search, I bump into a woman carrying two huge bundles of laundry.

"Oh! Sorry. I was distracted."

"Cute baby. Hi, sweetie," she croons, tickling Ari's hand.

"Say, you wouldn't happen to know of a clean, affordable apartment I could rent, would you?"

"Actually, I do. My husband and I are moving, and we're looking for someone to sublet our place."

It's more than I want to pay, $125 a month, but it's perfect. A small cottage duplex, it is cheery, flooded with sunlight. I point to the attached apartment in the back. "Who lives there?"

"Nice guy, Karl. A little weird, but very nice."

"Uh oh, what do you mean, 'weird'?"

"No, he's fine. Very helpful and considerate; he's just heavy into meditation. A yoga freak. Stands on his head a lot."

"Swell." My eyes roll. I've been through enough "weirdness" for a lifetime. How about a small dose of "normal" for a change?

"You'll like Karl," she assures me. "It's the ape that might drive you crazy."

"The what?!"

"Yeah, two houses down, a full-grown Gibbon. He screams a lot when his owners aren't home. And he runs up to hug strangers who pass their yard. A hug from a beast like that is no joke. But he's harmless. You'll get used to him."

"As long as I don't get them confused," I mumble. "The neighbor stands on his head, the ape hugs strangers. Or is it the other way . . .? Never mind, I'll take it."

I pass my neighbor's door, juggling a box of wallpaper rolls in one arm and holding Ari in the other. "Here, let me give you a hand with that." My neighbor steps out of his apartment and reaches for the wallpaper. "I'm Karl."

He's tall, blond and blue-eyed. Much better looking than I expected for someone "weird."

"Thanks. I'm Barbara. I live in front."

"I know." We enter my apartment. "Where are you going to put the wallpaper?"

"It might look good on the dining room wall. What do you think?"

"Yeah, it'll spruce up the place nicely. Tell you what, I'll do it for you."

"Hey, that's terrific. You know how?"

"Oh, yeah! My old man was a paperhanger. One of the best. I had to help a lot when I was a kid."

Perfect. I move next door to a professional paperhanger. "Have at it," I tell Karl.

There is a wonderful feeling about this sunny little apartment, my friendly neighbors, and the cheerful beach community with gardens and floral window boxes near the seashore. Never mind that my soul is shattered. We'll focus on the sun and the sea, Ari and I. We'll summon all our energy for living again.

Before long the dining room is transformed. "It's beautiful! How can I thank you?"

"You can come with me for a walk along the ocean." The beach is jammed with people. Street musicians work the crowds; vendors hawk goods and souvenirs. Karl wears my backpack with Ari in it and puts his arm over my shoulder to steer me through the crowd. A conga player in an all-black street band calls out to Karl, who smiles and waves back. Waving his hands with excitement, Ari enjoys the colorful sights and sounds.

Further along, on a quieter section of the beach, we sit near the water. Ari crawls about, playing in the sand. Karl tells funny anecdotes about his New England upbringing in a traditional Swedish family. He talks about his gentle mother and a father he remembers as hard, severe. "When he died, I ordered the biggest, heaviest stone we could afford," he says.

"As a memorial?"

"No. To keep the sonofagun down." Karl grins. "But the old man could be funny, sometimes. He always wanted me to marry a Swedish girl. I dated Jewish girls, Italian girls, Asian girls, a black gal—all of them were very nice, but none of them were Swedish. 'Why can't you go out with a Swedish girl?' he'd say all the time. It got on my nerves until one day I sassed him back. 'You wouldn't care if I dated a whore, as long as she's Swedish!' Furious, my ol' man shot back, 'There *are* no Swedish whores!'" Karl chuckles, remembering.

Ari throws sand in Karl's lap. "Hey, buddy, you want to build a castle?" Turning back to me he asks, "So, tell me. What brings you to our sunny shore?"

Karl and I talk about my divorce—more than I intended—and I ask about his work. Karl squints at the sun. "I'm a musician. Jazz. But I left New York a year ago to study Vedantic philosophy with a guru here in California."

"So Janice was right."

"About what?"

"She said you're into meditation and yoga and all sorts of—"

" . . . weird things!" he finishes my sentence. "Did she tell you I'm a vegetarian too? Might as well get it all out up front."

"She told me about the ape."

"Yeah, he's one of our more desirable neighbors."

"Oh, oh!" The baby is crawling toward the water. Karl jumps up to catch him, then carries him down to where the waves meet the shore. He holds Ari by his wrists and gently swings him back and forth with his feet dangling in the water. The baby laughs and kicks at the foam.

Great news! Lorna is now in Los Angeles. Her husband had been teaching at the University of Pau in France, but now has taken a position at the University of California. I am excited about living in the same town and sharing our lives again.

It's late, maybe 2:00 in the morning. Someone is climbing the steps to my front door, calling for "Carol." I yell out, "There's nobody here named Carol. You have the wrong place." He is banging on the door and I'm getting scared. I hate to call so late, but I don't know what else to do. I dial Karl's number.

"Karl," I whisper. "I need help. There's someone trying to break in."

"Huh? Barbara? Speak up, I can't hear you."

"Please, help. Someone's at my door."

"Louder . . . where? Here? Hold on, baby, I'll be right over."

I hang up, put out the light, and look out the front window. Karl is coming around the corner of the house. He has pulled on a pair of jeans, but he's still barefoot and bare-chested. The handle of a kitchen knife is sticking out of his pants in the back.

On my porch is a tall, unkempt-looking black man. He is still knocking and yelling. "C'mon, Carol, open up! Hey, baby, this is ol' Leroy!"

Karl steps out of the shadows. "Leroy," he says quietly, "better get your self out of here. You're upsetting my wife."

The intruder turns toward him, startled. "You live here?"

"Yes," Karl says, his bare feet planted firmly on the ground, his hands on his hips.

"I'm lookin' for a li'l gal named Carol," Leroy says.

"She doesn't live here."

The two men size each other up. Leroy moves away from the door. "She said she lives here."

"This is my home. Try someplace else," Karl says.

Leroy walks away, cursing and muttering.

Karl watches to make sure he's gone, and then climbs the steps. I let him in. I feel very vulnerable, alone in this unfamiliar community, with an infant child. My teeth are chattering.

"It's okay, he didn't mean any harm," Karl says. "He's just confused, like a lot of people around here. The hash turns their brains to silly putty. Did he wake the baby?"

"No." Karl appears bigger than life to me, heroic. It feels good, very good, that he's here. I point to the knife in his belt. "Were you going to use that? Oh, I was so scared!"

Karl lays the "weapon" on the dining table. "Me too," he grins.

"You risked your life! I was so sorry to wake you, but didn't know what else to do."

Karl wears a crooked, teasing grin. "We can make a hole through the kitchen wall. That way I can get here faster next time. Hmmm." His gaze fixes on my summer nightgown.

I go quickly into the bedroom for a robe. "I wasn't expecting company," I apologize.

He shrugs.

"You think Leroy's gone for good? Can you stay for just a little while to make sure? Oh, I must be a nuisance."

"Not at all," Karl says, "C'mon, sit down."

I sit.

"Over here," he says, motioning me closer to him on the sofa.

I look at him suspiciously.

"No heavy number." He reaches a hand toward me. "Now just relax a few minutes, then you can go to sleep." I rest my head on his shoulder and feel the tension start to slip away. "Nice," he murmurs, his voice low and throaty. "Now give me a good-night kiss." It's a gentle, friendly kiss. At first. Then it becomes more urgent, altogether consuming. I respond with a kiss that continues past the breaking dawn.

Waking to a cool, cloudy morning, I hear the baby laughing and smell fresh coffee percolating on the stove. I pad into the kitchen on bare feet. Karl is at the table with Ari on his lap. Ari digs into Karl's shirt pocket, pulls out little pieces of paper and gurgles with joy over each one he finds. Karl puts the paper back in his pocket, and the game begins again.

"How long have you two been at this?" I ask.

"Oh, she's back from the dead. Man, I've never known anyone to sleep like you. The kid was jumping up and down in his crib, laughing, singing, shrieking, and throwing toys at you. I could hear him clear over at my place."

"I never heard a thing."

"Obviously. I was getting ready for mouth-to-mouth resuscitation."

"Don't get fresh now."

"Wouldn't dream of it. Say, does your son always wake up in such a great mood?"

"Always. He's much sweeter than his mother."

We've been inseparable these last eight months. Karl makes me laugh for the first time since I don't know when. He makes me feel pretty. Exciting. Alive. I thought I never would again. When I'm not teaching or correcting papers, he entertains me with great stories of his life and people he knows in the music business.

We shop for vegetarian groceries. Karl cooks a lot of our meals; I clean up. We stroll along the beach, Ari happy high on Karl's shoulders. At a carnival booth on the boardwalk, Karl throws balls and hits the target. He wins a big stuffed mouse and gives it to Ari. Ari clutches the doll, who is as big as he is, and names him "Mouse."

It is nearly one o'clock in the morning. I am writing in my journal and listening to Mozart's piano concerto. Karl's car pulls up. He's back from a gig. I brush my hair, anticipating that he will probably knock at my door. The concerto plays to the end and still Karl isn't here. I reach for the phone. No, that isn't a good idea. It's very quiet on his side of the wall. I'd better leave him alone tonight.

Karl likes to listen to music and talk about his favorite subject: Eastern philosophy. Driven by a hunger to know God, he studies the great "masters" from India and spends hours every day practicing esoteric disciplines through meditation. "God, the creative force, is within us all," Karl says. "We *are* God. The only difference between Jesus Christ and the rest of us is that He knew it. Through study and meditation and the disciplines, we can eventually arrive at ultimate knowledge."

"What is that?" I ask.

"The disciplines lead to nirvana, where we transcend the physical body and the material world. Nirvana is a state of union with the cosmic One, the state of knowledge and peace. It is freedom from the agonies of passion, desire, hatred and delusion. When we reach this stage, we are free from the cycle of reincarnation and its consequent sufferings."

"Beyond the physical body? Can we transcend our own body?"

"Some people can leave the body at will. I'm told the Russians are far ahead of us in these things. They actually have astronauts trained in astrophysical travel." Reading aloud to one another from his books, we marvel at these things and talk late into the night about man's untapped capacity for knowledge, and how to develop our own.

Karl has been showing me how to practice the mental and physical disciplines—including a vegetarian diet—that bring us closer to cosmic wisdom, and freedom from our human limitations. "It's no accident that we met," he explains. "When the student is ready, the teacher appears. But you'll soon surpass me. You have a natural gift for this."

"How so?"

"I've been at this for six years and I haven't reached the point of 'going over.' But you, after just a few months, I think you can do it, if you'll just let it happen."

But I can't; something stops me. In my meditations, I've reached a point where, if I just "let go," I might be able to leave my body. Perhaps even project astrally into other planes of existence. It's like sitting on top of a wall. I just have to let myself fall to the other side. But each time, something calls me back, a sense of danger, a fear that I will never return. What calls me? Simply fear of the unknown? Or some greater, protective wisdom?

Karl pulls eggplant parmigiana from the broiler. "Now tell the truth," he says, serving a colorful array of melted cheese and tomatoes to Ari and me, "do I spoil you?"

"That's for sure. Mmmm. You outdid yourself."

I had come shattered to Karl and the cottage on the beach. Destroyed. After Stephen's betrayal, the fragile confidence I had developed through our love was left in shreds. Stephen confirmed everything I had felt growing up: I'm not pretty enough. I can't be loved. This world is a cruel, hurtful place.

But Karl is honest and loyal and wholesome—unusual among jazz players, where drink and drugs are all too common. And he truly seems to care for Ari and me. It is all good. And yet, deep down I know that he and I will never marry. Karl doesn't want the responsibility. He drifts through life on the winds of fate, landing when the breeze dies down. I call him "Peter Pan."

"You're right, I don't ever want to grow up."

Just as well. If I were ever to marry again, I'd want someone more in control of his destiny, someone who can deal with the realities of practical economics and make things happen. So why don't I look for that kind of a man? The answer is scribbled in green ink across the pages of my journal:

In the deepest part of me, I believe we are to marry only once. I have been married. It had been an extraordinary union, and it is no more. For my lifetime, that was it. You don't do it twice.

I release a weary sigh. The pain of separation from Stephen has never eased up. Awake or in my dreams, I relive that last disastrous year over and over.

So what is it we share, Karl and I? Karl always says, "I'll be with you for as long as you'll have me. I don't need a piece of paper blessed by bureaucracy to love you, or to keep me faithful." Sanctified or not, there is love. Maybe for a lifetime, maybe not. There's an exploration of music, art, spiritual mysteries and a friendship until death. We're sure of that. Whatever or whoever happens in the future, we tell one another, nothing will diminish the friendship.

And, of course, there's the powerful attraction of Karl's masculine presence. Until now, I've known lovemaking to be warm, affectionate, playful. But with Karl, it is fully sexual. He opens a realm of sensuality beyond my imagination, and I respond with a resonant force.

"Is it wrong?" I ask Lorna. "Nothing in my upbringing says it's wrong, although religions say it is. But Karl restores; he heals what Stephen destroyed. How can something so natural, so life-affirming be wrong?"

"Not all religions say it is wrong," Lorna replies. "Ask Karl about the ancient teachings of the Kama Sutra in India. Have you seen pictures of the stone friezes on their temples?" She laughs. "They look like a pornographic manual to erotic pleasures. Anyway, they say sex is a conduit to God. I'm sure Karl can tell you more about it."

A conduit to God? I wonder. Passion does bring us out of time and space and closer to the eternal. At least, that's as close as I can get for now.

I can't make ends meet teaching French literature at the university, but what else can I do? Research—I'm good at that. But who would use it? The movie industry? I have no idea how to look for a job.

I barge in, without appointment, at a number of studios and production houses, ridiculously ignorant about the thousands and thousands of talented people in Los Angeles trying to penetrate the entertainment industry. Remarkably, some are courteous and generous with their time. One particularly helpful producer on Sunset Boulevard suggests I look for work with Jacques Cousteau.

"Cousteau?" I idolize Cousteau. Years before, in France, Stephen and I had seen his film *The Living Sea*. I haven't forgotten our excitement at discovering a whole new world under the surface of the ocean. "Where can I find Cousteau? I thought he was in France."

"Yes, but he also has offices just three blocks from here."

I scribble the address and run out. I find the building and knock at the door. No answer. Knock again and try the knob. It opens. I slip into an empty reception area. "Hello?" No one. I look around and follow a short corridor with closed doors. No people, no sounds, no bustle of activity. Nothing. I open one of the doors and look in. A large, oblong conference table. And voices. In one quick movement eight faces pivot and fix their stares on me. All conversation ceases.

"I, uh . . . excuse me, I didn't mean . . . I was . . . I am looking for Mr. Jacques Cousteau, please."

"I am Captain Cousteau."

I turn toward the French-accented voice at the head of the table. Oh my gosh, it really is him.

"What do you wish to see me about?"

Do I have to say it before all these people? I am awkward, paralyzed. "Sir, I . . . please excuse me, I didn't mean to interrupt. You see . . . Actually . . ." (oh, just *say* it) "Captain Cousteau, I came here to work for you."

"Ah?"

"Yes, whatever you need, sir. I'm bilingual English and French . . . uh, good at research—"

He cuts me off. "Please leave your résumé on the reception desk. As you can see, we are in a meeting. I cannot discuss it now."

"Yes, of course, I'm so sorry. But, sir—"

"Yes?"

"I don't have a résumé." (How dumb is that? Why didn't I prepare a résumé?)

"You'll find paper out there. Just write down what you can do."

I nod, step out and close the door quietly. Whoa! Take a deep breath. They must think I'm an idiot! I find paper and pen on the desk. As oxygen seeps back into my brain, I try to write. Half an hour and two pages later I walk out and go home.

The semester ends, summer begins, and my job search continues. I'm armed now with a proper résumé and appropriate clothing. In August, if nothing comes through, I'll have to renew my contract at UCLA. I'm close to desperation.

The telephone rings. "Jean-Michel Cousteau, here. I'm the elder son of Captain Cousteau. You were seeking employment and left some information with us?"

"Yes, that's right."

"I could use help on a project. We're developing an undersea museum on the Queen Mary. Tell me what you know about marine biology."

"Nothing at all, sir, but I know how to find out."

"Good enough. Come tomorrow morning at 9:00 and ask for Mary Farber. She'll explain what we need in more detail."

I arrive bright-eyed, ecstatic, in the morning and introduce myself to Mary Farber. She cuts me off without a greeting. "You can start on those." Pointing to a sheaf of papers on a credenza near her office, her voice is sharp. "Find out everything you can on the topics listed." Training session is over. I quickly go through the files, but there isn't much help in there. I'm pretty discouraged by the end of the afternoon when Jean-Michel stops by to say hello. He has a few helpful hints and now, despite the chill emanating from Mary's office, I warm up to the project.

I've been at the job three days. This morning, as I crawl out of bed and stretch, I suddenly stop, listening. Something is wrong. I don't hear the usual playful, gurgling sounds from Ari's crib. He's lying flat on his back, hardly breathing, looking very gray. Frightened, I pick him up. He doesn't open his eyes; he just falls back limp, like a rag doll. I don't have to take his temperature to know he has a high fever; he's very hot to the touch. Karl doesn't answer his phone. I dial again. "Lorna, hurry . . . *please*."

I hold my baby close, pacing back and forth, weeping, talking to him until Lorna arrives. By the time we reach the hospital, Ari still hasn't opened his eyes, but his little body is wracked with convulsions. "Please, God, please," I keep mumbling. To whom it may concern. "*Please!*"

There is no waiting in the emergency room. They take one look at him and get busy. "Temperature: 108. Ice mattress!" Doctors, nurses, people rush around.

Pipes, tubes, heaven knows what. "Excuse me," a nurse says brusquely, "please go out to the waiting room." It seems like I live and die a thousand deaths before a doctor comes out. "Doctor . . . please! Will he be all right?"

"He's got spinal meningitis. We're trying to isolate the strain."

"Meningitis?" I've heard of that. It kills. If not, it brings on blindness, deafness, mental retardation, damage to the motor system. He can't have meningitis! "Does that mean—?"

"Lady, at this point we don't know what it means. We don't even know if he'll make it through the night." *Lady?* I'm not "lady"; I'm his *mother*! I have to know! The doctor barks orders at the nurses and I return with him to the room where my baby is shivering on an ice mattress. The day drags on into night.

As soon as Karl gets home and hears my message, he drives to the hospital and rushes up to the ward. He stops, breathless, at Ari's bed. Pricked with needles, probed with tubes, undergoing painful spinal taps, baby Ari's still little body is almost frozen on the ice mattress. One large plastic tube comes from a slit on the side of his neck, now covered with a bloodied bandage. Karl breaks out in perspiration, and tears well up in his eyes. Visibly shaken, he looks like he's about to pass out. He turns away. "How does it happen?" he whispers. "When did I get so attached? The little bugger sneaked in and stole my heart when I wasn't looking." I put my hand on his shoulder, recalling the endless hours Karl spends with my baby, teaching him, playing with him, disciplining and loving him. "Big help I am," he continues. "I come here to support you, and I'm the one falling apart."

The doctor comes to the waiting room and I jump up.

"I wish we could be more optimistic," the doctor says. "We have a very sick little boy on our hands."

"And—?" I don't want to say the words, but I have to know. "And brain damage? They said it's possible—"

"We're doing all we can, Mrs. Ilaynia. We've got two doctors at his bedside and two working in the lab. The fever is under control, but we can't tell yet how much damage there is. Go home. There's nothing you can do here. Get some rest and come back in the morning."

I fall to my knees in Ari's empty room. Mouse, his favorite stuffed toy, is all alone in the crib. I pick him up and hug him close. "Mouse looks as sad as we feel," Karl says. He and Lorna plan to stay the night with me, but I insist they leave. Pain envelopes me like a thick, isolating shield. No one can share this with me. No one.

I have to do something, but what? Pray? On my knees: "Dear God, please save my baby. Let him come out of this whole." Pacing the room: "Dear God, please . . ." It's not working. I am suffocating in my tiny cottage; the prayers are bouncing back from the ceiling at me. I go outdoors to breathe the sea air and see the stars. "Star light, star bright, I wish . . ." I fall to a helpless, crumpled heap on the porch.

I don't know how long I've been lying in this knot of despair before the fury hits me. I won't let Ari die! Infused with new energy, I channel all my force, my energy, toward Ari's consciousness. "Hear me, Ariel." I see his beautiful but inert little body. His eyes are closed. I go in behind his eyes to that precious little brain. It's shadowed, but there is still a faint, gold-colored spark.

"Darling baby," my heart calls to him, "an evil thing has caught you unaware and knocked the wind out of you. You were knocked senseless. But you've been down a full day now. You must get up, or it's all over. There is an enemy in there, son. It's bad. It will kill you. And there's absolutely nothing I can do. I would fight this battle for you, if I could. But this one is yours. Are you hearing me, Ari? Get up, sweetheart. It'll be tough, but you have to fight now—and fight to win!"

A tiny stream of blood flows through his brain and out again; there are unclean, unhealthy looking spots in it. Following the red stream as it travels through Ari's veins, I force up a tower of energy from within me, get it centered into a dense mass, and shoot it like a laser beam into his system. "Now, sweetheart. Up!"

Suddenly I notice the clock on the dresser. It is 7:00 A.M. I am spent, exhausted, anxious to get back to the hospital. And terrified of what I'll find when I do. I call Karl. Then Lorna. "Ready?"

"Be right there."

In the car, I tell them in a few words what happened. "Did you get through?" Lorna asks.

"How do I really know?" I break down and sob. "There's nothing more I can do." We fly through the lobby to the elevators and into the children's ward.

"You came at a good time." The doctor looks tired. He wipes his forehead with a handkerchief. "I'll be frank, it was a tough night. A couple of times we thought we'd lost him for sure." My head goes light and I come close to a faint. "But he rallied. At 7:00 this morning, he broke through. I think he'll make it."

"Oh, thank God!"

"Seven o'clock?" Lorna asks, "You're sure?"

"Seven o'clock."

"What does that mean, 'make it'? Will he be normal? Will he be able to—?"

"One thing at a time, Mrs. Ilaynia. He will probably live. Let's deal with the rest later."

Every moment is critical, and they can't isolate the strain to determine the most effective treatment. I am frantic. Karl comes with me to see Ari every day. "You'll have to call Stephen," he reminds me.

"Why? What's he got to do with this?"

"He is still Ari's father."

"Oh? What makes him a father? His faithful visits? His financial support?"

"I know, I know. But call him anyway. It's the right thing to do."

Stephen arrives. I see him striding down the corridor and nudge Karl to come with me to the cafeteria. Let him visit and get out of there. A big difference it will make in Stephen's life if Ari dies.

In the cafeteria, Karl and I are unable to eat. "Ari's in good hands, darlin'. They're doing all they can."

"I know," I sigh. "By the way, my supervisor, Mary, isn't taking this too well. I go in every morning to collect my work and bring it here to the hospital. When Ari sleeps, I work next to him. I don't care if I have to work day and night to get it done, but I want my baby to know I'm here when he opens his eyes. Yesterday, when I went in to pick up the work, Mary snapped at me, 'How long will *this* go on?'"

"The nerve!" Karl interjects. "What did you tell the witch?"

"I told her, 'Maybe you'll get lucky and he'll die tonight.'"

Karl shakes his head. "I'll never understand people. Animals are kinder."

We return to Ari's room. Stephen is gone, thank goodness. The baby is awake. Still struggling with pain and spinal taps, he is amusing his nurse by trying to balance green peas on a spoon. He laughs each time the peas fall off. Karl leans over the crib. "Hi, old topper . . ."

Ari reaches his hand through the bars and seizes Karl's fingers. With his other hand, Karl caresses his head. "Atta boy," he croons. "Look, Mama's here. Hold on, son, we're here. We're right with you."

I'd brought Mouse, and Ari clutches the toy to his cheek. His sweetness reminds me of the grandfather he was named for.

"This child is a blessing to everyone on the ward," the nurse says. She has an odd way of talking. Everything is "blessed" and "God's work" and "God's will." But she's nice. And she seems to really care for my little boy.

Ari remains in Intensive Care for three weeks. Three weeks before anyone can say to me, "He's out of danger; we're transferring him to the children's ward." It seems like forever before I can bring him home. We are instructed to disinfect everything in his room and throw out all stuffed animals.

"Even his favorite, Mouse?"

The doctor nods. "We had to take it from him."

Lorna scrubs his crib and cares for Ari when I go to work. I don't feel safe yet, leaving him at day care.

Four weeks later, we return for his follow-up exam. The doctor calls in a colleague and points to Ariel. "This is the case I told you about. The kid on Ward 6." They look, they check, they probe and they shake their heads in wonder. "I don't believe in miracles," the colleague says, "but I've never seen a recovery like this from what you described."

"Pretty amazing, huh?"

I wonder what they mean exactly. Just how bad had it been? If there's a God, why would He make a miracle to preserve my son? Why?

"We want to see him again when he starts school," the doctors say. "It'll be interesting to know if he has trouble learning to read."

"*Interesting*?" Doctors can be cruel. He's 18 months old now. Do they think I can wait until he's five to find out if my son is all right? No way. We start our alphabet lessons this afternoon. Months pass. Years. And I live daily with the fear of brain damage or an impaired motor system.

Ariel grows strong, graceful and athletic. Every day I have of this child's life is a miracle, a gift, and I never take it for granted. By the time Ari is three he starts to read. A few years later, in the third grade, his teacher suggests putting him in the advanced program for mentally gifted children. Clearly he's escaped the damaging effects of meningitis. But since the time of his illness—maybe it will always be this way—I live in constant fear of losing him. Every morning, I send him off to school with an almost desperate kiss, and I whisper, "Bring him back to me today. Please, bring him back."

His father's irresponsible conduct during his sporadic visits inflames my fear. When Ari is only two, I watch them cross a busy street. Stephen walks ahead, leaving the toddler unattended to make his way through traffic. Panicked, I run out after them, snatch Ari up and carry him home.

On another visit, Stephen takes Ari and promises to return him at six in the evening. Delayed in traffic, I arrive home seven minutes late. They aren't here, so I assume Stephen is also late. Six-thirty and they still aren't back. No answer to my calls. By seven, I call the highway patrol to check on accidents. Eight o'clock comes and goes . . . nine o'clock . . . ten. By now, I have the police searching.

An officer returns to my house at 11:30 with Ari in his arms. "Is this your child, ma'am?"

"Yes! Oh my gosh, where did you—?"

"He was left with your neighbor across the alley at six o'clock this evening." He hands me a piece of paper with the name. "I assume you know these people?"

"Why no, I don't! I don't understand why they had my baby."

"Your 'ex' told them that you'd be home in a few minutes. He couldn't wait for you."

"He couldn't wait *seven minutes*? He left my son with total *strangers* and didn't even let me know where he was?" That does it. It has been a history of ugly arguments, anyway, because Stephen won't commit to a regular schedule. The child never knows when, or if, he'll see his dad again. It is too disturbing. I move to restrict Stephen's visiting rights.

We are close to completing the Queen Mary exhibits, and I don't want to continue working with Mary Farber. I ask Philippe, the younger Cousteau brother, to let me work with him on the television documentaries.

"I'd like that too, but I can't 'steal' you away from Jean-Michel."

"I understand. I guess I'll be giving notice, then, at the end of the week. Sorry, Philippe. I'll miss you and Jean-Michel and the others."

I'm sad on Friday morning, as I pack up my office. Philippe pokes his head through the doorway. "Put that stuff in a box and follow me."

"Where are we going?" He cocks his head toward his end of the building. "No kidding!" I jump up and give him a hug. "How did you manage that?"

"Let's just go—we've got to get the film on sea otters started. Find out where they live and what time of year we can shoot underwater. Get the most respected scientist specializing in otters to join the expedition. Find a local guide, see what gear we'll need . . ." He continues the list as we travel to my new office down the hall.

I love my work with Philippe and his crew on the research ship *Calypso*. Philippe and Jan, married five years (over his mother's objection to an American daughter-in-law), are a great couple. She accompanies Philippe on his expeditions, the only woman besides the venerable Madame Cousteau, Senior, to set foot on the male-only domain of *Calypso*.

"I want to go too!" I tell Philippe.

"Ha, you can't even swim."

"If I could swim and dive, you'd take me?"

"Sure, sure . . ."

Calypso returns several days later, with two of the divers, Louis and Marc. After being away from home 8 to 10 months, the married guys are eager to get back to France. The single ones usually wait for the next expedition with us in Los Angeles. So it's always more fun at the office between expeditions, when the divers are there.

"Teach me to go underwater," I say to them. They take me to Jan and Philippe's house, where the divers stay when they're in town, and we get into the swimming pool.

"Start with this first." They slip a mask over my face and secure the band. Down I go under the surface. The mask fills with water; it gets into my eyes and windpipe as I breathe in. I come up sputtering. "Try again." And again. No use.

I can't master it in a domestic swimming pool, so how can I do it out at sea? I have to be content guiding the expeditions with research from my desk.

"Take the guys sightseeing, okay?" Philippe pleads with me for an evening alone with his wife. "There's a great restaurant down on Melrose." He drops money on my desk. "That should take care of the three of you."

"What about Ariel? I can't leave him home alone."

Another few dollars fall to the desk. "Yeah, yeah, take him too. Does he eat Mexican?" Ari eats everything, and the divers love him. When Karl is working (usually at night), they take us out to comb moonlit beaches, swim among the kelp beds and, when the season is right, watch the grunion run.

Lorna's marriage has been difficult from the start. Now her husband refuses to have children, and she's filing for divorce. She packs her bags, preparing to return to the Basque country in the southwest corner of France, near the border of Spain—the place where she and Steward had lived when he taught at the University of Pau. She feels a strong connection with that part of the world and it is calling her back.

My heart is breaking. I am losing my best friend. "Distance has no power over our bond," she argues against my tears. "We'll always be close."

"Being close 12,000 miles away is different. I want you where we can watch each other's kids grow up. I want to be involved in one another's daily struggles and joys."

"Perhaps one day we will."

No. I know with certainty it won't happen. Drying tears leave a caked, brittle trail on my cheeks.

Lorna hasn't been gone three weeks when Karl is ready to leave for India. It has been his dream to study in India at the feet of the great gurus. He's been saving and preparing for this trip as long as I've known him, reading about India, steeling himself for the confrontation with hardship, poverty, filth, and truth in its purest form. "I'll miss you more than I ever imagined I could miss anyone," he says, "but I can't give it up."

"How long will you be gone? Six months, a year, forever?"

"I wish I knew. I just have to go and do whatever is revealed to me when I get there."

So they're gone, Karl and Lorna both. Stephen is lost, and even Ari was almost lost. I can hardly bear to think about it. Am I always to lose the ones I love? My world is so fragile.

I board the plane, uneasy about leaving Ari behind with "Auntie Mae," the lady who takes care of him every day when I go to work. Mom and Dad will stop by every day to see him. It's important, everyone tells me, to take time off and restore my energy.

Settling into the comfortable seat, away from telephones, deadlines and responsibility, I have to admit this feels pretty good. As a single mom, there's no one to whom I can say, "Take him; I need a five-minute break." There's no one to take turns with changing a diaper, preparing a meal, or soothing a cranky, tired child. It's true; I need a break.

I haven't seen Lorna in almost a year now. I had called the little hotel in the Basque mountains of France and told her I was coming. Excited, we decide to meet in Paris; then we'll take a train to the Vallée d'Ossau, the corner of the Pyrenees Mountains where she's been living.

I open a long-neglected novel and begin to read. To be uninterrupted is luxurious, and time passes quickly; before I know it, we're landing at Charles de Gaulle airport in Paris. A taxi takes me to a cozy little apartment above the Cousteau offices where divers and others connected with the expeditions often stay between trips. It's unoccupied now, and Philippe said I could use it.

Paris again! The smell and feel and arrangement of a Paris apartment carries me back in time, tying together the loose threads of my life and giving them continuity.

The telephone wakes me in the morning. "What?! You're still asleep?" I can't recognize the voice addressing me familiarly in French. "Get dressed, someone's here to see you."

"Who is this?"

"Who is it?" The voice is indignant. "You really don't know who this is? Well, if you can't recognize your boss's voice, he should fire you! You're fired."

I laugh. Philippe "fires" me every other day. In Los Angeles, I had bought him a notepad with "You're Fired!" in big, bold letters printed on every page. "Here," I had told him, "you can just leave this on my desk and save yourself the trouble."

"Philippe, you've never spoken French to me before! And I didn't expect you to be in Paris!"

"Excuses, excuses. Hurry downstairs. Annette is here."

Annette Bouget! I can't wait to meet my counterpart researcher in Cousteau's Paris office. We've talked so many times on the phone, assisting one another on various projects and, in the process, we've become friends. How wonderful to meet her at last.

"Let's celebrate," Annette says with hugs and kisses on both cheeks. Philippe takes us to lunch in an out-of-the-way seafood restaurant and orders his favorite for the three of us: manta ray.

Back in the apartment, I pull out my old phone book and dial numbers that had been familiar to me six years ago.

Yves Monaud is delighted to hear from me and insists we have dinner. "At the Coupôle, of course—tonight." He has reserved a table on the restaurant side, the room with the white tablecloths. Stephen and I couldn't even afford the café section. "There will be no onion soup tonight," Yves insists. "Order a full-course meal, and don't look at the right side of the menu." How embarrassing! He remembers the onion soup.

Revisiting Paris recalls my former life and marriage. Ahh, I had believed that union to be indestructible. Nothing seems real since our love dissolved and I fell off the edge of the earth. I've been floating ever since, disembodied, with no up, no down, no gravity. Except for Ari, my life has lost its direction.

I catch my reflection in the window of the shop where Stephen bought boots for my cold feet. I walk through the open markets of the rue DaGuerre, as I did each evening when I'd meet Stephen at the studio and, oh yes, there it is, the little Moroccan restaurant where we'd eat hot couscous with friends who searched, as we did, for truth and beauty and justice.

On the right bank, in the gardens of the Bibliothèque Nationale, I recall the special moment when I felt the Creator's Presence. Such moments are rare, and they plant seeds. Standing in that same spot, I close my eyes, breathe deeply and try to recreate the moment. It is not possible.

I wind back toward the student quarter, toward the landmark English bookstore, *Shakespeare & Co.*, known for its history of writers who gathered there: Ernest Hemingway, Gertrude Stein, and others. *Shakespeare & Co.* is also where we first met Yves, and found our little bird with the broken wing. The store is still there, but George Whitman has since died, says the lady at the desk. *Who now publishes the stories and exhibits the paintings of young, unknown artists?* I wonder.

Around the corner is the restaurant where a whole lamb rotates on a spit in the window. Stephen and I had gazed hungrily at it a hundred times, but it was too expensive for us. Behind me, Nôtre Dame is lit up against the dark sky on the Ile Saint Louis.

Crossing a bridge to the other side of the river, I come to where Stephen and I lived at the Cité des Arts. What young artists and musicians live there now? Is there another genius composing music like our dear Stéfan? I must call and see him while I'm here. My memory is full with the richness of his music, those remarkable, spontaneous compositions, and his irrepressible dry humor. Impulsively, I stop in to see if Françoise still works at the reception desk. Does she remember me? Yes! She jumps up, surprised, for a warm embrace.

With every step, I hear the echo of Stephen's steps beside mine. Standing where we had lived and loved, inhaling deeply where we had breathed as one, I am assured of what I have to know: the beauty of my marriage was not a chimeric fantasy; it had been real. It flutters back to life, struggling against a heavy dark veil of deception and betrayal and of passing time, defying events that would have it all erased.

Paris. Within her hidden alleys, courtyards and studios, there pulses a secret life and activities of passion. Within her gates lie the treasured pearls of my past. I remember. I mourn. I say goodbye.

Lorna arrives at the end of the week. We share Paris for several days in a magical swirl of energy before boarding a train to the southeast corner of France, to her world in the Pyrenees Mountains.

The train takes us as far as the university town of Pau. From there, a bus brings us to the village of Laruns in the Ossau Valley. Sheep, drinking at the fountain in the central square, scatter reluctantly before the approaching bus and the two passengers alighting with their suitcases.

"It's right there." Lorna points to one of the larger houses facing us. "That's my hotel." As she leads me through the corridors, she explains there are only one or two other guests; we have the place almost to ourselves.

In her room, on the bed, is a letter from Patrick, her old flame from high school. She hasn't seen or spoken to him for 11 years. Now, Patrick, a successful copywriter in a Madison Avenue advertising agency, says he's compelled to see Lorna again.

"You two are writing regularly now?" She nods. "I bet you end up back in the States, married to him."

"Maybe, but I can't think about that now. There's too much to learn here."

"About what?"

She takes a deep breath. "Past lives, reincarnation, things that you and I have talked about, read about, wondered about for years." She pulls her honey-blonde hair away from her eyes with her left hand, a gesture I've seen a thousand times. It's Lorna's way of taking a few seconds to prepare the right words for what she has to say next. "But this is different, because I'm not studying it here; I'm living it. You saw Monsieur LeBastie, the owner of the hotel, downstairs?"

"I didn't take special notice. He seems reserved."

"Very. So you can imagine how surprised I was when he asked me—a guest in his hotel—I'd been here about two months . . ." her voice trails off.

"Asked you what?" I urge her to continue.

"It must have taken a long time for him to work up the courage—people here don't talk about such things. He asked if I thought we could have more than one life. I said, 'Yes, without a doubt.' Then he asked if I knew this place, and again I said yes."

"Why'd you say that?" I challenge.

"Several days after arriving here in Laruns, I sat on the grass over there at the river bank. The movement of the water was hypnotic, and I watched it tranquilly for a long time. Suddenly, where my own reflection had been, there was another. I mean it was me, but as a 10-year-old child playing on that same riverbank. When I came back to present time, I felt a profound familiarity with this Valley. Every inch of it. I know where all trails lead, what is hidden beyond the bend; I know this land."

"And let me guess. Monsieur LeBastie thinks he knew you before?"

"Yes. He believes that he lived with people in caves, in a Paleolithic society. He fished in that same river, and he remembers me as one of the women in his community."

"This is getting esoteric. Forgive a mundane question, but how are you living? Do you have any money left?"

"I work for Monsieur LeBastie. He's restoring an old estate—imagine, Napoleon III built it for his empress, Eugénie! Now Monsieur LeBastie is opening it as a second hotel, and I work there. But get unpacked; I'll tell you about it when we eat."

"Mmmmm." Inhaling the steaming aroma of a spicy hot beef ragoût, our conversation breaks just long enough to tear off a piece of fresh French bread and to savor the stew.

"What's your job?"

"Chambermaid."

"Scrubbing floors?"

"Yes, lots of floors. I relieve the barman and the receptionist too."

"Lorna, you don't have to stay, you know."

"It's something I need to do right now." Her left hand brushes her hair back again. "When I first got here, I couldn't speak a word of French. It plunged me into a solitude as total as being deaf. I saw people's mouths moving, knew they were communicating, but not to me. I couldn't reach out to anyone. All my life I've relied on words. Intellectual concepts. My ability to articulate. Suddenly I'm thrown into a world of silence."

She pauses for a breath and her first mouthful of soup since we sat down. "I scrub floors," she goes on, swallowing quickly, "because it's a labor of my body, not my brain. It takes me out of my head so I can develop acute sensitivities with my physical senses. There are no books to learn from. No dogma. No philosophical framework. The labor is breaking through a heavy block of intellect to an understanding of essence. Am I making sense to you?" I nod. "A different kind of knowledge is coming to me through this."

I gaze into the pool of her round blue eyes. I envy her ability to plunge totally into such an experience. Could I? Would I?

"I've spent my whole life in the academic world," Lorna continues. "But here I've lost my personal history. I'm known as the chambermaid, the one who scrubs floors. It's the lowest position. I own nothing, not even the money to get home. I'm in a vulnerable, humble place. And yet," she leans forward across the table with intense excitement, "from this vulnerable, humble place, I am learning what it is to have power."

I believe her. Because Lorna's power is electric. Overwhelming. I am in awe of her. I feel small, spiritually, next to her; but in her presence I also feel alive, totally alive as nowhere else. I'm recharged, reconnected. She brings abstract concepts into concrete reality. Lorna and I can share the most trivial things (cosmetics, gifts, humor), and we can also penetrate the cosmic truths of the universe. I have no other friendship like hers; I've missed her terribly.

Every evening after dinner, we return to my room or hers and spend most of the night talking, talking, talking. If Dad were here he'd tell us to get some sleep, but in that hotel of Laruns, in the Vallé d'Ossau, as everywhere else we get to meet, not a moment can be wasted. Living far apart as we do, our visits are rare and precious nuggets. Sleep is something we can do another time. We talk until we drop off, then rest an hour or two and go on.

In the morning, our conversation from the night before resumes as though it had ended with a comma. It doesn't skip a beat as we go into the dining room for a bowl of café au lait, hard-boiled eggs, and croissants.

"How is Karl's trip?" Lorna asks. "Is he finding what he was searching for in India?"

"I don't get that from his letters. Just descriptions of his travel adventures. Misadventures, mostly."

I confess to Lorna that since she and Karl have left California, my toughest battle has been loneliness. She warns against allowing the loneliness to eat at me, pull me down, and distract me from the fulfillment of caring for my son.

"It's hard. I seem to need affirmation that I'm not just a mother; I'm a woman too."

"Not now," Lorna counsels. "Give yourself to Ariel 100 percent; that's what's on your plate for this time. Fill yourself with him so there is no emptiness, no longing, no looking to your left or to your right to see what might be coming on the horizon. You are grieving a lost love, a great love, but in that child is a privileged happiness, and it is right in front of you. Grab hold of it and rejoice."

Our time in the Vallée d'Ossau is almost over. Where have the 10 days gone? Lorna, the one person who knows me deeply, who remembers every jot and tittle of my past, reconnects me with my history and makes me whole. Her probing, observant sensitivity leads me far below the surface of my circumstances to the essence of my response to them. I had left California lonely and shaken. Having time again with Lorna, I'll go home to Ari renewed. Centered. Refocused on my purpose.

It is our last day. Eager not to waste a minute of it, Lorna comes to my room early to wake me. She carries a large picnic basket she's filled with deli meats, cheese, a bottle of wine, Valencia blood oranges and country fresh bread.

After coffee and breakfast in the dining room, I'm wide awake (French coffee is guaranteed to do that for you). We scamper like children in a meadow of lavender and daisies and gather wildflowers to make our May basket. (We've exchanged flower baskets on the first of May every year since we've known each other.) Sunlight warms the hillside. It splashes on crystal-cold mountain streams that chill our legs. Old abandoned stone houses in the village whisper secrets of their long past.

One house in particular captures Lorna's fancy. It's just a ruin, a stone shell, but she loves it. "I'd buy this one if I could." Watching her wistful gaze, I have a sinking feeling. She will take root in this land and I'll lose her.

We pick up the picnic basket and walk on. Sheep and goats dot the landscape. "Goats are my favorite animal," I say, recalling the barn full of affectionate kids in Montélimar. "They show up in my life at the oddest times."

There's a change of planes in New York, just time enough for a quick visit to Grandma Kate. Food in France is a tough act to follow, but a bowl of Grandma Kate's hot chicken soup is unsurpassed. I tell her about the visit with Lorna. "She wants to buy a house there, Grandma. Do you think she will?"

You don't pose idle questions with Grandma Kate. She pushes away from the table and gets the tarot cards. "She'll marry Patrick, and he will buy the ancient house for her," Kate begins. "She will return many times to . . . what's the name of that place?"

"La Vallée d'Ossau."

"Yes. The Valley will wind as a thread through her life and the life of her children."

"She doesn't have children."

"She will. And the house will be a center for her Shamanic journeys in years to come."

"Her what? What's that, 'Shamanic'?"

"Honey, I don't know. I'm just telling you what is told to me. Don't ask questions I can't answer. Do you want me to go on or not?"

"Yes, of course. I'll look up the word later."

"Where was I?"

"You said the Valley will wind as a thread through Lorna's life. What about me, Grandma? Will I be with Lorna in the Valley again?"

She looks a long time at the cards, shuffling them slowly. "I don't think so. Your paths diverge widely."

There is a thud in my heart. "We are very close, Grandma. She's my best friend."

Katherine continues to stare at the cards. "Yes," she says, "but your chosen paths will drive you far apart." I feel so sad. I can't imagine anything that could drive me away from Lorna, especially not our spiritual quests; we've always shared that. But it's useless to argue with my grandmother. She just tells what she sees. She doesn't claim to understand.

Land of Vines and Fig Trees

*Leave your country, your people, and your father's household
and go to the land I will show you.*

GENESIS 12:1

*For the LORD your God is bringing you into a good land—a land with streams
and pools of water, with springs flowing in the valley and hills; a land with . . .
vines and fig trees, pomegranates, olive oil and honey.*

DEUTERONOMY 8:7-8

We are back in Southern California. It's time to say good-bye to the tiny house on the beach. Ari needs a neighborhood with families and children. But house hunting is a dreary business when you can't afford much.

I drive up a quiet, suburban street in Santa Monica to a large white house with green shutters and doors. The surrounding lawn is well-tended and lush with blooming fruit trees. A woman, perhaps in her fifties, answers the door with a smile. "Yes?"

"You advertised a guesthouse for rent?"

"We sure did. I'm Zada Clark. C'mon out back with me."

A pretty guesthouse attached to the garage is also white with green shutters. Inside are two bright, cheerful rooms. It's love at first sight. Not only for its charm but for its setting in the garden, and the energetic, lovely woman who would be my landlady. Let's see, I could use the room next to the kitchen for both dining and sleeping, no problem. But . . . I look around . . . there is no bedroom for Ari. My heart sinks.

"It's just beautiful. I can't tell you how much I'd like to take it, but there's no room for my little boy."

We walk outside past the open garage adjoining the guesthouse. On the back wall there are two windows and an electrical outlet. Click!

"Do you suppose . . .? No, I guess it's a crazy idea."

"What's that?"

"Don't laugh at me, Mrs. Clark, it's rather presumptuous. But since there's only one car in your double garage, do you suppose, would your husband be willing—? That back corner would be a perfect spot for the baby's room. It would take up about a quarter of your garage, so you'd still have some storage space—"

"Oh, no! Why, he'd have to knock out that wall and, oh no, I'm sorry; we've never had a problem renting it as is."

"Of course. I understand."

"On the other hand . . ." She leads me toward the garden. "My husband is right there. I can't imagine he'd agree to it, but I suppose you'd have nothing to lose by askin'."

"Lewis! This is Barbara. She's come to look at the guesthouse."

Tall and straight, Lewis Clark looks like a man who knows his strength. An honest man. He looks me squarely in the eyes as we shake hands. It's a moment of connection—there are just a few of them in a lifetime—when you know, you just know this stranger will be important to you. He feels it too. I can tell.

His wife explains the situation and my proposed solution. With thumb and forefinger cupping his chin, Mr. Clark doesn't say anything for a while. Then, slowly, "I'd have to charge a little more on the rent if I was to build a room . . ."

"Yes, of course."

He looks with squinted, piercing eyes at me, then turns back toward his wife. "Well, Zada, looks like we got us a little job to do this weekend."

Mrs. Clark is wide-eyed. "Well, I declare! I'd a never thought! Young lady, you must have cast a spell on him." We laugh. "Come on in and have some fruit juice. Let's talk a bit and get acquainted before you go back to work."

I won't feel so alone here; I'm sure of that. My heart sings with anticipation of the move.

If there were a God, I'd say He knew exactly what He was doing when He planted me in the Clark family garden. Like their other flowers, I am nourished, watered and protected. They are different from any family I have ever known. For one thing, they are very religious, and they live by their faith. They pray about everything they do and submit all decisions to their God for guidance. It's very strange to me, yet lovely in a way, like an Impressionist garden of soft watercolors in the glow of a gentle sun. In that garden I discover a family that blossoms in submission to their God. There's a love that holds its strength, both in times of provision and times of great loss. Not like any family I've known. It's pretty powerful stuff.

The youngest Clark, Evelyn Rose, sits cross-legged on my living room floor, playing for hours on end with Ari. Tall, blonde, and delicate as the flower she is named for, Ev has a combination of wide-eyed innocence and determined strength that carves a permanent place in my heart. I love her in a special way.

"Can I baby-sit for him?"

"You're only 12!" I protest. "How would you handle an emergency?"

"Please! I'll take a Red Cross class and get certified in first aid. And I'll never take my eyes off him, I promise. Besides, Mom and Dad are close by; I could call them if I had to." True to her word, Ev becomes the most dependable, most reliable caretaker I have ever had for Ari. "He's my baby too!" she declares.

Some evenings, her sister Patty, about 18, comes through the garden to sit at my round wooden table and talk. Patty is in love with a boy from her church. She agonizes over whether he'll ask her—or another girl he likes—to marry him.

Through my cottage window, lights from the Clark house cut through the dark blue evening and beckon me with fingers of a golden glow. Ari is asleep. I step outside to breathe the fragrance of night-blooming jasmine and knock softly on their kitchen door.

"Well, how nice! Come on in," Zada always says, and she carries fresh-baked cookies to the living room. Usually it's just the two of them talking there, she and Lewis, near the fire. The way they look at each other, like they are laughing at a tender secret, makes their pleasure in each other's company palpable. "We were head over heels when I was only 15," Zada had told me. Raising five kids has obviously done nothing to diminish the feeling.

Down the hall, Randy practices on his drums, or is absorbed in a project. Patty experiments with a new recipe. Evelyn Rose interrupts her violin practice to call, "Hi, Barbara!" Two older daughters, married with families, live out of town.

Lewis and Zada welcome Ari and me into their home without reserve. How drawn I am to them. How I long to be a part of it. But I can't. Because more than warmth and harmony characterize their home; there's also purity. I don't belong with purity.

Tapping on the window next to my bed, Lewis wakes me from a deep sleep. "What . . .?" It is only five-thirty in the morning. I slide the window open.

"Slip me the keys to your car."

I rub sleep from my eyes. "How come?"

"You've got a flat tire. Get me the keys and I'll fix it, so you can get to work." Lewis takes care of his own. As long as we live under his roof, we are counted among them.

On Sunday morning, I awake unusually refreshed. It's almost ten o'clock! How in the world did Ari let me sleep so late? I jump up and run through the living room into the beautiful little bedroom Lewis has built for him. The crib is empty. He couldn't have gotten out by himself. I search the garden. Not there. Fear creeps into my throat. I check the front lawn near the street.

"Looking for Ari?" Zada calls from the porch.

"Yes, have you seen him?"

She waves me toward her. "Guess you didn't see our note." I shake my head. "I hope we didn't scare you none. We figured you might like to sleep in just a bit, what with gettin' up for work so early and stayin' up most nights. Evelyn Rose slipped in real quiet this morning and took him to children's Sunday School at church. They should be back any time now."

I exhale a deep sigh of relief, make myself a cup of coffee, and enjoy the first moment of quiet solitude I've had in three years.

When Ari returns, he is excited about his adventure. "Can I go every Sunday?" he asks.

"We'll see." Once or twice is fine, but regular church? It doesn't occur to me there might be a connection between the faith that shapes the Clarks' family life and the peace that, for the first time, defines my own. In the garden guesthouse I am learning to feel "safe," to trust my world. I've always known that the planet on which I was born is not safe. It's a place where Cossacks and Nazis and sadists hunt innocent people; where animals and children suffer; where babies get sick and die without warning; and supervisors at work don't care. In the world I know, a man will love and marry you and father the flesh of your flesh, and then he disappears.

Lewis Clark and I sit side by side on the step leading to my cottage door, enjoying the smell of food from Zada's kitchen in the darkening evening. Lewis doesn't need to fill space with talk. He often sits without a word, appreciating the sweet surroundings with which God has blessed his life. But tonight, I can tell something's on his mind. Chewing on a blade of grass, he looks straight ahead toward the big house.

"Y'ever think of gettin' married?" he asks abruptly. In the long silence there is only the crickets' song. "I should think the boy could use a father. You too. You should have someone take care of you too."

That's a new thought. Someone take care of me? No one ever suggested that. Never. Not even Dad. He taught me to take care of everything myself. And Ari's father had been a child-man. A playful artist. *I* took care of us. The closest I've known to being taken care of is right here, in Lewis Clark's home.

"Actually, I do have a boyfriend. You haven't met him 'cause he's in India just now."

"Um-hmm." Lewis doesn't say more, but I can guess what he's wondering.

"He's a good person, very honest and trustworthy. But no, he isn't in a position to 'take care of me' as you put it."

"And the boy?"

"Oh yes, he loves Ari. He's wonderful with Ari."

"When's he comin' back?"

"Uh . . . I'm not sure."

"How long you been goin' with 'im?"

"Almost four years."

Lewis looks up at the trees, pensive. "Too long."

"Too long? You and Zada have been together 26 years!"

"It's different." He looks directly at me. "I married her. When it's right, you get married and get on with your life. When it's not right, you get out and move on. Give some fine young man a chance, Barbara. You and the boy deserve it."

He stands, stretches his long frame, and saunters toward the house. "Gettin' late," he mutters, as he waves goodnight.

Does he mean the evening is getting late? Or my life?

What Lewis said shakes me. First, because he cared enough to say it. No one, aside from Lorna, has spoken to me that way. Inside, something resonates to his words, and trembles.

We've lived happily in the Clarks' guesthouse for almost two years now. Today, Zada and I are plucking oranges from a tree.

"Zada, are you all right? You seem a bit tired."

"Sorry, dear. Does it show?"

"I don't mean to pry; I was just concerned."

"Of course you don't, dear. Been meaning to tell you, anyway. It's Gloria, our eldest. You haven't met her yet; she lives with her family in Utah." Zada pauses. "Well, Gloria's been diagnosed with cancer . . . of the bone marrow." I can hardly hear, as Zada barely whispers the last word: "Terminal."

"Oh, Zada, I'm so sorry." I reach my hand to her. "So sorry. I can't even imagine how one lives with such a loss."

"We live in God's hands." Zada twists an orange in her hands. "He knows His plan for us, and we have to trust Him."

"Do you trust Him now, Zada? You might lose your daughter!"

Her eyes fill with tears. "We might. Yes, dear, we might indeed. But I have to remember, He is greater than our earthly loss. And we have Him for eternity."

This sounds too preachy and I draw back. Is she saying it to console herself? No, Zada is brutally honest. I think she actually believes it.

Gloria's youthful blonde beauty belies the cancer riddling her body. She comes with her husband and three-year-old daughter to her parents' home. Lewis and Zada take care of her and the child during the day, while her husband works.

Two weeks after their arrival, Lewis knocks on my cottage door. "I have something to say, but it's not easy." He sits, long-legged, in the chair opposite mine. "You know how fond we are of you, Zada and I. You and Ari are like family to us." To my astonishment, Lewis drops his head, and a sob escapes.

"Lewis—"

"No, I'm all right. It's Gloria. She hasn't got much time left." He catches his breath. "She's wantin' to live in the guesthouse. We've got lots of room in the big house with us, we told her that, and it's easier to take care of her when she's right there, but . . ."

I don't want to hear the rest. I am about to lose my safe haven, our home in the garden of protection. I hold my breath, frozen with dread.

"She wants to live with Steve and the baby as a family. She wants that private time with them for as long as she can have it."

"I understand," I whisper. Lewis's pain is overwhelming. Gloria's pain is unimaginable. "I'll start looking for another place right away."

"I hate to ask it of you. We'll miss you."

"Don't even think about it," I assure him. "We'll find something close by and we'll visit often. The important thing now is Gloria."

Evening falls. The scene I witness in their living room is branded on my memory and will, I imagine, come back time and again over many years. Gloria's little girl plays on the floor with Randy, Pat and Evelyn Rose. Lewis and his son-in-law chat quietly near the fire. Gloria, clearly, is not feeling well. Lying on the sofa with her legs in Zada's lap, she is ashen and limp; her eyes are dull. But it is her mother, Zada, who captures my attention.

Zada's hands caress Gloria's legs and bare feet, rubbing tenderly, tenaciously, to soothe, to keep them warm with circulating blood. All her love and energy are focused in those hands. Her heart is in her hands, massaging tirelessly, desperately transmitting pulsing warmth and strength from her own body into the pale, assaulted young woman. The caressing massage of Zada's hands, her eyes on the fading beauty of her daughter's face, communicates an intensity of maternal love to her treasure, her first-born. For me, that love, wordless and mute, fills the room with the power of a Presence I can never forget.

Suddenly, I see myself with humbling clarity: a young woman fleeing what she imagines is the "living death" of an ordinary life, with a family in suburbia. She had fancied herself an artistic soul on a quest for "significance." She looks so stupid to me now. In this moment I realize all that is meaningful, all that has ever been important from the earliest time of man to this day, is right here in the Clarks' living room. This is what I've been searching for, traveling the world for, longing for, since the day of my birth. None of the books I have read, the artists I have met, or the sages I have studied could tell me the true meaning of life. But here it is, right in front of me. It is in the loving touch of a mother's anguished caress on the cold, limp foot of her dying daughter.

We find a nice two-bedroom apartment on Harvard Street. The landlord allows me to manage the six units in exchange for my rent. It's a terrific arrangement, because I get to choose who moves in and who doesn't. Within 12 months I create a close-knit group of neighbors. It is not the Clarks' haven of family love, but there's friendship here and camaraderie. Zada would say God is meeting my needs. Uh oh, I'm starting to think like her. I know nothing of God or what Zada calls "His watchful eye over me." In fact, with the exception of the Clark family, I don't know anyone whose faith or God is central in his or her life. I don't run into people like that.

I rent the rear unit to Aviva and Sari, two Israeli women, my age and single. We exercise together before work in the morning, and they are wonderful with Ari; I can leave him with them on occasion, when I have to.

In the front unit are Bob and Linda. Friends gather in their apartment, some of whom are young producers and actors. Bob has been working out of town for two weeks, and Linda has her hands full with their two kids. "Now I know what it feels like to be a single mother like you," she complains. "There's no one around to help!"

"No," I tell her, "you haven't a clue. You're busy, sure, but Bob's out there earning a paycheck to take care of you all. You are at home with the kids; you don't have to build a career and deal with that whole set of problems. Besides, Bob will be back on Monday." If she's looking for a sympathetic ear, she picked the wrong person. People really don't understand what single-parenting is about.

In the unit just below us are Cassandra and her little girl, Rebecca, who is just Ari's age. Cass is a single working mother like me, developing a marketing career. Our circumstances give us much in common, but in temperament we are very different. Blonde, blue-eyed and fair, Cass is pretty in a robust sort of way, exuding a no-nonsense energy. Nothing is impossible for her. While I battle with anxiety, she takes on monumental problems with an indifferent shrug. I am idealistic; she is practical. I seek poetry and aesthetics; she deals in concrete realities. I live from moment to moment, wholly in the present tense; Cass lives by goals, objectives, and five-year plans. How do two such people come together to fulfill one another's need? Zada says God knows our needs better than we do ourselves. Okay, Zada, God must have known Cass was just right.

I have to get to the day-care center before they close the doors at 6:00. But typically, when I'm about to leave work, there's something urgent. "Barbara! Good thing you're still here. We need to reach the nautilus expert in Australia. Like right now."

"But . . ." I swallow my words. One word about getting to the day-care center and I'll hear that litany again about how they should have hired a man. "Give me a second, I'll be right there." I reach for the phone frantically. "Cass, can you pick up Ari tonight and feed him?"

"Sure." We're both used to these last-minute calls. "I've got hamburger meat," she says, "but no vegetables. You have any?"

"Plenty. Bottom shelf. See you later, and thanks." By the time I get home (or, if it's her turn, when she gets home) the kids will be fed and, if it's late enough, put to bed. They are as used to sleeping in one apartment as the other.

Cass and I live as a single family in two separate apartments. Our lives are intricately entwined. Preparing meals, caring for the kids, creating recreational activities, celebrating holidays, vacation traveling—we do all of it together. The kids, strong-willed both of them, play and fight, amuse and annoy one another. We take them camping, cook over fires, and sleep under stars.

Single parents have to have some kind of support system. Some have parents or ex-husbands who help out. Some have live-in maids. I have Cass, and she has me. God's provision and protection? Who knows. But I wonder how I'd survive without her.

Karl is back from India. "The trip was a major disappointment," he says. "Traveling alone, in primitive conditions, was harder than I anticipated. I was expecting answers to core questions, enlightenment, an end to mystery and the finality of nirvana. Either it doesn't exist, or I don't have what it takes to find it. I'm not a world traveler like you, I guess. Home is where I belong, and I'm back to stay."

To celebrate, I'm cooking hummus, an Israeli dish. Sari said it's easy. Just put the garbanzo beans in boiling water, let them get soft, mash them and add the spice. She forgot to say the beans expand and swell. By the time Karl arrives, the beans have overflowed the pot. They are all over the stove and covering half the kitchen floor. He finds me on my hands and knees, scooping garbanzo beans into the trash.

I work during the day; Karl works at night, when he's got a gig. He's good with Ari; he teaches good values and provides a strong masculine model. When clearing the dinner dishes, I hear him remind Ari, "Did you thank Mama for the good dinner she made?" Sometimes Karl pats my bottom and says, "You sure got a pretty mama, Ari, don't you think?" Ari sees a lot of affection and teasing. He knows love can be fun.

But Karl does lose his temper on occasion. Tonight, he snaps because we've been trying to get Ari to sleep for over an hour. Every few minutes there comes a plaintive cry from the bedroom. "Mama!"

"What is it, Ari?"

"It's too hot in here."

"Take off your blanket."

"Okay."

Fifteen minutes later: "Mama!"

"Yes, Ari?"

"I have to go to the bathroom."

"So, go."

Then it's, "I need a glass of water" or, "I can't sleep."

Karl has had enough. He drops his book and leaps off the sofa, stomps into Ari's room and yanks him out of bed.

"What is it you really want? You want to play?"

"Yes." Ari's voice is shaky. He knows Karl is mad.

"You want to play? Fine, you'll play." Karl sits Ari firmly on the floor and pulls toys off the closet shelf, throwing them on the floor. "You'll play through the night. You'll play until you're so tired you beg me to let you go to sleep. Then you'll play some more. You'll play until you can't stand it anymore."

Ari is in tears. "No, Karl. I'll go to sleep."

"Too late for that. You'll play." He sits on the floor next to the child and takes up a box of Legos. "Let's start with this."

I throw up my hands. Two hours later (it's now 11:00) I peek in on them. The Legos are put away and they are playing Monopoly. I crawl into bed and read. At midnight they are playing and—is that laughter? I guess Karl has gotten into it—I drift off. I wake up at . . . oh my gosh, it's after 4:00. There's still a light from Ari's room across the hall. I tiptoe over. Yes, they're still at it. At least Ari is going full swing. Karl is looking weary. I go back to sleep and wake up again at 6:00, when I hear the click of the closet door.

"Just taking him out for a run around the block," Karl groans. "Got to tire him out."

"How's Ari?"

"Having the time of his life. Never had so much 'quality' time with me before! But he shows no sign of slowing down."

I hide my giggles in the pillow. Poor Karl. This "punishment" of Ari is killing him. They return from their walk in half an hour and the games resume. They're still playing when I leave for work. "Be sure to take time out for breakfast," I remind them. "You'll need energy."

When I get back at dinnertime, the two of them are asleep on the floor. Karl is holding Ari, and Ari is holding his bunny. Looks like Karl sure taught Ari a lesson.

Most Sunday mornings we have brunch with my aunt and uncle. My cousins usually come, and sometimes Cass and Rebecca too. We look forward all week to these Sundays for relaxation, humor, lively discussion, games and laughter. "We're here for just a little while," we always say, "we've got lots to do today."

"Fine." Aunt Evelyn spreads the tablecloth. "Stay as long as you can; go when you must." Next thing we know, it's nine or ten o'clock at night. Where does the day go?

Karl and I return home from an afternoon out. Dad has been watching Ari. "I have a surprise for you," he says, leading us into the living room.

My mouth falls open. An entire wall is covered with handsome wooden bookshelves, from floor to ceiling and wall to wall. He had taken all my books out of their boxes to line the new shelves. "Thank you, Dad! This is just beautiful. I can't believe you did this!" I hug my dad and tell him I will cherish these bookshelves.

"How's Ari?" Karl asks, "Was he a good boy for you?"

"Hi, Mom. Hi, Karl. Can I have ice cream?"

"Hi, darling, give me a hug. No ice cream now; we're about to make dinner. Dad, can you stay and eat with us?"

"But, Mom! The truck is here and all the kids are getting ice cream. *Please!*"

"Tell you what," Karl says, "you can get the ice cream if you promise to put it in the freezer and save it until after dinner. Will you do that?"

"Sure!" Ari grabs the quarter from Karl and runs out. When I call him in for dinner, he returns. "Where's the ice cream?" we ask.

"Ummm, I didn't get it."

"Oh, well then, give us back the quarter."

"Ummm, I think I lost it."

Karl takes Ari's arm. "Look at me, son." Karl's voice is deep and stern. Ari lifts his eyes with effort. "What happened? Did you buy the ice cream or not?" Ari looks at me, then at Karl, then at the floor. If he didn't buy ice cream, he has to give us the quarter. He says nothing.

"Look me in the eye, son, and tell the truth." Karl gets down on one knee so they are face to face. He holds Ari's arm at the elbow. "I don't care what you did, or how bad it is. But when you look me in the eye, I want to know I can trust you to tell the truth. I want to know the five years we've spent together aren't for nothing. Do you understand?"

Ari looks uncertain.

"Do you care about our relationship, Ari? About your relationship with your mother?" Ari nods. "Well, if we don't tell each other the truth at all times, we can't trust each other, can we? And if we can't trust each other, what do we have?" Ari shakes his head. It's beginning to sink in. "I have to trust you, Ariel. Let's say someone tells us you did something really bad. Like stealing. If I trust you, and you tell me you didn't do it, I'll go to bat for you. I'll fight a whole police department for you, if I have to. But first I have to know you always tell the truth. We'll get past it if you do a bad thing. Maybe you'll have to take some punishment, but that's no big deal and it won't destroy our relationship. But if you lie to me, son, we have nothing left. Is it worth it?"

Ari starts to cry. "I ate the ice cream. I couldn't help it. All the kids were eating theirs. I'm sorry. I promise I won't lie anymore."

"Okay." Karl pats his back. "I'm glad you're man enough to say it."

It is a tremendous risk, writing the letter to Mom, but I have to take it. I'm 32 years old and it is my first attempt to communicate honestly with her. Between Mom and me there's always been tension, a constant anticipation of rejection. If I don't speak up now, it will never change.

> *Mom, there are things I have to say to you. I'm afraid of your response, as I write this, but what's new, I've always been afraid of your reaction to me, and that's what this is all about. I am no longer willing to live in fear of your rejection.*
>
> *The issue between us isn't very complicated, but it's taken me 30-plus years to find the courage to say it. Very simply, I feel that you don't like me. Kids know their mom's love by the look in her eyes, the softness in her voice, the tender caress of her touch. I know you don't like me very much, that the sight of me is not pleasant to you. When did I first become aware of it? On the day of my birth, I think. Or within a few days thereafter. I always knew. In your eyes, I am not pretty. I have no appeal, no charm. My presence provokes only your impatience and irritability.*
>
> *One can't win them all, of course. But if my own mom can't feel an affection for me, how can I expect anyone in the world ever will?*

My letter listed every grievance I could remember. I talked about her explosive temper and constant disapproval. I told her I had no memory of ever being held in her arms or kissed by her. She touched me in practical ways, to get me dressed or to brush my hair, but I have no recall of a tender caress or an approving smile.

Mother—that's the person you're supposed to feel safe and protected with, the one you turn to for comfort, no matter what. Kids run to their moms if someone bullies them; they hide behind her skirt and she defends and protects them. Not mine.

I've never been comfortable with my mom. I'm afraid that I'll use the wrong word, the wrong intonation, or the wrong look and unleash a lightning fury.

As a child I wondered how my mother appeared to other people. Was she pretty? I couldn't see her past the cloud of my fear. Growing up hasn't helped. I still cringe when her voice gets brittle or shows an edge of annoyance.

I avoid "touchy" subjects—like baby-sitting. In my letter, I remind Mom of the first and last time I had asked her to watch Ari. It was five years ago, when he was about a year old. I'd been invited to a ballet and it would have been my first night "out" since Ari was born. Mom had said, "Okay," begrudgingly. Understandably, after her divorce, she was not happy, but I had hoped that once she had the baby there, she'd enjoy him.

Looking forward to a special evening, I took pains to look nice, packed Ari into the car, and knocked on Mom's door. She greeted me with, "Oh, don't you look just fine! Off you go for a night on the town while I'm cooped up here alone with a kid to watch. That's what my life's come to. Everybody's out having a good time, everybody's got someplace to go, but I'm stuck at home . . ." she spat out the word "baby-sitting." A bitter outpouring of resentments followed me as I turned away from her door and carried Ari back to the car.

I drove home and canceled the date.

With Mom, anything can set her off. It's worse than walking on eggshells, more like walking on spikes and broken glass. I send the letter because if I don't speak up now, I'll always be afraid of her. Afraid of everyone.

I didn't think she'd answer, but her response to my letter just arrived. I'm afraid to open it. Is she going to write me off? Wipe me out of her life? My hand shakes as I open the envelope.

"My Dearest Barbara . . ." *Dearest?* I'd better reread it to be sure. She doesn't normally use language like that.

My Dearest Barbara,

Your letter broke my heart. How stupid we parents can be, reacting out of our own hurts and limitations. What terrible things we do to our children. I am so sorry. I'd give anything to be able to do it over again—I'd do it so differently. Can I spend the rest of my life making it up to you?

There's more—pages and pages. Mom explains her insecurities, tells me about things from her childhood with immigrant parents that made her who she is. She had felt inadequate as a wife and mother under the stinging criticism of her mother-in-law. It helps me to understand her better. But most important, the words "I'm so sorry" and "I love you very much, more than I ever told you" make me feel as if my whole life is starting over again—clean, fresh, and full of opportunity. Her letter tells me she really listened and she understands.

For the first time, I believe she really cares; she wants to be in my life. Maybe, just maybe, it can be different. Even at my age, I still want my mom. I long for her approval, her support, her love. But who is the woman who wrote this letter? It might be awkward getting reacquainted.

I reach for the phone. "Mom? Yes, it's me. I just got your letter." I can't say any more; tears are washing the words away. *Uh oh, Mom hates it when I cry; she always says, with contempt and disgust, "Don't get sensitive on me, now."* Instead, there is silence. "Sorry, Mom. I just called to see if you want to come over for dinner tonight." She doesn't answer. "Mom?"

"Yes," her voice catches, "I'd like that. What time?"

It is 10:30 at night when the telephone rings.

"Bar-r-r-bar-r-r-a, this is JYC. I just ar-r-r-ived in Los Angeles."

"Yes, Captain. Do you need a ride to your hotel?"

"No, I'll take a cab. But I want to start you on a new project. It's a book on energy resources."

"Sounds interesting. I don't know much about the subject, but—"

"Not a problem. We have collected all the material."

"Good. Where is it?"

"In my office at the Museum in Monaco. You'll have to do the work there."

Wow! My heart is pounding. "When?"

"Can you leave immediately?"

"For how long?"

"I'm not sure. Six months? Twelve? Whatever it takes to do the book." Captain Cousteau is constantly relocating his diving crews; moving people around means nothing to him.

My mind is racing; I can't fathom all I'll have to do. "Can you give me five days?"

"If necessary. My secretary will meet you at the airport in Nice."

Karl is incredulous. "Just like that?! You're up and gone for you-don't-know-how-long on Monday?"

Cass is more practical. "You'll have to find a tenant and sublet your apartment, get Ariel into a school, find a place to live in Monaco. Is your passport expired? Will you store your furniture? You need time to say good-bye. Can you do it all by Monday?"

Dad is excited; he sees this as an adventure. Mom's reaction surprises me. "You'll be so far away . . ." She looks sad.

"Mom, I've traveled overseas before."

"I know." She shakes her head, unable to explain. But I understand. It is different now between us. She'll miss me. What's more, I will miss *her* too. She's been a real mother these past months, and I love it. There is a sting of apprehension on my heart. Do I really want to be so far away? I reach over to hug her. She doesn't stiffen.

"If we stay a long time, promise you'll come visit. It'll be a fabulous vacation!" Her smile is weak.

Sunday night, exhausted from all I've had to cram into four days, I snap the last suitcase shut. "You don't know anyone there," Karl mutters, trying to hold me back, "not a soul."

"If I decide to stay, what's to keep you from joining me?" In my mind I am four years old again, with Daddy sitting on the edge of my bed, telling stories of faraway places to discover. I have to do this, have to push through the boundaries of my daily life. Didn't I vow to live before I die? Yes, it's a little scary, but it's an adventure. How often does a chance like this come along? There might never be another.

In the tiny, sun-bathed airport of Nice, in the south of France, we pass through the arrival gate. A woman with brown hair, probably in her forties, steps forward with a boy of seven or eight.

"You are Barbara?" she asks in French.

"Yes, and this is Ariel."

"I am Marie-France, secretary to the Captain, and this is my boy, Claude. We thought your son might like to meet someone close to his age. Please come this way. My car is in front."

Driving to Monaco from Nice, Marie-France and I chat easily. I like her. The boys babble happily in the back seat. Claude, in French, tells Ari about his dog, Sacha, and his favorite toys. Ari responds in English, of course, the only way he can. He says we live in America, but his mama has to work here, and we'll be staying for a while. They seem totally oblivious to the fact that they can't understand anything the other says. They are completely content in one another's company. Until Claude begins to tickle Ari.

"Stop." Ari tells him. Claude continues. "Stop!" Ari repeats, louder, and more urgently. When several more "Stop!"s are ignored, Ari's annoyance reaches a shrill pitch.

I turn toward the rear seat. "He doesn't understand 'stop,' Ari. Tell him '*ar-rête.*'" Ari takes a deep breath when the tickling permits, and then bellows at the top of his voice: "*ARRÊTE!*"

Claude freezes. Ari, startled that it worked, gives me a triumphant glance. He has just learned his first word in French; one he won't forget.

"We would have invited you to our house for dinner tonight," Marie-France continues when the back seat settles again into quiet, happy chatter. "But Simone—Madame Cousteau—requested that you join her for lunch at the museum. You may want to rest after that. We'll do it another time."

"You're very thoughtful, thank you." I appreciate her invitation, knowing that it's rare to be invited to someone's home in France unless you're family or an intimate friend. "By the way, what is she like, Madame Cousteau?"

"She's . . . how shall I say, she's . . . *spéciale*. You'll see."

Marie-France drives into the heart of Monte Carlo and turns into the Place du Casino, a meticulously landscaped green with tall palms. Directly in front of us is the famous, ornate Casino de Monte Carlo. To the right, the magnificent Hôtel de Paris with its splendid steps and golden entrance. On our left is a lovely café with white pillars in a garden of geraniums and roses. Partially hidden beyond the garden, between the café and the Casino, stands another hotel, Le Métropole, all white stone and marble. Less pretentious than the Hôtel de Paris, Le Métropole is elegant in a *Belle Epoque* sort of way.

Marie-France pulls up to the white hotel. "You'll stay here until we can rent an apartment." Our luggage is whisked into the lobby. I can hardly take it all in. The high sculpted ceilings, the gold trims and marble balconies and richly carpeted floors. I've never walked into such a place, let alone registered as a guest.

Our room is bright, a soft peach with white moldings. The furniture is French provincial. There are two beds, a writing desk, a large armoire and—oh this is wonderful—two sets of French doors open onto a large balcony overlooking trees down to the sea. A small round table and chairs make the balcony ideal for reading and breakfast.

"Marie-France!" I whirl around to thank her, but she cuts me off.

"We must hurry. Madame is waiting."

Marie-France drives swiftly. "You'll lunch with Simone at the restaurant on the roof of the Museum. After that, come find me on the lower level, where the library and administrative offices are located. That's where you'll be working too. Also, we rented a *mobylette* for your transportation. Believe me, it is better in this dense traffic than a car."

"A what?"

"A motorized bicycle. Everyone uses them. Now pay attention as we go, so you won't get lost."

Some people hate moving to new places, new jobs, new surroundings. Not me. But when I first arrive, I go into an intense visual orientation mode. I locate on a local map and make careful mental notes of the streets.

The principality of Monaco is shaped like a "U" around an ocean inlet. We drive through the affluent resort center, Monte Carlo, then go around the curve of the "U" through *Le Condamine*, the congested commercial section. I note the grocery stores, a laundry, a place to buy soapsuds, and a dentist. Approaching the other "leg" of the "U," the road becomes a steep cobblestone climb on the side of a cliff toward the Old City.

Marie-France explains, "*La Vieille Ville* (Old City) is preserved as it was in medieval times. We call it '*Le Rocher*' (The Rock) because it is built on the flat surface of a high cliff. On this end of the cliff," she points to the gates, "is the palace where Prince Rainier Grimaldi lives with his beautiful *princesse américaine*, Grace Kelly, and their three royal children."

At the gates, candy-cane guards on prancing horses are oblivious to my stare. It's hard to fathom real people living within the walls of the fairy-tale castle.

Holding Ari's small hand, I follow Marie-France through narrow, twisting, stone streets with fascinating little shops and restaurants. We pass the Cathedral where the Prince and Grace Kelly were married, an open-air amphitheater built by the Romans, City Hall and the Post Office. On the other end of The Rock is a large plaza, dominated by the Oceanographic Museum towering on the edge of the cliff. I catch my breath. This is where Captain Cousteau has his offices, and it's where *I* will come to work every day.

Marie-France points to a building across the street. "Ariel will go to school there. He can join you for lunch at the museum cafeteria every day."

"Oh, boy," Ari says when I translate. "I can come see all the fishes!"

"Yes," I hug him. "And I get to see *you*. At home, I never got to see you during the day!"

"I will take you now to Madame Cousteau, then I must return to my office. Can you find your way back to the hotel with the mobylette?"

My glance sweeps past the imposing museum to the small sea-based industries, oyster fisheries, net makers, and diving equipment suppliers at the foot of the cliff directly below. The entire principality is the size of a small town, built on cliffs rising from the sea. "Sure. We can find our way back." Like my five-year-old son, I absorb what I see. I don't wonder why we're here or if it's a good thing. I simply melt into the fiber of our new surroundings. Fascinated by the maze of narrow, intricate streets, I am drawn to mysteries that lurk behind ancient doors, in hidden courtyards, in lives I do not know. I can't wait to explore.

❧   ❧   ❧

It is 2:00 P.M., past the hour for lunch. The terrace restaurant is empty but for the single occupant of a distant table. Sitting next to a low stone wall over which is a perfect view of the sea, she looks sideways at us, almost with indifference, as we approach.

"Simone, this is Barbara and her son, Ariel. Bon appétit." Marie-France withdraws.

"I'm happy to meet you," I say with enthusiasm, despite my exhaustion. In the excitement of our arrival, I forget that it's been at least 48 hours since we slept.

"Are you?" she responds dryly. "We'll see."

Taken aback, I press on. "Oh, yes. I've heard wonderful things about your expeditions with the Captain. You two have achieved so much!" I explain the work I do with The Cousteau Society. That meets with a skeptical "Hmmph."

I'd better let her do the talking, I think, focusing on the meal set before us, making sure Ari has what he needs. *Don't get restless,* I plead inwardly with him. *I know you can't understand a word we're speaking, but sit here like a polite little statue. Please.*

I'd expected a refined, regal counterpart to the Captain's gentlemanly grace. But his wife is a gruff, mannish, disgruntled sort of person. In a gravelly voice, and the coarse language of a truck driver, she presents a rather bitter view of life.

Ari tugs at my arm. "What is it, sweetie?" I ask in English. He tugs again to bring my ear down closer to his lips.

"Mama," he says in a loud whisper, "I don't like this lady."

I flush crimson, hoping she doesn't understand. "Hush, Ari," I say urgently. "That isn't nice. We don't say things like that."

"It's quite all right," the gravelly voice interrupts in flawless English. "I don't think *he's* so hot either."

We've barely landed, and my career may be over. I offer profuse apologies, explain that my child is tired, and lunch finishes quickly.

I tend to my job, and Marie-France, bless her heart, tends to putting my life in order. She enrolls Ari in the public school across the street and, four weeks after our arrival, finds an apartment just outside the borders of Monaco, in the neighboring village of Rocquebrune. And none to soon. I'm getting used to the service at the hotel. Having my bed turned down at 5:00, with chocolates on the pillow, my dry cleaning whisked away and returned, no housekeeping to do . . . it's starting to feel pretty good.

The one-bedroom furnished apartment is high on a hill and full of light, with French doors in the living room that open to a balcony over the sea. I set

our breakfast table out there, so we can look down over the Principality of
Monaco on the twisting coast, the beaches, and the ever-changing colors of the
ocean. At night, multicolored lights twinkle like a brilliant Christmas tree laid
out beneath our feet.

Best of all, as far as Ari is concerned, there is a television. He flips on a
channel and, to our surprise, the characters of his favorite show, *Sesame Street*,
come alive in our room. They dance and sing, teach arithmetic, sing-song
spelling words (all in French, of course) and tell delightful stories. Ari sits on
the edge of the bed, enthralled and laughing.

"What are you laughing at? You don't understand a word of French!"

"I know what they're saying, Mama; I've seen this one already."

We develop a routine of shopping, ironing, cooking. The motorbike whizzes
us around town with Ari on the back, holding groceries, laundry, or books. He
does the daily breakfast run, trotting down the street to the dairy store, the deli
meat store, and the bakery, stopping to look at matchbook cars in the toy shop.
Everyone loves the little boy with the dark eyes and auburn hair.

"What's your name, *petit cowboy américain*?" neighbors and shopkeepers ask.

"Ariel," he replies. My name is irrelevant; I am simply "*la maman d'Ariel.*"

In Monaco, Ari enjoys a freedom he never had at home, where he's not allowed to cross a street or play out of my view. Here, there is no fear of crime,
kidnapping, or violence. He goes by himself to the beach or school. When he
crosses a street, the nearest adult takes his hand and sees him safely to the
other side. It's a different world.

Friday evenings, we putt-putt up the hills to Marie-France's house for dinner. The *mobylette* gives out on the steepest half mile before her house; we push
it the rest of the way up.

"Don't leave the table without knotting your cloth napkins," Marie-France
explains. "This means you are part of the family. For guests, we set out a new
napkin each time. In the family, we knot our napkins, each in a different way.
At the next meal, we get our own napkin back until it is soiled."

Madame Cousteau is often at Marie-France's house. With her two sons living in California, and her husband traveling constantly around the world, Simone is a woman with only a few carefully selected friends.

She nods toward Ari, curled on the sofa. "He's awfully quiet tonight. Is he
all right?"

Feeling his forehead, I realize he has a fever. "Marie-France, have you got a
thermometer?" She produces one immediately, but it reads in centigrade; it's
meaningless to me.

Simone picks up the telephone and dials several people. No one has a Fahrenheit thermometer. She calls her personal doctor. "Come right away, and
bring a Fahrenheit thermometer."

Ari's illness, thank goodness, is not serious. I expect the doctor's bill in the mail, but it never arrives. Simone, apparently, has discreetly taken care of it.

Apart from Marie-France, I haven't developed much of a social life. Jeanne and Analiese, two women my age who also work at the museum, often invite me to join them for lunch, but they have men in their lives and aren't free in the evenings.

Marie-France anticipates my need before I say a word. "You'd like my friend Andrea. She is single, like you, and she's going to a concert with her friends on Saturday. There's a party afterwards. Go with her. You can leave Ariel with us."

Andrea comes to pick me up. "The concert will be very special tonight, with Zino Francescatti on violin," she says, excited. "Prince Rainier and Princess Grace will be there too."

I twist around to catch a glimpse of the royal couple in their box high above us in the rear of the theater. By the second half of the concert, the Prince's royal head and eyelids droop. He is awakened by his beautiful consort's gentle elbow in his royal rib.

Musically, the concert is memorable. Andrea leads me backstage afterwards and introduces me to a dozen or so members of the orchestra. "They are taking us to a wonderful restaurant in Villefranche tonight!" she says.

Twelve of us pile into three cars and climb the hills above the sea to an exquisite, ancient village. Amongst the nooks and crannies of the old stone walls, we approach a door that looks like all the other doors but opens into a warm, rustic, candlelit restaurant.

We settle with noisy laughter at a long table, and get louder as the evening progresses. These classical musicians have an unrestrained capacity for stories and pranks. I laugh until it hurts. People at home always say I'm too serious. What is it about French humor that makes me laugh so hard? Lively music gets us singing and dancing between copious courses of soup, pasta, fresh seafood, salad, cheese, fruit, dessert and coffee.

One of the men in the group, Jean-Luc, sits next to me and takes charge of my well-being. He orders for me, makes sure my food is perfect, and asks me numerous times to dance. Andrea says we have to leave, she has to get up early, but Jean-Luc prevails upon her to let me stay. "We'll see her safely home, don't worry." Andrea doesn't look happy, but she leaves alone.

Jean-Luc calls the following morning. "Our group generally meets at Calypso for lunch. It's a small restaurant on the dock beneath the museum. Come join us." I pick up Ari from school and take him with me to the dock. "The team," as Jean-Luc calls them, is seated at one of the round tables with an umbrella shading them from the sun. They are a jovial bunch, but Andrea appears quiet.

After lunch, we spread towels on the cement dike and lie in bathing suits to soak in the sun, and then dive off the pier for a swim. The musicians don't have to work until evening; only Andrea and I have to get back to our offices.

On second thought, it occurs to me, there's no set schedule for my work. No one cares where I write or at what time of day, as long as the book meets deadline. I can actually allow my biological clock to shape my days! So now I wake up at 8:00, get Ari to school on the *mobylette* and shop at the central marketplace. I return home to put the food away, work on the book until noon, then grab my bathing suit and join "the team" for lunch. At about 2:30, I zoom up to the museum on the *mobylette* and work until Ari gets out of school at five. I pick him up and we go home for dinner. I work another three or four hours, until orchestra rehearsals are finished and Jean-Luc picks me up to join the others for a "nightcap" and dancing at one of the nightspots.

I'm quite caught up in the book Cousteau is having me write. We are trying to show there is enough power available from various solar and hydroelectric sources that there is no need, no excuse, to be developing nuclear power, with all the dangers it entails. The more I research the risks of plutonium and the careless, irresponsible way it is managed, the more irascible I become on the subject. I don't understand the greed that is willing to endanger a planet full of people.

Jean-Luc provides a wonderful balance to the work. He loves his land, *Le Midi* (Southern France), and it is his pleasure to show its treasures to Ari and me. One weekend he takes us to his family farm to pick cherries. Another is spent exploring the backcountry between Monaco and the Alps. He takes us to the hidden underground tunnel city of Eze, the neighboring towns of Villefranche, Saint-Jean-Cap-Ferrat (where the Rothschilds and others of their class maintain stately villas) and the seaside city of Nice. When my friends Gary and Thérèse come to see her mother in Sainte-Maxime, Jean-Luc arranges the three-hour trip to visit them.

Jean-Luc shows me where to shop, which stalls in the market have the best produce, and he repairs everything that doesn't function. Through his good-natured teasing, he challenges Ari's linguistic skills and wits as they banter back and forth. Ari is so busy laughing, he doesn't realize he's becoming fluent in French.

Today, at the office, Marie-France is not her usual warm self. "Marie-France, is something troubling you?" No response. "Would it be all right if Ari and I come up to the house on Saturday? We could bring fresh fish."

"Not this weekend. We are very busy."

"Marie-France, talk to me. What's wrong?"

Putting down her pen, she looks up at me. "I am very disappointed about how you have treated my friend Andrea. She was kind to you. She introduced you to her friends, and this is how you repay her."

"What? What have I done?"

"Andrea hasn't heard from her boyfriend since he first met you. She's devastated."

"Her boyfriend? Who is—?"

"Don't pretend you don't know. Everyone knows Jean-Luc is Andrea's boyfriend.

"Oh, no," I moan, "you can't be serious. Please believe me, Marie-France, I had no idea. I'll tell him not to call again."

I confront Jean-Luc this very night. "Why didn't you tell me Andrea was your girlfriend? How could you spend so much time with Ari and me and hurt her like this?"

"Who said she's my girlfriend?"

"It seems everyone knows. Except me."

"Wait. If Andrea tells people we're a couple, she's jumping to conclusions. We've been dating, but I never gave her reason to think it's serious. It has nothing to do with you. I'm simply not in love with her. She knows that; we've talked about it. Andrea is free to see anyone she wants, and I thought I was too."

"Obviously that's not her understanding." I slump, unhappy, into a soft chair. "Now I've lost a friend. Two friends."

Jean-Luc wastes no time. He tells Andrea he values their friendship but doesn't want her to nourish false hopes. I speak with her too. "I'm so sorry, I didn't know. Jean-Luc and I are merely friends. Nothing more. I never suspected you two were dating."

"Well we aren't now," she says. "I hope you're satisfied."

That's the end of my friendship with Andrea and, I realize with deep regret, with Marie-France as well.

Jean-Luc has a remarkable spirit of joy, despite hardships life has brought him. He watched his wife die a slow death from cancer. And during the war, when he was active in the Resistance against the Nazis, he was imprisoned and tortured. For a year and a half he was kept in solitary confinement.

"A year and a half! But how did you survive? People lose their minds in just a few weeks of solitary."

"One can, of course. For me, salvation was my music. I played over and over in my head every symphony, ever concerto, every piece I had ever learned. I played solo, I played duets, I played full orchestra. I sang every note of the trumpet parts and listened to the others behind me. Music I had forgotten came back to me. It was good practice time," he says, smiling. "It got me hired in the national orchestra when France was liberated."

Jean-Luc takes delight in everyday pleasures and playfulness. He is considerably older than I. Considerate, witty, and in every way a gentleman; he is not wealthy; but he is financially comfortable, with money for travel and recreation.

When I am at work, Jean-Luc takes Ari to the plaza where he can roller skate and play with neighborhood boys. He teaches him to play the trumpet, and to love the outdoors. When Jean-Luc isn't lavishing attention on him, his two sons are. Ari begs me to marry Jean-Luc. I wish I could. I have boundless affection and respect for him. I just wish I could love him as he deserves to be loved.

Ahh, love can be the most refined, most elegant instrument of cruelty. What keeps me from Jean-Luc? Is it the physical passion I have for Karl? Can I know what is good for me, and crave something that is not? Karl is a fine man, a man of integrity, but he can't handle responsibility; he has never grown up. Jean-Luc, in contrast, is the consummate protector, a man who embraces commitment and responsibility. Jean-Luc is a rare gem.

Is it not enough?

This morning, Ari went to the beach with Jean-Luc's eldest, Jérôme, and his girlfriend, Danielle. Now it's close to dinnertime and they still aren't back. Jean-Luc and I cast nervous glances at the kitchen clock. Another hour. At seven o'clock, Jérôme and Danielle arrive. They are visibly upset and out of breath. "I don't know how he slipped out of our sight; one moment he was there; then he was gone. We've searched everywhere . . . everywhere!" He cups his head in his hand. "If anything should happen to him—" Jérôme picks up the telephone. "I'm calling the police." My stomach twists. Danielle begins to cry. Jérôme identifies Ariel and the beach where he was last seen to the police. We wait, helpless and frightened.

The front door opens slowly and Ari walks in, crying. Jérôme springs forward to meet him, conflicted with anger and relief. Hands on his hips, he looks down from a height of six-foot-four to the small boy whose head is just above his knees.

"Where have you been?" he thunders.

Ari is not intimidated. Mirroring Jérôme, he also places his little hands on his hips and stretches his neck back to look high up into Jérôme's face. "Where were *you*? I had to find my way back all by myself! *You* were supposed to be watching me! You were responsible for me! I'm just a kid and—" he tries to maintain his indignant tone but dissolves into tears, "—and you *lost* me!"

Jérôme scoops Ari into his arms and hugs him. "Thank God you're all right. That's all that matters."

Five o'clock on Friday afternoon, Marie-France neatly arranges file folders on her desk and prepares to lock up. Her "Goodnight" is polite but cool. She has not invited us to dinner in a long time, and I miss her.

I pick up Ari from school. One of his classmates comes running toward me. "Your son, Madame, he is not nice."

"Oh, dear. Is he fighting again?" Normally such a gentle child, on occasion Ari's frustration with his limited French comes out through his fists.

A colleague of mine at the museum offers a suggestion. "Ari isn't learning French because his *maman* is close by to translate. Why don't you let him go with my son to camp in the Alps this summer?"

"What do you think?" I ask Jean-Luc that evening.

"Oh, yes, Val de Blore. It's a terrific camp run by the church fathers. My boys loved it when they were kids."

For the next three evenings, together with Jean-Luc, his sons, their girl-friends, and "the team," I sew labels into Ari's clothes and mark his name, "Ariel," in big blue letters on the soap dish, flashlight, and coffee bowl with the picture of a funny little man.

"A coffee bowl, Mama?"

"*Oui*, Ariel," (I speak French to him as often as I can), "kids in France drink their breakfast milk hot, with a teaspoon of coffee for flavor."

He piles into the school bus, waving as they pull away. "We'll be up to see you on the weekend, Chief!" Jean-Luc calls.

It's a three-hour drive through the backcountry and gorges leading to the Alps. The camp, an old stone chicken farm in the mountains, is charming. Ari runs toward us, arms outstretched. Off we go for a hike in the forest and a picnic near the cold mountain stream. But as we pull food out of the basket, a sudden rain sends us under a wide oak tree for shelter. We wait for the sun to return.

Ari, normally giddy with joy when he's with Jean-Luc, lies quietly on the blanket, moaning softly. "My tummy hurts, Mama. I want to go home."

I'm not sure if there's something really wrong with his tummy or if he's just lonely. He still isn't very fluent in his French. "Tell you what, *chéri*, stay just one more week. We'll come back again on Saturday, and if you still want to leave, we'll bring you home then."

On the second weekend, we play with cows and deer in the mountain meadows. "How is your tummy?" I ask.

"It hurts every day."

"Do you want to come home?"

"I . . . I'll stay one more week."

"You're sure?" He nods.

The third week, we find him chattering like a magpie in French with his buddies. He waves, and tears himself away reluctantly to greet us. "Come," he tugs at my hand, "I'll show you the new baby chicks." He is happy now; he doesn't want to come home with us.

"No more tummy aches?" I ask.

"Yes, all the time. But I don't want to leave the camp." As soon as he becomes fluent, Ari's temper completely disappears. But his tummy aches do not.

When camp season is over, we resume our daily routines. Ari climbs onto the back of the *mobylette* and we head down the hills toward the outdoor market in the center of town. Suddenly he doubles over and wails in pain. I drive to the pharmacy.

"This will help, Madame. It's pure carbon."

"Carbon?" I take the capsules doubtfully. "Is this all right for children? There are no chemicals in it?"

"I beg your pardon, Madame!" The pharmacist is indignant. "We do not give chemicals to children."

"Glad to hear that. Because in America, they do. Frequently."

"Fortunately, Madame, we are in France."

BOOM! I am jerked out of my sleep by the sound of a bomb exploding. Boom! BoomBoomBOOM! Lots of bombs. Oh, God, it must be war. You never know in Europe. Who's fighting whom? Whose side am I on? What are we doing here? It's midnight. A sneak attack? The French doors on the balcony are open. Jean-Luc had always teased me about being a fresh-air fiend; he said he'd never met anyone before who didn't close his or her shutter-doors at night. Creeping in the dark toward the balcony, I reach to shut the doors and see the sky ablaze with color. BOOM! More color, sparkles, thundering showers of light. It is a dazzling, elaborate display of fireworks. Grateful that no one is here to witness my foolish fear, I sheepishly take a glass of warm milk to calm my nerves and sit on the balcony to enjoy the spectacle.

I lunch with the "team" the following day, as usual. At Restaurant Calypso, below the museum, conversation centers on the International Festival of Fireworks, which had begun the night before with an exhibition from Japan.

"They'll be hard to beat. I'm betting on them." Guy throws a 50-franc note on the table. "Here's a hundred on Italy," Jacques counters. With a cool display of patriotism, I place my bet on the USA. Everyone laughs.

"What's so funny?"

"No offense, Barbara. Your country can boast of many achievements, but when it comes to fireworks . . ." they laugh again, "save your money."

Three hairpin-turn roads run parallel above the Principality of Monaco. They are "The High Road," "The Middle Road" and "The Low Road." Between ten o'clock and midnight, every night this week, thousands of people line the walls of the three-tiered roads to watch the fireworks.

Below us, in the famous harbor of Monaco, some of the world's most spectacular yachts are docked, including the one belonging to Aristotle Onassis. The boats, too, are full of people, their colored lanterns bobbing on dark waters, sending upwards, towards us, the sounds of music, clinking glasses, and festivity. When the fireworks display is spectacular, in addition to shouts and applause from thousands of onlookers, there wells up a deep, reverberating chorus of foghorns from the yachts, a powerful low-pitched bellow of approval across the water. For 10 consecutive nights, as the international competition continues, the citizens of Monaco party.

Guy had bet on the winner. "Since you're all paying for my lunch today, I'm ordering the best the menu has to offer." He hesitates when choosing his dessert. "The ice cream looks good, but so does the apple pie."

"That's easy," I advise, "make it pie *à la mode*." They all look blankly at me. "Pie with a ball of ice cream on top of it," I explain. The puzzled looks continue.

"*Une tarte au boule?*" The restaurant owner translates it literally. "Pie with a ball?"

"We do it in America. It's very good." This is hardly convincing. As far as the French are concerned, Americans are not civilized when it comes to food.

"They don't go together. One has pie, or one has ice cream. It isn't done." All the heads nod.

"It *is* done," I insist. "Please bring me a *tarte au boule*." The waiter leaves, shaking his head, and returns to set the revolutionary piece of pie before me. I pass it around to my friends. "Taste it, all of you. Tell me what you think."

The oohs and aahs vindicate me. "Pierre," Jean-Luc tells the waiter, "bring out seven *tartes au boule*."

Every day now, when our crew gathers for lunch, Pierre prepares the *tartes au boule* for dessert. Within a few weeks, it's a featured item on the menu, and people are coming to the restaurant for a taste delight unique to the creative chef of Restaurant Calypso.

This summer, Ari and I travel to Normandy, in the far northwestern corner of France, to visit an old friend from my student days in Paris. Pierre has since married and they have a son the same age as Ari.

Normandy is as different from Monaco—physically and culturally—as New England is from New Orleans and we enjoy discovering this different part of France. But on the train, when we return to Monaco in the south, Ari doubles over, moaning in pain, for most of the eight-hour ride. This is the first time, since taking the carbon, that he has had a problem.

Jean-Luc and Guy are waiting for us at the station but, in my anxiety over Ari's condition, I miss the stop and we have to take a cab back from Menton, across the Italian border. I put Ari to bed when we eventually get home, and knock on a neighbor's door to inquire about a doctor. None of my neighbors are home. Sunday, darn! They go for picnics in the country. I run down to the corner café to call a cab. Closed. I'll have to find a way to a hospital, but can Ari withstand the bumpy trip on the back of the *mobylette*? What to do? I am bordering on panic when there is a knock at our door.

"Jean-Luc! You are an angel of mercy! Thank God you're here!" It's just a figure of speech, of course, but who—what—does one thank? If Jean-Luc hadn't come just now . . . a shiver of dread overtakes me.

We drive rapidly to the Hôpital Princesse Grace. In the emergency room, Ari is diagnosed with acute appendicitis. "Doctor Amiens will operate in just a few minutes, Madame," a nurse assures me. "Your son will be fine."

"Thank you."

"Amiens?" Jean-Luc interrupts. "No way. Call Dr. Lomas."

"Doctor Lomas is not on duty tonight, Monsieur. Doctor Amiens will do the surgery."

"Find Doctor Lomas right away," Jean-Luc replies. "I insist."

"Jean-Luc . . ." I protest.

"Amiens is no more a surgeon than the 'butcher of Buchenwald,'" Jean-Luc whispers to me. "Don't let him touch the boy." Dr. Lomas arrives in 15 minutes. Ari surrenders his inflamed appendix, and I collapse, crushed by dual emotions of fear and relief.

On my own, I now realize, I'd been unable to get medical help when my son needed it. Then, at the hospital, I almost put us in the hands of an incompetent. I'm overwhelmed with our vulnerability. What if Jean-Luc hadn't come to our house when he did? (He almost didn't, he tells me. When he didn't see us get off the train, he assumed we were staying longer in Normandy.) What if we hadn't gotten to the hospital before Ari's appendix burst? Good God, it's the second time I almost lost him, but for the intervention of . . . of . . . what? Luck?

Life is very frightening if "luck" is all there is.

My work at the museum is coming to a close. For a last sortie before we return to California, Jean-Luc takes us to the artistic villages of St. Paul and Vence, about an hour to the west. We wander the alleys, museums and galleries cut into stone walls that stand since Roman times, and pretend this joy can last forever. Then, as evening falls, we head back toward Monaco.

"I have chosen a special place for our dinner tonight," Jean-Luc says. "It's my favorite restaurant, and I've been saving it for the right moment with the right person." He turns off the coast road to make a narrow, steep climb above the town of Cagnes-sur-Mer. Good thing he knows where he's going. You can't make a mistake here, can't turn around on the one-lane hairpin road until you reach the central plaza of Les Hauts de Cagnes (the Cagnes Highlands), a carefully preserved, beautiful medieval village.

We walk the winding alleys toward the restaurant. Within the ancient stone walls are apartments that, on the inside, people of wealth have refurbished and modernized with elegance. At the restaurant, called *Le Puits Fleuri* (The Flowering Well), there is indeed a well within the courtyard covered in flowering vines and surrounded by lush gardens. Tiny sparkling lights dance in the trees to make a magical setting. A singer sits on the ledge of the well with his guitar, singing songs of the southern Midi region, and the character all its own.

Seated, Jean-Luc gazes intently into my eyes in a way that makes me uncomfortable, because I can't gaze back the same way. I turn my attention to the singer. "I love his melodies, Jean-Luc, but his southern accent is very thick. I'm missing some of the words."

"He is singing about his accent. He says that wherever he travels, his accent goes with him. In this way he takes a piece of his land along and he is never in a foreign place. Like the soil on his shoes, a part of his home is with him always, and it brings comfort to the places that he visits."

"How lovely! I never thought of an accent in that way."

"Bar-r-b-a-a-a-r-r-a . . . *ma petite américaine*." Jean-Luc takes my hand and looks longingly at me. "You, too, bring your land here to the Midi. You color my world with it. Stay here with me, Bar-bar-a, *mon amour*. Marry me."

Can I stay? Ari and I have adapted nicely to life in Monaco, but I do miss my family. Mom and I were just starting to get to know each other; I don't want to lose that. Would they visit? Do I want to make this my home? The song of the guitarist fills the long, awkward silence. "Jean-Luc . . . I don't know what to say."

"Say yes. Ari will be happy too. I love the boy, you know I do."

"Let me think about it, dear Jean-Luc. I'm so honored . . ."

We make the remaining time of that last evening as festive as we can, knowing that morning will see me off, away from this land I love so much, this man who has been so wonderful to me and my son. We focus with intense concentration on the present moment until no moments are left.

Back on Harvard Street in Santa Monica, California, Karl is shaken when I tell him about Jean-Luc. "You want to get married? I didn't think it was that important to you; it certainly isn't to me. But if that's what you want, baby, we can get married. No problem!"

For eight months, Jean-Luc has been calling every night, long tender calls. "We are thousands of miles apart, Bar-bar-a, but we can open our window to the sky and wish upon the same star at the same moment. Look at the star, *chérie*. I am wishing for you . . . wishing you will come back to me. Forever. What are you wishing for?"

I wish to feel the same way. I want desperately to love Jean-Luc, to live the life he can offer Ari and me. But my love for him is not what a woman should feel for her man. I cannot marry him without that, and I don't know how to make it happen.

It's good to be back with family, good to be at Sunday brunch with my aunt and uncle and my cousins. But Ari and I miss Monaco, and Jean-Luc, and the feeling I had known only twice in my life (with the Clarks and with him) of being cared for and protected. Without Jean-Luc, I am the only one who takes care of us, who makes sure Ari can survive and thrive. I protect his childhood and create a path to his maturity. I'll see him grown and educated, and make all the decisions along the way. Some decisions will be good; some won't. But there is no one else to help; they'll have to do.

"What concerns me more than anything in the world," I tell my aunt Evelyn, "is who would care for Ari if something happened to me? His irresponsible father? No thanks. I don't even want him around Stephen's strange ideas. My mom? She'd crack under the demands of a child—"

"Why, Barbara, I'm surprised to hear you worrying about this," Evelyn interrupts. "Karl loves Ari as his own son. He'd be the one to raise him!" All eyes in the room turn to Karl. He clears his throat, but the reassuring words we await do not come. "Wouldn't you, Karl?" my aunt urges.

"Ahh, well . . . you know I love the boy, but, I . . . well I can hardly support myself; how could I take responsibility for him?" Silence fills the room. "I mean," Karl rushes on, "I'd always be in touch with him; I'd make sure he was in good hands . . ."

This is a life-defining moment. Inside, from the top of my neck to the pit of my stomach, a heavy iron curtain comes down, crushing my gut with a resonant clang. My tie to Karl is stamped out. It is over. Finished.

The Woman at the Well

*"I have no husband," she replied. Jesus said to her, "You are right when
you say you have no husband. The fact is, you have had five husbands,
and the man you now have is not your husband."*

JOHN 4:17-18

*At one time we too were foolish, disobedient, deceived and enslaved by
all kinds of passions and pleasures.*

TITUS 3:3

I reach for the ringing telephone. Somebody from the Sherman Oaks Burn
Center says my dad is there; he'd been trapped in a fire. "There was a gas explosion. His house burned to the ground and he was found barely alive."

"Oh, no." This is not real. "What is his condition now?"

"Touch and go."

The blood freezes in my veins. "Where are you located?"

The Burn Center is not a place you forget. It is a state-of-the-art treatment
center with a brilliant and caring professional staff, but it is also a house of unbearable, excruciating torment, and many within its walls long for death.
Mummies wander the halls wrapped head-to-toe in bandages with little holes
for their eyes. There are little toddler mummies and big adult mummies. Screams
of the tortured echo ceaselessly, as one imagines they would in hell.

I find Dad's room. His dark eyes, showing through bandages, are con-
torted with pain. "Dad—" Words freeze in my throat as unshed tears sit like
ice pellets in my eyes. I reach out with an impulse to hug him and withdraw,
afraid I'll hurt him more.

He tries to move and cries out, "Aaagh!"

"Oh, Dad, you're in so much pain, I can't even imagine it. I wish I could do
something."

His voice is weak behind the bandage mask. "They're doing all they can
for me."

"I called Mom and told her what happened. She is coming to see you."

"Yes. Nice . . ." his voice trails off weakly, "of her to come . . . a long time."

The head of the burn center, Dr. Richard Grossman, steps in. "Morning, Jordan. You ready for your whirlpool bath?"

Daddy groans.

"What's that?"

"It's how we remove dead skin," Grossman explains.

"It's how they torture us," Daddy says. "Just kidding. He's a good man, Bobs; I wouldn't be able to bear this if it weren't for him."

They take Daddy out. He winces, and little yelps of pain escape at every touch of the aide.

"Will he make it, Doctor?" I ask, when Daddy is further down the hall.

"He's a fighter, your dad is." Dr. Grossman smiles. "He complains about the food, says his body can't restore itself with the 'garbage' we're giving him. He wants whole-grain breads, fresh fruit and vegetables. Refuses to eat anything with artificial colors or preservatives."

"That's my dad. He's always been a nut about healthy food. Sorry if he makes it tough for your staff."

"Don't be sorry. We'll accommodate his wishes. I'm just glad he cares that much about getting well. You see," Dr. Grossman explains, "I can treat the burns, but I lose a lot of patients because they can't take the pain; they *will* themselves to die. So when a patient wants to heal, I'll support him every possible way."

I come every day and bring Daddy's mail. He dictates letters I am to send, tells me what checks to write, how to pay his bills. We make a little office in his room. Dad has daily treatments and therapy to help him move again. Nurses come frequently to pour water on the bandages so they don't stick too badly when they are changed. I wince, aware that all the nerves, all the pain receptors are in the torn and burned skin. We wonder if the pain will ever go away. But Dad is grateful for the attentive care and the staff's capacity to deal with the unloveliness of rotting skin.

Daddy has had different roommates these past several days. Can't tell if they are young or old; their heads are covered with bandages, and they scream unceasingly.

"This goes on through the night, Dad. How can you sleep?"

"Haven't slept in a week. When they moved the first guy into my room, I was going nuts, but I tried talking to him. Don't know if he heard anything I said through his noise, but after a couple of days he quieted down. I thought great, finally some peace and quiet. So what do they do? They move him out, and that same day they bring in another screamer. This guy's the third one. He's been here for two days. I don't know how much longer I can take it."

I speak to Dr. Grossman. "Is there any other bed for that poor man? My father is desperate for a night's sleep."

"I know," the doctor acknowledges. "I'm very sorry about that. It's just that . . ." he seems to be deciding whether to tell me something or not. "It's not that there aren't other beds. We put these people in with your dad for a reason. They are the ones who want to die, you see. And usually we lose them. But your dad has a way of talking with them, encouraging them, and they come around. I guess I have to admit we're using him. But if he's willing, I'll keep sending them as long as he can stand it."

I tell Dad what the doctor said. He groans.

"Grossman will move him out right away if you just say the word, Dad. He understands."

"No, it's okay. If it's doing some good, it's okay. I'll put up with the noise."

After 40 days in the Burn Center, they are preparing Dad to go home, teaching him about the complex bathing rituals and treatments he will have to do for months to come. His home is burned down, and it's best if he's not alone; so he's going to stay with my sister. Julia has a guest room.

I bring his clothes and help him gingerly—trying not to touch the tender skin—to get dressed.

"Say, it's quiet in here today," I observe. "Your friend is sleeping peacefully for a change."

"Yes," Dad says. "He won't be screaming anymore. Says Jesus came in the night and touched him. Says the pain is gone now."

"What? Has he flipped out?"

"Didn't seem like it. He sounded rational, calm, very sure of himself."

"Dad!" I'm astounded to hear my dad talk like this, and to be so matter-of-fact about it. In the same tone of voice he could have said he had chicken soup for dinner. "Do you believe him?"

"Don't know. But if somebody could touch me and make all the pain go away, he could say his name was Jesus or anything else, and I'd believe him."

Dad closes his eyes and lies back on the pillow, exhausted. Poor Daddy. Normally, I'd slip out when he falls asleep and run some errands. But today I stay to gaze upon this wonderful man who continues to surprise me.

"Don't know," he said. He doesn't know? So Jesus *might* have come? This blows my circuits. Obviously, my father isn't hallucinating. So what could he have seen in his roommate's transformation to even *consider* such a possibility? Who is this Jesus that touches people in the night and takes away their pain?

❧   ❧   ❧

My Israeli neighbor, Aviva, is working with an immigration attorney to get her green card. She says Ivan is a terrific guy; she wants me to meet him.

"But I don't need a green card."

"Why don't you tell him that? Tonight. My house at 8:00."

When Aviva introduces us, Ivan takes my hand. It is electric. I try to look away, pretend not to notice, but he locks my eyes with his. This man is intense—and intensely attractive, with thick black hair and beautiful brown-almost-black eyes.

I disengage from his look and hide behind the safety of conversation. "So, Aviva, you're staying in the States? Doesn't Israel need good teachers like you?"

Aviva explains that life in Israel is very difficult for a single woman. "Sure, I miss my family," she admits, "but I don't miss feeling unaccepted by society." I am aware of Ivan's unrelenting gaze as I focus my attention on Aviva.

After dinner, I clear the dishes, carry a pile to the sink and turn back for more. Suddenly, Ivan is standing close, very close in front of me, one arm on each side, leaning on the sink so that I am "trapped" in between.

"Don't go," he says. "I haven't had a moment alone with you."

"I want to help Aviva clean up," I squirm out of reach but am breathless. This man has an effect on me.

I stay close to Aviva for the rest of the evening; but when I prepare to leave, Ivan is ready too. He escorts me outside. "Let me take you for coffee before you go home. I'd like to get to know you better."

In a quiet coffee house, we talk a long time. He is bright; his humor is sharp. But it's late and I have to leave.

"I can't let you go," he says. "I'll miss you."

I laugh. "You're nuts. We've just met; how did you get along all your life without me?"

"I've been asking myself the same question. I think I've just come alive tonight for the first time. Don't leave."

"My son is with a sitter."

"Have breakfast with me in the morning."

"I go to work in the morning."

"Me, too. I'll bring breakfast to your house before we go, okay?"

He's bold and persistent and, I realize as I climb into bed, he's intriguing. It takes a while to stop thinking of him and fall sleep. But sleep is fitful because of a vivid, disturbing dream.

I am on a narrow dirt path high on the ridge of a hill. Below my path, a small French village, with its stone houses and red tile roofs, faces a beautiful lake. It is late night, almost dawn. Ivan is on the far end of the path, coming toward me. We run to close the distance between us, drawn with longing to meet. As we get closer, the cry of a woman's voice rises from the village below. We continue toward one another, the night giving way to the first light of day. The woman's shrill cry grows louder. The closer we get, Ivan and I, the louder the cry, until it becomes a haunting wail. I ignore it. He ignores it. We focus only on one another and the compelling force that thrusts us together. The wail has reached a frightening pitch when, at last, he is holding me tight, enclosing me in the magic of his arms that block out the sound, block out the world, block out all reason.

In the morning, I try to shake off the unnerving effect of the dream. Only once in the past—just before my marriage to Stephen—have I dreamt so vividly. I had ignored that dream and lived the consequences. Dare I disregard this one? Nonsense! Ivan is different. Unlike the artistic, irresponsible men to whom I'm usually drawn, he is an attorney, a practical profession, and he wants commitment.

"It's great that you have a little boy," he had said last night, "I always wanted a son." Then he had taken my hand across the table. "You'll say we haven't known each other long enough, but I know what I feel, and I have never felt this way about anyone. You've entered my life like a thunderburst." And then the magic words: "*I want to take care of you.*"

I dress quickly for breakfast. I have to get Ari ready and let him know Ivan's coming. Uh oh, there are dishes in the sink. The doorbell rings. "My goodness, you're early! I'm not quite—"

"You're fine. Beautiful! If I'm lucky, I'll get to see you without makeup every day for the rest of my life, so don't worry about it."

He hands me a bag. "Can you heat this? Where's your little boy? I'd like to meet him."

When Ari leaves for school, I tell Ivan about the dream. "Who is the woman who would cry if you and I get together?"

"Dalia. We went together for two years, but it's been over for months. Don't even think about it. You are the only woman in my life."

"How can you say that? We've just met!"

"You don't understand the importance of that meeting, Barbie-Doll. But you will."

Ivan brings dinner when I get home from work. "I'll be here tomorrow too," he says. "And the day after. And the next."

My breath catches in the whirlwind. "Let's slow this down. It feels like we are racing downhill without brakes."

"You are a foolish girl." Ivan wraps me in his arms and presses close to me. I can't pretend his nearness doesn't weaken me. "We are faced with the love of a lifetime, and you're scared. Thank goodness I'm here to protect you from your foolishness."

For the weekend, Ivan has rented a cabin in the San Bernardino Mountains. We walk, wade in streams, eat leisurely, and get to know more about one another. Ivan loves to talk about the law. We sit for hours near the fire as darkness comes over the forest. Ivan expounds on the differences between civil and criminal law, the historic roots of civil law in old England, examples of decisions that changed society, and the role of Justice Cardoza (a Sephardic Jew like Ivan, and his hero) in shaping the American justice system. Ivan should be a law professor. Brilliant, articulate and witty, he makes it fascinating.

We breakfast on the grassy bank of a hill overlooking the valley and stream below. The mist on the mountains recalls a Chinese waterbrush drawing. "Extraordinary, isn't it?" I muse aloud. "Whoever created this world is a consummate artist."

"You have any ideas on that?"

"I'm not sure, except that there's a great one-ness to it, and I know I'm part of it."

"How so?"

"I see the universe like a biological body, one huge body, and each of us is a simple cell within it. All of us together, plus animals and plants and atmosphere and planets and stars and suns make a single whole. And, as tiny a cell that we are, look what extraordinary complexities lie within each of us. My dad says the human body is the most marvelous, most intricate wonder in all creation. There are limbs with different functions, systems within the limbs like blood and lymph, cells within the systems . . . Doesn't it boggle your imagination?"

"I don't usually indulge in spiritual fantasies." He looks down at a twig he breaks with his fingers. "But it makes sense the way you describe it."

I draw a picture of the Chinese Yin-Yang in the dirt and explain the male-female symbol for complementary completion. "It's like you and me together. You complete my ignorance of law and economics, and I can fill your empty spaces with art and spirit."

Sometimes Ivan leaves his office during the day or rushes home from a court-room during recess to steal an hour with me. When I check my daily calendar on the kitchen wall, I find he's scribbled a message in large letters: "*Ivan misses you.*"

Flowers come to my office. The card says, *"Just because."* Anywhere we go, in the streets, at family gatherings, Ivan finds a hidden corner where he can hold me, nibble my neck, and cover me with hot, biting kisses. "I can't wait to be alone with you," he whispers, and his outrageous desire is delicious. It's head-turning.

"It's uncomfortable being around you two," Cass complains. "There's a circle of exclusivity keeping you apart from the rest of us. Can't you just be with us once in a while?" My aunt and cousins nod their agreement. Why? Can't they see that Ivan is devoted to me? That he takes care of me?

Last week, for example, when I was sick, he called around to find the finest specialist in the city. "I won't let you go to that HMO; I want the best doctor in town treating you."

"But, Ivan, I can't afford a private doctor. I'm sure the HMO is fine."

"You don't have to afford it; I'm paying the bill." There had been a minor surgery and three follow-up visits. The bills are mounting quickly, but Ivan assures me not to worry. I am only to get well.

Can't my family understand that he is wonderful? Except for Lorna, no one has penetrated so deeply into my psyche and my heart as Ivan.

I work late, pick up Ari, and arrive home. Ivan is waiting for us in the living room, reading my notebooks. He doesn't lift his head to say hello.

"Hi, what are you doing?"

His voice is quiet, deliberate. "Getting to know you better."

"Since when have you been reading my notebooks?"

He cuts me off. "You had quite a thing going with Karl."

"I've told you about him."

"Not all of it."

"Ivan, put those away. I'm going to start dinner." I haven't seen him in a mood like this before. Dark. Brooding. Oppressive. Nothing I do can make him smile. A cloud hangs over the evening. And over my heart.

Karl calls me at work. "How's it going, baby? You all right?"

"Yes, fine. What about you?"

"Yeah . . . well . . ." When Ivan came into my life Karl had been gracious. There had been no recriminations, but I know he's hurting. "Whatever makes you happy, darlin'," he had said. "I want what's best for you, I really do. If he's the one, then go for it." Karl is making it as easy for me as possible.

"Look, I have a favor to ask," he gets quickly to the point. "My new apartment, it's fine, but it's tight. One small closet. I have some things that I'd like to store. Any problem with my leaving them in the little shack out behind your place?"

"Of course not. It's fine."

"Yeah. I can go in and out from the alley. You won't even have to see me."

"Karl, please. Why wouldn't I want to see you?" But even as I say it, I know it's best not to. Ivan hasn't been the same since he read about Karl in my notebooks. He broods about Karl, wondering if I think it's as good with him as it had been with Karl.

I should not have told Ivan that Karl called. I didn't expect his outburst. "I knew it! You can't let go of him—keeping his things here, he's got a reason to keep coming back. Next thing you know, he'll want visiting rights with Ari!"

My stomach tightens. Karl can't see Ari? But they should see each other! Karl loves him. "Ivan, this is ridiculous. His things won't be here in the apartment, only in the shed behind the building. We won't even know when he comes and goes." My words are like oil on a fire. Ivan's rage is an explosion, but he doesn't lose his ability to articulate, to reason, to make it sound right.

The black mood hangs between us for hours until I agree to tell Karl he cannot leave his things. Right now. It is devastating. To say Karl can't use the storage shed is bad enough. But with Ivan standing there, I can't explain what's going on. I'm hurting Karl, and it crushes me to do it.

"I can't believe this is you," Karl says. "What's happening to you, kid?"

In the morning, I call Karl from work to explain.

"Look," Karl says, "I don't know who or what this guy is, but I don't like the sound of it." His voice is flat. "I just hope you know what you're doing. For your sake and Ari's." We are both silent. Then Karl asks, broken. "How is he? How's my boy?"

"Good, Karl. He's doing fine."

"Does he miss me?"

"Yes, as a matter of fact. He does."

"Yeah, well . . . have a good life, kid."

We rarely spend Sunday mornings at my aunt's house anymore, but today is an exception. Ivan will grow to like them, I'm sure, when he gets to know them better.

"Barbara, come with me for a second." Aunt Evelyn leads me to her bedroom. "I want you to look at a dress I bought yesterday. Tell me if you think I should have it shortened."

The dress is fine. That isn't why she brought me in. "Karl was here last night," my aunt says, "and I'm disturbed by what he told us."

"He was here?"

"Oh yes, he comes by. With you and Ari gone, and his mother in Massachusetts, he says we're all the family he has. You don't mind, do you?"

"Oh no, no. I'm glad you're there for him. I really am."

"He says you've let Ivan sever your friendship. It's hard for him to get over that. And I'll tell you frankly, dear, we're concerned, too. The idea that Karl can't see Ariel! I hope you'll think about what you're doing."

Ivan is back to his old self, I note with enormous relief. That scene about Karl must have been an aberration. The notebooks made Karl too real for Ivan. I wish he hadn't read them. But he's cheerful and ebullient now, and he has arranged a vacation. "You need a break," Ivan says, waving two airline tickets. "You need to get away from work, the house, the kid—"

"I don't need to get away from Ari."

"Nonsense. This is time out for the two of us." I give in, hoping to overcome his tension about the time I spend with my son.

"What do you say to visiting the Deep South? It's a big part of our history, a culture within a culture, and neither of us have ever been there."

Dad offers to stay with Ari while Ivan and I explore the land of plantations and Scarlett O'Hara and cotton mills. He's almost completely recovered from his burns; there are scars, of course, but he walks almost without any drag to his feet now.

The South is a feast of lavender and magnolia, a gentle rhythm of living. Ivan makes keen observations as we travel and, as we visit old courthouses, explains how the law has affected history. I link my arm through his and hold tight as we stroll through Bourbon Street in New Orleans, alive with hot music all night long; Savannah, a city dressed in old lace; Atlanta, where Ivan says there's a large settlement of Sephardic Jews.

We drive along the Gulf Coast to Alabama and swim in a "crick" with local kids. Mississippi, for all its ugly history, has an exquisitely beautiful countryside. In South Carolina, we ride a tandem bike through lush grasses and weeping willows. Plantations recall a civilization of refined formality and genteel manners rooted in a horrific evil, an evil to which the Old Slave Mart Museum is a devastating monument.

Our flight home stops in New York, where Lorna and her husband now live. She had returned from the Basque country several years ago to marry Patrick,

and he is a successful writer at a Madison Avenue advertising agency. I am excited about introducing them to Ivan.

We arrange to meet in a Greenwich Village nightclub, but a subtle tension
stresses the evening. When Ivan steps over to the bar for a second round of
beer, I lean toward Lorna and ask, "What's going on?"

"He's poison!" she whispers.

I'm very angry when I call Lorna, after our return to California. "You shut
him out from the moment we arrived—it was positively rude! You made no effort to get to know Ivan, and then you came out with that vicious remark!"

"I'm sorry, but I had a powerfully negative reaction to him. He's bad for
you, Barbara. Watch out."

"You're all-knowing, aren't you? Well, this is one time you know nothing.
Maybe you've met your match, Lorna. And maybe you can't deal with it."

"Barbara, please, what I said is for your own good. If I'm wrong, I'm sorry.
I just don't think I am."

"Give him a chance, for heaven's sake. Come out here and spend some time
with us. Get to know him before you jump to conclusions."

"Okay." It's a reluctant assent. "I'll try to manage a visit before winter."

"I have to go now. I'm calling from work."

Thanks to Ivan, I now work as a copywriter in an advertising agency, and I'm
learning a lot about the business world. Working for Cousteau, I had put
in 10, 12, 14 hours a day, writing books and doing research. But I was earning peanuts. "You should be paid what you're worth," Ivan had insisted, "and
the only place that will happen is in the corporate world. Once I get my practice on solid footing, you won't have to work at all. Until then, you should be
well paid."

"But I don't know anything about the business world. I didn't even know
they use writers."

Ivan explained the structure of a corporation, how it works, and where I
could fit in. He wrote an impressive résumé for me, using language that sounded
"bottom-line" oriented, and he taught me how to interview, using buzz words
that indicated I understood their issues. He suggested that advertising would
utilize my writing and design skills.

"I know who can help me!" I called Lorna and asked if Patrick would teach
me the principles of marketing and advertising.

"Are you sure you want to do this, Barbara? That's not a world where you
belong. You're a writer, an artist. It's all wrong. They'll chew you up and spit
you out. Don't do it . . . please."

"You know, Lorna, for all your penetrating insight, you are surprisingly short-sighted about practical realities. You're married to a man who earns half a million dollars a year writing advertisements for the business world you hate so much. That allows you to stay at home with your kids and paint canvases in your studio. I'm a single mother. I've got to earn a living. Do you have any idea what that's like?"

"Okay, okay. Here's Patrick."

"Hey, Barb. Tell you what. Create 10 ads, then call me back."

"What kind of ads? What products?"

"Anything. Look around your house. Look under the sink. It's full of products."

I had spent three weeks cutting pictures from magazines, drawing, designing, and creating headlines and body copy. I put the 16 x 24 mockups in a new portfolio, picked Ari up from school, and boarded a plane for New York. For three solid days, Patrick and I locked ourselves in a room while Lorna took care of Ari. He used each of my ads as an object lesson.

"Spic 'n Span." He held up the TV storyboard. It began with a close-up on a nun scrubbing a floor, Bach's B-minor mass playing softly in the background. Camera pulled back to show two more nuns scrubbing pillars and pews close by. The B-minor Mass got louder. Pulling farther back, as the Mass reached a sonorous climax, a long shot revealed a magnificent cathedral where dozens of nuns scrubbed and cleaned like a hive of busy little black ants. Superimposed, the caption: *"Cleanliness Is Next to Godliness."* Voice over: *"Spic 'n Span: the Big-Job Cleanser."*

"Clever. Very clever," Patrick had said. "Now explain the positioning statement."

"The what?"

"What is the product's position in the market? Dominant? Struggling? Who are their competitors, and what do they offer? Who buys it? Why? Why not? What, if anything, is its USP?"

"You're going too fast."

"USP. Unique selling point. Look, Barbara, it's not enough to be clever. There has to be a reason for everything you do. It has to be the solution to some kind of problem. So let's start at the beginning, shall we?"

Patrick and I went through 10 products this way, working steadily until Sunday night, when Ari and I boarded the 6:00 plane for Los Angeles. By then, I knew how to position a product, research the competition, and determine buyers' wants. I had some understanding of how to develop a creative concept.

Normally, without a portfolio of real, produced work, you can't get an appointment. No one will see you. Without experience, they expect you to begin as a secretary or in the mailroom. I didn't have time for that. I had to earn a living.

I took three more weeks to redo my ads and storyboards, preparing a make-believe portfolio. Because I used Patrick's name, the creative director at Doyle Dane Bernbach made time to see me. Slowly, carefully, he went through my portfolio of fictitious ads, making comments as he read. Then he closed the leather case. "You're talented. I wish I had an opening on my creative team, but I don't." He scribbled on a piece of paper, then handed me six names and telephone numbers. "Use my name with any of these people; it will get you in the door."

Six names led to a mushrooming list of others. I got past closed doors at every major agency in town. Creative directors said I was audacious, innovative; they liked my ideas. They got on the phone and called colleagues in other agencies. "You have to see her portfolio." And new doors opened. It took three months, but I was finally hired as a copywriter by one of the largest ad agencies in Los Angeles. Now I am writing to make the public fall in love with Peugeot, Pennzoil, Merle Norman Cosmetics, and Ballantine Scotch. I still work long, 12- to 14-hour days, and it's hard; but I have a future.

"I have to get up at 5:30, Ivan. I'd better get to bed."

Ivan is at the desk in the corner of the bedroom, poring over mail. His jaw is tense. "Wish I could join you, but I'm behind in paying my bills. Look at all these."

"Okay." I yawn. "See you in the morning." I fall immediately into a deep, dreamless sleep of fatigue. Dark nothingness. My brain and body begin to relax.

Loud, angry shouting awakens me. I sit bolt upright, jarred and frightened. "Ivan, what's the matter?"

He is waving papers at me. On his face there is what I now call "the dark look" of his internal frenzy. "One thousand three hundred and fifty dollars! Where am I supposed to find that kind of money?"

"What? What is it?"

"Your medical bill, that's what! The fancy doctors and a surgical procedure. I can't make ends meet as it is; how am I supposed to pay this?"

My stomach tightens with a sickening dread. The "best doctor in town" had been his idea, not mine. I would have gone to the HMO. "I'll take care of it." There is a stone in my gut. "I'll pay it, just stop yelling. Stop!" He had to wake me for this? Could it not have waited until morning? Is this angry man the knight who rode into my life on a white horse to protect and take care of me? Fear and shock and disappointment shatter my world; it collapses into a thousand unsalvageable pieces.

We are going out to a nice restaurant with another couple tonight. I've been look-ing forward to it for a long time and we should be there in 15 minutes. "Ivan, you still aren't dressed. Shall I call the restaurant to say we'll be a little late?"

"I'm not feeling well. Got a headache. I don't think we should go."

"Perhaps you can take something for it? They'll be there in a few minutes. I hate to disappoint people."

"I said I don't feel well. Is that all you care about, disappointing other peo-ple? Doesn't it matter how I feel?"

"Yes, of course. But you often seem to get these headaches just before we go out with friends."

That provokes a tirade. "You only care about other people; everyone is more important to you than I am; I'm your last priority." On and on, for hours into the night. Of course, we do not leave the house. It's close to sunrise before Ivan calms down. Now he tries to soothe me and plead for forgiveness. He says he loves me more than life. Which is the real Ivan?

I bought a desk for Ivan and set it up in the living room. "Hey, that's terrific!" He is very pleased. He stands behind me, encircling me in his arms, "With a place to work at home, I can leave the office earlier and get back faster to you!" He walks to the desk and rubs his hand on the surface. "Salvation Army, huh? Looks pretty good. Say, what's this?"

He bends over to read the inscription I had carved on the penholder:

Ivan the Terrible, Prince of Darkness.

" 'Prince of Darkness'? Isn't that another name for Satan, the devil?"

"I don't know anything about that," I say. "It's a title I'm bestowing on you because of your dark moods."

He looks contrite. "Am I that bad, Barbie-Doll?"

"Worse. But you are also the prince of my blazing nights."

He laughs, takes me in his arms and kisses me deeply.

Marriage. We talk often about how we want our wedding. But I have serious concerns about Ivan's ability to include Ari in our life; I have to see real changes there. He had said, when we met, that he was glad I had a little boy, that he had wanted a son. But he doesn't pay any attention to Ari except to criticize. He won't take him places with us, and he resents the time I spend with him.

Ivan has reservations too. He's never sure enough of my love. No matter what I do, it's never enough to prevent the dark moods. I wish he'd lighten up. I'm lying on the sofa, my head in his lap, and he's running his fingers through my hair. "They say you never marry the great passion of your life," he murmurs.

"Who says? I never heard that."

"Think about it. How many people do you know who married the person they are passionately, madly, in love with?"

"Not many, I suppose. The Clarks. And my aunt and uncle, they did."

"For most people, true love ends tragically. Then they 'settle' for someone else and marry. It's a horrible thought, isn't it?"

"Horrible, yes. I couldn't bear to be with anyone else."

"Me neither. Forget I said anything. We'll work things out; we've got to."

"On the other hand, maybe burning passion isn't something one can live with forever. Maybe people want it to be peaceful and comfortable for the long haul."

"Maybe. But we'll be the exception," he says, sliding down next to me. "For us it'll be a marriage of great passion."

"We might be consumed by the blaze."

I close the photo album. "I've gone on for hours about my life in Paris and Monaco, you must be bored to death."

"You never bore me. Never. I want to hear every detail, everything you ever did, everyone you ever knew. I can't get enough of knowing you." Ivan leans back with a slow, sly grin that makes me melt. "Show me the real thing. Walk me down the streets you walked. Sit me down face to face with the people you knew. I want to share all of it with you. Let's make France *ours*, not just yours."

"You mean *go* there?"

"Yes! You have vacation time; I'll shut the office. Let's just do it."

Two weeks later, we're packed. Ari is with Dad again, and we start our trip in a playful spirit.

As we approach the airport, I mention that "I looked up places I loved in my notebooks so I wouldn't forget to show you any of them." Ivan's mood changes suddenly. The word "notebooks" triggers a dark cloud. After that, nothing can lighten it. He looks for the smallest thing to criticize, to attack. Now, carrying our luggage across traffic, toward the check-in counter, he is out of control, raging in the middle of the street.

I'm at my wits' end. "Let's call it off! Obviously we can't travel like this." I turn back toward the parking lot.

That quiets him down. "No. Just get on the plane."

As soon as we are seated and belted, he begins again, whispering, but the impact is just as deadly as when he shouts. I want to get up, move away, but we are preparing for take-off. The ranting focuses on Karl again. In that diabolical whisper, he's calling me ugly, degrading names.

"The minute we land in Paris, I'm taking a return flight," I sob hysterically. "I hope you stay in France and never come back." I put my hands over my ears and turn away to block him out. I'm afraid—very afraid—of his anger, but I'm also seething with my own. I am furious that he would ruin our trip, and furious at what he is doing to us. When the seatbelt sign goes off, I escape to an empty seat as far from him as possible. I cry so long and hard my sight is blurry. My stomach feels sick.

Hours later, somewhere over the Atlantic Ocean, Ivan comes down the aisle and signals for me to rejoin him. I turn away. Not wanting a scene in front of the people next to me, he returns a few minutes later with a note:

Forgive me, Barbie, I'm such a fool. Please come back to your seat, I miss you. We'll have a wonderful time in France, I promise. Come back to me . . . come back.

I turn away, my energy drained. I'm a wrung-out rag. He drops another note on my lap.

There's no life for me without you. I love you more than you will ever know, and I want the chance to prove it. I'm sorry, jealousy gets the better of me sometimes. Give us a chance; I'm working on it.

He stretches his hand toward mine and leads me back to our seats.

"You won't be sorry. It'll be all right."

On our arrival at the Paris airport, I consider turning around and going back home; but to have gotten this far to Paris, and leave? Ivan is back to his normal self; it would be a shame to throw away this wonderful trip together.

Our cab pulls up to a narrow house with a mansard roof and large shutters. Inside the wrought-iron gates, ivy-covered walls surround a rose garden. We ring the bell.

"*Ba-a-r-r-ba-a-r-a! Te voilà, enfin!*" Annette rushes to give me a hug and kisses on both cheeks. She extends her hand to Ivan.

"This is Ivan, Annette. He doesn't speak French."

"Oh, this is good! I practice my English, *alors.* 'ow do you do?" She ushers us into her small but artistically charming home.

Ivan and Annette hit it off from the start. What a relief! She appreciates his quick humor. And how could he not like her? She's so cheerful and positive. But, we'll see. Ivan had liked other friends at first. Then after a second or third visit, something they said or did offended him. I wondered, at times, if there was a pattern to it, but each time the explanation was different, airtight, and logical.

Annette is a gracious hostess. For five days she's shown us the hidden corners of Paris and shared her favorite spots. This sunny afternoon, having walked for miles through the narrow streets of St. Germain, browsing the antiques shops and portfolios of etchings and drawings in the art galleries, we've worked up a good appetite.

"There's a terrific little restaurant close by with food that is native to my region. Do you like—'ow do you say, *saucisson et choucroûte?*"

"Sausage and sauerkraut," I translate. "Yes, we love it."

The familiar aroma causes Annette to reminisce about the customs of her region. "You must come with me to my parents' home one day. I would love to show you Alsace."

She excuses herself for a moment to find a restroom. Ivan turns to me. "I'm not feeling very well."

"What is it?"

"Dunno. Kind of nauseous."

"Annette is almost finished with her dinner. We can leave in a few minutes."

Annette returns, oblivious to his discomfort and, as most French people do, takes her time to savor the meal, enjoy the people-watching, and entertain us with her conversation. Ivan signals to me. "I want to leave *now*."

Turning to Annette, I apologize. "Ivan isn't feeling well."

The three of us leave the restaurant and walk back along the river toward Annette's house. "We'll get him into bed with some tea immediately," she says, and heats water in the kitchen.

I pull the spread off the bed. "Here, Ivan, get in. If you don't feel better soon, we'll call a doctor." Ivan explodes in a whisper. "That's not the point. I said I wasn't feeling well, but obviously it's more important that your friend finish her meal."

I'm in for it. A tirade is coming and nothing will stop it. It won't end until I'm reduced to tears and ready to walk out. Until the doctor arrives, Ivan volleys an incessant undertone of anger at me. He is quiet when Annette returns to say good night, but by then I'm devastated. I know what the rest of the night with him will be like, and he is true to form. Ivan seethes and vents his poison until the tension is broken by the smell of fresh-brewed morning coffee and Annette's bright "*Bonjour, mes amis!*" In her presence he controls himself, and I have shelter from his anger.

Annette waves us off at the airport and we board our plane for the south of France. She'll join us down there for a long weekend on Friday.

The plane takes off and so does Ivan. No longer ranting about my neglect of his health, now it's his jealousy of my friendship with Jean-Luc. I dread our arrival.

"Stop it! You are ruining my trip—no, my whole life! I hate you!" But I don't hate him. Impossible as he is, I understand his torment. "Only you can heal my pain," he always says. "You're my salvation, Barbie-Doll, my angel of mercy, the sunshine of my life." He smiles when I respond, "And you, my darling, are my Prince of Darkness."

He has regained his good humor by the time we land. Jean-Luc and several others are at the airport to greet us. Jean-Luc's good cheer and friendliness reassure Ivan, but I wouldn't push our luck by accepting the invitation to stay at his house. Instead, we are guests of Pierre, next door.

The following 10 days, with our crowd from the National Orchestra and Annette, are wonderful. They make me forget that anything ever went wrong. Lunches on sunny stone terraces, centuries of secrets, fresh flowers, *crèpes* with Grand Marnier, walks in the Old City, and dinners in cavelike wine cellars. We walk the oceanfront from Monaco to the town of Menton on the Italian border, through sea gardens, beaches and stone paths. Ivan gets to see the famous fireworks festival and the Calypso Restaurant on the pier. There is animated talk about the legal profession in France, fresh fish just caught from the sea, concerts at the casino, and a party on a huge yacht in the harbor. My head aches from continuous translation, but I rejoice at Ivan's enjoyment of my friends and the wonder of seeing them all again.

Jean-Luc generously lends us his car so I can show Ivan where Ari and I lived in Roquebrune, and the hidden underground city of Eze. We stroll through a shaded meadow and sink to the soft, scented bed of grass for love in the noonday sun, then lunch at a cozy little restaurant on the town plaza.

In the afternoon, we drive to what I believe is the most beautiful spot in the world. Jean-Luc had once brought me here, to the village of Sillans-la-Cascade. A mile walk into the woods takes us to the secret treasure. When Jean-Luc and I had discovered the thunderous waterfall, hidden under a moist, shady canopy of massive oaks and willows, we had gasped in shared awe. We had stood motionless and silent, in worship and wonder in the cathedral of majestic old trees, blessed and baptized by the sun-sparkled crystal spray. There was a once-in-a-lifetime magic to it.

Now, leading a reluctant Ivan along the path, the mile seems longer. But, ah! The waterfall comes into view with its splashing roar. I turn, expecting to see Ivan marvel. But he doesn't. "I know you love this sort of thing," Ivan says, "and I go along to give you pleasure; but to me woods are woods and plants are plants."

I'm so disappointed. *Is something missing,* I wonder, *in someone who can't respond to nature's awesome beauty? Is there is no spirit in him?* I brush away the thought.

Hiking back to a neighboring fish farm for lunch, I tell myself not to let Ivan's indifference dampen the ardor of my memory. I vow to keep the image of Sillans pure in my heart, overpowering, as it was the first time I saw it, with a man who comprehends the wonder of nature's most extraordinary creations. But I regret coming here with Ivan. It feels like I have dishonored the magic of that day with Jean-Luc. I owe him an apology I cannot pronounce, but in my heart I say it.

Back in Monaco we are caught up in a whirlwind of parties and fond farewells. Ivan is at his finest, his most charming, and the visit ends on a note of happiness and hope.

Less than a year after our trip to France, I feel increasing isolation and loneliness. My friends are disappearing. Ivan has found something offensive in almost all of them. If he isn't attacking someone directly, he creates an incident to separate me from them. Like the time we celebrated New Year's Eve with friends of mine, a Cousteau diver and his wife, in Santa Barbara. The following night, they had a commitment and left us for a short while. "No problem," we assured them. "We'll enjoy a quiet evening watching television."

Quiet evening, right. I don't remember what set him off this time (the verbal violence of his wrath blots out all but the force of it), but it was Ivan at his ugliest, most vitriolic, accusatory rage. He never laid a hand on me, but I found myself curled in a ball on the floor, feeling beaten and bruised deep in my soul. Because Ivan knows me so well, he knows where I'm vulnerable. That night he used words like a whip with iron hooks to shred what was left of my spirit. Unwilling to expose my friends to what was happening—and having no transportation but Ivan's car—I couldn't leave the house. I was so crushed, I couldn't fight back.

We left early the next morning. My friends can't possibly know what happened in their home while they were gone, but my shame was so profound, I'll never call or see them again.

Rifts are forming in my family too. At the dinner table in her house, Aunt Evelyn said or did something that set Ivan off. He had ranted and railed all the way home. Still seething when we got back to the house, he grabbed the phone and yelled cruelly at her. I had no idea what Aunt Evelyn did to upset him, and neither did she. But my cousin later told me she cried the whole night through. I was so shamed, I didn't know how to apologize to her or what to say. Aunt Evelyn, whom I loved and looked to as a role model since childhood, now maintains a strained, polite distance.

Cass will never ask—she doesn't confront personal issues like Lorna does; but in her eyes I can see the question: *Why do you stay with Ivan?* Actually, I think of leaving him every time he gets into one of his terrible moods. But for every bad day there are 10 good ones. And the good ones are better than good. Besides, Ivan had said the magic words: "I want to take care of you and help raise your son." Those words had melted my heart; I believed him.

When I complain that he ignores Ari, that he tries to separate me from my son and pretend he doesn't exist, Ivan reassures me, "It will come. This is a big adjustment for me, but you'll see; it will be fine."

I explain to Lorna, "I need his passion; it restores the confidence my ex-husband, Stephen, shattered. It's hard to walk away from it."

"You're a fool," she says. "You don't know how attractive you are. Men are drawn to you, you idiot; I see it all the time! What will it take to convince *you*?"

It takes Ivan to convince me. As long as I'm with him, I feel beautiful.

Dad needs legal assistance. He owes more than $300,000 to the Burn Center, and his insurance company is denying the claim. Dad is here tonight to discuss it with Ivan at my small round table in the dining room.

Ivan has always been warm and respectful with Dad. He enjoys an exchange with a great mind. But they've been talking for about an hour now, and I hear a different tone, an edge of impatience from Ivan. Dad asks for clarification about something Ivan said and Ivan's voice is suddenly louder, irritated, even intimidating. I'm extremely uncomfortable. Dad shouldn't be subjected to this.

"Anybody want a cup of coffee?" I ask to break the tension.

"No thanks," Ivan says, "I'm okay with my beer."

"Dad?"

"No, honey. I think I'll head home now."

I walk to the door with him. "I'm so sorry, Dad . . . I don't know why he suddenly took off on you. I don't understand."

My father lowers his voice. "I hate to say this, Bobs, but that's very typical of addictive behavior."

Ivan? Dad must be mistaken. Ivan doesn't drink or take drugs. Oh, a beer with dinner, sure. But he has a high tolerance; he can drink a lot and show no sign of it. His speech never slurs, his perception never dulls. So he's had a few on occasion, but addicted?

Lorna has come from New York to visit. She and Ivan are talking in the living room as I dry the supper dishes. Suddenly Ivan bolts up from the sofa and heads for the bedroom, grim-faced. I follow and find him packing a bag. "Ivan, what are you—?" He slams the bag shut, grabs it, and flings the apartment key at me.

"I've had it," he spits out. "Keep your apartment, your friends, your clinging family, and your brat. I'm out of here." His footsteps echo on each descending stair.

"Lorna! What's going on? What did you say to him? Why did he leave like that?"

"Come into the kitchen," she says softly, taking me by the arm. "I'm making tea. It's time to talk."

The hot honey tea is soothing. "You want to know what I said? I told Ivan to look at what this relationship is doing to you and to Ari. What it's done to your spirit and your creativity!"

"Oh, Lorna, how could you? Ivan has done so much for me. He got me started on a real career."

"He's launched you into the grinding machine of the business world. You'll be crushed by it."

"Isn't this a bit melodramatic?"

"Is it? When's the last time you wrote in your notebooks?" I don't answer. "Never mind, I know exactly when. You stopped the day he was reading them, didn't you?" I nod. "How many of your old friends do you still see?" I shake my head, mute. "Okay. So much for friends. How about your aunt? Have you restored that yet?" I look down. Of course it's fine on the surface. But the closeness we used to know is gone. She doesn't trust me now. "And your father?"

"He thinks Ivan has an addictive personality."

"And you don't? Between the beer and the Valium—"

"Hold on, the Valium is for chest pains. He has chest pains. And he only has a beer with dinner."

"Are you blind? Or just stupid?" Lorna leads me to the trash bin and removes the lid. It is stacked with beer bottles.

"That's just from today. He empties it every night when you're brushing your teeth."

I become indignant. "How do you know that?"

"I've been here four days now and I keep my eyes open. I lived with an alcoholic, remember? I know what to look for. And it's all here."

"Impossible," I whisper.

"I can't believe you don't know," she says.

"Lorna, I've never been around alcohol. My parents never drank. I don't drink. My husband and Karl didn't drink. I've never been near it."

"You are now. You've been living with it for two and a half years."

Lorna drinks her tea while this sinks in. Then, "You know what's next, don't you?" I don't want to hear it. "Ariel's next, kiddo. This man has it in for him. After having been totally neglected by his father and losing Karl, now Ari is suffering major rejection from another man in a parent role."

My tears fall. Lorna puts her arm around me. "Barbara, you have always been such a positive, optimistic person. Whatever you've been through, you always maintained your capacity for joy. But Ivan is continually raking the coals of your past. In a 'caring' way, with sympathy and understanding, he makes you relive times that were tough, betrayals you've suffered. By making you remember and focusing on the pain, he nurtures bitterness and regret. He's injecting you with a dark force that is eating at your spirit."

"Why? Why would he do that?"

"So you will depend on him, and him alone, for your happiness. He wants you completely within his control. To do that, he has to get everyone you love out of your life. He's done his best to get rid of me, but I understand his game. It won't work."

The truth of her words hit me like a shower of stones. I slump under their impact. "Well, he's gone now. I suppose it's for the best."

"Remember what your Grandma Kate said when she read the tarot cards for you?"

"That was 15 years ago, when Stephen and I first returned from Europe. You remember that?"

"She said she saw two more men in your future: one fair, one very dark. Karl was fair. Ivan is dark. Very dark!"

Lorna collects her things and prepares for her return flight. Picking up books she left on Ivan's desk, she sees the inscription I had carved on the edge: *Ivan the Terrible, Prince of Darkness.*

Lorna bends closer to read it again, then straightens up and looks at me. "So you knew," she says softly. "You knew!"

At the advertising agency where I work, we lose two major accounts. Several of us junior "creatives" are let go. I pack my things with shaking hands. I loved this job. It's devastating. Frightening.

The phone rings on my desk. It's been four long months since I've heard Ivan's voice. How does he know just when to call, when I'm most vulnerable? "Barbie-Doll, are you okay? What's wrong?" He hears my sniffle. "I had a feeling you needed me," Ivan says gently. "What is it? Your job? Has something happened?"

"Uh huh."

"I'll be right there. Meet you at the house in 10 minutes."

I let him take me into his arms and he rocks me like a baby. "What will I do?" I sob. "I've lost everything—my job, and . . . you . . ."

"You haven't lost me, I'm right here."

"It'll take months to find work again. I have a child to support, and I feel so alone."

He cradles me and holds me close. It's a weak moment, and the obsessive electricity still sparks. Darn, it still sparks. No matter, I won't let him stay long. I just need him right now. Like a fix. To make the hurt go away.

In the morning, I tell Ivan he must leave. "You got me through a difficult night, and I appreciate that, but we both know this won't work; it's over."

"Give it a chance," he says. "I've done a lot of soul-searching, and things will be different now. Better. I don't expect you to believe me right off, but give it some time so you can see."

"It's daylight now, Ivan, and I see clearly." Words, long imprisoned in my heart, pour out. "What you liked about me when we first met—my spirit and my poetry—are the very things you will destroy. Because of your jealous rages, I hide the notebooks and silence the music. I don't dance anymore. Under the guise of sympathy, you focus on my misfortunes until all I feel is bitterness and self-pity."

Ivan puts a tender finger across my lips. "Shhh, sweetheart, that's all over now. I was wrong. I'm so sorry." I back away from his touch. "You cut me off from everyone I care about: friends, family . . . even my memories!" My anger mounts, remembering that he had insisted I destroy all photos of Stephen and Karl. (I never did, of course; I hid them.) "You had the audacity to trample the ties to my past! It's unforgivable. But what is worse, I allowed it. I let you suck everything and everyone out of me. And I can't forgive myself."

"I never meant for that to happen, Barbie, believe me. I just loved you so much I couldn't get enough of you, couldn't bear to share you. But it won't happen again. Give us a chance. No one in this world understands and loves you like I do." He stretches out his arms to me. "Come. You won't be sorry. We belong together. I know it, and you do too."

I watch carefully for several weeks, not trusting him. I keep my eye on the beer, the Valium, and wait for a dark mood to descend. Nothing clouds his good nature. Could he really have turned a page? "It's different now," I assure Lorna. "He recognizes the harm he's done and he's sorry for it."

"I hope you're right; I truly hope you're right. As for the job, good riddance! You never belonged in an ad agency. Hold out for the right kind of work, and don't give in to fear."

"It's pretty scary when you can't pay the electric bill."

"Yes, of course. But I'm talking about something deeper. I'm referring to the fear that took over when your marriage ended." Her voice softens. "You were so shattered, Barbara, so wounded. Alone with the baby, you turned away from your creativity, the artistic world you and Stephen had shared, that Ivan said betrayed you, and you went into survival mode. When Stephen abandoned you, you abandoned the artist within you and turned to the business world to protect you. And what happens there? They pull your job out from under you. You're back to square one."

"I'll find another job. I have to."

"Okay, but find something that leaves some energy for your writing. Write, Barbara. Open up the notebooks."

"Soon, Lorna. One day soon."

It's been eight good weeks since Ivan returned. No quarrels. I start to relax a bit.

"I'll be right back," I say. "It's Ari's bedtime."

"Don't you think he's a little old for this nightly tucking-in routine?"

"No, I don't."

Ari is playing quietly in his bedroom. I long to stroke his beautiful little head and see him off to a gentle sleep. I cherish our nighttime ritual of brushing his teeth, reading stories, and sharing about his day. Especially, I love the hug when we say good night. Ivan's resentment of this special time used to create unbearable pressure on me. I thought we'd gotten past that.

"It's important to have time for ourselves," Ivan says. "Many couples forget that when they have kids." Ivan demands my full attention from the moment he gets home from work. He wants focused conversations—adult talk—the kind that shut Ari out. I resent this.

"Ari plays in his room alone too much. And when we go out, you won't take him with us. You insist on a baby-sitter. Now back off. I'm going to say good night."

"Let's not quarrel." Ivan puts his arms around me. "I love you." He caresses me and shuts the bedroom door, clearly intending to make love.

"No, Ivan!" I'm furious that he would shut the door to Ari, leaving him in the apartment with no one to talk to. "Don't you understand you're tormenting me? I won't do this to my child."

He lets go abruptly. "But what you do to *me* is okay? I'm supposed to schedule my feelings? When I can hold you and when I can't? When we can talk?"

"Yes! People who have children schedule themselves. You want me all to yourself. It isn't fair to my son."

"You aren't fair to *me*. Obviously my needs are the last to be considered. What am I anyway, background music? You don't want a marriage partner, you want a robot who responds on cue. Seven o'clock: time to play with baby. Eight o'clock: bedtime stories. This is no life."

"You said you wanted children. Well, kids need your time! They require attention. You don't stick them on a shelf and pull them down when you're in the mood."

"No. That's what you do with husbands!"

We've had this argument a dozen times in the past; nothing's changed. It eats into the little time left after work that I can spend with Ari. And just as before, it escalates to rage, with Ari lying in bed listening.

I walk away from Ivan and enter Ari's room. I want to hold and comfort him. I'll pay for it later.

As it was before, it is again. I'm torn between my son's increasing loneliness and Ivan's intense demands. It's the most painful torment imaginable. People say I look drawn. Yes—drawn and quartered.

In Ari's room, I tuck him in and hurry through a story. I don't stay as long as I'd like, but he settles for what he can get. I return to Ivan in the bedroom. "He's asleep now. It's only eight o'clock and we have the rest of the evening to ourselves."

"The leftovers, you mean."

"Oh, please!" I've reached my limit. "There's no give with you, no compromise! What would you have me do? Give him up for adoption? Is that what you want? This is never going to work. Ariel is my son, do you understand? He's my son!"

In one swift movement, Ivan lifts his boot from the floor and flings it with all his force at a large drawing framed on the wall. Glass shatters with a loud crash.

Ari wakes up and cries. *I* wake up, as well—to the realization that there is violence in this man. I have to get him out of here. Tonight he smashes a picture. Tomorrow?

I'm working now as the Advertising and Public Relations Manager for an international computer manufacturer, a job with good career potential. Lorna keeps reminding me not to neglect the notebooks, what she calls my "true life's work." It's hard to find the energy for that; work takes a lot out of me. I feel a tug in two directions.

"The tug," Lorna says, "is between the 'survivor' in you, and the 'creator.' The two parts of you do not coexist harmoniously. Survivor is big and strong. He's street-smart, tough and action-oriented. He gets things done."

"Is that bad?"

"No, of course not. What's bad is that Survivor overshadows Creator. Creator is delicate and feminine. She's the spirit of playfulness and spontaneity and flirtation. But she's crushed and cowering, hiding in a corner. I hope she's still alive."

"I don't care about her anymore! I don't trust her; I have to be practical. My work as a marketing professional is how I feed my family. It's where I have to be for now."

I throw myself completely into the job, learning everything about the high-tech industry, the products, the competition, and the marketing issues. Now *I'm* the client; I get to hire and direct the work of the advertising and public-relations agencies.

I travel too. This year the trade shows are in London, Frankfurt, Milan and Paris. Long walks after dinner with local colleagues from our company bring back the magic of Europe. After the Paris show, I take a week's vacation to visit Jean-Luc and my friends in the Midi. It is a peaceful time-out, re-capturing, for a few days, what had been a long-ago season of almost-perfect happiness.

Traveling gives me lots of time to think. Snug in my window seat, I stare at white, puffy clouds, unaware of the passenger next to me and unwilling to engage in conversation. I am on my way to Lorna in New York. She's in her Soho loft.

My affair with Ivan ended six years ago. Clouds embracing mountain tips swoosh by. I remember it as the relationship that took me down to the lowest pit in my life. Months after we broke up, we were still obsessively drawn back to one another. Sometimes there'd be a late-night knock on the door when I was tossing, sleepless, in bed—he always knew when. And I'd open the door because I wanted to believe the promises that he'd changed; because I needed to calm the craving and ease the agony of withdrawal. I read a book that said one could be addicted to another person. Ugh! What a bondage. Thank God it's over.

But what have I done with my life since then? Professionally, I am proud of what I've learned and achieved. Personally? It's funny: we can be so smart in one part of our life and so dumb in another. It doesn't seem I have any brains when it comes to choosing men. Starting back in college, when I had given up a solid, good-looking medical student for Stephen, an irresponsible but artistic, fun-loving flake. Then Karl—also artistic and exciting, and equally unable to accept responsibility. Ivan, of course, was a psychopathic disaster.

And there had been others. Najit was a Ceylonese biologist I met while working for Cousteau. Beneath his success as a scientist, I discovered another irresponsible, but charming, child-like man. Worse, he manipulated with deception and lies. After about three or four months, I discovered he had a wife and baby at home in Sri Lanka. "It is only a marriage of convenience; it was arranged by my family," he explained. "It's not a marriage of love." So, according to Najit, that marriage didn't count. I threw up my hands and walked out.

That happened last year, at the time I was to meet Lorna in France. When I lifted my suitcase onto the airport check-in scale, a dark, long-fingered hand closed over mine. "I've got it." Najit lifted my bag onto the scale with one hand and took my arm with the other, leading me toward the boarding gates.

"Where do you think you're going?" I pulled away from him.

"To our flight. Paris, you said, right?"

"Our what? You booked on my flight?"

"Of course. You refuse to see me in Los Angeles; what's a guy to do? By the way, I upgraded your ticket. Hope you don't mind." I slump down in my first-class seat. "I booked two rooms at the Georges V Hotel—two separate rooms, mind you, not adjoining—and I made reservations at an intimate, charming restaurant, just off the Champs Elysée, so do me the honor, as my guest . . ."

It was a dashing, romantic gesture, and I'd be less than honest to say I wasn't tempted. But I have strong feelings about adultery. I had been its victim; I would not do that to another woman. I took a hard look at Najit and realized that, attractive as he was, life could have no form, no meaning, without ethics. Finally, I've reached a point where I recognize that commitment, loyalty, a willingness to sacrifice—those are qualities that make people beautiful. Najit was wrong. Wrong about life and wrong for me.

"Sorry," I told him, "I have other plans."

Makes me wonder, though, what about me attracts the wrong kind of men? Dieter, a handsome German professor who pursued me shortly after my divorce, seemed promising—until I discovered he was having an affair with a good friend of mine who was betraying her husband with him. Sounds like a cheap soap opera, but it was real life.

Winston might have been "Mr. Right," but I never gave him a chance. Dr. Winston James was a distinguished, attractive and impressive man. A consultant on one of Cousteau's expeditions, he was an internationally renowned authority on sea mammals, and a professor at a prestigious university. Winston had taken me to an elegant restaurant to meet some of his friends, and asked if he could see me again. What in the world made me back away? Did I not believe I was worthy of his attention? Did his success and prestige scare me in some stupid way? Ah, if we could turn back the clock.

And what about Stéfan? No longer the struggling student Stephen and I had known when we all lived at the Cité des Arts in Paris, Stéfan had since won the Prix de Rome for his composition and was now a professor at the Conservatory of Music in Paris. "I'm sorry about your divorce," he had said on my last visit to Paris. "I cared very much for both of you."

"Thank you."

"There is a child, yes? A son?" Smiling, I had pulled out Ari's picture. "Your husband was a fool."

"Yes," I agreed. "Ari is a treasure."

"I am referring to you," Stéfan said. "You are a treasure. I always knew that."

A nervous laugh hid my astonishment. I changed the subject. "Things have worked out nicely for you, Stéfan. Your work is recognized and you say you just bought an apartment. Congratulations! You have it all now, don't you?"

"No, not everything." A mischievous smile lifted the corner of his lips. "It needs the right woman. And children. It is incomplete."

"Ahh . . ."

"Barbara, marry me. Bring the child, Ariel. I'll adopt him as my own. I am only a professor at the Conservatory, but I will be director one day. It can be a good life."

Alas, I never said yes to the good life. Not with Phillip, not with Stéfan nor with Jean-Luc or Winston; and now, probably not with Robert, either.

"Who's Robert?" Lorna opens the blinds to let the morning light flood into her Soho loft.

"He's a nice man I met in our company's London office. He calls me two, three times a week and arranges to work in Los Angeles every couple of months . . . Robert is pursuing a transatlantic courtship, and I shouldn't let him."

"Why not? What's he like?"

"Energetic. Fun. Thoughtful—a wonderful man, actually. He has two little daughters. He's great."

Lorna doesn't mince words. "And in bed?"

"We haven't been."

"In a *year*?"

During his last visit, Robert had surprised me with tickets for a vacation in Hawaii. He was so disappointed when I said I wouldn't go. But that would have put us on a whole different footing, and I wasn't ready. No, the truth is, I wasn't attracted. But Robert is too good to lose. He's everything a woman should want.

"Lorna, it's not going to happen with Robert."

"No sparks, eh?"

"No sparks." I put my cup down on the coffee table. "What is it with me? Why can't I be attracted to the *nice* men who want to marry me?"

"Maybe," Lorna muses, "you're still trying to avoid the conventional marriage that made your mother so unhappy. She delivered a powerful message to her little girl: she taught you that cooking, housekeeping and child-rearing are drudgery, a fate worse than death. And that's what 'nice,' solid men are offering: a home and kids. For you, passion and excitement are how you run away from that."

I stand, walk to her window and stare down at the narrow street, Each of the houses below hides a personal drama behind its brick walls. "When Robert is back in Los Angeles at the end of the month, he's going to propose; I know it."

"And you'll say no."

Still gazing through the window at the street, I murmur, "Yes. I'll say no."

"Too bad. You could have fun times and a good life with a guy like that. So what if you don't thrill to his touch? Does it really matter?"

We are silent, the question hanging between us. Yes, it matters, this passion I pursue at such a price. Life would slip away from me without it. It's the measure of being alive. In a funny way, I've always felt it was a gateway to the Divine Force.

Suddenly, a new thought strikes me like a thunderbolt. What if it isn't? What if, on the contrary, illicit passion is actually a deceptive *substitute* for God? What if, instead, it can be—as it was with Ivan—a force of enslavement, a gateway to hell? What if the preachers in churches know something I don't?

I turn toward Lorna on the sofa. "I may not be ready yet to accept a 'Robert,' but one thing I know for sure: there will never be another Stephen or Ivan in my life. Never again, I swear! And if that means there will never be another man, so be it. I'm prepared to live and raise my son alone."

"Good. Stay with that. Frankly, I don't give a fig whom you marry or if you ever marry. What I really care about . . . oh, Barbara, it's been 14 years since your divorce and I see no healing, no restoration of the woman I once knew. There's no joy, no energy in you anymore." I wave my hand to cut off her words. "No, listen to me. You look beaten. Anxiety-ridden. Your fear is ugly."

I glimpse, reluctantly, at my listless reflection in the mirror.

"Barbara," she whispers with urgency, "there was a time you lived with courage, with a spirit of freedom and daring that was so attractive! Everyone felt your magnetism. You were a force, a fire that took our breath away! What's *happened* to you?"

I remember. I recall the energy, the strength of the woman she describes. It seems so long ago and far away. A tear escapes the corner of Lorna's round blue eyes, but her gaze does not waver. *"Snap out of it!"*

Her voice, barely audible, reverberates across my heart like the deafening gong of a carillon from the other side. "You are crossing a point of no return," she whispers lamenting. "You are . . . *unrecognizable.*"

Road to Damascus

As he neared Damascus on his journey, suddenly a light from heaven flashed around him. He fell to the ground and heard a voice say to him, "Saul, Saul, why do you persecute me?" "Who are you, Lord?" Saul asked. "I am Jesus . . ."

ACTS 9:3-5

The phone rings. Startled out of a faraway dream in a deep sleep, I grope toward the sound. It is four o'clock in the morning.

"Barb? It's Grace." My cousin's voice is tense. "Aunt Evelyn is dying. Can you get to the hospital right away?"

"What do you mean, 'dying'? She was at the bridge club last night. She's as healthy as I am."

"It happened in the middle of a game. She was chatting and having a good time, and . . ." Grace catches her breath, "she fell off her chair, and that was it. An aneurysm to the brain." I snatch my purse and head for the hospital. By the time I arrive, Aunt Evelyn is gone.

Aunt Evelyn was one of the bright lights in my life. She inspired gusto for living. Once, when greeted by a friend, "Hi, Evelyn, what's new?" my aunt had replied with her clipped Canadian accent, "Every day is new! I can't wait to get out of bed to find out what today's adventure will be!" For Aunt Evelyn, life was as delicious as the strawberry sodas we shared. I spent the summers of my teen years with my aunt and uncle in their Queens apartment. Aunt Evelyn made me carry myself tall and proud and taught me to buy clothes that made me look good, rather than clothes that were in fashion. At night, she sat with me on the pullout sofa bed in the living room and we talked and laughed about "girl things," about the secrets of womanhood I could look forward to when I grew up. Aunt Evelyn was vital in her femininity, in love with her husband, and ardent about the mysterious pleasures of marriage. In the flashing cut facets of everyday life, she saw diamonds.

Now she's gone? In the waiting room, my uncle is sobbing, his head between his knees. He looks gray. I can't imagine him without the wife he adores.

"Dearest Uncle," I place my arm around his shoulder, "I'm so sorry. I understand how alone you feel. I lost a spouse I loved too."

He looks up, puzzled. "Yours was a divorce. That's different; it was your choice."

My choice? His words cut deeply. Is that what he thinks? Is that what everyone thinks? Is that why no one had been there to mourn with me, to help keep me together when I was suddenly alone with a four-month-old infant? Do people think divorce is something you choose?

The years with Stephen remain for me as an island in a sea of loneliness. In our home, I'd been loved, I belonged, I had a place in the world. I've never recovered from the loss of my husband, my friend, my soul mate, my love. Since the divorce—has it been 14 years already?—my life has been shaped and defined by abandonment and loss. By my anger toward Stephen, and hurt for the marriage that failed. By guilt and grief for Michael, the baby I did not have, could not hold, or see grow up. By the tearing of my heart when my little boy wonders why his daddy isn't here. And people think it was my choice? Some day—this isn't the right time—I will have to deal with the wound reopened by those hurtful words.

A rabbi comes to console my destitute uncle. He's young and means well, I'm sure, but he doesn't know my aunt or my uncle, and his condolences sound hollow. The trite sentiments fall flat, inept before the infinite chasm of death. Frustrated, I leave the room. I want *real* answers.

I roam, aimless, through sterile hospital corridors in the quiet early-morning hour. Real answers. Where do I find them? Straight ahead, there is a small sign with an arrow pointing left: "Chapel." Sure, why not?

Alone, in the quiet white room with stained-glass windows, I hope, if there is a God, he'll make himself known. Silence. Nothing.

A nun enters. An elderly woman, thin, she has a hook where her right hand used to be. She kneels in a pew across the aisle from me, prays about 10 minutes, then rises to leave. She sees me and nods.

An impulse drives me to call out. "Sister . . ." She waits. "My aunt just died."

"Ahh." She reaches her good hand to touch my shoulder and sits beside me. "I'm sorry, my dear. I did not know your aunt, but I can understand your love for her. And how you miss her. Why God took her at this moment, only He knows. But I do know this: His love for you is greater than any you can imagine. He will walk with you through your pain."

Her eyes drift off, seemingly fixed on something beyond this room. "Death is not the end, daughter. So much more awaits. Seek Him," she urges. "He promises that if you do, He will reveal Himself."

"Seek where, Sister? There are so many paths. I'm Jewish. You're Catholic. Others follow the way of Buddha or Vedantic sages. Where do I begin?"

"Ask *Him*."

I cover my face with my hands. "Dear God," I say inside . . . it's weird talking to someone you can't see or know for sure exists. Is this a prayer? "Dear

God, if You are real and can hear me, I don't mean to offend, but I'm not sure You are there. No one I ever knew believed in You, and I have no experience with this . . ." Take a deep breath and start again. "Dear God, I want to know if You are real. I want to know who You are and what You want from me. Where do I start? The Sister says You will show the way. Can You do that? Will You?"

The gentle nun sits with me until dawn, when the hospital awakens. The day shift, fresh from sleep, is now organizing charts and paperwork for their rounds.

I return to the waiting room, where my uncle slumps in a chair, sobbing uncontrollably, surrounded by my mute cousins. My heart weeps for him. My own sorrow is enveloped in a cloud of mystery that, one day, might open to the light of God. I can't remember much of what the nun said, except that her God knows exactly what is happening and, if I seek Him, He will take me on a journey far beyond my pain. For my uncle, there is no journey. There is only the pain.

The funeral is over. The people—there were so many, where did they all come from?—have left my aunt's house and I am mercifully busy, along with Julia and my cousins, clearing the table and cleaning up. My cousins and I brought suitcases; we'll stay here with my uncle for the week.

Julia gives me a hug as she prepares to leave. "Will you be all right?"

"Yeah, fine . . ." I slump to the couch. "No, I'm not fine. This is bad." Too much happening all at once."

"Besides Aunt Evelyn, what?"

"Well . . ." I don't really feel like talking about it. "I guess I was caught in the chaos of corporate politics; I lost my job a few weeks ago."

"Oh! I'm sorry." Julia understands it's no small matter for a sole-supporting single mother.

"I'm so afraid we'll lose our house, now that the paychecks stopped. And since the break-up with Ivan . . . it's been so lonely these last years. I guess I've been spinning in a whirlpool of insecurity, and now, losing Aunt Evelyn—" I can't say it's sucking me close to the center of despair.

"Put it all in your God bag." Julia's hand is on my shoulder. "You don't have to deal with it. Ask Him to handle it."

"'Him' who? What are you talking about? Since when do you believe in such stuff?"

"I don't, but they taught us that in Al-Anon." Oh, yes, she'd gone to 12-step meetings years ago, when her boyfriend was an alcoholic. "They said to put all your problems in a big bag, then lay it at God's feet and ask Him to take care of it." She shrugs, aware of how silly it sounds. "Somehow it works."

"Right. Along with my Santa Claus list."

But the phrase rings in my head, repeatedly, all night long. "Put it in your God bag." My "God bag." Santa-God will take care of everything. Ridiculous. But every time the phrase comes to mind, the wrenching pain of anxiety in my gut lessens, and a calm washes over me that I can't explain. The sweetness of the calm spreads through me like a pool of soothing red balm, and it brings tears. Red balm? Did I say "red"? Why do I see red? That's the color of blood. Hardly soothing.

I recall the man who had shared Dad's room at the Burn Center. Is this what he had felt? This lifting of pain, an almost euphoric peace in the midst of it? He said he'd seen Jesus in the night. Perhaps he'd been hallucinating, poor thing. But his moment of hallucination removed his pain, even into the light of day and throughout his healing process after that. How? Who is this Jesus?

When I was a child, my Catholic baby-sitters warned that if I didn't believe in Jesus, I would burn in hell. We felt sorry for them, poor ignorant people, enslaved in fear. Was that the same Jesus of the nun at the hospital? She was clearly neither ignorant nor enslaved in fear. She was basking in love. Exuding joy. What had she said? "Seek God."

"Where?" I had asked. I expected her to tell me to go to church. Instead, what she said was, "Ask *Him*."

So I'm asking You, God. If You really exist, reveal Yourself and the path that's right for me. How am I to reach You? Which truth is true for me? I'm asking. And what do I get? Someone who says to fill a bag with my garbage and lay it at Your feet. Okay, I can do that. But I need a sign. Let me know my mind isn't playing tricks on me. I need a sign.

It is a beautiful spring morning. Susan and I are hiking in our favorite canyon, as we always do on Saturdays. As we climb, Susan points, startled, at a black goat in our path. We climb further and see another goat—a white one. Then another. Reaching the crest, we look down over the other side of the hill and see a whole herd of goats, hundreds of them!

Goats? My memory flies back to a barn in Alba, a tiny village in south-central France. Kids and goats frolic on fragrant hay, greeting us with animal joy, dancing in the golden beam of our lantern. But this is Los Angeles, California. There have never been goats in this canyon before.

Susan and I watch, mesmerized. The goats graze, driven by three trained dogs. In the midst of them, a goatherd with long white hair and a wide-brimmed straw hat shading him from the sun. Under his arm, he carries a big book. He walks tall, his staff tapping rhythmically upon the soil. It is fascinating, this time-warped, nineteenth-century pastoral apparition.

"He looks unreal!" Susan says.

"Yes. C'mon, Susan, we've got to talk to him and see what he's about." We approach the goatherd and ask about his animals. He welcomes us, happy to talk, and explains the difference between grazing goats and milking goats, and how you train the dogs. As we chat, I wonder about the worn leather book he carries and ask what it is. The goatherd holds it out so I can see it is a Bible. Then, fixing me hypnotically with his gaze, he speaks words that spill over the hills with fervor. He talks and talks—something about Isaiah . . . prophecies . . . I don't understand any of it. And yet, I can't tear myself away.

Susan tugs on my arm. "C'mon, let's get out of here. It's almost noon." In deference to my friend, I take my leave. "I'm so glad to have met you, but we have to go now. Thank you for telling us about all this."

He turns the brilliance of his crystalline blue eyes on me and, half-smiling, softly utters these astounding words: "I had to be here. I came to tell you. You prayed for it."

We return to town. I can't get the goats and goatherd out of my mind. Not trusting my memory, I ask Susan what *she* had seen and heard. "Tell me. Tell me word for word."

"He said he *had to be here; you prayed for it*," Susan repeats. "What's that supposed to mean?"

I look away, embarrassed. "I've prayed . . . two or three times now—"

"Prayed what?"

"For a sign. For God to show me where to find Him."

"Well! He certainly put Himself through a lot of trouble to create a goatherd and a whole flock of goats, just to point you in the right direction."

I ignore her sarcasm. "Susan, did you understand any of it? You went to Sunday School as a kid; do you know what it means?"

"Hmmm. Most of it was from Isaiah, I think. We can look it up."

"Show me," I insist when we return to her house.

Susan pulls a Bible from her bookshelf. "Here, Isaiah 35:5-6: '*Then will the eyes of the blind be opened and the ears of the deaf unstopped . . .*'"

"Slower, go slower."

"'*Then will the lame leap like a deer,*'" she reads, "'*and the mute tongue shout for joy. Water will gush forth in the wilderness and streams in the desert.*'

"There was more, something about angels. Let's see if I can find it. Oh, here—first chapter of Hebrews, verse 14: '*Are not all angels ministering spirits sent to serve those who will inherit salvation?*'"

"Angels sent to . . . what?"

"Angels sent to minister . . . to serve those who will inherit salvation. Oh, no! You don't really think he was . . .?!"

"I don't know what to think, Susan, except that he said he had to be here because I prayed for it."

"Yes, and you prayed for?"

"A sign," I whisper, as the incredulous begins to penetrate. "He's the messenger, the sign!"

"Signs point to something. What's he pointing to?"

"The Bible. He's saying I'll find God in the Bible."

I can't wait for next Saturday, to return to the canyon, to see the goatherd again. I have questions for him, lots of questions! But the rolling hills and expansive vistas are empty. Puffy white clouds lie quiet above the unbroken horizon of the hills. No goats. Not even one.

I return the following Saturday and several more after that. No goats. No goatherd. I inquire at the park ranger station, "Do you know when the goats will come back? I'd like to talk to the man who herds them."

They stare blankly at me and at one another.

"The grazing goats. Do they come every year at this time?"

"Sorry, miss," says the one behind the desk, "we don't know anything out here about goats."

Spring. Summer. Fall. I take in secretarial work to keep food on the table while searching for a "real" job, but it doesn't begin to meet the monthly bills. As my debt mounts, so does my anxiety.

I'm up at 6:00 to get Ari ready for school. Flicking on the morning news program, I try to still my fear with the friendly voices of the morning news anchor team. If I don't get a job very soon, we'll have to sell the townhouse. Our first home. Oh, well. Get dressed. Put on makeup. Keep up the discipline.

I don't watch the television actually, I just listen, because it is behind me as I apply cosmetics, brush my hair, and dress. There are banks going under, third-world massacres, civil rights issues . . . (*that's odd, no local murders?*) . . . a call to share our wealth at Thanksgiving and Christmas with people who have no money, no homes (*nice, maybe I can qualify?*) . . . presidential decisions . . . (*um hmmm*) . . . and a call to recognize God as the ultimate power of the universe and give my life to Him.

The eyeliner pencil stops in its tracks. That last bit doesn't compute. I swivel around to look at the screen. Oh darn, it's tuned to the wrong station.

But how did it get switched from the news to a program with a religious crackpot? And why doesn't the "crackpot" look the part? He's an attractive, intelligent-looking, rather captivating man. *Agh!* It's nonsense. I flick back to the news channel and go on with my life.

Next morning, I make sure the channel is set correctly. But half an hour into the political debates and local murders, I can't resist an urge to see what the interesting man on the other channel is saying—just for a minute, mind you, not that I care, I'm just curious . . . just for one minute.

The following morning, "one minute" becomes five; the day after, it's fifteen; and before a week goes by, I wake up so eager to tune in that I flick the TV on before I'm fully awake. I can't say what draws me; certainly TV ministry is not my sort of thing. But every word seems directed straight to me. Some of it sounds like hocus-pocus, like when the preacher gets "a word of knowledge."

Almost always this is about healing people's illnesses. But this morning, he catches my attention big-time. Years ago, when Stephen and I lived in Paris, we'd gone to a party. A dark, curly-haired woman who claimed to be a palm reader took my hand. "Oh," she said. "Not a long lifeline. Not very long at all."

"What does that mean? I'm going to die young?"

She hesitated. "I don't like to say, but . . . well, yes. Doesn't look like it goes beyond 40 . . . 43 maybe. I'm sorry."

Sounded like bunk to me. I dismissed it. At least I thought I did. But over the years, the thought keeps creeping back. "I won't live past 43. Now I'm 29. Now I'm 32. Now I'm 36 . . ." Each time, I brush it off as nonsense, but it does come back.

Today, when the TV preacher gets his "word of knowledge," he says, "Someone out there was told by a fortune-teller they would not live beyond the age of 40. The Lord wants you to know this is not true. You are not to believe it. Your days are in the Lord's hands and He will give you many years to live in His service. Trust not in soothsayers; trust in God and His holy word only."

I listen very carefully every day after that for similar words of knowledge but never again hear one that is not related to physical illness.

The issues he and his guests discuss are precisely those I'm struggling with. Their teaching speaks specifically to my heart and offers a glimpse of God's embracing love, His promise to provide and protect. I experience moments—isolated moments—when the pain of my losses disappears, shrinks to insignificance, and is overpowered by the awesome, brilliant, humbling Presence of God.

I fall to my knees and pray with the preacher, sometimes joyful, sometimes weeping. Traveling the airwaves through a television monitor, the Holy Spirit of God enters my room. This is no abstract cosmic force. His Presence is *real*. It's personal. And wonderful, except . . . except for the Jesus part. I try to ignore it, go around it, deny it. I struggle for God without Jesus.

If you are even nominally Protestant or Catholic, you probably can't understand how upsetting it is for a Jew to be confronted with Jesus. Time after time, Christians massacred my people, *in the name of Jesus*. In the Middle Ages, crusading Christian knights murdered, raped and pillaged us, *in the name of Jesus*. *In the name of Jesus*, the Spanish Church tortured and burned us at the stake. In East European ghettos, my own grandparents escaped marauding Christian Cossacks. And when I came into the world, six million Jewish men, women, adolescents and babies were tortured and killed in Germany and Poland: Christian nations.

Jewish kids learn early on that Christians don't like us. Christian kids would chase me, yelling, "Christ killer!" Our dads were not accepted into good colleges and jobs. Many started small businesses to feed their families and survive. So what is "spiritual" about the way Christians hate Jews? How could I ever be one of them?

Yet, I do feel God's love in the message of the man on television. And he talks about the nation of Israel as the "apple of God's eye." Back and forth between my mind and my heart, back and forth. Back and forth.

To consider the Christian faith is ridiculous, both historically and intellectually. If there really were a God, little children wouldn't be hurt or hungry, would they? History books and newspapers testify that the inhabitants of Earth are unspeakably cruel to one another. Since I was a little girl, I've been tormented by the question: Why? That's my challenge to people who believe in God: Tell me why does evil ravage the innocents?

The answer is obvious: There is no God. Humans invent God, because we can't accept the brutality of life and deal with it in our own strength. I think it's cowardly and weak to depend on anything outside ourselves. One must be courageous. Self-sufficient. Tough enough to deal with *real* life.

But still, the spirit of the gentle, one-handed nun I met in the hospital chapel haunts me. Daily now, I pray, as she suggested, that God show me the way, that He direct me to the path of truth. The image of the goatherd keeps coming back (*how did he know who I was?*) pointing to his big book and saying, "The Way is in the Word." And the television teacher I stumbled upon also points to the Word. *The Word*. Okay, the Jews are people of the Word. My people. Perhaps I am being directed back to my origins.

I call a local Temple. My son is 11; it's already two years late to start his lessons if he is to be bar mitzvah at 13. "You must be a member of the Temple to prepare him." The director quotes the annual membership fee.

I gasp. "That's much more than I can afford!"

"We'll set up a meeting with the finance committee," she says with ice in her voice. "They make allowances in certain cases."

Five weeks and a dozen forms later, I walk, trembling, out of the finance committee meeting. I've been grilled, drilled, and through the mill. They've combed through my bank accounts, savings, tax returns, lists of monthly expenses. But I hid nothing. And now they present a figure somewhat less than the original fee but still so far out of reach, I give up. God will have to accept Ari as a Jew without a bar mitzvah, but I still want us to be part of the community, to be better Jews.

I call another local Temple for an appointment to speak privately with the rabbi. In the rabbi's study, I ask the two questions that haunt me: "Who is God?" and "What does He want from me?"

The rabbi talks to me about our heritage, the traditions, the holy days.

"But who is God," I repeat, "and what does He want from me?"

The rabbi folds his hands and looks across the desk at me. "We cannot know the mind of God, but I'm sure He wants us to be good people, good Jews, and good citizens."

I attend services on several Friday nights and seek God. He is not there to meet me. Afterward, at the *oneg shabbat*, I attempt to join the congregants at the pastry table and look around. No one says hello. No one asks who I am. I am a stranger and alone amongst my own. Watching the people who belong, I envy their social comfort. I envy the children who grow up with a sense of identity. I watch. The cold, uncomfortable chill of feeling like an intruder creeps around my heart and I can't wait to get back to the shelter of my home.

I crawl, lonely, into bed and wait eagerly for morning to bring the solace of loving prayer and the palpable Presence of an Almighty God. In the privacy of my bedroom, in the secrecy I can share with no one, the Presence of the Holy Spirit is real. In prayer, I disappear into insignificance and am reborn precious in His love.

It's wonderful—until the end of the prayer, when they say, "In the name of Jesus . . ." That's when I stop praying and go cold. It's like an ice cube sliding down my back. Chilling. Unnecessary. Why can't they leave Jesus out of it? It's perfect with just God and me, until they say "Jesus." Why can't they let me have God and leave it at that?

When they say the name "Jesus," I am torn between longing and rage. Day after day, I steel myself when the prayers draw to a close and press my fists against my ears. After several weeks, the rage melts into tears. Hearing the dreaded name, I tremble and cry, "Why can't you leave me in peace? I don't want him!" Until one day, broken, I crumble to my knees, my face to the floor, and hear a whisper escape my torn, Spirit-filled heart.

"In the name of Jesus. Amen."

In My Father's House

*Everyone who drinks this water will be thirsty again, but whoever
drinks the water I give him will never thirst. Indeed, the water I give him will
become in him a spring of water welling up to eternal life.*

JOHN 4:13-14

What impulse drove me to call Ben and ask him to meet me? Ben had been a friend when I worked at the computer company, and we have kept in touch since the layoff. Every few months one of us will call to say hi or to suggest going for coffee or a beer after work, but why this compulsion to tell Ben, of all people, about the nun, the goatherd, the television evangelist and my recent encounter with the Almighty? Ben is so reserved, so practical. Is it because he said something once about going to church with his wife? I don't know anyone else who goes to church. Still, I've never talked to Ben about anything except work. Never about anything personal

Face to face, in a Mexican restaurant with sawdust on the floor, my confession tumbles out. There is no expression on Ben's face. Occasionally he says, "Um hmm." He must think I'm loony tunes.

"Am I losing my mind, Ben? Does it sound crazy to you?"

"No." Ben clears his throat. "Sounds to me like God wants your attention. And . . . for reasons neither of us need to understand . . . He'll do what it takes to get it."

"Why me? Whatever for?"

Ben shrugs. "You'll know when it's time, I'm sure."

This is Ben speaking—my hard-core realist friend. "You believe in stuff like this? In miracles?"

"After what you've just told me, don't you?"

Toward 6:00, we pick up Ari from his friend's house, then return to my place for dinner. We continue talking, even after Ari has gone to bed. The next thing I know—uh oh!—it's 1:00 in the morning.

"You haven't called home, Ben. This isn't going to go over well with your wife, and I'd hate to see you in trouble." I had met Ben's wife once, at a company sales meeting in New Orleans. As fair, blonde and blue-eyed as Ben is dark and Asian, Deborah had impressed me as sharp, intelligent. "She must be worried, wondering where you are."

"I'll tell her we had dinner together."

"Until this hour? That's just what she'll want to hear."

He shrugs. "Come to church with us on Sunday. You'll find out more about what's happening to you."

"I don't know. Church isn't my sort of thing."

"Do what you want." He scribbles directions on a small piece of paper and leaves it on the dining room table. "If you change your mind and decide to come, give me a call. I'll get there early so I can introduce you to people."

Ben means well, but there's no way I'll give up a Sunday morning. It's my once-a-week chance to take a cup of coffee back to bed or out on the patio and read lazily in the morning sun.

How annoying. It's only seven o'clock and I'm awakened by a thought. *Get up; go to Ben's church.* No way! The idea is nuts. I'm going back to sleep. *Get up . . .* No. *Yes, now; you'll be late.* Can't be late; I'm not going anywhere. *Yes, you are.*

I'm up and dressing. Ben had said to call him if I'm coming. Shoot. What if his wife answers the phone? After keeping him out so late, I'll be embarrassed. Dialing, I pray: *Please, please let Ben pick up . . .*

Deborah answers.

"Hello, Deborah." Don't let her hear my voice shaking.

"Yes?"

"This is Barbara. I'm a friend of Ben's, from Per—"

"I know who you are."

"Uh . . . Ben invited me to your church this morning."

"Hmmm, yes. Well, there's a very nice little church closer to where you live. You might want to try that one."

"I don't know anyone there."

"Ben's in the shower now. I'll let him know you called."

I pull the car out of the garage and follow Ben's instructions. *Why am I doing this? I don't like churches . . . I don't belong . . . Deborah doesn't want me there.*

Ben waits at the entrance. He leads me to the Sunday School class the pastor teaches before service. I slip quietly into the last row, hoping to enter unseen. The class is informal, with people participating spontaneously. The pastor is young, enthusiastic about his lesson. Book of Luke, did he say? What's that? Something about Mary being a single mother after Joseph died? That gets my attention. Now he's talking about *Jewish customs* of the time. But he doesn't know who I am . . . is it a coincidence?

Class is over. I slip out to find Ben. "I can't sit with you today," he says, "because I'm ushering. Sit down there about halfway, beside Deborah." Is he kidding? Or just insensitive? Finding Deborah's pew, I slip into a seat on the other side of her, leaving room for Ben on the aisle. I smile a weak, foolish smile. She doesn't respond.

Worship begins with music, announcements, and prayer for the health problems and upcoming marriages in the congregation. Then singing, followed by the sermon. Halfway through, to my humiliation, tears roll down my face. Overcome with an unfamiliar emotion, I can't stop the tears. I feel the fool. I brush the tears away inconspicuously and sniffle as quietly as possible.

What's this? A white tissue floats down over my left shoulder. (From heaven, surely.) More quiet sniffles. Another tissue floats over from the pew behind. Somebody noticed, shoot! This is unbearable; I have to leave. But I'm trapped. I'd have to climb over Deborah and Ben. I can't stop the tears.

Deborah looks over at me. I flush and look away, swiping at another tear with the providential tissue. She leans toward me and whispers, "Don't be embarrassed; the Holy Spirit brings your tears."

Embarrassed? I'm mortified. When service is finally over, I try to escape, but Deborah takes my arm and turns to her husband. "Ben, let's take Barbara to lunch."

I don't belong here. I am an alien in a community of wholesome, stay-at-home wives who were virgins when they wed; where men hold responsible jobs, and two-parent families raise children within white picket fences. This is not a life I know, and I can't relate to many of their issues. I'm astounded, for example, to hear women complain that their husbands spend too much time at work. Spare me! Don't they know they are lucky to *have* a husband, one who works and provides for the family? Conversely, I can't expect them to understand my problems as a single mother and working woman either. If Grandma Kate were alive, I'd ask her if I should stay here. Ha! How would they like crystal balls and tarot cards in the church? (But give credit where it's due; Kate was good at it.)

God provides Deborah as the bridge between the world from which I come and the one in which I now live. Deborah has been through a lot. She understands the miracle that brings people like me to God. We've become inseparable. We share books and secrets and prayers; we share even the bread of my first Communion, when the plate passes by me because my eyes are closed, and Deborah gives me half of hers. We spend hours studying, exploring what God is doing in our lives. Deborah comforts, encourages and mentors my journey with the Holy Spirit. She sees to it that I meet everyone. With Deborah at my side, I cross the threshold of the little church where tissues float over one's shoulder to blot Holy Spirit tears and know, for the first time in all my journeys, that Barbara, the stranger, the foreigner, has come home.

Watching the couple in front of us, a stab of pain washes over me during the service. I nudge Deborah. "Look how he holds her. Stephen used to hold me like that." In everything we did, Stephen and I, we did it together, thought together, loved together. People always said we had an ideal union. And we thought so too. "If *our* marriage doesn't work," we had always said, "marriage itself doesn't work." What on earth had gone wrong?

The woman in the pew in front of us snuggles into her husband's arm. "I bet they're still in love after all these years," I murmur, envying their perfect life.

"Yes, they're in love," Deborah whispers. "They are also raising a Down syndrome child, nursing his dying father, and dealing with unemployment right now."

One would never guess. There is an aura of peace and contentment about them. Contentment. How do they maintain that, dealing with such problems? Others here in the church also seem to radiate a quiet, gentle joy. Is it a mask? Don't they have troubles like the rest of us? If the joy is real, what's their secret?

I can't help noticing how the mothers with small children share baby-sitting, car-pooling, child-care. A stab of regret squeezes my heart. "How different it would have been to raise Ari in a community like this. He could have gone to this wonderful school—they even give scholarships if you don't have the money! Oh, well. He's in junior high now. Too late."

Deborah reminds me, "Jesus was with you, even back then. Didn't He provide Cass to help you as a single mom?" I hadn't thought of that. Cass was a gift. A lifesaver. Deborah's effect on me is just the opposite of Ivan's. She dissipates the bitterness he had nurtured. "Take your focus off of what you don't have, Barbara. Focus on what you *do* have. See what God has in store for you."

Since that day I fell on my knees and prayed in the name of Jesus, remarkable changes have been taking place in me. First, my addiction to cigarettes is gone. I'd been a heavy smoker since I was 15 (that's 26 years). My body, the temple of God, is being cleansed in preparation for receiving Him.

Another addiction falls away too, freeing me from the obsessive need for sexual romance. It is so clear now that what I'd had with Ivan was not love. Real love isn't pain or madness. It does not destroy. Love is a quiet ecstasy, a peace that becomes joy. Love is light. Health-giving. At last, I can open the fingers of my heart and really let it go.

Old wounds are healing. Driving home, my car fills with a soothing Presence, a light balm, patching broken places. I can't wait to tell Ari. He is doing homework at the dining room table when I arrive.

"Ari, the most extraordinary thing . . ." He looks up, suspicious. He thinks his mother's gone daft ever since all this God stuff. "Tonight," I continue, undaunted, "I was healed of so much pain from my past. I felt like a smashed pottery jar, and all the pieces were being glued and fitted into place by a loving hand, so that the original form was taking shape again. God is doing a marvelous work in me."

"What's the big deal?" Ari shrugs. "He made you, didn't He? So why can't He fix you?"

When Sunday service ends, some of the women ask me to join their Tuesday morning Bible study. "I'd love to, but I work during the day. And I don't like leaving Ari in the evenings; I see so little of him. I guess Bible study isn't possible for me now."

A tall gentleman appears on my left and introduces himself as Allan Anders. "When and where *would* a Bible study be possible for you?"

"Ideally? Oh, maybe a Monday night. At my house."

"Very well," he says, "if you give me your address, I will be there next Monday to teach you." Allan is an ordained minister, currently without a pulpit. He works at a bakery to support his family, while waiting for a pastoral opportunity. Seeing a new believer with much to learn, he offers his knowledge.

Allan arrives at my front door on Monday evening, and we open the book of John. Every week we study that rich little book. To fully understand what Jesus and the disciples are saying, Allan takes us back frequently to their points of reference in the Torah and other books of the Old Testament.

"You must understand the Old Testament concept of atonement through the sacrifice of animal blood to really understand the meaning of Christ's blood at the cross," Allan explains. "The animals sacrificed for atonement, for the most part, were lambs and kids and goats—lovable, affectionate creatures who lived in the household as pets. They played with the children." (Just as the goats and kids had played with Stephen and me in the lamp-lit barn on a small farm in Alba, France.) "They slept with the family and kept them warm. These were not impersonal sacrifices, but sacrifices of beloved, innocent family pets. Just as when God sacrificed Jesus on the cross, it was not impersonal; it was the sacrifice of His beloved son, His own flesh—a sacrifice so terrible that, in His mercy, He didn't make Abraham do it with his son Isaac."

Delving deeply into the Old Testament, it takes a good year and a half to finish the Gospel of John. That's okay. I'm learning the foundation of Judaism, the Law of Moses, and the history of my people.

A Bible verse circles maddeningly in my mind. I want to look it up, but I'm too tired to get out of bed. I try to sleep, but the question plagues me. I give up. Stumbling downstairs, I light a lamp in the study and look up the passage. *Romans, maybe? Oh, here it is.*

The next thing I know, the sun is up. Oddly enough, I'm not tired, just reluctant to tear myself away from the power of this reading. This happens often now, these all-night Bible readings. Once the book is open, I float free of gravity, resting on the hand of God in ecstasy, awed by His wisdom. How have I missed this all my life? I've got 40 years of ignorance to catch up on! Hungry for the Word, I feast on it. I read. I study. I listen daily to teachers like John MacArthur, David Hocking, R. C. Sproul, Jack Hayford, Walter Martin—all of them. When I'm not in the Word, I'm at prayer meetings, drinking in all I can of the Spirit's blessings.

This is nothing like studying with Krishnamurti in Paris, or reading the Vedantic sages with Karl in our cottage on Venice beach. Those were intellectual explorations. This is an indwelling of the Spirit within me. I live and breathe the exhilarating discovery of God. Night after night I read Scripture and, for hours every day, I listen to teachings on the radio and on tapes from the church library. I can't get enough of the Word. Unlike the passions that destroy, this one nourishes and grows and protects.

Monday nights I study with Allan. Wednesday evenings I am at the church for prayer. Sunday mornings, before service, we have a dynamic Sunday School session. Jason, who leads the class, says he remembers his initial hunger and thirst. "What I wouldn't give to recapture that beautiful time of insatiable immersion. It's like falling in love."

"You mean it will go away?"

"No. But there comes a point, of course, when the honeymoon is over. The relationship matures and it settles with peaceful certainty within you. You are entering a marriage here, Barbara. Marriage starts with passion, transforms into a comfortable assurance, and is lived out in peaks and valleys. You take each other for granted at times, and sometimes it's hard to live with your commitment. Dry spells, you know? Especially when worldly problems like finances, illness, or failed relationships press in on you. But then the passion wells up and you fall madly in love again.

"Quiet or tumultuous, calm or intense, your life with the Lord is a journey, an adventure. Sometimes difficult, but always deeply satisfying. Delicate and powerfully thrilling. And it is forever."

Delving again into my Judaic heritage, some of the Scripture in Leviticus and Deuteronomy is hard to swallow for today's American woman. I bring indignant objections to Sunday School. "What is this? What kind of a God sets down such a law?"

"I don't like it either," Jason admits. "Personally, I'd write the Scripture differently, very differently. But it's a good thing I'm not the one in charge. I know nothing about how to form a planet or create trees and rivers and ecosystems. I can't design and manufacture a human being with its automatic moving parts, its brain and tissues and reproductive system. I can't sculpt mountains or hang a moon in the sky, or run a universe and tend to every single one of the billions of individuals within it. So if you don't like what His good Word says, talk to Him about it."

"Very funny."

"No, I'm not being funny. Ask Him what it means and why He does it that way. Keep asking until He shows you. Sooner or later, He will."

"You believe that?"

"I know it."

Part of me holds back. Something I'm afraid of . . . Africa? If I give my life to Him completely, will He send me to Africa as a missionary?

"I'm not worthy to be a Christian," I confess to Jason and his wife, Patti. "I hate bugs. I hate camping. I hate villages without running water."

"Then missionary work is not your gift—as it's not ours! If God wanted you in Africa, He'd put it in your heart to go there. Obviously He has work for you somewhere else."

"The French Riviera," I hope.

But Pattie knows my weak spot and teases me with it. "*Boom* boom boom boom . . . *boom* boom boom boom," she chants. "Africa awaits!"

Questions arise as I study, lots of them. "Question everything," Dad had always said. "If it's real, it'll hold up." I throw questions at Allan and at Jason in class. I spend hours in my pastor's study, challenging passages I don't understand.

One thing especially bothers me. "Am I accepting God because I'm at such a vulnerable point in my life right now? Would I believe if I hadn't lost my aunt, my prospect for marriage and my job? Is it possible, if I were in a better place, that all this would seem like nonsense?"

Pastor listens patiently, elbows on his knees, fingers touching like a tent between his long legs.

"You see, Pastor, I have to overcome a lifetime of doubts. I was taught that it's a weakness, that it's ignorance, to believe in God. So I can't help wondering: Is God just a security blanket, an everything-will-be-okay fairy tale that I'm swallowing now just because I'm weak?"

"We are all weak, Barbara; it is the human condition. What would you say about a two-year-old child who tries to cook on a stove?"

"Whoa! Dangerous!"

"Right. At two, there are other things the child is supposed to do, like learning to talk and exploring his world. Not cooking. He's not equipped for it. He has a mother for that. In the same way, we are not equipped to go through life without God. We are unwise to try; it's dangerous."

"So it's okay to need Him?"

"Very okay."

"It doesn't mean we're unable to cope with harsh reality?"

"Oh, you'll have to cope with reality, harsh or otherwise. God does not promise a life without tribulation."

Pastor leans back in his leather armchair and looks through the large picture window at the garden. He is quiet. I look at the bookshelves lining the wall behind him, reading titles on the bindings. I wonder what "tribulations" he might be dealing with in his own life. "Believing in God won't make your troubles disappear," he cautions, "but you can draw upon His divine guidance for wisdom. And you'll feel His gracious Presence with you as you struggle through them."

"You feel His Presence? Really?"

"Yes. And you will too. The Holy Spirit, now within you, will make Him real."

"It's happening, but I'm reluctant to admit it. It goes against my whole upbringing."

"God has given you a good mind, Barbara. Use it to study and learn more of His ways. Soon it will seem quite irrational *not* to believe in Him."

In the sessions with my pastor, I broach the subject of marriage. "The Bible says we are to marry once, and not divorce. I, too, always believed we are to marry only once—and that's it. My marriage was wonderful while it lasted, and I believe that's it for life. I don't think I'm ever to marry again."

"The Bible tells us how to live in a way that's best for us," Pastor explains. "But God knows we don't always live to His standards, that we aren't perfect, as

He is perfect. Our imperfection, our inability to meet God's standard of holiness, is what we call 'sin.' Your divorce was the result of human imperfection. Of sin. But through the sacrifice of His Son, God bought atonement for our sins."

Pastor leans back in his chair, his eyes tranquil. "When you accepted Jesus in your heart, Barbara, you became a new creature. The sins of your past are gone. In the sight of God, you are a new, virginal creation."

"Oh yeah. It's been so long since I've been with a man, I probably am a virgin again."

He laughs. "Trust God. Perhaps this is a time of purification for you, a preparation for something better. Find a man who loves God, and give your son a father."

Ahhh. An echo of what Lewis Clark had said to me a long time ago.

In my bedroom, a large upholstered maple armchair that Mom and Dad bought when they first got married has now become my "prayer chair." I'm having a good session this morning, the kind that connects (you know it when you have it). Oddly, though, I pray to Jesus as "Elder Brother." This term comes back to my mind over and over again, and I'm ashamed. It seems so presumptuous. Jesus is my Lord. My Savior. My compassionate advocate before the high throne. But to call Him "brother"—isn't that putting myself on the same level?

I am careful not to let that repeat in my prayers, but it comes again in a dream. "Why does it keep coming to me like that?" I am in Pastor's study again, confessing my arrogance, the notion that I can pray to Jesus as Elder Brother. "I don't mean to be disrespectful, but somehow it feels right."

"Do you understand your position in the family of God?" Pastor picks up his Bible and turns to Ephesians 2:19. "Listen . . ."

You are no longer foreigners and aliens, but fellow citizens with God's people and members of God's household.

"It says that?" I am astounded, "No longer foreigners and aliens? That's who I am: my name, 'Barbara,' means 'foreigner' or 'stranger.'"

"No longer! It says you are now a member of His household. And there's more. Here, Romans 8:29: *'For those God foreknew he also predestined to be conformed to the likeness of His Son, that He might be the firstborn among many brothers . . .'*"

"Brothers!" I exclaim.

Pastor holds up his index finger and continues. "Turn to Ephesians 1:5: *'In love He predestined us to be adopted as his sons through Jesus Christ . . .'* and in the second chapter of Hebrews, verse 11—listen to this: *'Both the one who makes men holy and those who are made holy are of the same family. So Jesus is not ashamed to call them brothers.'"*

"So it wasn't arrogance . . ." I sink back into my chair, breathless. "It was *revelation.*"

I'd like to discuss something else with my pastor, but it's too awful. He says God forgives everything, but he's never had an abortion. *Dear God, ask my baby to forgive me. Take care of him. Give me hope that one day I can see him, hold him. Let him know I love him.*

Things that used to frustrate me are now blessings. Small, simple things, like kitchen chores. I always hated washing dishes. Just when you get them done, there's another meal and another sink full of them. "Dishes," I'd often said, "make me feel like Sisyphus pushing the bloody rock up the hill. Once you reach the top it rolls back down, and you have to start over again." Now, soaking my hands in suds, I sing praises to God who provides beautiful dishes to wash and fills them continually with nourishing food.

Just this morning, driving home from church, the car overheated. I pulled off to a call box and dialed AAA. (I wish I could have dialed up a husband and said, "Come get me," but AAA was second best.) They asked for my card number. But I'd left the house in a hurry without my wallet; I didn't have the card with me. Unbelievably, they sent a tow truck out anyway. If that weren't strange enough, when I got to the gas station—on a Sunday, remember—there was a mechanic on duty! Unbelievable. Even more unbelievable, when I told the mechanic I hadn't brought my wallet, he completed the work on the car and trusted me to drive home for the money! That might not be so strange in a small town, but here in Los Angeles, it's a miracle.

Such things are happening all the time, now—the piano-tuner who wouldn't take money for his work; the lady who rewrote my résumé without charge. I live in a world of blessings.

I learned from Krishnamurti that no political or philosophical system can eradicate violence and suffering in the world. "Only a change in the human psyche can do that," he'd said. "If only a dozen people are transformed, it can change the world." Yes, it can and it did. Twelve disciples were transformed through Jesus and, through them, the entire Western world. But Krishnamurti relied upon the strength of the human mind. God takes us far beyond this finite resource. In Him, we have the infinite power of the Alpha and Omega.

How do I tell my Jewish family that I am now a Christian? They will feel it is such a betrayal. Ari knows, of course. He's not sure what to think, but he's watching. I dread having to tell the others. Some Jewish families sit *shivah* when their kids leave the faith (that means they spend a ritual week in mourning and prayer for the lost one), and never speak to them again, for they are considered dead. I don't want that to happen, but I can't live a secret life.

I tell Mom first. She doesn't like it; you can tell from the way she says "Oh?" in a tight, controlled voice. And then, "Look, whatever makes you happy. I just don't want to hear about it." (Translation: "Don't even *think* of trying to convert me!") But she isn't kicking me out of her life, bless her heart. There's no anger, no guilt, none of the negatives I was bracing for. But Mom was never into guilt. There are jokes about Jewish mothers and guilt, but that's not my mom. This is a hard moment for her, but she accepts it as long as I don't try to change her. That's pretty fair, don't you think?

Mom is not the person I knew as a child. She can still go to pieces over the small stuff; but in a crisis, she comes up on the right side. There's a lot more to her than I've recognized.

Dad might be tougher. He always said, "Never forget you're a Jew, and never be ashamed of it."

I pick up the phone. "Hi, Dad."

"Hi, honey, what's happening?"

"Not much. Well, that's actually not true. Dad, are you sitting?"

"Of course not; when do I sit? I'm refinishing the kitchen cabinets."

"Dad, please sit."

"If I must. Something serious?"

"I hope not. I . . . Dad, I don't know how to say this." My mouth is dry. "I've become a Christian, Dad." A long silence. Very long. "Dad?"

He clears his throat. "But . . . how can you be a Christian? You're a Jew."

"Yes, of course, Dad! And that'll never change. But I'm a Jew who believes in Jesus."

"Hmmm." Then, after another lengthy silence: "Why?" There is no condemnation, no anger in the question, only curiosity. I breathe easier, settle into my recliner, and tell him everything. We talk for hours.

Months pass, a couple of years, and we still talk about it. Dad's an engineer; his work depends on rationality and precision. Even so, he's no stranger to the world of spirit. Growing up with Grandma Kate as his mother, he's seen things and had experiences. Now he's curious. And that's the beauty of him. He's curious about everything; he always wants to learn.

Dad and I meet every Thursday for a quick dinner, and then drive together to my Bible study. Dad likes the study and the people in the group. Our prayers are strange to him, at first. Prayers at Bible study are spontaneous, personal conversations, straight from the heart to God. They aren't like the written collective prayers in synagogue. But he gets used to it. Eventually, he brings his own prayer requests to the group.

At church, our choir is doing a beautiful Easter concert and Dad is singing with us. He doesn't read notes; but he listens. He picks out the tenor part and sings it perfectly. I don't know who is more surprised: me seeing Dad in the church choir, or Dad hearing me sing on key. "When did you learn to sing?"

"I guess God didn't want me messing up His choir, so He gave me a new voice."

Julia, my sister, had told me to put my troubles in a bag and lay it at God's feet. That was last year, when things were so bad. She had said He would take care of everything. She was not sure she believed it herself, but it seems that God was preparing her heart. So she is not shocked now when I tell her I found God. In fact, she agrees to come with me to a prayer meeting.

Toward the meeting's end, the leader prays for any unbelievers who might be in the room tonight. Tears run down Julia's cheeks. That's odd, because Julia never cries. She was strong-willed and stoic even as a child. Even when she got punished, she was tough and refused to cry. Tonight she embraces Jesus in her heart, and she cries. I guess the Holy Spirit is stronger than the strap.

This opens up a new relationship for us. Julia becomes part of my church and Bible study group. My friends become her friends; we attend social events together and see each other several times a week. What a blessing to share my new life with her.

I pray continually that both Mom and Dad will come to know Jesus. "Coincidentally," both of them are now encountering Christians in their lives. Mom's cleaning lady talks incessantly about the Lord. And Dad, who has just moved into a new house, discovers his neighbor on the ranch next door is a Christian. Music brings them together as friends. Joy is a pianist—she's been Dale Evans's accompanist for many years.

"Yes, I believe in God," Dad tells Joy, "after all, I'm an engineer. I know *design* when I see it. But Jesus . . . I can't accept that Jesus is God."

Mom and Dad have Jewish friends who, when they hear their two daughters have become Christians, lament and pity them. "What a terrible thing. You should live so long to see this?"

Mom and Dad both respond the same way. "What's so terrible? My daughters live a rich and meaningful life. To tell the truth, I envy what they've found."

There are still my uncle and cousins to be told. (Aunt Evelyn isn't here, of course. My "betrayal" would have probably broken her heart.) Uncle says nothing; he just looks down and sags a little. "I was hoping someday you might enjoy a new marriage. Now I won't be able to attend the ceremony."

"But that's silly! Why wouldn't you be there?"

"No, dear. When you marry, I want to celebrate wearing a yarmulka and tallis. One doesn't wear these in a church."

"In the church where I worship, Uncle, you would be honored wearing a yarmulka and tallis. And I would be proud of you." He merely shakes his head; it's beyond him how this could have happened. Still he loves me.

Cousin Martina is easy. She shrugs and says, "Whatever." She couldn't care less about religion, except that it doesn't fit her image of me as a "free-thinking" existentialist. Ha! If I could only put Martina in a room with some of the exciting Christian thinkers I've encountered!

It's different with my other cousin, Howard. "So!" Howie hugs me. "What's new? I haven't seen you since—when, just after Mom died? That was a pretty extraordinary week, all of us staying at the house with Dad."

I recall my uncle's grief. "I'm afraid a week wasn't enough. He's still so lost without her."

"I keep an eye on him," Howard assures me. "So, Cuz, what's been happening in your life since then?"

"You know most of it. I lost my job, Ivan is out of my life for good, Ari's fine, and I miss your mom terribly . . . I guess that's it."

"What else?" (He's hoping there's a new love.)

"Howard," I hesitate, "we've always been honest with one another, right?"

"Sure, Bobs. Why? Something on your mind? Spit it out."

"Right. Well, there *is* something, but I don't think you'll like it."

"Oh, c'mon! There's nothing you can't tell me. This is Howie, remember?"

"It's something I believe in, something that has taken over my life."

"Sounds heavy. Shoot."

I look down at the floor, not knowing where to start. The silence is awkward. He puts his hands on my shoulders, serious for a moment.

"Look, Bobs, you're my cousin and I love you. Nothing you believe in can change that. Unless . . ." A ludicrous, zany image crosses his mind. He can't help laughing.

"Unless what?"

Still chuckling at the absurdity of it, he continues, "Unless you've become one of those freaky, born-again, fundamentalist nuts!"

I freeze.

"Bobs?"

I say nothing, but a mischievous smile tugs at the corners of my mouth. I bite my lip.

"Oh God! " he groans. "You aren't *serious*, are you?" I hold my silence. "Say it's a joke. Please . . ."

"I said you wouldn't like it, Howard."

"Yeah, but 'not like it,' that's different. This is killing me!"

"I'm sorry."

Now it's his turn to be quiet. He makes a visible effort to pull himself together. "You *are* serious?" I nod. "Okay." His voice is flat.

"Okay, what?"

"Okay. Just okay. I'm sure it's okay, whatever you do. I said nothing is going to change how I feel about you, and I meant it. So it's okay."

"Really? You aren't just saying it to be nice?"

"I am saying it to be nice and, yes, it's true." He hugs me. "You must be some kind of a nut. But I've always loved you; I always will."

I can't wait to tell Lewis and Zada. They lost their daughter not long after Ari and I moved out of their cottage eight years ago. We still visit from time to time, and I keep up with their grown kids and their expanding families. They'll be happy to hear my news.

"The big white house is quiet now with everybody gone," I observe.

"Yup." Lewis winks at his wife. "It's our turn now. We give our free time to the church, we visit the kids and we travel around the world. We've discovered how much fun we can have, just the two of us!"

"Sounds like a second honeymoon," I say.

"Well, we sure do have a good time," Zada says, looking at Lewis with the eyes of a bride.

At the dining room table, they listen attentively when I tell how God revealed Himself to me and how He is carrying me through this long, frightening period of unemployment. "I thought for sure we'd lose our home," I say, "but I'm finding just enough freelance work to squeak by for another couple of months. Hopefully, something will open up soon."

Zada and Lewis look at one another, shocked. "Dear, why didn't you call us?" Zada asks. "There's always room for you at our house; rent out your condo for some income and come live with us!"

Lewis nods in agreement. "Absolutely. You just bring Ari and move right in."

It had never occurred to me to call upon anyone for help. But they mean it. I reach for Zada's hand. "If the day comes when I have to, I surely will. I'll call." I breathe deeply. Their home is still, as always, my safe corner on a hostile planet.

The added dimension of spiritual intimacy enriches our relationship. Together we seek God's blessing on our food and His guidance in our lives. We speak of things never given voice before and enter the sanctuary of sharing the Presence of the Lord; the anointing of the Spirit; the private, innermost journey of a human life illuminated by prayer.

My family accepts. The Clarks understand. There remains only Lorna who must know, and whose reaction matters. Lorna has a more intimate knowledge of who I am than any person on Earth. For 20 some odd years, we have shared everything: emotional upheavals, intellectual concepts, the aesthetic process, and the exploration of spiritual realms. We've counseled one another through broken love affairs, childbirth and raising children. We shared the near-death of my child, the ravages of divorce, and the practical matters of everyday life. Unfortunately, since we left the university (she for Baghdad with her first husband, and me for Paris with mine), we have never again lived in the same city—except for the very brief time in Los Angeles, when she struggled through her divorce and helped me while baby Ariel recovered from meningitis. Since then she's lived in France, married Patrick, and now they live in New York.

Even so, Lorna is my living calendar, my memory bank. Often I ask, "When did such-and-such happen? Was it before or after so-and-so?" Or, "Who brought us to . . .?" In her steel-trap memory, every date, every step of my internal and external life is recorded and stored in minute detail. When new situations crop up, it is Lorna who sees the connection points to my past, sometimes in early childhood, and understands where they can take me in the future.

Spiritually, Lorna is a powerhouse. She was when we were 20; she still is at 41. She meditates with unbroken concentration for hours to commune with the cosmic "force." I've seen her fast for nine days, ingesting only water. She knows no fear, leading journeys several times a year to Peruvian jungles and living for weeks on herbs and local "medicinal" plants. Lorna marches into men's prisons and teaches art to violent criminals. She walks (*walks*, mind you) across a vast Israeli desert and leads a pilgrimage across 1,200 miles of a Pyrenees mountain range. Nothing—physical, emotional or financial—constrains her quest.

We are 3,000 miles apart, on opposite ends of a continent, traveling divergent spiritual paths. Lorna is a nationally recognized shaman, a healer. I am a born-again disciple of Jesus. She's disappointed with the choice I've made. She doesn't say it, but I know.

It's not that Lorna doesn't know Christianity. Her father raised her in the church, but he worshiped with a cold rigidity and used Scripture to ward off relating. She hates it when I quote Scripture. "Just *talk* to me, in your own words!" she pleads, frustrated.

Conversely, I have studied and understand her path. We had explored together, in earlier years, and I had studied more of it with Karl, but I have serious concerns about her practices. Not about her sincerity—I trust the integrity and the depth of her quest—but about the source of her power and where it can lead.

I grieve the widening distance between us, both in physical miles and spiritual vision. I mourn, because I believe God has given Lorna wisdom far beyond her personal experience, and hers is a voice through which He often speaks to me. Our relationship remains my special treasure. If not for my connection with Lorna, I often think, mine might have been an ordinary life.

Ari is a good kid; he doesn't give me trouble often. Once, when he was 11, we took a ferry trip to Catalina Island. He had wandered around the boat, looking for amusement. I found him on the upper deck, playing cards with a man and his little girl. *Fish, probably,* I guessed. But why was he sitting there in just his undershorts? Where were his clothes? And why did he look so unhappy?

"There you are!" Ari looked up when I approached, startled and ashamed. "What's going on?"

"We're playing Poker, and Ariel is losing," the man explained.

"But he has no money!"

"Right. He's bet his clothes. We're on the last hand now. It's all or nothing." Ari shot a pleading look at me.

"I didn't know you were into gambling, Ari. The stakes are high."

Ari was caught between a rock and a hard place. He couldn't walk away without his clothes, but he didn't want to play this hand and risk losing his shorts either. "What if I lose?" he wailed. He weighed the situation, put the cards down and said, "I'm out. I know you'll be mad about the clothes, Mom, but I can't take the chance."

A chuckle escaped my serious mask. "Tell you what, Ariel. If you promise this is your last bout with gambling, I'll get the clothes back and we'll forget it happened."

"Oh! I swear, I promise. Never again, Mom. Never."

That was about the worst of it, except for a series of jackets he lost in junior high, but that stopped when I made him raise the money to buy a new one. Oh yes, and the one time he put his fist through his bedroom door. When I returned from work, there was a note tacked over the hole: *Dear Mom, sorry about the door.*

I had been pretty angry, at first; but by the time he got home, I was cool. "No problem," I assured Ari. "All you have to do is raise $125 to replace and hang a new door."

His mouth dropped. "Huh? How am I going to do that? Give me a break, Mom, I'm just a kid!"

"Find a way, and find it fast. I want that door replaced in two weeks."

"Uh . . . can I just fix it?"

"Do you know how?"

"I'll learn."

"You'll have to do it so nobody can tell there was ever a hole. If I see even a trace, you'll have to come up with the $125. Deal?"

That turned out to be a learning experience in woodwork. Ari asked a neighbor to lend him tools and show him how. Two weeks later the door was back in place. The hole was gone. It was sanded, planed, painted and perfect.

Ari is 14 now, and he's still a good kid. But he parades around in black T-shirts with the sleeves rolled up, and spiked heavy-metal armbands. I worry about what the clothes represent and the music that goes along with them. "I've listened to some of those heavy-metal lyrics," I tell Ari. "They're grotesque, evil. About torturing girls, necrophilia, stuff like that,"

"Oh, Mom, no one pays attention to the words."

"Yes, they do. Listen, Ari, the church is holding a parenting session on teen music next week. Come with me."

"Why should I?"

"Because we parents don't know as much about the music as you do. The guy speaking is a musician. If what he tells us isn't true, we won't know. With you there to speak up, we'll have a reality check. What do you say?"

Ari comes to the session and spoke at length with the speaker afterwards.

"So, Ari, what do you think?"

"He's cool."

"From what he said, your clothes and music reflect a pretty scary culture, don't they?"

"Don't sweat it, Mom," he says. "I'll grow out of it."

We quarrel tonight because Ari wants to go with his friends to heavy-metal concerts. "But, Mom," he whines, "all my friends can go. *Their* parents let them."

"What their parents do is none of my business. *You* are my business. Now listen to me, because this conversation is as old as the hills. Every kid, in every country in the world, has this same argument with his parents. I had it with mine, and your kids will have it with you. I know it by heart, and pretty soon you will too. So decide. We can go on with it for another hour or so, or you can give up now. You won't win."

He sulks. "You don't want to accept my authority? You don't think Mom knows best? Okay. Go to a higher authority." He looks up, puzzled. "I mean it. Go to your room and talk to God. Ask Him if a heavy-metal concert is what He wants for you. Ask Him if it'll help you become a man, and wait for an answer. When you get it, let me know. I promise I'll abide by the decision."

Now he's grinning. "You will? Even if He says I can go?"

"Even if."

Ari bounds upstairs, very pleased.

Waiting, I pray. He's gone for 40 minutes.

Now the bedroom door opens with a click. Ari comes, subdued, into my study. "Well?"

"Nothin'. I'm not goin' to the concert."

Ari doesn't want any part of becoming Christian. "I already have a religion, thank you."

"Okay, but I'd like you to study the Bible."

"Fine, I'll study in synagogue." At the synagogue, however, the courses for 14-year-old kids focus on Jewish traditions; we couldn't find a study of the Bible. A young man from church who is fluent in Hebrew offers him lessons in Hebrew and the Old Testament. Unfortunately, our friend is not a dynamic teacher, and Ari squirms with boredom. He says he'd rather join Allan and me on Monday nights, but here, too, Ari can't stay awake for more than a couple of minutes—five, if he really tries. It's embarrassing. Poor Allan teaches his heart out, but we can't get Ari to stay awake.

In church one Sunday morning, I observe a teenage boy at the far end of the pew. Leaning forward, elbows on his knees in prayer, his head rests on his clasped hands. He is beautiful. *Lord,* I pray, my heart aching, *Lord, let me see my Ariel like that one day, bent in prayer, in submission to You. Just grant this one request, oh*

Lord, and I promise I'll never ask for anything ever again. (Oops. Is that a promise I can keep?)

"Ari, will you come to church tomorrow?" Up until now, I haven't asked him to go with me, but the time seems right.

"Okay," he says. (Whew! That was easy.) "But Donovan invited me to spend the night at his house. Is that okay too?" (Ah, the catch.)

"Will his parents be there?"

"Of course."

"Well, if it's all right with his parents, it's fine with me. Only promise to be home by 7:30 in the morning, so we won't be late."

True to his word, Ari arrives home on time. He lies on the couch while I get ready.

"Are you feeling all right, Ari?" His head is warm. "You look a little gray."

"My stomach's real upset. I think I'm going to throw up."

"Oh, I'm sorry. Maybe you should stay home."

"No, I'll go. I'll be fine."

At church we sit on the aisle so Ari can slip out easily to the men's room if he has to. He's a good sport, coming with me when he feels so bad. A good kid. "Take it easy this afternoon," I say when we get home. "Lie on the sofa; watch some TV."

The telephone rings. "Hello, is this Ariel's mother? I'm Bill Weaver, Donovan's dad. Sorry to call you with unpleasant news, but I think you should know what happened last night."

"Last night, Mr. Weaver?" My eyes flash to Ari. When he hears Mr. Weaver's name, he looks scared. "My wife and I returned home this morning from Sacramento—"

"Sacramento?" I interrupt. "You weren't home?" Ari shrinks, desperate, into the sofa pillows. His lips mouth the words "I'm sorry, Mom. I'm sorry..."

"That's right. We returned to find the house in shambles. Beer bottles... marijuana butts everywhere. The carpet's ruined and the smell is unbelievable. What's more..." He doesn't sound angry, just sad. "...there's jewelry missing. Almost every valuable piece my wife had."

I gasp. "I'm so sorry! I was assured you'd be home and they had permission."

"No, not at all." He sighs. "We've had problems with Donovan for some time. In fact, he sees a therapist. But my wife and I had to leave town, and he'd given us his word there'd be no parties, no funny stuff. We believed him. I guess we wanted to. Excuse me, I don't mean to burden you with our family problems, it's just... for the sake of your son, I thought you ought to know."

"You're quite right, and I thank you for calling. I know it wasn't easy for you." I hang up, glaring at Ari who is in tears by now.

"I drank beer, Mom, but I swear I didn't touch the marijuana. Just the beer. And the lie . . . I'm sorry I lied."

"What about the jewelry?" He looks blank. "Jewelry is missing," I insist. "Who did it?" His eyes are wide now, wide like quarters.

"I don't know," he says almost in a whisper. "Oh, God, I had no idea what was going on."

"What kind of people do you hang around with? I want a complete list of names, everyone who was there!" After blowing steam and yelling about not being able to trust my own son, I blurt out, "Six months! You're grounded for the rest of your ninth-grade school year, do you hear?"

"That's five months, Mom."

"Right. Five. You'll go to school, you'll go to church if you choose; but outside of that, you don't leave this house. Not even for sports. And when you get to see the light of day again, if I ever catch you near Donovan or anyone who was there last night, even once, for a minute, I'll keep you under house arrest until you're 21. *Do you understand?*"

Later in the day, when I am calmer, I wonder how you ground a kid for five months. Did I put my foot in my mouth? If I don't do what I said, my word and my authority are mud. And if I do?

Ari never much liked to read. He's an action-oriented, athletic type, but he reads books now—good ones, like Jack London's *Call of the Wild*. He builds models, draws, and we spend a lot more "quality" time together. The five long months are passing peacefully and, I hope, there was a lesson learned.

Set free at last, he's back on the gymnastics team. He attends church regularly too, not because he's made any commitment, but because he likes the teen group, the camping trips, and the activities. Joe and Dave, two young men who lead these groups, are great with the kids. "It's weird, Mom," Ari had said the first time he went with them. "They pray about everything. Before we took off, they prayed for safety, driving to the site. Before we ate, they gave thanks. Before we played soccer, they asked for a fair game with no injuries. They don't take a breath without God."

"Does it bother you?"

"No . . . 'cause they . . . it's weird for kids my age, but they love each other."

After completing our study in the book of John, the weekly study sessions with Allan come to an end. Allan and his family are moving to Atlanta for a new job. But the Lord fills the gap when Jason and Patti bring their Bible study group to our house. Ari loves the difference in tone. With Allan, Bible study had been quiet. His voice was soft, contemplative. He allowed long pauses to make us think and ponder what the Lord would have us learn. With Jason leading the study group, our house is filled with animated discussion, laughter, even hilarity. As we grow spiritually, God reveals His humor and exuberant joy. Ari doesn't fall asleep anymore. He looks forward to Thursday nights, not because he believes in this "stuff," he's quick to let me know, only because he can't wait to see Jason again.

Ari adores Jason. He looks to him for counsel and direction and he wishes Jason were the father he never had. The feeling is mutual. They are happy together, whether scrutinizing a passage of Scripture or rolling on the floor, wrestling. Having lost both Stephen and Karl, and having experienced rejection from Ivan, Ari deeply needs to be loved by a father figure.

Jason discovers that Ari has a real affinity for the Bible. He absorbs it like a sponge and remembers everything he reads and hears. Sometimes, when the rest of us discuss a difficult or perplexing passage, Ari pipes up, "I get it, I see what it means." And he's able to give a clear, illuminating explanation.

"Just as Moses lifted up the snake in the desert, so the Son of Man must be lifted up, that everyone who believes in him may have eternal life."

"What does that mean, 'Moses lifted up the snake in the desert'?" Jason asks us.

"It refers to the story in Numbers 21," responds one of the men. "When the Israelites wandered through the desert complaining, the Lord sent serpents to bite them and many died. They were looking to Moses for help."

"What did he do?" Jason prods.

"He mounted a bronze serpent high up on a pole and told the people who were bitten to look up at it. He said if they looked up at the bronze serpent, they would live. Frankly, I've never understood it."

"Me neither," I admit. "If serpents were biting my leg, it would be very hard not to look down. And it seems absurd that a bronze idol on a stick is going to help. I'd want a doctor or medicine to cure it!"

"We all have serpents biting at our legs," Jason says. "The car breaks down. We lose a job. A child gets sick. Those are our serpents."

"Yes," Ari interjects. "But we aren't supposed to focus on those things. We're to keep our eyes upward, looking toward Jesus. Jesus high on the cross— He's the serpent on the pole. Look to Him, Jesus tells us, and we'll survive the circumstances. We'll live forever. Death and pain have no power over us if we are looking up at Him."

I am stunned. Ari is repeating, almost verbatim, what Allan had taught while Ari had slept.

"Right, Ari," Jason thumps his shoulder. "Absolutely right. And the Lord is commanding something that seems irrational here, isn't He? He says to do something completely against our instinct and logic. There are many, many instances of this in both the Old Testament and the New. Let's look up some other examples."

After everyone goes home, I ask Ari, "How do you remember what Allan taught while you were asleep?"

"Did Allan teach that?"

"Yes. You've shared his teaching on numerous occasions these last weeks. How do you remember it? You were asleep!"

"I don't know, Mom. It just comes. God gives it to me."

"Do you believe what you said, Ari? Do you believe in God?"

"I guess so, but . . . I'm not ready . . . I still want to have fun. There are things I'm not ready to give up."

"Girls?"

He looks embarrassed. "Hey, whatever."

※   ※   ※

On Thursday, when Jason, Patti and the others come again, Ari says he can't do Bible study tonight.

"How come? You never miss."

"I have a term paper due in the morning. It isn't started yet."

"Give your time to God first," Jason suggests, "and He'll help you get it done."

"Get real," Ari says. "We don't finish until nine-thirty!"

Jason shrugs. "If it were me, I'd trust Him."

Ari is torn. Casting a nervous eye up the stairs toward his room, he sits with us. We complete our study, and everyone leaves except Jason and Patti.

"So, Ari, what's the paper about?" Jason asks. "We'll work on it with you."

Ari isn't used to grown-ups helping with his homework. We go to his room, the four of us, and two hours later, when we come out, Ari has the draft for a good paper. Polishing it up a bit won't take long. "Wow," he says. "This is great!"

"Did I tell you to trust Him?" Jason swings a high-five. "Focus on Him first. The rest will come. Guaranteed."

※   ※   ※

It's Good Friday, and they are passing the Communion plate. Ari sees it coming and looks at me, unsure.

"Don't take it unless you mean it," I counsel. "The Lord will respect your honesty. He knows anyway, so who would you be kidding? It's no sin to pass it by if you aren't ready."

"How do I know if I'm ready?"

"I can't answer that, son. Ask Him."

Ari stares at the plate, still two rows in front of us, but on its way. He squeezes his eyelids tightly shut and bows his head. Elbows on his knees, he looks just like the young man I'd seen praying. Except that Ari is struggling; his hands are balled into fists against his forehead. He remains in that position until he feels a tiny nudge from his neighbor on the left who hands him the plate. I reach out to take it from him, but he holds it. Pauses. Reaches his free hand slowly toward it. Withdraws. Then reaches in again to take the piece of matzoh. He looks at it between his thumb and forefinger, passes the plate to me and, with his head bowed, continues to hold it between his knees. For many minutes he sits, eyes closed, holding the matzoh.

"Mom, should I take it?"

"I don't know, son."

It's a moment of no return, and Ariel knows it. Slowly, he raises it to his lips, places it on his tongue, and receives the broken body of Christ into his heart.

Manna for a Tentmaker

You will know that it was the LORD when he gives you meat to eat in the evening and all the bread you want in the morning, because he has heard your grumbling against him.

EXODUS 16:8

My remarkable journey with Jesus doesn't change the reality of being unemployed. When I had been manager of advertising and public relations for a high-technology manufacturer, I loved the fast-paced excitement of it, the creativity, and the travel to European trade shows. Not to mention the paycheck and benefits—I loved that, too. Now it's all gone.

I've been searching almost a year for a new position. A single mother with a teenage mouth to feed is no joke. Two years ago, I bought our first home, so there's a mortgage to meet as well. With no paycheck coming in, it looks like our home will soon be gone, too.

My lovely townhouse—I remember the first time we saw it, Ari and me. We had wanted to move closer to my job, because the long commute gave us so little time together. After working late hours, if I had to stop for groceries, it was almost his bedtime before I got home. Too often, Ari ate his dinner alone. That wasn't good. So we had gone looking for something affordable near my office. Not an apartment, this time, but something of our own.

When we saw the three-level townhouse, we fell in love. It was beautiful. Sloped, beamed ceilings; fireplaces in the living room and master bedroom; a large patio; two communal pools, jacuzzis, and tennis courts surrounded by flowering gardens.

Instantly my mind's eye envisioned the patio paved with old brick and filled with multicolored flowers, vines and trees. Room by room, I mentally designed it for the pages of *Home & Garden* magazine, converting the family room to a floor-to-ceiling, book-lined library . . .

Ari had broken into my reverie. "Forget it, Mom . . . we'll *never* own a place like this!"

He's right, I had agreed. Then a powerful thought surged through my head: Why not? Why *not*, indeed! I put my hand on the cheek of my sweet, disappointed boy, his dark auburn hair sparkling in the sun. "We *are* going to live in this house, Ari."

"How?"

"I have no idea. But we will." Certainly, I could never qualify for a loan. But I would move heaven and earth to find a way. It didn't occur to me, back then, that this house was part of God's plan for revealing Himself in my life. In fact, it didn't occur to me that there was a God.

I was able to obtain the loan only because Julia agreed to cosign. I had old brick laid on the patio. I planted vines and flowers, pored through decorating magazines, and made the pages come true. What fun we had, Ari and I, choosing furnishings, colors, dishes. After all those years of watching every penny, working two jobs, and living without much sleep, we had a real home of our own. And we made it beautiful!

Now, just two years later, I've lost my job, and we are about to lose our house.

Dad urges me to give it up. "The house is an albatross around your neck. You're killing yourself to meet the payments."

I can't bear the thought of selling it. But it can be many months before finding work in my field. I take a temporary bookkeeping job, but my entire salary comes to less than two-thirds of the mortgage payment. And there's still food to buy, utilities, insurance, gas for the car, and job-hunting expenses! You don't get my kind of work from a classified ad. You have to network and schmooze with media reps who have the scoop about who is moving where, and who is about to lose their job, long before it reaches a newspaper or trade ad. By then it's too late; you're competing with 500 applicants. But schmoozing is expensive. I can't afford $30 lunches and bar tabs. And I can't afford not to. Out of sight, out of mind, out of the loop!

Months slip by. My savings account approaches zero, and debt is climbing. Anxiety eats away at my sleep. I share my worry with Jo, our new Sunday School teacher. She puts an arm around my shoulder and quotes Jeremiah 29:11:

> *"For I know the plans I have for you," declares the Lord. "Plans to prosper you and not to harm you, plans to give you a hope and a future."*

The words go straight to my heart. How wonderful! But, Lord, (reality check) how do I know they are meant for me? How do I know I can trust them?

In the morning, driving to my temporary bookkeeping job, I listen to a Bible teaching broadcast. Suddenly, sharply, the verse is spoken out:

"I know the plans I have for you," declares the Lord. "Plans to prosper you and not to harm you, plans to give you a hope and a future."

Twice, from two unrelated sources within 14 hours. Nice. Reassuring. Maybe even something to depend on?

Deborah stops by in the evening, as she often does when Ben works late. Tonight she carries a small package. "I brought you a present," she says. "The colors match your bedroom." How thoughtful! The first time she brought me a gift was shortly after I first arrived at her church. It was a beautiful new Bible, signed by everyone in our Sunday School class, as a welcome gesture. Now another gift? I tear the wrapping off and look at it, speechless.

"Do you like it?"

A decorative oak picture frame with a cloth-covered, floral-print mat frames a verse in hand-drawn calligraphy:

"I know the plans I have for you," declares the Lord. "Plans to prosper you and not to harm you, plans to give you a hope and a future."

"How could you know?" I stutter. This is the third confirmation in one day. A message clearly meant for me.

At this point, there is only $275 left in the bank. I send $180 of it to support the Christian Broadcasting Network. Dad says that was irresponsible and reckless when I can hardly buy groceries. But I was led in my heart to do it.

My Father in heaven, on the other hand, seems to be pleased. There comes in the mail a check for $300 from a most surprising source: Stephen! It is the first time in 15 years, and maybe the last. He owes me $37,000 for child support by now, but $300 is better than nothing, and nothing is what I've been getting. No letter. No explanation. Just an unexpected, unprecedented check.

Another miracle of provision comes when Ari begs to go to baseball camp for the summer. Baseball Camp costs $625—enough to get us through another month. "Please, Lord, be with him," I pray. "It's going to be a long, lonely summer."

Four days after that prayer, I am called to do a small brochure for a private-label shampoo. "I can pay $400," the client says. Four hundred dollars! Manna! I mustn't let him slip away.

It's an easy job, and $400 is fair. But I need $625 for the baseball camp. "I have to charge you $625," I say.

His eyes narrow. He stands, as though to end our meeting, and then says, "Okay."

At home, I fall on my knees to thank and praise God for His generosity. "You are so good to us, Lord," I say. "I'm ashamed at how often I doubt You. Forgive me. You are all we need. I've been clinging to the house, unwilling to give it up. It isn't mine, anyway; it's Yours. You gave it to us; You can certainly take it away. Just give me a little while to get used to the idea, okay? Thanks."

From that day forward, whenever I drive through poor and disadvantaged neighborhoods, I look closely at the small, dilapidated houses and the cramped, dingy apartments. I try to picture us living in one of them. Eventually, as weeks go by, my queasiness transforms to familiarity. I can finally feel comfortable with the idea of living there. I can fix up one of these old places, I tell myself, and make it cozy.

Tonight, back in my beautiful slope-ceilinged bedroom, in my "prayer chair" next to the fireplace, I'm prepared to give it up. *I'm ready, Lord. This house is Yours to take. I'll put it up for sale.*

I look around the pretty room I'll soon be packing up. My heart breaks just a little. I'm beginning to learn to trust.

Then I hear it.

Never before this moment have I heard God speak directly to me. It sounds crazy, but I don't know any other way to describe it. During that intense prayer session, just as I tell God I'm ready to sell the house, that's when I hear the soft rumble of words in my head:

Keep the house. It is My gift to you.

It isn't loud. It isn't earth shattering. It just is. I don't believe, at first, that this comes from God. *Nonsense,* I tell myself, *it's just my own desire speaking. It's what I want to hear.* Still, I obey, despite my family's continual urging to sell. I must admit I'm afraid, because if I'm mistaking my own thoughts for God's message, it can lead to disaster.

You say the house is mine, Lord? That's good. Now please tell it to the bank; they expect a payment every month!

We give up meat. Sometimes we give up meals. Debt is mounting on the credit card. I am paying bills with checks that have no cash behind them. I wonder if I'm doing the right thing. But in this desperate situation, my friends at church promise, God will show me who He is and how He works in our lives.

Maybe the Lord will find me a job in a Christian company. I hope so. I would like a Christian boss, Christian friends, a Christian husband. I'm applying to every Christian company that advertises, even if it means a drastic cut in pay.

The Lord closes all those doors. There's no money left for networking luncheons at the professional societies, and that puts me out of the circuit. I'll *never* get a job if no one sees me!

Please, God, do something!

I pray this on four or five occasions. Every time I do—*every* time—the telephone rings and I'm invited to interview for a position. None of these particular opportunities materialize, but God is letting me know, unmistakably, that He doesn't need networking lunches to open doors. His message is loud and clear: *Don't depend on networking to get a job. Depend on Me.*

The call that comes in this morning has got to be "it." The job fits my background and experience to a tee. I'm invited to a nice restaurant for a dinner interview by the president. It goes well—I know it does. I'm convinced the job is mine.

But it's not mine; it goes to someone else. Lord, are You asleep at the post?

Silence.

Friends and family say I'm nuts to keep the house; but to sell it feels like a breach of faith. Unemployment has been dragging on for 16 long months. Temporary office jobs and freelance work don't pay a fraction of our bills. Savings are long gone, and we're in debt for $8,000! This is as far as my faith can go.

I prepare to put the house on the market; and that's when two job offers come along. One is with a software manufacturer—something I have lots of experience with. The other is from one of the largest, prestigious international accounting and consulting firms. But I don't do accounting firms. My specialty is high-tech and product marketing. Professional services require a completely different set of programs, and I imagine they'd be boring. Besides, a 90-minute commute to work downtown is crazy. The software company is only 10 minutes from home.

The right choice is clear: accept the company close to home, where I know the industry and the market well. I want to call in my acceptance right away, but something holds me back. I go quickly to my prayer chair for a discussion with you-know-who.

Dear Lord, thank You for these two opportunities. Two is better than one for lifting my morale after such a long time unemployed! But I don't want to make a move without seeking Your guidance, Lord. Obviously I belong at the software company, right?

The still, small voice again . . .

The accounting firm.

He's joking, of course.

Silence.

The silence sits heavily on me. Heavily. Admonishing me. I prayed for guidance, and I got it. Now I want to ignore it, because it doesn't make sense. And yet . . . something tells me I had better obey.

Obedience, at this moment, is very hard. It's so *scary* when you're in desperate circumstances and you have to obey something that defies all logic. This must be what the Israelites in the desert felt like when poisonous snakes were biting at their feet and they were told to look upward, toward the top of a pole.

Trembling, I pick up the phone and tell KPMG that I am honored to join their firm as marketing director.

Six months pass. Ben calls with news that the software company I had wanted to join, the one that was "perfect" for me, has gone belly-up. "If you had taken that job," he says, "you'd be out on the street again now!"

See? I can almost hear God say. *I watch over you, My child of little faith!*

And my fear it would be boring at the accounting firm? Ha! My position is turning out to be the most interesting, the highlight of my career. In my own limited wisdom, I'd have passed it up. Once more, the lesson is driven home: *Father knows best!*

At KPMG, I develop the first marketing and public relations program for the Los Angeles area. It is so well received that the national firm applies a modified version to their 144 offices throughout the country. And my initiative in taking an "industry-specific" approach to marketing the firm's services now has my department juggling 16 full-scale marketing programs. By the third year, there are such impressive results, they appoint me to the Executive Steering Committee, which sets marketing policies for the firm nationwide. So now, four times a year, I travel to headquarters in New York—and I can see Lorna!

It is funny: the job I thought would be dull turns out to be an exciting and privileged entrée into the top echelons of the Los Angeles business community. I'm developing a network of powerful contacts. It's an experience for which I thank God, one that few people get to enjoy. Materially, the firm provides abundant benefits and a salary that generously fulfills the Lord's promise that the house would be mine. Paying the mortgage is no problem now. By the end of the first year, my $8,000 debt is repaid.

In my fourth year, we merge with another international accounting firm and establish global headquarters in Amsterdam. At last! For so many years I've longed to live and work in Europe again. Now I can do it! Ironically, however, the opportunity comes when my son is no longer "portable." In earlier years, I'd have picked him up and taken him along. But he is in college now and has a life of his own. I couldn't live so far from him.

God comes to work with me every day. When I have projects I don't know how to handle, I ask for His help and they get done extremely well.

There is a problem, however, with my secretary. She had wanted my position and resents that they hired me. She tries to sabotage everything that I do. I try talking kindly to her. I offer to train and mentor her. Nothing works. Frankly, I want to fire her, but her father is a big client of the firm and my boss won't let me. Meanwhile, her sullen face and refusal to cooperate make my job a living hell. "Lord! Please help!" He helps. Three days later, she walks into my office and resigns. Now I can hire a secretary who will really support me.

Another situation needs help too. I had hired a graphics artist, a good kid with a fine aesthetic sense. But she doesn't understand marketing, and she screws up occasionally on proofreading.

The senior partner on a major account we're proposing to bursts into my office. "I want that idiot fired!"

"Please, Walter, let's discuss this. Firing someone is very serious."

Placing both hands on my desk, he leans across, his face close to mine. "Running a slide presentation with a client's name in bold, back-lit, *misspelled* letters is very serious. See that she's out of here today." He stomps out, slamming the door.

I rush into my boss's office. "I don't want to let her go, Dennis. She has to improve her proofreading, but she's a fine artist and hardworking. What can I do?"

"Don't antagonize Walter."

"Dennis! I can't fire her for one mistake. Granted it was bad . . ." Dennis shrugs. It's amazing how little someone's job means to these people. "If I'm forced to fire her, Dennis, I'll leave too. It's not right."

"You'll have to deal with Walter. There can be repercussions."

In Walter's office, I apologize humbly for the error and promise it won't happen again. "I'd like to give her a chance," I entreat.

"What comes out of that department is a reflection on *you*," Walter hisses. "We expect you to set standards."

Now both our jobs are on the line. I call Victoria into my office. "I understand you were focused on the aesthetics, Vicki, but you must be meticulous from now on; we have a lot at stake." She promises to be careful. "I'll be praying for you," I tell her, "for both of us." It's uncomfortable saying that in a corporate environment. You never know how someone will react.

"Please do," Victoria responds. "I've been thinking lately that I should go back to church. It's been a long time."

My heart leaps. It is hard to integrate God into my work world. But I need Him here as much as anywhere. Others do too.

Julia and I spend a weekend in the mountains, at a retreat. The program has built-in periods of silence four hours a day. Walking in the woods or near the stream, reading, praying, sleeping or eating, together or alone, we speak not a word. Evenings we come together in the fireside lodge to share our experience of the silence. For some of us, nothing happens. For others, there are revelations.

The fire crackles. People share what they experienced during the silent time. Where is my sister? Oh, she's in the back of the room, next to a blonde woman in our group, about 50 years old. I had noticed her the first day. Noticed and dismissed. Without having spoken a word, I decide she's not my type, not "interesting." These aren't conscious thoughts, of course, just an instantaneous impression. She's attractive and well dressed. Too well dressed, actually. Perfect grooming and accessories, perfectly coiffed hair, a perfect drape and fit to her clothes. Her understated style speaks of money. Lots of money, lots of time spent on creating that tasteful perfection. I assume, in my omniscient wisdom, that she must be superficial, must have her priorities out of whack. I'm not surprised that Julia is with her. Julia is attracted to people with money and "status."

I pull my attention back to the group. The sharing reveals a lot about people. Someone behind me is talking about horrendous ordeals she's experienced in recent years and how, in the silence of the afternoon, the Lord has revealed His constant protection of her. The speaker's voice conveys humility and a rich spiritual maturity. I'm impressed; it will be years before I walk that closely with God. I'd like to get to know this person better. I turn to see who it is.

Blondie! No, it can't be. Perhaps the voice is coming from her right? No. It's Blondie, all right, Blondie revealing the richness of her walk and the depth of her communion with the Holy Spirit. It belies her appearance. The incongruity makes her interesting.

My sister introduces us and I join them for a walk. Irene is a woman who once had everything and lost it all. A modern-day female Job, she had lost her husband, her business, her home, her health and her daughter's affection. Most recently, her 20-year-old grandson, a wonderful boy and her closest love, was diagnosed with bone cancer. "In all this," she is assured, "the Lord preserves, shelters, and keeps me safe."

Irene's spirit, her gracious outreach, and her adoration of Jesus are an inspiration. If she knew what I'd been thinking about her earlier, I'd die. But I can't hide my presumptuous thoughts from the Lord, and I feel Him laughing at me. *Okay,* I concede, *You made Your point; I'm in no position to judge Your loved ones. Forgive me. I'm an arrogant fool, and I've learned a lesson.*

Apparently the Lord accepts my apology, because He gives me the gift of Irene's friendship. Several months later, she invites Julia and me to her home in Rancho Mirage, near Palm Springs. Since we'd last seen her, the Lord has worked miracles to restore Irene's circumstances. She now lives in an exclusive country club, plays golf with Bob Hope, visits with Betty Ford, and moves in the social circles of her upscale past. I wonder how she reconciles her spiritual life with her affluent material surroundings.

"It's a desert out there," I say.

"You noticed," Julia says dryly.

"I mean spiritually. Irene, isn't it hard to find people you can relate to?"

"Not at all. My life is here. My friends. It's my world. And it's my mission field." I squint a skeptical eye. "Yes, it's true. Most people in Palm Springs don't know the Lord. Many of the women, married to rich absentee or philandering husbands, are alcoholics. Believe me, in a land that worships a green-backed Baal, I have my work cut out for me."

Irene gives us a tour of the community. "I'm a good missionary for these neighbors, because they trust me. I wear the same fashion labels they do. We know the same people and speak the same language. When I invite these women to hear the gospel, I send engraved invitations to meet a celebrity. They come to an elegant house in an upscale neighborhood and partake of refreshments on fine china and sterling silver. You understand? I create an environment where they're comfortable. I'm credible. Then they're willing to listen." Aha. The Lord restored her home in the country club and uses it for His work. Irene smiles gently. "The Lord Jesus isn't prejudiced, Barbara. He comes to nice houses too."

I swallow hard. Does she know what a self-righteous idiot I was? Or is the Lord enjoying His joke on me?

On Sunday we visit Irene's church, a Christ-centered, Bible-based congregation of wealthy, influential people who love the Lord profoundly and consecrate their holdings to His work. Irene, the woman I'd been quick to snub, becomes a spiritual mentor. I learn a lesson in humility as, once again, the cosmic Script Writer brings forth treasure from a fool's colossal arrogance.

The telephone is ringing. It's Irene, and she's excited. "Remember my grandson, Brett?" I remember. A terrific kid about Ari's age who'd been ill with cancer. "I'm taking him to Israel!" she says.

"That's wonderful, Irene. I'm so glad to hear he's well again. What a fabulous way to spend time with him."

"Our church is doing the tour. I was hoping you and Ari would join us. What do you say?"

"Israel?"

"It's a Bible study tour to trace the life of Jesus. Oh, say yes; it'll be so fun to do together."

Israel! What a special thing to share with Ari, especially now that he'll be going away to university. It would be a vacation to remember. What the heck, I'm working now. What better way to spend our money? "When?"

"In two months. We meet with our pastor every Tuesday night for an overview of Israel's history and geography before we go. It's a good way to get to know one another too. Come next Tuesday?"

The trip, 14 days of non-stop extraordinary experiences, leaves us breathless. We are led by Irene's Christian pastor. Our official guide is Baruch, a Jewish professor of archeology; Mahmoud, the Arab bus driver, is our unofficial guide. What we learn about archeology's verification of biblical history is astounding.

Baruch leads us on a trail that climbs a hill. Up, up, up. To still our groans, he promises a great view at the top. Finally, reaching the high plateau, we pause, look around, and gasp. He didn't tell us—and we didn't expect—this sudden, spectacular vision of the Sea of Galilee spread out in a calm, sun-speckled blue beneath us. The Sea of Galilee! Where Jesus walked the shore, talked with His disciples, taught and blessed all who crossed His path. It's as if we all stop breathing collectively. In the hushed, awestruck silence, Pastor reads from Jesus' teachings. We pray. In these magical moments, even Baruch admits to feeling Jesus sit among us and embrace us with His love.

Mornings we are up at 5:30, and we go nonstop until evening. We trek miles under a burning desert sun. We swim in the salty Dead Sea. We climb Masada and relive the story of the Jews' mass suicide to avoid having their women and children enslaved by the cruel Romans. We see the rejoicing of a bar mitzvah at the Wailing Wall.

An angry Arab accosts us with a knife when our pastor opens his Bible and reads to us at the Dome of the Rock. We even meet a Samaritan (yes, there are still a handful of them left today), and I am horrified to see the sacrificial pit in which they continue the practice of offering animals for atonement, as in ancient days. By evening, we are too tired to lift a fork to get food into our mouths; we crawl, collapsing, into bed.

Tonight we decide to "go out on the town" in Caesarea. It's ten o'clock, but Mahmoud, our driver, says that's too early. "The good night spots don't open until after twelve, or one. The others, pah! For tourists. Wait. I'll take you later."

With three hours to wait, we wander the quiet streets and grassy areas in the dark. People nod, greeting passersby. A man plays a guitar, singing for his wife and small son who sit with him on the lawn. The danger Israelis live with is not like ours. We cannot stroll our streets at night. Their towns are peaceful, friendly and gentle. Their killings are political, not random, like ours.

At one o'clock we rejoin Mahmoud. Even though it's a Tuesday night, the place he takes us to is jammed. Israelis play hard and they play late. When do they sleep? How do they get up for work in the morning? It's one of the unexplainable mysteries of Israel.

Mahmoud's second daughter is getting married. He invites four of us to the wedding, and we leave the group to attend. This is my first Muslim wedding. We sit on cushions in a room full of veiled women who chat, animated, in Arabic. Many fine dishes are spread before us on mats across the floor. The men eat somewhere else.

After the meal, I follow the women and their small children into another room, adjacent to the wedding hall. When it is their turn to dance, the women pull me along with them. They gyrate with graceful, undulating movements, an embodiment of feminine sensuality. The men watch from afar; they do not dance with the women. When it is their turn, they dance robust, masculine dances that the women watch. Never do the bride and groom dance. They sit stiffly, side by side, in high thronelike chairs and observe. Most likely they are wondering, *Who is this life partner my family chose for me? Please, God, let it be someone I can find attractive.*

The wedding goes beyond the end of night and the break of dawn. How will Mahmoud be in any shape to drive as our tour continues? And, having paid for this celebration, how can he afford not to?

The pastor guides us, chronologically, from one site to another, through the life of Jesus—where He was born, where He grew up; and to the Jordan River where He'd been baptized by John. Several in our group are baptized now in that same river. The rest of us, perched on rocks along the riverbank, watch our brothers and sisters dip beneath the water's surface. We witness the continuity of 2,000 years. Then, standing on the spot where Jesus looked into the eyes of Peter and asked, "And you, Simon, who do you say that I am?" Pastor faces each of us in the group and, one by one, asks each of us the same question.

"And you, Barbara," his eyes fix steadily on mine, "who do *you* say Jesus is?"

This is the moment of my true confession. Words come trembling from a deep place in my heart. "He is the Son of the Living God, the promised Messiah, the Lord of my salvation."

An old rabbi guards the tomb of Joseph. He is suspicious of Christians coming to visit this sacred son of Jacob. "Joseph is beloved of the Jews," he growls, unwilling to stand aside and let us pass.

"He is the beloved of our faithful ones, as well," Pastor Paul assures him. While the rest of us visit the tomb, our pastor engages the rabbi in discussion. The rabbi comes to realize this pastor knows Old Testament Scripture well, and that it is sacred to us. Our reverence for the tomb also does not go unnoticed. By the time our visit ends, the old rabbi has a warm embrace for the Christian pastor and a fond farewell for the group.

On to Jericho, to Herod's winter palace and the caves where David hid from the wrath of Saul. Along the road are Arabs, camels, nomads, the site where Jesus gave His sermon on the mount, the Via Dolorosa where He carried such a heavy cross, and the tomb where Jesus was buried. On a grassy area, just outside the tomb, our pastor conducts a Communion service. It is overwhelming to take the body and blood of Jesus into ourselves at the very spot where He was laid to rest after His supreme sacrifice.

Churches mark the sites where something significant took place in the life of Jesus. "This is where Mary drew water daily from the well, the center of village life. Her little son, no doubt, came with her to play with other children at the well," the guide explains. I see no well, no village. I see only a church. "This is where Jesus delivered His sermon on the mount to the crowds gathered around." What mount? What crowds? I see a church. I don't like the "marker" churches in Israel. Why couldn't they leave the sites as they were?

Filing into the Church of Saint Anne, we begin, in soft voices, to sing the *Alleluia*. Gentle melody fills the white stone space with the Spirit's love. A group of German Christians arrives. They stop near the entrance, silenced by our song, then enter and join in with quiet, reverent harmonies. These German brothers and sisters sing with us in a language we don't understand, in ancient Israel, whose time warp we cannot enter. It is a moment when the voices of angels join the worship of God's humblest servants, a brief, ephemeral moment when the heavens open to let us in.

Israel carves indelible pictures on my mind. One above all others is a small dungeon where Jesus was held prisoner for several days after His interrogation by Pilate, and before His crucifixion. It's a tiny cavelike stone room. Pastor guides us down tight, narrow steps to enter. Three people would fill this space, but we are 40, packed like sardines, and pressed against the walls. Claustrophobia attacks and I am hyperventilating. I have to leave.

Quietly, but forcibly, I push my way through the crowd to an opening in the wall. I squeeze through to escape the sad little room where Jesus must have contemplated His impending torture. What terrible days they must have been for Him! *Ahhh . . . I can breathe now!* The adjacent room is even smaller, but I am here alone. I press against the coolness of the stone wall, overcome. It is dreary, dismal. A nasty little place. *Dear Jesus, I'm so sorry You had to be here and go through all this for us. So sorry we are hopeless sinners and that Your atonement is the only way to bring us into communion with God. How I would love to be with You, to know You, see You, hear You. Will You come to me?*

In the dark and dreary places, says the still, small voice, *I will come to you in the dark and dreary places where you are afraid.*

I have returned to the elegant, glass-walled, carpeted halls of KPMG in the high-rise tower of downtown Los Angeles. Is this where I'm supposed to be?

"You wondered if Palm Desert could be a mission field," Irene reminds me. "How about the corporate halls for you? You think God can't work through you inside tall office buildings?"

I am at my desk, concentrating on drafting a report. A thought breaks in, more of an urge, really, to walk down the hall to the office of the firm's senior national SEC partner. Not sure why I'm to go, I follow the prompting, and knock on Abe's door.

"You read my mind," Abe says. "I was just about to call you. Here is some additional information for your report." We discuss the report, and I am about to leave when I notice books on Abe's shelf about Yiddish literature and theater. They have his name on the cover.

"My gosh, you wrote these?" Abe nods. "I know nothing about Yiddish literature and theater. Can you enlighten me?"

"Sure. If you have time for lunch, I'll give you an overview."

Settled in a booth at the corner Chinese restaurant, having talked for an hour about his favorite subject, Abe abruptly asks, "You're Jewish, aren't you?"

"Yes." I could let it go at that and not complicate my life at work. But it feels dishonest. "Actually," I brace myself, "I'm a Jewish Christian."

"A what?"

"A Jew who believes that Jesus, the Messiah, has come."

"Jesus? So you're a Christian. Jews don't believe in Jesus."

"Some of us do. And we don't stop being Jewish. One can't."

Abe shakes his gray-bearded head. "I'm confused; I never heard of such a thing."

"Well, I hadn't either. But I discovered there are thousands of Jewish Christians in Los Angeles—and everywhere else in the world too."

"Strange." Abe picks up his chopsticks. "Very odd."

What possessed me to say that to a senior partner? Is God using me here? Or is Satan jeopardizing my career? At various times, Abe and I chat about Yiddish literature, our families, his books, even my activities at church. I am afraid, at first, that I will offend him, but he seems, despite my "defection," to have an affection for me.

Several months later, Abe is hospitalized with a stroke. I send get-well notes to his home. After his recovery and return to work, he introduces me to his wife. "Sylvia, this is the little gal I told you about. She says she's a Christian. But she's so sweet, we know she must still be a Jew."

Kelley is my counterpart in the firm's Phoenix office. We've worked together on several projects. Today she calls to ask if I'm going to the national marketing meeting in New Jersey next month.

"Yes. Are you?"

"Yes! Want to go together?"

We coordinate our flights and plan to stay the weekend after the company meeting ends.

"You know what," I propose, "I grew up in Princeton. It's a beautiful town. Let's drive up and I'll show you around."

"Great," she agrees. "I also grew up nearby, in Greenwich, Connecticut. Let's spend a day there too." For three fun-filled days we revisit our childhood and teenage memories.

"This is the little Catholic church I went to as a child," Kelley parks our rented car near the entrance. "Do you mind stopping in for a minute?" We enter the quiet sanctuary with wooden pews under arched, stained-glass windows lining the sidewalls. "There's a lot of nostalgia for me here." Kelley slips into a pew and kneels.

"Do you still go to church?"

"No. It seems like an empty ritual now."

"Would it seem like an empty ritual if you knew God personally, and felt He knew you?"

"I never had that feeling."

There are Bibles in the pew racks. I pick one up, open to John 10, and read aloud:

I am the good shepherd; I know my sheep and my sheep know me . . . He calls His own sheep by name and leads them out . . .

. . . by name, Kelley, you hear?

My sheep listen to my voice; I know them, and they follow me. I give them eternal life, and they shall never perish; no one can snatch them out of my hand.

Kelley bows her head and tears course down her cheeks. I put my hand on her hair. "He must have forgotten my name by now," she whispers.

"Do you recognize His voice, Kelley?" She nods. "Only His sheep recognize His voice, so you must be one of them. And no one can snatch you out of His hand."

"I want to follow Him," she sobs. "It's been so long."

"His hand is outstretched for you. Reach up and take it." Kelley and I remain a long time, praying together, in that little church in Greenwich. It's the town where she was born. Today it is the town where she is reborn.

"Something happened in there," Kelley says when we drive to the airport. "My life won't ever be the same. I have to tell my daughters. Oh, there's a lot I've neglected in their upbringing."

"Don't get 'religious' on me, now. I still have to work with you!"

She lightens up. "I know. Not religious. Learning at the feet of Jesus."

I've been summoned for jury duty. I don't mind; the firm pays me while I'm here. Waiting to be selected for a trial in the jury lounge, I catch up on reading. Two men, probably in their early thirties, sit together every day at the back of the room. They are engaged in a nonstop discussion, their voices very low, their heads close. I look up frequently from my book, wondering what they can be talking about.

On the eleventh day, a group of us are called for jury selection. One of the two men I've been watching stands right behind me in line. "Hope we get chosen for a jury," he says. "It's pretty boring just waiting."

I smile and dare to observe, "*You* haven't seemed bored. Looks like you were involved in some pretty intense discussions."

"Yeah." He hesitates, then decides to confide. "That guy back there," he shifts his eyes in the direction of his companion who sits alone now in the rear of the room, "I don't know why he picked *me*, but he's a Mormon and he's been trying to convert me for three days. There's no stopping him."

"Oh." So there's been a spiritual battle going on back there. I had no way of knowing, but I'd been drawn to watch by the Spirit! "And what do you think? Is it for you?"

"It doesn't feel right."

"Why not?" Our line has moved up now. We won't have much longer to talk.

"I can't say exactly. Don't get me wrong; he's a very nice guy. But the more he talks about God and the Book of Mormon, the more uncomfortable I get."

"Do you believe in God?"

"Don't know. I suppose. We weren't religious in my family. Didn't go to church except, sometimes, on Christmas. But I guess we believed in God."

"Oh, by the way, my name is Barbara. What's yours?"

"Taylor. Nice to meet you. Looks like we're next. Why don't you meet me here after the interview and we'll see if either of us gets picked for a jury. Maybe take a break for lunch?"

"Great. There's a little Thai place across the street."

My interview is not long. I'm chosen as a juror on a car theft case. I wait outside for Taylor who arrives 10 minutes later. He grins. "They picked me! The case is supposed to last two-and-a-half weeks. Car theft."

"Ha! We're sitting on the same jury!"

"Would you believe that? It's 1 in 100. I guess we're destined to spend some time together. C'mon. Thai food sounds good."

He was just kidding about the "destiny," but I know it's true.

The restaurant is small and quiet. We chat about our work, our families, all the usual introductory stuff. But I'm burning with curiosity. "So tell me, Taylor, why were you uncomfortable talking with the man in the jury lounge? It looked like you were interested."

"I can't tell you why. I tried to argue with him, but he had answers to everything. Not that I know anything about it; I was just arguing instinctively."

"What point of view were you arguing? What is your understanding of God? Who do you think He is?"

He laughs. "Boy, you sure ask the tough ones. I don't know! I suppose He created the universe. Who do *you* think He is?"

We are into it now. Sharing what I understand of Jesus, and what I've learned about God from the Bible, our lunch flies by quickly and we have to return. Before they usher us into the jury room, Taylor leans over to whisper, "I like talking to you. Okay to have lunch tomorrow?"

"Sure."

We have lunch every day for two-and-a-half weeks. The trial is engrossing and we are dying to talk about it, but we're not allowed. Taylor picks up our conversation about God and the Bible. I have to be careful. "I don't want to bore you with all this. It's my favorite subject, but I *can* talk about other things."

"No, no. I *want* to talk about it. This is what's missing in my life."

The trial is over. Time to go back to our work, our families, and normal life. Taylor walks me to my car in the parking lot for the last time. "I probably won't see you again," I say, shaking his hand, "but before we go, I'm wondering where you stand." He looks puzzled. "I'm just wondering . . ." Take a deep breath. "Taylor, who do *you* say Jesus is?"

He is still holding my hand. "Jesus . . ." he begins. The hold gets tighter and his hand shakes. Taylor closes his eyes and tears squeeze through. He lets them flow. A grown man, in a public parking lot, with people passing in broad daylight, his tears splashing on our hands, which are still locked in a farewell shake. "Jesus is the living God." The realization hits him. He says it again. And again. He tells me he is going to start a new life, a life for himself and his family, with Jesus as their Lord and Savior. He says they'll join a church and study the Bible.

"God bless you." We hug, and part. He heads north. I turn west. We both follow the same Master.

Breakfast is served promptly at 7:30 in the California Club, an exclusive conclave that few Jews or women get to see. I have to be there for the monthly meeting of executive partners. It won't do to be late. Unfortunately, I left the marketing status report in my office, just across the street; I can run up quickly and still be on time.

Seven-fifteen. There are few people this early in the lobby of the downtown high-rise where my office is located. The elevators wait, doors open. I enter one of them and press the button for the twenty-ninth floor. Just as the doors begin to close, a young black man (27 or 28?) jumps on board. He reaches past me and presses the button for 35. We begin the ascent, each of us standing in opposite corners, as strangers in elevators tend to do, looking up at the changing floor numbers, wordless.

The elevator stops. The lights go out. In pitch-black blindness, the car lurches violently back and forth, swinging on its cables, and plunges downward. Down, down—I don't know how many floors, but we're headed for a brutal crash—down, down, and . . . the elevator jolts to a stop.

The lights come back on. Where are we? The numbers indicating the floors do not function. It is small and stuffy in the car. Claustrophobia clutches my lungs. I swallow my breath.

"Excuse me." A voice from the other corner. I almost forgot he was there. "My name is Thomas Davidson and my heart is about to burst through my chest."

"Oh! I'm Barbara Ilaynia. I'm not feeling too great either right now."

Thomas presses the alarm button. It clangs loudly through the elevator shaft. "That should get some attention." He forces a smile to reassure me. But moments, then minutes, pass and there is no response. He rings again, repeatedly. Surely they won't ignore such a loud alarm. Fifteen more minutes, and nothing.

"Wonder what is going on?"

Claustrophobia has gone into hyperventilating. Unable to breathe normally, panic creeps in. "Thomas," I gasp. "Talk to me. Tell me the story of your life."

"Sure." He sees I'm in trouble. "Okay. I was born in Washington, DC. My mom is still there . . ."

"What's she like, your mom?"

Thomas talks, bless his heart; he keeps on talking. Another half hour passes. I take off my high heels and we sit on the floor, pretending not to be terrified. We hit the alarm three or four more times. No response.

"Here." I hand Thomas a pad of paper from my briefcase. "We can play tic-tac-toe."

"Great." He wins five in a row. "Shall we try something else? Hangman's Noose?"

"Maybe this isn't the best time."

"Oh, sorry."

I dig into my briefcase again. Where is . . . ? I always carry a tiny little Bible in here, never knew why, maybe for occasions like this, but it's gone. Just when you need it most, right? "You wouldn't happen to have a Bible on you?"

"No, sorry." His eyebrows shoot up and he reaches into his back pocket. "Wait. It's not a Bible, but will this help?" He hands me four small pages from a daily devotional. On each is a verse, and several paragraphs about the meaning of the verse.

"You carry pages from a devotional?"

"Not usually. My roommate asked me to read it. Today, when I was leaving the apartment, he shoved these pages into my hand and said 'take this with you. You might need it.' I figured it was easier to take it than argue. Could he have known . . .?"

"He didn't know; but God did. So let's see. It isn't much, but it's sure better than nothing." I read aloud. Thomas and I find ourselves in a theological discussion that carries us through the next hour and a half.

We've been in the elevator now for more than two hours. I need a bathroom. They don't give you instructions for when you're trapped in an elevator and need a bathroom. No laughing matter. Claustrophobia flares again and chokes me.

We hear sirens—the kind that warn you when a building is on fire. Fire! And we are trapped where you should never be in a fire: the elevator shaft. Thomas and I look at one another, at the person with whom we'll share the second most important moment of our existence: our death.

I'm hyperventilating again. "I don't mind dying. I'm ready to go home when God will have me. But I don't want to suffocate first. Or burn."

"Tell me about 'going home,'" he says.

"Wait!" I hold up my hand. In the elevator, a moment ago, there were only Thomas and me. Now . . . "Thomas! Do you feel it? It's Jesus! He's here with us. There were two of us in here, and now we are three. Yet, somehow, it's less crowded." Safe, now, in the comfort of His Presence, I recall another claustrophobic space, the sad little dungeon in Israel, where a small, still voice had said:

In the dark and dreary places, there shall I be with you. I will come to you in the close and dreary places where you are afraid.

My heart is calm. I can breathe. The claustrophobia, the pressure in my bladder, and my fears are gone. Thomas opens his eyes with a smile that reflects my own like a mirror.

"You feel it, too, don't you?" Thomas nods, unable to speak. "What're you going to do about it, Thomas?"

"I'll follow Him all the days of my life," he whispers.

Okay, Lord, if You had Your finger on this man's heart, if this is one of Your chosen, I'm proud You trapped me in the elevator with him to get his attention. And if we have to die now, to live with You forever, that's okay, too. But do me a favor. We've been inside this narrow box close to three hours now. Bring it quickly to an end.

The elevator moves. Down. Slowly, controlled, it is moving down. The floor numbers light up and function again. Five, four, three, two, lobby. We stand up, put on our shoes, and try to straighten our wrinkled clothes. The doors slide open.

We see no evidence of a fire. Dozens of people stare at us, shouting, "There are people in there!" Didn't they know? We are helped out, given coffee. One voice says, "Sorry, we didn't know anyone was in there."

"Didn't you hear the alarm? We kept ringing the alarm!"

"Security was away, shutting off gas valves and water pipes . . . the biggest earthquake since '69. Here, miss, can we help you up to your office?"

Get into that elevator again and ride up 29 floors? No way. I have to find another job. Where's Thomas? I can't see him in the crowd. Thomas is at my elbow, guiding me through the crowded lobby. "Come on, we'll get some fresh air and a bite to eat. We need to settle down a bit."

"I need a bathroom."

"That, too."

"Oh my gosh! The meeting at the California Club—I was supposed to present a report. Oh, this might mean my job!"

"I don't think so." Behind me, a distinguished gentleman puts his hand on my shoulder. It is our managing partner, Mr. Sanders. "The meeting was brought to an abrupt end by the earthquake. We'll hear your report another time. Why don't you take the day off."

I glance toward the elevators. "Tomorrow I'll have to ride up to the twenty-ninth floor." I shake at the thought.

"You've had a terrible experience in there."

"Yes, Mr. Sanders, but you know what? It was extraordinary too." Thomas approaches. "Mr. Sanders, this is Thomas . . ." He steps forward to shake Mr. Sanders's hand. "He was trapped in there with me."

"The two of you, eh? Well, it's merciful you weren't alone."

"Actually . . ." I can't believe I'm going to say this to the Managing Partner . . . "Actually, Mr. Sanders, it wasn't two of us. It was three." He raises one eyebrow, waiting for the explanation. I take the plunge. "Jesus was in there too. We both felt His Presence."

Mr. Sanders says nothing for a moment. Then, "Hmm, yes."

How stupid to have said that. It was a career-limiting move.

Mr. Sanders clears his throat. "Yes, well, it's been a long time, a very long time, since I've been to church. Perhaps I should focus a little more in that direction." He returns to the building.

Thomas and I head for a coffee shop. When we've eaten a bite and settled down, we say good-bye and go home. I sleep well and wake refreshed. The idea of returning to my office via the elevator is unappealing, but one does have to work, after all.

In the lobby I steel myself, wait for another passenger or two to arrive, then enter the elevator and hold my breath until we stop at the twenty-ninth floor. Mr. Sanders is in the main lobby when I arrive. I flush, embarrassed at how I had blurted out my experience of Jesus to him.

"Good morning, Barbara. I see you made it."

"Good morning, Mr. Sanders. You'll have to excuse me for yesterday. I was very shaken."

"There's nothing to excuse. You've given me something to think about."

He's a gracious man. Or could he be sincerely thinking about it? I'll never know. God uses us in strange ways.

"Morning, Barbara." My secretary hands messages to me. "Would you like coffee?"

"I would indeed, thanks!" I enter my office and there, on my desk, is a glorious bouquet of yellow roses. Who in the world . . .? There's a card.

Dear Barbara, the Lord knew what He was doing when He put us together in the elevator. How can I thank you enough? How can I thank Him? You are, and will always be, very special to me. I will never forget you. Love, your brother, Thomas.

The corporate world is where God has me for now and where He has His work for me. Irene was right; the glass high-rise towers of downtown Los Angeles are my mission field. This is where the Lord has me speak to people like Vicki, Abe, Kelley, Tyler, Thomas, and Mr. Sanders. There can be others.

The Lord has blessed me beyond all I asked for here at KPMG. I get to see how movers and shakers in the international business community get things done. I'm developing professional and leadership skills; I can afford to buy nice things, eat in elegant restaurants and, best of all, travel. Apart from vacations in Europe and Israel, there are the quarterly company meetings in New York that make it possible to see Lorna.

Lorna cannot understand my interest in the business community; she's convinced it pollutes my existence. "You don't write anymore, you don't grow artistically. You use all your energy and talent to make money for an international mega-corporation. There's no meaning in that."

But I don't seek "meaning" anymore. Not in art or politics or work. I don't seek it because, as a child of God, I have found it.

This year, the annual conference of the Public Relations Society is in Toronto, when the colors of October are ablaze. I find a little church where I can worship on Sunday. The service ends at 10:30, and I prepare to leave. Oddly, no one else is going home. The singing and praising continue spontaneously. Some songs are mellow and poignant. Others are foot-stomping and energetic, joyous and celebrating. People lift their hands high in the air and close their eyes. Others dance and clap in the aisles. Some leave to feed children, then return. At 2:30, I decide to leave, but there is still no sign of worship winding down. I wonder if it's like this every week.

A meeting takes me to Washington, DC; it's my first time here. The beauty of the architecture and monuments in the nation's capital amazes me. One monument, in particular, shakes me to my soul as I walk through the park at night and approach its white splendor: it is the Lincoln Memorial where Abe Lincoln, towering above me, sits on his white throne.

He is huge, brilliantly lit against the black sky, carved of smooth alabaster stone, yet somehow very human. I look up in awe and whisper, "Hello, my brother. I wish I had known you. But I will one day, won't I?" It isn't a feeling; it's a certainty, a knowing. I will be in his physical presence and know him. "My brother?" Why did I call him that?

I do a little research. Abraham Lincoln had, in fact, become a born-again Christian at Gettysburg. How did my heart know that, standing before the memorial aglow against a dark night? From what source had I been filled with such certainty, a whispered knowledge that transcends my own experience?

Grandma Kate didn't even know what the word meant when she foretold that Lorna would become a shaman. Lorna says it means a healer; her purpose is to serve those who are ill. She uses "medicines," the natural drugs of the earth.

I'll be in New York again this winter. Lorna is pleased that I will be there in time for her Shamanic Fire Ceremony. I'm curious to see what it is, and I'm glad Lorna wants to share it. But from the deeply visceral, intuitive part of me comes a warning. Entering the realm of these spirits, one should be well prepared, fully protected by the armor of God. Lorna would be furious, profoundly offended, if she thought I attributed her source of power to anything other than God—or the god-force—as she calls it. Our friendship struggles with our spiritual differences. If we really respected each other's choice, it would be all right. But she has contempt for Christianity (she denies that, but it comes out continually in subtle and sometimes not-so-subtle ways). For my part, while I do recognize her honesty and commitment, I believe Lorna has chosen a false and dangerous direction, one that draws from spiritual realms that are not of God.

There are longer and longer stretches of time between our calls. We are becoming more comfortable, each in our own community, than we are with one another. Are we slipping apart?

I pray for wisdom about the Fire Ceremony. Something Joshua said in the Old Testament keeps coming to my mind, and I pray it over and over. "Lord, whereupon I plant my feet, I claim that land for you." Through prayer, my faith grows bold and I am unafraid—indeed, eager—for the encounter. I envision bringing with me the presence and power of the one true God.

Pastor Paul and others in our midweek prayer group pray about it too. They surround my chair, each laying a hand on me. Prayer is intense and long. For 20, 30, 40 minutes we pray in the name and authority of Jesus against spirits that would pull us away from God. With my eyes closed, the hands upon my body feel like a cushion on which I rest my weight, reclining, it seems, in the very palm of God's hand.

"We will lift you up during service next Sunday," Pastor says. "You'll be well covered in prayer when you arrive at Lorna's, I promise."

The meeting in New York ends on Friday afternoon. I call Lorna to let her know what time I'll be at her house tomorrow.

"Good. I'm preparing for the Fire Ceremony, rearranging furniture so we can form one large circle and connect everybody by holding hands."

A circle. A closed circle. For some reason, the image makes me uncomfortable. "I won't be in the circle, holding hands, Lorna. I'll just watch from a corner where I won't bother anyone."

Lorna is appalled. "You won't join our circle? I thought you were coming to participate?"

"Well, I'm coming to learn more about it, to see firsthand what it is. I don't know yet if I'll be right in it."

"I'm sorry, Barbara," her voice is crisp with disappointment, "that's not acceptable. If you aren't participating, I prefer you not be here. Just come the morning after."

I hang up, deflated. My spiritual preparation was all for nothing. I won't even get to see what happens. I'm locked out! Frustrated, I call Pastor Paul.

"I'm relieved," Paul says.

"I'm disappointed."

"Don't be. God knows exactly what He's doing. If He wanted you to go in there alone and do battle for Him, He'd send you. Just thank Him for His protection. You risked your friend's anger to remain true, and I believe God will honor that. Now," Paul advises with the practical wisdom I love about him, "get a good night's sleep and be at peace. You could be in for some intense discussions in the next few days."

Jesus warned that to follow Him would cause strife and separation from loved ones. Will I have to sacrifice my friendship with Lorna to remain faithful to Him?

Lorna welcomes me on Sunday morning, but her embrace is restrained. We talk of many things, skirting the issue that drives us apart. For the first time, we relate on the surface and avoid the intensity that characterizes our relationship. We do not look directly into one another's eyes.

Members of the Body

*You are no longer foreigners and aliens, but fellow citizens with
God's people and members of God's household . . .*

EPHESIANS 2:19

Life is lovelier with a steady paycheck, notwithstanding Lorna's concern about my corporate career. It allows for comfort and even little luxuries. One of the luxuries I really appreciate is Maria, who comes every two weeks to clean my house. Through Maria comes a miracle, one that reveals God's power.

Maria arrives every other Tuesday. She is a dark, round bubble of energy determined to restore order to my universe, scrubbing as though it were an act of worship. No corner is left untouched; and when she leaves, it sparkles. Maria, a devout born-again Christian from Peru, prays while she cleans, and sings while she scrubs.

It's hard to say how old Maria is. Short and squat, with a large head and pock-marked face, she chants while traveling on the bus, mutters prayers and praises Jesus everywhere she walks with her heavy step. She is a comic figure to the casual observer, a "character" mocked by the passengers on her bus.

"They say Mar-r-r-ia iz-z cr-r-azy, Meessus," she admits, picking up the broom. "They laugh at Mar-r-ia, yes, but when they are afraid, Meessus, they come to me. 'Mar-r-ia,' they cry, 'you pr-ray for me, Mar-ria, ask your God He watch for me.'"

"And do you pray for them, Maria?"

"Oh yes. I pray, and my God, He listen. I pr-ray for you, too, Meessus."

One Tuesday, Maria doesn't arrive. The day passes with no sign of her, and no sign the next day. This is unlike her. On the third day, a nurse calls to say Maria is in the hospital. Hoping it isn't too serious, I cut some flowers and drive over to see her.

Entering her room, I catch my breath, shaken. Maria is sitting up in bed, moaning, rocking back and forth. Her large head is encased in a heavy iron cage that rests on her shoulders. Her eyes are closed, and tears stream down her cheeks. Touching her gently so she knows I'm there, I offer the flowers. She clutches them to her chest.

"What's that around your head, Maria?"

"Oooh, Meesus," she moans, touching the iron contraption, "it iz-z the torture of Satan."

I turn, puzzled, to the nurse. "It isn't pleasant," the nurse explains. "We call it a 'halo.' It is screwed and bolted directly into the bone of her head. In four places."

"Oh, my poor Maria! How long must you wear it?"

"Five months, my doctor say. Maybe. But Meesus, you tell him Mar-r-ia, she no live five months with thees in her head. She die. You tell him, yes?"

"I'll talk to him, Maria. Anything else I can do for you?"

"Yes, Meesus. My Bible." She points to the bedside table. "Please, you read to me."

"Sure, Maria.

"Juan. Juan catorce."

I open the sacred book and read John 14. *"No dejen que se angustie su corazón. Confíen en Dios; confíen también en mí."* ("Do not let your hearts be troubled. Trust in God; trust also in me.")

"A-men. A-men. Hallelujah, Jésus!" Maria's interjections punctuate my reading. Hearing the Word sends her into an ecstasy that, for a moment, transcends her pain. "A-men. *Gracias, Jésus.*" She prays and mutters a few minutes more. *"Gracias,* Meesus, you bring joy to Mar-r-ia."

"Keep your eyes on Him, Maria, not on your pain. I'll be back to see you in a couple of days."

In the corridor, I find Dr. Horowitz. "Why must she wear that hideous device?"

"Because if she doesn't, to put it simply," he says, "her head will fall off."

"What?!"

"In a manner of speaking. There is cancer in Maria's neck. Her neck bones have degenerated to the point where they can no longer support her head."

"Can they be repaired? Or regenerate?"

He shakes his head, closing his eyes to emphasize the impossibility.

"Oooh," I groan. "That means . . ."

" . . . we can't ever take it off. She must learn to live with it."

"Easy for you to say."

Every week, Maria asks me to pray with her and read from the Bible. Always John, chapter 14. Weeks turn into months. The pain of the heavy metal cage drilled into her head has weakened her. Today, Maria clutches my hands. "God tells Maria it won't be long. Soon, He say, we take this off."

My heart sinks. Only the hope of removing the cruel contraption is keeping her alive. "Maria, dear, Jesus is merciful. But if it turns out to be longer than you hope, He will give you a way to live with it."

"No, no. Jésus say it will go. My neck is strong now. I feel. You tell doctor I need new X-ray, yes? I ask him many days, but he no listen to me. They no like people who have no money, Meesus. He no give X-ray."

I promise to ask the doctor.

Maria sits back and smiles. "You read now. *Juan catorce.*"

When leaving, I stop at the nurses' desk. They are preparing papers to release Maria from the hospital. "How can you let her go? She can't manage by herself!"

The nurse shrugs. They don't keep patients who can't pay any longer than they have to.

Maria panics when they tell her she is being discharged. "No! You take new X-ray." Her finger touches the heavy head cage, and she cries, "You take thees torture from me! I no leave with thees!"

"When will she have the X-ray?" I ask Dr. Horowitz.

"There is no point; nothing's changed."

"The woman is suffering horribly," I plead. "If the X-ray makes her feel better, it's reason enough." The doctor walks away. "Is this the way you'd treat your mother?" I call after him. "Or is it just the way the hospital deals with the indigent?"

He stops and turns around. "That has nothing to do—"

"Let's be honest, Doctor. It has everything to do with it. This has been an eye-opening experience—one the newspapers may find interesting too."

His lips pressed tightly against his teeth, the doctor hisses, "We'll schedule the X-ray for Friday morning."

Maria is ecstatic. She grabs my hands to thank me. My heart sinks at how disappointed she will be. "Help her, dear Jesus. I know You love this short, funny woman they laugh at on the bus." Her dark eyes burn to see the Savior she loves with such passion. Her faith must be a jewel of rare beauty in His kingdom. I am privileged that He had her path cross mine, allowing me to behold and learn what God treasures above all else.

I return on Friday to drive her home. Maria is sitting up in a chair, beaming. "I no leave today."

"Why not, Maria? Have you had your X-ray?"

"Yes." Her eyes roll up toward the iron cage. "And I stay until they take thees off."

I don't know if anyone has explained what will happen to her if the cage is removed, but it can't be me. I can't face her overwhelming despair. "She won't leave until you take it off. What do we do?" I ask her doctor.

"We'll take it off."

"You said her head will fall off without it!"

Doctor Horowitz looks left and right, as if afraid he might be overheard. He mutters in low tones, "The X-ray we took this morning indicates her neck bones have regenerated. They are strong enough to hold her head."

"You said that was impossible."

"It *is* impossible."

I shake my head, confused. "Were the original X-rays a mistake?"

"Not at all. They're here for anyone to see."

"So . . . Doctor, are you saying this a miracle?"

He exhales a deep sigh. "I don't know anything about miracles; that's Maria's department. She says Jesus healed her."

"Ha!" I laugh aloud. "If you didn't, I guess He did!"

"The Lord commanded baptism," my pastor says, "but understand it has nothing to do with your salvation. Think of it as a wedding ring. The ring itself doesn't make you married; it's just a symbol, a public statement of your relationship. Perhaps, my dear, it is time for yours."

We stand before the congregation. My pastor's eyes are crinkled in a smile. "What's a nice Jewish girl like you doing in a place like this?"

I scan the pews. Ari is in the third row with Mom and Dad. They are showing their love by attending the rite of my conviction. And God's gift to me, this day, is seeing Mom and Dad, divorced almost 20 years, sitting next to one another!

"The Bible says," Pastor continues, "that angels in heaven rejoice when a new believer comes to the Lord. Should we do any less here on Earth? After Barbara's baptism, my wife and I invite you all to celebrate at our house."

Everyone comes: adults, teens, kids. There's singing, lots of laughter, practical jokes, and the animated conversation of intimate friends who don't need small talk. This is our new church family, with whom we rejoice. With whom, sometimes, we cry. And from whom, for the first time, we learn to ask for help.

My life is a current in the river, rushing over a bed of sharp stones toward an unforeseen, thundering waterfall that crashes brutally on jagged rocks below.

By contrast, in my church family, lives seem to flow gently, like droplets in a stream over smooth, well-polished stones. They flow past sleepy weeping willows and nourishing grasses. Occasionally, when rain clouds the sky, there is cold or discomfort, but a warm sun eventually breaks through. The droplets continue to flow in the stream, reflect the light, and then evaporate softly to their destiny.

The pleasure and peace in the way these people relate are foreign to me. I've always been around artists, intellectuals, scientists, poets—people who seduce with their creativity, romance and adventure. In our little church, unpretentious souls seduce with caring, devotion and sensitivity. Some of them are dynamic, like friends I used to know. Some are not. But they are kind and gentle. They are more concerned with meeting one another's needs than about being brilliant. If I had to call someone at three o'clock in the morning, someone outside my own family and the Clarks, I know—and this is new to me, but I know it with certainty—there are a dozen people here ready to help.

I am coming to value goodness above brilliance and originality. How ironic. I spent my life on a search for *truth*. What God brings to me, instead, is *love*.

A waif on a cold, dark night, I peer through windows lit with a warm glowing lamp at families that live within like the fifties TV show *Father Knows Best*.

Patti opens the front door. "Hey! C'mon in, the girls couldn't wait for you to get here."

Her daughters, seven and nine, rush up to greet Ari, Dad and me, holding out baskets of colorful Easter eggs, chocolates, and hand-drawn cards with poems and pictures. "We made these for you! Do you want to come see our rabbits?"

A year ago, I would have said such families don't exist. But they do. Ari and I discover that marriages can be playful and loving after 30-plus years; that parents and children partake, with real pleasure, in one another's activities. Jason and Patti Towers have that kind of a home—integrated, enthusiastic, enjoying their time together. Growing up, I had never seen families like this. And it's a funny thing. Generous, grateful, God-loving people tend to raise productive, cheerful citizens who, in turn, marry and propagate caring human beings. But what I love best is their fun and humor.

It is Patti's fortieth birthday. The invitation says to be at her house at midnight, with a gift related to camping. "But Patti hates camping," I protest. "And she's an early riser. By midnight she'll have been asleep for hours!"

"I know." Jason's grin is wicked. "I know. Just be there."

More than 20 people are partying on Patti's lawn when we arrive. Her daughters giggle and hop around in anticipation, their faces glowing orange in the light of a bonfire next to a large tent. At midnight, everyone runs through the house and into the bedroom to wake Patti, singing "Happy Birthday" around her bed.

"Wha . . .?" Dazed with sleep, she protests as Jason throws a bathrobe over her bare shoulders and leads her from the room to the front door. She sees the tent, the bonfire, and sleeping bags strewn around. People are singing with guitars, roasting marshmallows, and telling ghost stories. They greet her with a birthday cake and presents. The elegant little packages contain mosquito repellent ("keeps husbands away too," Jason moans), folding cookware, a portable potty, flashlight, pocket knife and everything one needs for camping. Patti, laughing, shakes her fist, and swears revenge. We party under the stars until dawn. These fun-loving people don't fit my stereotype of grim, forbidding Christians. For them, any occasion is an excuse for festivity and creative celebration.

But it is not always fun and games. Some of our church families struggle with heavy issues: kids on drugs, unemployment, illness, spiritual peaks and valleys. This morning, for instance, when service comes to a close, our pastor announces that Samuel has something to say. Samuel, the son of one of our elders, is married to a talented soloist in our choir. He devotes a lot of time to the junior-high youth group, taking them on camping trips and to sports rallies. Ari adores him.

Samuel steps up on the altar, plants his feet firmly and faces us. He has a hard time getting started, clears his throat and says, "I need your prayers. I've been battling drug addiction for some time now. It's destroying my marriage and my service to God." (Samuel? Not Samuel!) His head drops. "I'm going to a rehabilitation program for help." His wife and parents watch intently from their pew. "I'm sorry." Samuel struggles against tears. "I'm ashamed. And I'm deeply grateful to God for this church family."

He steps off the altar. Immediately, people rush to embrace him and promise their support. Deborah puts an arm around Samuel's mother. "I can help. I've been through this, as you know, with my eldest son."

It is an intimate community. One woman is starting a retail business. She tells our Sunday School class that she's rented a store, but the place needs a major cleaning and "face lift." She asks that we pray for its success. Saturday next, 12 people show up to scrub and paint and refurbish her store. Another woman, divorced with three sons, hasn't got enough to pay her utilities bill; they have disconnected her telephone line. We pray about it and pass a basket around the room. Bill, the class leader, collects the basket and counts the money. "How much will it cost to get caught up?" Bill asks.

"Four hundred dollars," she says in a low voice.

Bill holds up the basket. "Four hundred six dollars and thirty-two cents," he announces with a triumphant smile. "Keep the change!"

As for me, I still find it difficult to accept help from anyone! I had been talking to Bill about working long hours and feeling the pressure of an overfull schedule.

"Can you cut some of your activities?" he asks.

"I don't see how. And I spend a lot of time commuting. Work . . . the church . . . Everything is so far from home."

"Let's have lunch and go through your calendar. Maybe I can help."

"I work downtown, Bill. That's a long drive for you."

"No problem."

In a small downtown restaurant, Bill goes through every page on my calendar, and we have a long talk about priorities. He helps me identify and eliminate what I feel are obligatory commitments to make more time for Ari and the church activities I really enjoy. What a gift of his caring and time!

Others do for us too. One of the men, Marc, takes Ari out flying and target shooting and to ball games—guy things for a fatherless boy. Pastor Paul and Jason, men Ari wants to emulate, provide important role modeling. Ari beams with joy when Paul puts a hand on his shoulder and says to Jason, "Between us, we have five beautiful daughters, you and I. But this young man—this is the son we'd love to have had."

Patti is an early riser. The best time for us to talk is at 5:30 in the morning, when I get up for work. But at that time of day, I feel like death on a cracker. I drag the phone to the bathroom sink. "I'm brushing my teeth," I tell her, "you talk." By the time my teeth are done, she has me laughing so hard, I'm ready for the day.

I don't laugh every morning though. Some mornings, I wake up in a grip of fear: nauseated, paralyzed, unable to come out from under the covers. It's my morning panic attack. I've had it for years but hadn't told anybody until last Thursday, when I mentioned it during Bible study. I wake up feeling abandoned, helpless, alone. I worry about what will happen if I lose my job again, how I'd meet the mortgage, how I'd get Ari through school, and who will take care of me when I'm too old to work? Silly thoughts, but they torture me. Eventually, when I force myself out of bed and into the shower, when blood flows through my veins, I'm okay again.

It's 5:30 A.M. I've been awake since 4:00, agonizing, before the alarm goes off. *Hit the snooze—just a little while longer. Uh-oh, the phone.* "Yes?" I struggle to produce the sound.

"It's me, Jason. Figured your alarm must be going off about now."

"Right on time."

"How're you doin'?"

"Not too good today."

"Would you like me to pray with you?"

"Yes."

"Father God," he begins, "thank You for Barbara, for bringing her to us, and for all You're doing in her life." I clutch the telephone to my ear and sink lower into the soft blanket and pillows, my delicious buffers against the world. "Lord," Jason continues, "we ask that You be with Barbara in a special way this morning. We know, because Your Word says it, that a spirit of fear is not from You. So we come against this spirit of anxiety, Father. By the authority vested in us through the name of Jesus, we come against it. We open ourselves to Your spirit, Lord, the spirit of love, of protection. Satan is strong, Father. Alone we cannot battle against him. But You are greater, far greater than he who is in the world, and we claim Your protection. Be with us now and throughout the day, Lord. We praise You in the name of Jesus. Amen."

"Amen. Thank you, Jason. Thank you for thinking of me at my most vulnerable time of day. It means a lot."

"How are you feeling now?"

"Much better. Yes, really. Thanks again."

At 5:30 every morning for three weeks, the phone rings at the same moment the alarm sounds. Every morning, Jason prays the demons away. Then I get out of bed, willing to face the day. One morning when he calls, I say, "Guess what? No demons today! None." The next day is the same.

"Wonderful," Jason says. "If the demons come back, try praying on your own and let me know how you do. If you need to, call me. Anytime, night or day, hear?"

They do come back a few times, but I pray as Jason showed me, and it works. It works! Even more important, I don't feel so alone anymore. The God of widows and orphans, the God who promises to be a father to the fatherless, provides these wonderful people who care about me, think of me, pray for me.

Pastor Paul and his wife, Erica, watch protectively over us too. Paul expresses concern that I put money away for my future. "Let me introduce you to a good financial planner. I'd feel better knowing a professional is helping you." Financial planner? I didn't know such a thing exists, or that I could afford one. And how did Paul know I've been worrying about my future? How blessed I am that he cares!

"Oh, he cares, all right," Erica assures me. "Why just this morning, when Paul gave me a 'good-morning' hug he said, 'I'm so grateful to have you to wake up to. Barbara faces her mornings alone; no one's there to give her a hug.' If God put that on Paul's mind, we assume He wants us to pray about it."

"I truly appreciate that," I say, and I do. But I'm embarrassed that my loneliness is so apparent.

"It's nothing to be ashamed of," Erica says. "God created us male and female, to complement each other and share our life. It's tough on your own. We know that. We'll keep praying about it."

"I envy the two of you," I confess to Erica. "To live with someone for 38 years, raise kids, build a career together, watch the grandchildren come—and still be in love! I guess that's the way God designed it to be, but I botched it."

"Envious . . . you?" Erica sounds surprised. "God's been good to us, there's no doubt; but to us, Barbara, *your* life seems so adventurous. I can't imagine you wanting it different!"

Miracles: Some are major, show-stopping miracles, like Maria's head. Some are in the minor leagues. But they occur almost daily now. Like when Allan's car falls apart, and he simply can't afford another. The church prays, and a car is offered by an anonymous donor as a gift. And I mustn't forget the lump that showed up in my breast, near the lymph nodes. I had been so scared! We gave that to Jesus in prayer and the next X-ray showed it had completely disappeared. What God is doing with my own family is amazing too. We had all gone our separate ways these many years: my sister . . . my long-divorced parents . . . He brings us all together weekly, faithfully, to study Scripture in Jason's living room.

Minor miracles like these bless me almost every day. Bigger ones still to come make me sit up and take notice.

Curious, as a new Christian, I visit other churches. The Vineyard has a younger congregation and a contemporary, exuberant style of music. They speak in tongues and raise their hands in song. Tonight, I attend one of their midweek prayer meetings at a parishioner's home. Fifty people crowd into a very small house; I don't know any of them. In the kitchen, a group is chatting near the chips and soda. One fellow stares at me, astonished.

"Do you know there are two angels alongside you?"

Angels, huh? This guy is certifiable. What have I walked into?

"I'm not kidding," he persists. "Never seen anything like it. They are plain as day. Only . . . it's kind of strange—"

"I'll say. Do you see angels all the time?"

"No. And certainly none like these!"

"Like what?" I humor him. I don't want to sound smug, but it makes you wonder if he's smoking something.

"One is huge; looks like a big tough guy. A street thug. The other, she's . . . gee whiz, I didn't know there were lady angels . . . she's very delicate. And so pale."

I can't help laughing. "Most people only get one guardian angel, you know. They're luminescent, dressed in white and all . . . but you say I've got 'Big Louie' and 'Tinkerbell'?"

"I'm telling you what I see. Make what you want of it." He tries to turn away but can't take his eyes off his vision. "Remarkable . . ."

Loony as he sounds, his words chill me. The similarity between what this stranger sees and what Lorna described years ago is staggering. Lorna always says I am split between the "survivor" and the "creator" in me. "Survivor," she says, "is strong, street-smart, tough and action-oriented. Creator is delicate and feminine, the spirit of playfulness. But she's overpowered by Survivor, and she's dying."

"Wait!" I call the stranger back to the kitchen. "You really see this?"

He nods. "They're fading now."

We take seats in the living room. The meeting opens with praise songs and prayer, then moves on to Scripture study, and closes with prayer. The man who saw my angels holds out his hand. "My name is Mel. You care to stay for healing prayer?"

"I don't know what that is. You think I should?"

"Definitely." He leads me to the back of the room where a dozen or so people are gathered to pray for specific requests or concerns. They encircle the individual and lay hands on him or her, praying fervently for the person's needs.

"How can we pray for you?" Mel asks.

"I'm not sure. Whatever you think is best."

Six people surround me, including Mel, and I close my eyes. They lay hands on my head, my shoulders, my upper arms. There is a minute or two of silence, then one of them begins chanting with sounds I don't understand. Others softly murmur "um hmm," or "yes, Lord," until the one "chanting" starts speaking in English again.

"Lord, we thank You for our new sister." (How do they know that I'm a new Christian?) "Heal her of fear, Father, and restore to her the bold spirit she has lost. Help her, Lord, to discover its true source and fill her with Your everlasting joy."

This is really spooky. These people have never seen me before, yet they pray about the very same things Lorna observed.

Another voice: "The Lord found you at a velvet-green grassy place in the thicket, dipping your cup into a creek." (Oh, no! This goes way back to when my marriage was falling apart, when I took an "underground" trip seeking spirit guides.) "You are dry and thirsty, but drink not the water of the creek. Jesus says, ask *Him* for drink and He will give you living water. Drink from the creek, and you will thirst again. But drink of the water Jesus gives, and it will become a spring of water within you, welling up to eternal life."

I hear You, Lord. Your promise of healing is loud and clear. I trust You for it.

I drive through Topanga Canyon to visit Lewis and Zada. The narrow, hairpin road climbs to the crest, then twists downhill to the ocean. I know this road well, every twist and turn, but I misjudge one curve. It's sharp. The tires squeal. I skid and turn the wheel frantically. It's no good; it's totally out of control! The front end of my car is plunging headlong past the right shoulder, toward a 30-foot drop. In just a few seconds I'll be dead.

"God help me!" I scream. "Send Your angels!"

I'm at a complete stop. Silence. The motor isn't running. All is still, save for my heart, pounding like it will break the wall of my chest. The front end of my car now points in the opposite direction, toward the center of the road. I am alive. How does my car, racing straight off the edge of the road to my right, now sit, dead still, pointing at the center dividing line on my left? As though it were picked up by a giant hand, turned completely around, and set down, solid.

I have to move off the road. Anyone coming around the bend will plow into me. I must stop shaking and move. And take a moment to say thanks—a moment to wonder. The Bible says angels protect us. Was that "Big Louie" who flipped the car around?

It's been several years since my last visit with Lewis and Zada Clark. Ari is soon to be an engineering student at the university, and the number of Clark grandchildren has grown to 28 or so. I drive up the familiar street. The white house is still beautiful, but the lawn is not manicured as before. The paint not quite as fresh. At the door, Zada's greeting is very warm, but her eyes are tired. "Come on in! Lewis is at the table. He can't wait to see you."

Entering the dining room, I catch my breath. Lewis is smiling, but he has aged so much! "Lewis. How are you?"

"Fine. Just fine. Have a seat." His words come slowly, without his usual strength.

"I will in just a moment. Let me first see if Zada needs help in the kitchen."

"Is he all right?" I ask in a lowered voice.

"He's had a stroke." She smiles and pats my hand. "But he's coming back just fine. Doin' real good." We carry the fresh, steaming fish, green beans and rice to the table. Lewis leads us in prayer, and we begin to eat. His movements, I observe, are slow, deliberate, difficult.

With the joy of being together and so much to catch up on, time flies. It pauses, however, for a minute or two, when Zada reaches over to Lewis's plate and, as unobtrusively as possible, cuts his fish. Patiently, in small pieces, as for a child.

I look away. Tall, strong and proud, Lewis the protector, the caretaker of all within his household, cannot be liking this at all. The rhythm of our conversation slows a beat while Lewis works with labored movements to manage the rest of his meal. The peas are difficult; they won't stay on the fork. But he manages.

Ari discovers that the world isn't always friendly to believers. He is at his friend's house one evening when Larry's father announces he got a promotion at work. Everyone is excited, and Ari exclaims, "Praise God!"

"What are you praising *Him* for?" Larry's father asks irritably. "*I* earned the promotion. *I* did it, not God!"

Later, in private with Larry, Ari mentions his dad's response. "Well, my dad's right," his friend says. "We're Jewish, you know."

"There's only one God, Larry, and Jews are supposed to love Him too." Ari is learning what it is to be in a minority with unpopular opinions.

Ari's high-school graduation is upon us. I had assumed he'd go to school here in town and live at home, because it's so expensive to live away on campus.

"Mom, remember the stories you've told me about campus life at the university, how those were the best years of your life?"

"Yes, Ari. They were exciting years of discovery, and learning to be independent. It's a special time."

"Well, I've been thinking. I want to live on campus like you did. I want that experience too."

He's right, of course, he's absolutely right. But where do I find an extra $15,000 a year?

"And so you should, my love." God knows how, but we'll have to trust Him for it.

When Ari goes off to college, our life together will come to an end. I won't be functioning as a mom anymore; he'll be responsible for his own life. He'll shop for his food, manage his money, and schedule his own activities.

He'll be back, of course, but only as a guest. His "real" life will be elsewhere, separate, building a path to his adulthood. It's good. It's in the natural order of things. And I can't stand it. The nest is emptying in one fell swoop. For other women, when a child leaves home, there are siblings left behind. And when the last one goes, Mama has Papa. Ari is my only one; his departure looms on the horizon like a death sentence. I'll miss him so much.

"It isn't fair," I tease. "Just when you get old enough to take out the trash, vacuum the floors, haul in the groceries . . . just when it feels like all that child-rearing is reaping its rewards, you up and leave."

"So you'll miss me, huh?" he grins.

"No, of course not. I just don't want to take out the trash."

Scouting campuses creates mini-vacations, precious time together in Santa Barbara, San Diego, Santa Cruz. Our weekend jaunts are wonderful fun, and each campus has something good to offer. When we get to San Luis Obispo, however, both of us feel something more. We are impressed with the academics, the faculty, and the programs to facilitate campus life; but there is also a spiritual welcome. An embrace. A sense of joy and safety. Wandering through the campus, and perusing a bulletin board in the Student Union, suddenly Ari and I turn to one another and say simultaneously, "This is it." We are sure.

Unfortunately, the Engineering school is full, and most incoming student registrations are rejected. We pray about that. The Lord opens this door, and Ari, thankfully, is enrolled. It calls for celebration, something special! But what?

The "something special" is an invitation from Gary and Thérèse to have Ari spend the summer at their home in south-central France. "Ari can travel with us when school lets out in June. You can join us later, when you get your vacation. It'll be a great way for our kids to get to know each other better."

Summer in a small French village! What could be better? If we use my frequent flyer miles, and stay with Gary and Thérèse, it won't cost any more than a local camping trip. God is so good!

After one month in the tiny village of La Bruyère in the region of Le Languedoc, Ari calls home. He and the Haynes's son, Marc, are not getting along. Ari is unhappy and wants me to come get him.

"Ari," I suggest, "You are with a religious Catholic family. Ask them to pray with you about getting along better. God can intervene."

"No, Mom, I can't. God doesn't live in this house. They visit Him at church on Sundays, but He doesn't live here. They get mad when I talk about God."

"Oh," I sigh, defeated. "I can't leave work until August, but I'll call Jean-Luc in Monaco, and see if you can stay with him until I can get there."

Jean-Luc, bless his heart, is delighted to see Ari again; it's been 10 years. He arranges with Thérèse what train to put Ari on, so he can meet him at the station in Monaco. Jean-Luc will keep him until I can get to La Bruyère.

August at last. I board a plane to Paris, take a train to Mileau, then a bus to Le Vigan and, from Le Vigan, a taxi to their ancient farmhouse in the village of La Bruyère. I've been traveling 46 hours, and I'm exhausted. Looking forward to a friendly place to land.

My welcome, however, is not what I had hoped.

"We've been under a lot of strain," Thérèse explains, "and there's been a string of visitors all summer. We're just not up for a houseguest now."

I can't believe it! Why'd they wait for me to arrive before saying anything?! I've been planning this trip for months! After our long years of friendship, this is unimaginable. Thérèse had been my roommate when we lived in a house for

French-speaking students at the university. I'm the one who introduced her to Gary. I had been her close friend all the years we lived in France, attended her marriage and had become part of her family, especially close to her younger sister, Aimée. We've watched each other's kids grow up. After our husbands obtained faculty posts, with Thérèse and Gary in Maryland, and Stephen and me in California, we continued to call and write and see each other every Christmas when they visited Gary's parents near our home. Gary and Thérèse are part of my life!

I'm devastated. "Please," I say, "Ari is arriving on the six-o'clock train from Monaco tonight, and I'm very tired from the trip. I haven't made any plans to travel elsewhere. Give me a couple of days to figure out what to do and where to go."

I drag my bags to their guesthouse in the renovated two-story barn. The old stone kitchen reminds me of our house in Alba, a lifetime ago, when Stephen and I were in love. This is where Ari and I planned to spend a quiet, peaceful four weeks. I was going to catch up on my reading, start some writing, do a lot of Bible study, and take long walks in the country. How I'd looked forward to a complete escape from urban and corporate pressures! How I longed for the luxury of time to visit with good friends and connect with life in a small village! Now it isn't going to happen.

Six o'clock. There is no call from Ari at the train station. I wait with increasing anxiety. At 7:30, the phone finally rings. "I missed the station, Mom." He is frightened. "I couldn't get off until Grasse."

"How far is Grasse?" I ask Thérèse.

"About two hours."

"Ari, is there a taxi near you?"

"Yes."

"Find out what it costs to get to La Bruyère."

He returns a moment later. "Seven hundred fifty francs."

That's $150. No way. "I'll come get you, honey. It's going to be a while, but don't move."

I get directions from Thérèse and borrow their car. I do wish one of them had offered to come with me. After 46 hours of traveling, and the blow of finding we are unwelcome at La Bruyère, now there's the tension of trying to find my son in an unknown region, alone, at night.

By the time I get to the station in Grasse, Ari and I are both pretty shaken. I clasp him to me, and we cling to the comfort of being together. Driving back, the two hours fly quickly as Ari tells me about his adventures with the kids in the village, his reunion with Jean-Luc, and his difficulties in the home of Gary and Thérèse.

"Ari, I don't understand why they want us to leave. Do you?"

"They get mad when I talk about Jesus," Ari says. "They don't like it."

I'm confused. They are devout Catholics. Why would Ari's faith alienate them to the point of kicking us out? Ah, well. At least he's fluent in French again. The trip isn't a total waste.

We arrive back at La Bruyère at 3:30 in the morning. I fall into bed, unnerved. Tomorrow, I think, tomorrow I'll figure out what to do.

In the morning, after breakfast in the barn, I stroll down to the main house. Gary is sunbathing, facedown, on the patio and barely utters hello. Thérèse is straightening up inside.

"Have you got a minute to talk?" I ask.

"*Bien sûr,* of course." We sit side by side on the hill next to the house, looking down at the dirt road flanked by thick, tall sunflowers.

"I understand you've had a lot of visitors, and you're both tired," I say. "But there has to be something more; what is it?"

Thérèse tries; she tells me about irritating incidents and friction between the boys, but it still doesn't explain.

I spend the morning walking and chatting with Thérèse's mother and her hearing-impaired aunt. Over the years, these dear ladies have received me with affection into their homes. When the shadows stretch into late afternoon, Ari and I pedal into the village to buy food for dinner. I pick up a bottle of Gary's favorite brandy. After a simple meal in the barn, just the two of us, Ari runs off to visit friends in the village. I take the brandy to the house.

"For you." I wave the bottle at Gary.

"How nice! We can enjoy a taste of it as soon as I finish these dishes." I help him dry and put them away. He's more talkative than he was this morning. "We've been under a lot of stress this summer," he apologizes. "Marc has been in trouble again. He's really out of control now."

"Gary, we talked about this years ago; the kid needs discipline."

"Yes, well, it's a sore spot with Thérèse. She gets pressure from me and her family about it, but it's something she can't do. It goes back to her father. His discipline was too severe, and it left a mark on her."

The dishes finished, he calls Thérèse down to join us. We open the brandy, turn on some music, and sink into a few peaceful moments in front of the fire. I'm beginning to hope things might get back to normal. Suddenly Thérèse announces, "It's almost 7:00, Gary. We'd better get dressed."

I look first at one, then the other, puzzled. Gary gets up and says, "Uh, yes . . . our neighbors invited us to a party next door."

"Oh?"

"Yes. They're from London. Very nice people." They glance uneasily at one another but offer no invitation to join them.

"Ah . . . well, then." I stand. "I guess I'd better let you go."

Upstairs, in the barn loft, I watch through the window as they walk to their neighbors' house and knock. The door opens. Laughter and festivity welcome them. With a crowd that large, I'm sure the neighbors wouldn't have minded one guest more. It was Gary and Thérèse who didn't want me there.

With laser focus, all my years of loneliness wrap around this one moment: rejection from my mother in infancy; rejection in grade school from my peers; rejection from my husband who preferred a taller, more slender, blonde. The night is oppressive, full with the anguish of the outcast, the cold chill of the leper who never sees the eyes of another, only the back. Curled on the bed in the big, lonely barn, I wonder why I am here—why I'd ever been born. In the solitude of the charming converted barn, I ask over and over again: Why? Is God teaching me something here? Is it that I hold too tenaciously to earthly friendships, trust too much in them? It's true, friendship is important to me. I enter into it with the kind of commitment one brings to a marriage. "For better or worse . . . in sickness and in health . . . until death do us part." A lot of good my commitment did to keep my marriage alive. Now a friendship of 24 years is dying.

I open my Bible, hoping to read myself to sleep. Instead, the pages awaken me in a way that happens rarely in a lifetime. The Lord speaks to me in this lonely night through His Word, filling me with confidence that I am in the palm of His hand. I was left out of a party, but I am brought into the love of a universal family, a God who never forsakes me. His Word lets me know I am no outcast in the Lord's family; I am His beloved. He had preferred to die than have me separated from Him.

It is painful, nevertheless, that my friends treat me this way. I clutch the Bible to my breast, grateful for the special way God reaches out to me in this low, low moment and transforms it into a memorable, life-changing union with His Spirit. If they had asked me to the party, I would have missed out on this special rendezvous.

Three days later, after dozens of phone calls, studying maps, and plotting an itinerary, Ari and I board a bus to Le Vigan where we will rent a car. I had called Analiese at the museum in Monaco. She was so happy to hear from me, she spontaneously dropped everything to meet us for a few days in Avignon. Dear Analiese. She has written faithfully every year for 10 years since I left Monaco. We'll have a wonderful few days with her. After that? I still don't know.

We drag our luggage from the bus depot six blocks to the car rental agency, only to discover the price is three times what they quoted on the phone. I can't pay that much. We argue vigorously with the clerk, insisting they honor what their agent said. Eventually, she calls headquarters to authorize leasing at the price I understood. Even so, I don't know where the money will come from, not to mention gasoline at French prices, hotels, and all the rest of a trip that we hadn't planned.

On the road . . . finally. I grin at Ari. "Here we are, just the two of us, our suitcases in the back, the road in front, and the exquisite beauty of the French countryside all around." *Take a deep breath.* As I exhale, tears roll from my eyes. The fight with the car rental agency was the last straw. The rebuff of Thérèse and Gary, then the night they went to the party and left me behind, the pressure of planning an unexpected trip—all the tension and disappointment of the last few days pour out in hot, salted streams.

"Why are you crying, Mom?"

"I'm grieving the loss of old friends, honey. It's the end of something I cared a lot about. But from here on out, we're going to have a great time. Let's ask Father God for His blessing on this trip, okay? Let's put it in His hands." Ari bows his head. "Guide us, Lord," I pray, "and show us how to use this time in some way for Your glory."

"Cool," Ari says. "It feels good to be in touch with Him again."

Analiese's smile, in front of the hotel in Avignon, greets us like a friendly breeze. We exchange hugs and repeated *bises* on the cheeks. "Ariel, how you've grown!" We stroll through town to a sidewalk café, order lemonade, and catch up on the last 10 years of our lives. Analiese tells about her work, her broken marriage, and the struggles of her recent years. In turn, I tell about how my life has changed since I've given it to Jesus, and the miracles occurring with regularity.

"I envy that, but I can't believe it."

"You don't have to believe *me*, but if it's something you want for yourself, pray directly to God. Ask Him to reveal the truth to you. Ask Him. What He gives to you might be very different from what He gives to me."

"Different? How?"

"He gives to each of us what we need most. I don't know what that would be for you."

Analiese and Ari and I run around like three kids set loose in a sand box. We tour the Pope's palace, stroll across arched bridges built by Roman engineers, and picnic near a river with houses on grassy banks. We eat well, sleep soundly, and play hard. Four days pass in a flash. Analiese has to go back to work.

Ari and I continue northeast toward Aix-les-Bains, a town famous for its mineral waters and spas that cure arthritis. Aix is magnificent: cobblestone streets, prolific gardens, music in the park at night where people—old, young, and in-between—come to dance. I stop a woman walking her dog and ask where, if she were a visitor, she would most want to stay.

"Oh!" she says without hesitation. "Le Manoir. It is beautiful! But you cannot get a room; you must reserve many months in advance." Ari frowns.

"Not to worry," I tell him. "God will find something for us."

"Let's just call the place," Ari says, "just see."

"*Non, Madame*," the receptionist says, predictably. "There are no vacan—oh, hold for a moment *si'l vous plaît*." The line goes silent. Then, returning, she says "Are you still there? Good, because a room was just canceled on the other line. It is small. Do you want it?"

"How much, please?"

"*Cent francs*." Twenty dollars—can that be a mistake?

"We'll be there in 10 minutes."

Following her directions, we wind up the hill, up, up, up until I wonder if I've missed a turn; then up some more, until we dead-end before a magnificent patio garden. Le Manoir is an old, exquisite manor house. Wood beams, stone fireplaces, a panelled library, terraces, and an elegant restaurant overlooking the gardens. Our little room has a sloped ceiling and dormer windows. Ari and I fall to our knees. "Thank You, Jesus, for opening up this room. Thank You for this atmosphere of rarified loveliness. It's wonderful to have You traveling with us." We shower and change for dinner.

Aix is a cure indeed. In just a few days my depression is lifted. We are ready to travel on to Switzerland in search of a Christian study center called *L'Abri* (The Shelter). Circling Lake Geneva on the French side, we cross the border, pass through the resort towns of Montreux and Vevey, then climb mountain roads to pastoral alpine meadows.

I've always imagined Switzerland as it was pictured in the story *Heidi*. And so it is! In the midst of summer snow-capped peaks are green flowered meadows and lazy grazing cows. Halfway up the mountain, darkness descends, and with it comes a torrential rain. We can't see anything on this narrow country road with no lights and no signs. We are soaked by the time we locate the humble cluster of small log houses that is the tiny village of Huémoz.

There, well hidden and unmarked, *L'Abri* was founded by theologians and authors Francis and Edith Schaeffer. A shelter from the stresses of the modern world for those who seek the peace of God, *L'Abri* is open to travelers, believers and questioners.

At the door of a modest wooden house our knock is answered by a woman with gray hair tied in a knot behind her head. "They are just beginning Bible study. Would you like to join them?"

"Yes. And may we stay a few days?"

"There is no room here; we are full to capacity. But there is a lady three houses down who will take you in. Come."

The study is warm in the soft orange glow of a fire, a gentle refuge from the dark night and the rain. At the end of the lesson, an American teenager, Jonathan, approaches Ari, while a woman from Geneva talks with me. They help us find the house where we can stay the night, and the four of us visit, cross-legged on the rug, sharing how God has shaped our lives. Jonathan reaffirms and encourages Ari's newfound faith. We spread our store of wine, bread, cheese and tomatoes on a blanket between us and talk until dawn dries up the rain.

Ari and I bid our two new friends farewell in the morning, exchanging addresses and promising to write and visit again one day. God has not opened the door for us to stay at *l'Abri*, but He has given us an unforgettable moment there. We carry the glow of the evening and the memory of the two travelers who offered friendship in Christ.

Returning to the French shore of Lake Geneva (*Lac Léman*), we are drawn to the charm of Thonon-les-Bains. A small town nestled between the magnificent lake and alpine mountains, Thonon is green, friendly, and easy to get around. A wonderful *pension,* or guest house, situated on acres of wooded lawns and flowerbeds, offers a sunny, spacious room and three meals for $20 a day. It isn't a gourmet cuisine, but it's homemade, hearty and wholesome. "This is it, Ari. Until we return home, this is where we park and rest."

An aerial tram (the *funiculaire*) takes us down to the lake. I stretch out on the grass with a book while my son heads for the water and windsurfing lessons. Ariel, now 16, can't ignore the topless wonders that populate the grassy shore. Left, right, straight ahead, he doesn't know where to look first. "Oh, man! Did you see *that*?"

How can I not see? She is tall and blonde and walks slowly, right in front of us, toward the water.

Ari's hormones bounce ecstatically. "It's great, Mom, don't you think, that they're free to go topless?!"

"Is it?"

"Oh, yes. It's healthy, uninhibited. The body is exposed to sun and air, and it gets to breathe." Ari goes on for two days, extolling the virtues of topless sunbathing. I'm getting tired of it.

"Okay, fine, maybe it *is* better. I'll go topless too."

Ari's eyes widen, appalled. "You can't do that!" he sputters. "You can't. You're . . . you're my *mother*!"

Some days we drive to nearby alpine ski resorts; other days we stay close to the narrow streets and markets of Thonon. Daily, we thank God for guiding us to this beautiful place. "God is traveling with us, Mom, can you feel it?" I nod, amazed at the strength of that Presence.

Sunday morning, we find a Protestant church (they are rare!) in the town of Evian, a few kilometers down the road. It's a simple, lovely service. A gentleman greets us. "You are new here. May I introduce myself?" Monsieur Fenêton, it turns out, is a director at the Evian water bottling plant.

"Really," I exclaim. "I love Evian water! You should think about selling it in America. We're ready for 'designer' water in the States. It would be a great market for you."

"You make a timely observation, Madame. Actually, we are launching Evian in the United States this coming fall. We have created the advertising campaign; everything is set to go." Monsieur Fenêton lights up with an idea. "I tell you what, come to the plant tomorrow. I'll give you a personal tour; then you can join my wife and me at our home for an *apéritif*. My son is about the same age as yours—you are 16, more or less, no?" He turns to Ari who nods. "Good. Thomas can introduce you to other young people."

At the Evian water bottling plant, Monsieur Fenêton takes us to the source of the spring. "We produce three million bottles a day." Incredible! So much just from this natural little fountain bubbling to the surface. Then, at the other side of the spring, he shows how Evian created a detour on the tracks of the French national railroad. A train pulls right into the plant to be loaded daily for distribution all over France, and soon to go all over the world.

Monsieur and Madame Fenêton welcome us into their home and introduce us to their friends. Ah, we could be happy staying a long time in Thonon, even living here, if I didn't have to work!

Alas, we have only two weeks, then off to the airport in Paris. On the *autoroute*, we're doing 95 miles an hour. I don't like driving this fast, but unless we do, we'll be run over by the cars shooting past at speeds of more than 100. I grip the wheel, stop breathing, and close my eyes. No. I don't close my eyes. But I want to. The experience is terrifying.

"You people are crazy with speed," I complain to a Parisian taxi driver after we return the rented car.

He shrugs. "*C'est normale.*"

"In my country, we have speed laws."

"*Ah, oui.* Of course, we have them here too."

"But we have police on the highways to *enforce* them," I persist.

At this, he turns his head completely around to glare at me while weaving his way through four rows of traffic without lane markers. Indignant, he huffs, "Now *that*, Madame, is not civilized!"

We are scheduled to return on a charter airline, but the check-in counter is closed. The company has just declared bankruptcy. There will be no flight. And no refunds. I slump, defeated, against a pillar. Somehow we've got to get home! But an Air France ticket costs $688. Each! Lord, this trip has cost thousands more than planned. Guess we'll have to trust You for that too.

Ariel is in love. "Puppy love," people call it. But I don't take it lightly. This relationship will mark him, I'm sure. Nicole has qualities that remind me of Ivan. Very possessive. She's uncomfortable with his friends and family. She pulls him off to the side, away from others. It's having an unwholesome effect on Ari's normally cheerful nature. He's troubled but won't admit to it. He cares too much for her. And we've just found out . . . she's pregnant.

"I can't leave her now!"

Ari's right. I can't encourage an abortion. The poor baby didn't ask to be created; he's entitled to his life. And God frowns on divorce; so it looks like this is it for Ari. He's not yet 18. He hasn't gone to college. Still, they could make a good life for themselves—if she were a different type of person. I fear she will drag him, and the child, down into her depression and paranoia.

"Pray for us," I ask my church family. "Pray the Lord will make Nicole a happier person; pray for their future, and for the life of this innocent child. Pray that I'll have the wisdom to support them and that she'll let me into their lives."

I'm on my knees every day. *Dear God, protect and bless them. Their lives, and the baby's life, are in Your hands. Hear me, Lord, please. We really do need Your help.*

Weeks pass. Ari returns home one evening exhausted and drained. "What's the matter, son? Did you two have a quarrel?"

"No."

"Want to talk about it?"

"She was bleeding. We rushed over to the hospital, but they couldn't save it. We lost the baby."

"Good heavens, is Nicole okay?"

"She's fine. She's sleeping. Her mom's with her."

"How are *you*, son?"

"I'm sorry about the baby. I loved the baby . . ." his voice trails off. "Mom, I feel bad about this, but the truth is, I'm kind of relieved. Like I was rescued from a rushing river."

"Perhaps you were."

"I know you don't think Nicole is good for me, but I can't abandon her now. I said I'd marry her, and I don't want her to think it was just because of the baby."

"I appreciate your integrity, son. Have you considered the possibility that God is giving you a chance for a fresh start and a new direction? Think about it."

Pastor Paul and Jason have also been praying these past weeks. Yesterday, Paul took Ari out to lunch with him. "He doesn't think I should keep seeing her," Ari had said when he got back, "especially after I leave for college in September."

"What do you think?"

"I can't leave her."

Today he's out with Jason. Thank God for these two men who care so much for my Ari. There are some things a woman can't say to a son. Oh, I hear the garage door opening; he's back. Entering the house, Ari passes me as though I weren't there, walks into the study, and picks up the phone. I cannot hear his conversation, but the tone is subdued and firm. After just a few minutes, he hangs up.

"It's over." His voice is flat. He goes into his room and closes the door.

The car is loaded. I force a festive mood as we drive off to get Ari settled in his new room at the Cal Poly dormitory. How I've dreaded this moment and prayed for God to prepare me. But I want this day to be a happy memory for us. Laughing, and sharing funny college stories, we drive through farmlands and rolling hills into San Luis Obispo. We locate the dorm and his room. It's empty, but his roommate has evidently been there earlier. There's a suitcase on one of the beds, a jacket thrown across one of the desk chairs, and . . .

"Ari, look!" An *NIV* Bible sits on the desk. "Looks like your roommate is a Christian!" The sight of that Bible, worn and well read, is the sign I'd prayed for. A peace settles within me, a certainty that Ari is safe, that he'll be just fine without me. God is his guardian now. In my heart, for the first time, I release my son and hand him over to God's watchful care.

Oh, I pray these will be happy years full of learning, adventure, and wonderful friendships in preparation for a productive life. I pray, too, that God will provide a way to deal with my loneliness when he's gone.

Bill finishes the Sunday School lesson and asks if there are any prayer requests. My hand shoots up. "Pray for my mother's husband. His name is Leo."

"Anything in particular?"

"No. Actually, I'm not sure why I want to pray for him. In fact, I'm not sure I even like him. The words just popped out."

"Perhaps it's a prompting of the Holy Spirit," Bill suggests.

One week later, Leo is dead. He's had a heart attack while driving a tour bus. No one else is hurt, fortunately. I drive out to Mom's house and look for words to comfort her.

"Don't worry," she assures me. "I'm fine. I feel like a bird let out of a cage."

"Mom!"

"No, listen to me. My life with him wasn't what you think. Leo was difficult. He kept me in the house like a prisoner. He didn't want me to see my family or have any friends. I put up with all of that, but today I found out other things. Trust me, I'm better off." She waves a hand to ward off further questions, but I want to know.

"Fine, you want to know?" She pours a cup of coffee and sits in her favorite chair, gazing through the window. "For starters, he was having an affair and spending huge amounts of money on another woman. She had the gall to come here this morning and demand $10,000 he had promised to give her."

"What?! He was a bus driver; where would he get so much money?"

"From *my* retirement account. I don't know how he got into it, but he's been stealing me blind."

"Oh, Mom!" I sit heavily on the sofa. "You said 'for starters.' There's more?"

She doesn't answer. Her lips are pressed together in a tight, bitter line. Then she says, in a voice so hoarse I hardly recognize it, "and he's a filthy child molester. I found that out today too. Don't ask me any more; I don't want to discuss it."

Julia and the kids come to help. We make funeral arrangements quickly, with minimum fuss. Mom just wants to get this over and into the past as fast as possible. I can't blame her. "I'll be all right," she assures me. "Look at it this way. If he had lived, I'd have been abandoned and penniless a few months from now. Maybe there's a God after all, and He's protecting me."

"The only thing that would redeem what you're going through right now is if you were to discover Him through it. I pray that happens for you."

A couple of weeks after the funeral, I'm at Mom's house for dinner. "It's odd, isn't it," she muses. "You prayed about finding money for Ari at the university, and then you prayed for Leo; and just a few days later, Leo died."

"Yes, but what's the connection? What does Ari's school have to do with Leo?"

She smiles and hands me a piece of paper. It's a check for $5,000. "Leo died on the job, driving the bus, remember? This morning—I couldn't believe it—this check from the workmen's compensation fund came in the mail."

"Mom, that's great! It'll help replenish your losses!"

"Put it toward Ariel's education."

"No! Oh, Mom, I can't!"

"Yes, you can and you will. There's nothing in the world I'd rather spend it on." She looks so happy. "It's too bad I wasted those years with such a man.

Obviously, I completely misread him. But your God is showing me that something good can come from anything. If this helps get Ari through school . . ."

"The Lord *is* good! And, Mom, just for the record, He's your God too."

Susan and I are in a country-and-western dance hall. We had come to enjoy the music and, hopefully, be asked to dance a time or two. But it's late, and tomorrow is work. We push our way through a dense, smokey crowd toward the exit.

"Excuse me . . ." I mumble, worming my way past the mob at the bar.

"Here, let me help." A man with a swarthy face and thick, velvet-black hair takes my elbow. He moves ahead to part the crowd and let us through. At the door I breathe in a welcome blast of cool night air. "Thank you," I say. His eyes are dark and beautiful. Susan and I head for the car.

"Wait!" he calls. "Please, I'd like to see you again. If you leave now I won't know how to find you."

I don't give my number to people I don't know, but his eyes are compelling and, in a strange way, I trust them. I give him my number at work and rush off behind Susan. "Hey!" he calls after me, "My name is Joseph."

Joseph has come to see me almost every day this week. Relaxed on my patio this warm evening, I'm telling him about how I came to know Jesus.

"I don't like religion," he says brusquely.

"Me neither. But I love Jesus, and if you're going to be hanging around here very much, you'll be hearing about Him."

"I may not be around much longer then."

"Suit yourself."

But he keeps coming back. And in between telling me about his life, his divorce, the successful business he used to have and lost, he says things about God and Jesus and the Bible, things that reveal a greater familiarity and spiritual understanding than he wants to admit.

"How do you know so much about it?"

Joseph shrugs. "My mother. She's a born-again Christian."

"Really! So you hate your mother, is that it?"

"No! I love my mother. She's a beautiful lady. I love her. Poor thing's had nothing but trouble from me, but she prays for my salvation all the time. Ha!" He laughs. "This is a funny scene." He lifts his coke glass in a toast. "Where else can you find a Presbyterian Sicilian enjoying dinner with a Presbyterian Jew?"

Joseph parks his car near the ocean, at the marina. He cuts the motor, turns to me and asks, "Are you a cop?"

"What?"

"A cop . . . you know. Are you?"

"No! Why are you asking that?"

He pulls out a packet of white powder and a tiny, hollow pipe. He inserts one end of the pipe into the powder and the other into his nostril. He inhales sharply.

I'm aghast. "Joseph, for heaven's sake, what are you doing?!"

"This is what I do. It's who I am. Sorry," he says.

"I can't deal with this; it makes me sick. Please, take me home."

Driving back to my house, he makes a detour and heads north toward Granada Hills. He drives into a lovely, upscale residential neighborhood alongside a golf course and stops in front of a large house. Joseph steps out and opens the passenger door, waving me out of the car. He extends his hand, palm up, toward the house.

"This was mine."

"I don't understand."

"This house, the golf green behind it, a golden retriever, and a beautiful wife. I had built a fine business in industrial chemicals. Sold to every major company south of Santa Barbara. I had it all."

"So what happened?"

"I sucked it up my nose." He stares wistfully at the house. "Do you have any idea how much money passed through my hands and disappeared up my nose?" I shake my head, speechless. "A million and a half."

He drives me home without another word and walks me to the house. "I was going to cook us a good Italian dinner tonight," he says wistfully, "but you probably want me out of here, huh?"

I nod. He turns to go.

"Joseph." He turns back. "Joseph, tell me something. Have you . . . have you ever—?"

"Ask."

"Have you ever been in jail?"

"Yes."

"And," swallowing hard, "do you carry a gun?"

"Yes." He leaves.

Three days later, Joseph is at my front door. "Don't worry." He raises his hand to stop my protest. "You have my word I will never bring a piece into this house. No dope either. Never."

"That will be hard for you, won't it?"

"Yes. But this house is my refuge. It's all I have on Earth that's good and clean and full of hope. I want to keep it that way." He paces up and down and around the living room. "Why'd you give me your phone number that first time I saw you?"

"I don't know. Normally I wouldn't."

"'Course not. You think it was an accident? Don't you understand you were sent to me?"

"Sent?"

"Barbara, sit down. I have to talk to you." Joseph sits on the sofa opposite my chair and takes a deep breath. "You're a Christian, right?" I nod. "The Holy Spirit dwells in you?" I nod again. "Good. 'Cause it's the only way you can understand." His head drops toward his hands clasped between his knees. "I may die soon." My eyes open wide. "That's right. I'm fighting for my life, and I'm losing. At least I was, until you . . ."

"Joseph, are you ill?"

"Not ill. Under attack." He stands and paces again. "Cocaine—it's the highway Satan rides into your soul. First he took my possessions, then my loved ones. Now he's going in for the kill. And he's using that she-demon."

"Who?"

"Lucille. She's death. Kinky sex, drugs, far-out fantasies. Satan knows our weak spots; he uses her to get right in there. And Lucy's good! Every time, I swear, 'never again.' But she's under my skin. That's an addiction, too, y'know. No, you don't know about stuff like that."

"Joseph, you said you're not a believer. Only a believer can recognize that Satan is attacking his life and soul."

"He is. And God is battling it out with him."

"Why have you told me?"

"Because you, my dear, are my angel. I'm torn between you, Angel-pie, and Lucille. With her it's passion, fury, excitement so intense I can't breathe. Here, it's fresh and fragrant. It's healthy. It's life."

"It sounds so . . . this isn't something you cooked up so I wouldn't throw you out?"

"I don't lie to you."

That's true. Even when the truth is ugly, he never has lied to me. I reach for the Bible on my coffee table and open it to Deuteronomy 30. "The Lord would have me say this to you, Joseph."

See, I set before you today life and prosperity, death and destruction . . . I have set before you life and death, blessings and curses. Now choose life . . . Love the Lord your God, listen to His voice, and hold fast to Him. For the Lord is your life (vv. 15,19,20).

Joseph has his head back, his eyes closed. He reaches for my hand. "Pray for me, little angel of God. The battle is on."

"I'll pray for you every day. He to whom I pray is greater than the one who is in the world."

"What will you pray?"

"That Jesus will take your soul in the palm of His loving hand, that He will prepare your body as His holy temple, and that the powder you sniff into it will be rendered powerless, as if you were sucking in air."

Joseph chuckles and pats my hand. "Keep praying, little angel. With you on my side, what can come against me?"

Bravado. But sometimes, when he's afraid of the power that pulls him back to the downward spiral of Lucille, I let him stay on the couch. I read the Bible to him before he goes to sleep. "His peace He leaves with you," I say, "to vanquish the fearful moments when the battle is at its worst. Claim his promise, Joseph. God loves you, and I do too."

I put a timer on the TV. It wakes him in the morning tuned to a good program of Christian teaching. He complains bitterly, but those are the terms. If he wants to stay here, he'll wake up with the Word of God. "It was like this in my mom's house. Clean and disciplined and normal. I miss it."

I pray daily for Joseph's submission to Jesus, and his release from the power of the powder. His mother, in Arkansas, prays with me on the phone. Deborah and some of the women at church also pray regularly for him. Deborah knows the drug scene; her practical suggestions are helpful.

One evening, Joseph rushes into the house. I've never seen him like this; he's furious. "What're you doing?" he yells. "Keep your bloody prayers to yourself. I don't need them; I don't want them. You're ruining me!"

"Whatever are you talking about?"

"Your damned prayers about the cocaine. The stuff I buy is *primo*. You have any idea what it *costs*? And now it's worthless. Less than worthless! I might as well be sniffing air."

"What's wrong with it?"

"What I said. There's nothing in it. Just powder. Can't even get a buzz, let alone a kick."

"You're sure it's the same stuff you had before?"

"Of course I'm sure. I'm very careful with my supplies." Yes, he would be. Joseph is neat, organized, meticulous. So that can only mean . . .

"God is more powerful than Satan, Joseph." I stifle a smile. "Which side did you *expect* to come out on top when you asked me to battle for your soul?"

"Damn!" He storms out of the house.

Hours later, he returns, apologetic. "I appreciate what you're trying to do for me. Maybe I'm just a lost cause and you shouldn't be wasting your effort.

I'm going to . . . I've decided to go back to Arkansas."

It feels like someone just punched me in the stomach. I didn't realize how much I'd miss him. "I have to leave," Joseph continues. "Not just for me, but for you." He puts his finger under my chin to lift my face. "There's a lovely future waiting for you, Angel-pie, but for you to have it, I've got to step aside."

"Since when are you a fortune-teller?"

"I know." His voice is firm and gentle. "I know, because your God talks to me too."

Ariel is now in his second year at the university. I have good friends, an active life at church, and lots of travel opportunities. Joseph is keeping clean and has started a new business. He calls, from time to time, to stay in touch. "I had a strange dream last night," he says. "I dreamt I could buy back my beautiful house, my wife, the dog, the whole shebang. I could have it all again if only," he chuckles, "you're gonna like this, Angel-pie, if only I give my heart to Jesus."

"You're right, ha! ha! I like it. So when do we celebrate?"

"Not yet, Angel. But hang in there, we're getting close."

Joseph's next call, some months later, is to let me know he's getting married. His calls become infrequent. In March, when my plane to New York stops in Arkansas, he and his mother meet me for dinner at the airport.

The following June, he calls again. "I'm at LAX," he says. "Coming in to see about that land I own near Wrightwood, you remember?"

"I remember."

"You want to take a drive out there with me?"

It's a clear, sunny day on the open road, and our mood is light. It's vintage Joseph, good laughs, good time. "Are you happy, Joseph?"

"I'm married. Can a man be married and happy? What about you?"

"I'm single. Can a woman be single and happy?"

The car stops in an open, seemingly endless, field. Joseph takes my hand and we walk silently across the acres he'd once had hopes and dreams about. "Maybe we could've built a little place up here, you and me," he says.

"Nah. You need a woman for a wife, not an angel."

"You have a point there," he concedes.

I turn toward Joseph and take both his hands in mine. I may never see him again. He knows it too. I kneel on the soil and draw him down. "Pray with me, Joseph."

"Don't know how."

"Yes, you do."

We bow our heads. "Father God, thank You for allowing us to share this lovely afternoon. Thank You that You have a plan for each of our lives, a plan for our welfare and our highest good. Thank You that, for a brief time, You caused our paths to cross, and created love in us for one another. Bless us, Father, and give Joseph the assurance that hard as he may try to run, he is one of those who dwell in the palm of Your hand. In the name of Jesus we pray. Amen."

God is with us out here in the field. Our meeting those years ago at the country-and-western dance hall was a divine appointment, an assignment, a ministry. But God was right to send Joseph away. Had he stayed, I probably could not have maintained a Christian life; the temptation was becoming too great. It's better this way.

"Bye, Joseph!" I wave him off at the airport. God's purpose is met; Joseph's war is over and he has survived the worst of it. My part is finished; it's time to move on.

So Joseph is married. Will that ever happen to me? After Stephen, I didn't want to ever marry again, didn't believe I had the right. And years later, when I was willing once again, Ivan destroyed my ability to trust. But Pastor Paul says I am a new creature in Christ. I have no history, no past, no sin to stain my heart. I am pure in His sight, thanks to Jesus. My church family has given me a new view of what marriage is meant to be, of families that love and enjoy and grow together. I want that.

I leave church late one night after a meeting. The library door is open and the light is on. It's an odd hour for the library to be open. I wander in and peruse the shelves. A title jumps out. I reach for the book and hold it close to my chest. Before switching off the light, I leave a note on the desk: "Checked out to Barbara—*The Right to Remarry: A Study Through Scripture.*

If We Forgive

For if you forgive men when they sin against you, your heavenly Father will also forgive you.
MATTHEW 6:14

We discuss the concept of forgiveness in my Bible study. Jason and Patti tell me I must forgive.

"Forgive whom?"

"Anyone who has sinned against you."

"Okay."

"*Everyone* who has sinned against you."

A nervous laugh escapes me. My bitter divorce 16 years ago and Stephen come to mind. People always say, "Get over it." Some things you don't get over. For 10 years, Stephen had been my best friend and love partner—until we returned from Europe, and the California drug scene seduced him. Then I saw a warm, affectionate, out-going person turn into a cruel, intensely hard, and unfaithful man. It was frightening. It was ultimate betrayal. The disgrace of rejection. That's when the joy of my spirit died.

Stephen remarried shortly after we broke up and, with his second wife, had three more boys. I'm still trying to restore my life. Year after year, he forgets Ari's birthday, he is silent on holidays, and there is a complete absence of child support or any evidence that Stephen cares. My resentment burns anew every time my boy is hurt. Even when I was unemployed and needed money for food, Stephen had said, "Sorry, I can't help you; I have three kids to take care of."

Fire rockets had gone off in my head. "Three? Three kids? You don't have *three*," I had answered between gritted teeth. "You have four! And one of them is going to be hungry!"

"Things are tough here now."

"If things are that tough, why doesn't your wife work?"

"She can't work. She has three kids to watch."

That fried my socks. "And just who is watching over *my* kid while *I'm* out at work?" It gets harder and harder, as time goes on, to remember the things I once liked—loved—about Stephen.

"Why must I forgive *everyone*?" I ask.

"Because Jesus tells us to. If it is too hard, if there is no forgiveness in you, God will provide the love you need to do it. Pray about it."

I close my eyes and pray. "Lord, You know I hate Stephen, and You know why. So if You want forgiveness here, You'll have to give me what I need to do it. It is just not in me. And let me know when it's over."

A year passes, and my anger, aggravated continually by new offenses, does not lighten up.

Late one night, sorting through files in my study, I come upon Stephen's buried letters from Alba. *Ahh, Alba!* We'd been so happy in that tiny village in south-central France. Now here are the letters he'd written every day when I'd returned home to visit my parents. Wonderful, loving letters full of passion and humor and colorful anecdotes about the villagers. Letters that bring back, for the first time in all these bitter years, what I had liked about this man, why I had married him, how it felt to be loved.

I sit on the floor for hours, reading. I laugh at the little stories about our friends and neighbors. I weep where it says he longs to see me and misses me desperately. I ache to recapture what had been. So long ago.

It is close to midnight (three o'clock in the morning on the east coast where Stephen lives). I reach for the phone. "Stephen?"

He hasn't heard from me in many years. At the sound of my voice, he awakens abruptly and tenses. "Yes?"

"I found . . . you'll never guess . . . I found . . . the letters from Alba."

A long silence, and then a soft, involuntary, deep-throated chuckle.

"You remember?"

"Of course." He is still laughing softly. I laugh too. It is the first time we've heard each other laugh in 17 years.

"You wrote good letters," I say.

"Those were great times."

"Yes, well . . . try to get back to sleep." I hang up. The brief, so brief, connection is cut. There's no sleep for me tonight. Do I forgive him? Sort of. The hatred packed hard into my heart is beginning to melt. But in the months and years to come, I'm sure I'll have to forgive him again and again as waves of anger and hurt repeatedly wash back. Still, it's just anger, not hatred. God is surely working a miracle if I can even *begin* to think of forgiveness.

My prayer group rejoices when I tell them about the letters and the call. Jason says, "You're in the process of forgiving, and that's the first step toward your healing. The next step is asking *him* to forgive *you*."

What?! Ask Stephen to forgive . . . *what*? His infidelities? His drugs? His abandonment? All the years he's ignored and neglected Ariel? Why should I ask *his* forgiveness?

After Stephen, there had been Karl, then Ivan. Since then, it had been a nine-year dry spell. Well, except for the brief but purposeful time with Joseph—and a hopeful but short-lived episode with a Christian man from Washington, DC.

It was a bicoastal, DC-L.A. courtship that made me remember how good it felt to be important in someone else's life. And sexless dating taught me a new path to intimacy, a clearer way to contemplate the possibility of marriage. It was fresh and cool and clean, like a blue-green mint.

Adam met my plane when I flew to Washington, DC, for a conference. We strolled through art shows and museums, ate in candlelit basement restaurants, and walked the streets late at night in the shelter of his umbrella against a cool autumn rain. We wandered the isles of bookstores, reading aloud to one another. Remembering my enthusiasm for Monet, Adam bought me a big book of color reproductions. On his salary, at a Christian organization, a gift like this was tantamount to giving me a jewel.

Even Lorna loved Adam! Challenging our Christian perspective over pasta and Chianti on a red-checkered tablecloth, she laughed, "I didn't expect you to know so much about shamanism, New Age thinking and other spiritual paths. Frankly, my dear Adam, you are intellectually dazzling!"

He lifted his glass in a toast. "The surprise is mutual. I didn't expect a shaman to provide such a stimulating exchange!" They bantered until the restaurant closed and Lorna had to drive back to New York. Kissing me good-bye, she whispered, "He is formidable, your Christian."

But alas, it was fleeting. Both of us had been too badly burned and scarred in the past; what it would take to make it work was just too scary.

Months go by without a date, sometimes a year or two. Then I venture out because I think I should. Some of my encounters are worthy of a television sitcom about dating. Actually, I hate dating. The forced, stilted conversations and dinners that drag on so long make me wonder why I was stupid enough to give up a soft bathrobe and a good book.

For the most part, I spend my free time alone. I celebrate birthdays with my closest women friends and hope for an invitation (which usually does not come) to someone's house at Christmas. Saturday nights are especially hard; it seems the whole world is dancing, coupled in elegant and exotic places whose doors are closed to me.

If only God would give me peace with celibacy. But no, I long to enjoy the pleasures of the flesh again; s-o-o-o, it would be nice to find a husband. In the singles group at church, I make some friends, share holidays and ski trips. But I cringe when guest speakers talk to us about the virtue of chastity and how, when your body is aching with unsatisfied desire, "God's grace is sufficient." Most of them have been married since they got out of college. They've never known the solitude of singleness or the agonies of solo parenting. They say, "Have patience and trust God for His timing." Then they go home and snuggle into bed with their wives.

It's April, time for our quarterly marketing meeting in New York. As always, I stay on a few extra days to spend with Lorna. Sunday morning, at her country house in the rural upstate mountains, I thumb through the yellow pages looking for a good church.

"We have so little time together. Do you really have to spend half the day in church?"

"I don't have to, Lorna, I want to. Oh, this one looks inviting. Where's Riverstone?"

She gives me directions and I drive the beautiful country roads through thick forests, flower fields, and small towns. "Riverstone." That has a familiar sound to it.

I find the modest little church and worship with a sweet body of believers. The pastor greets me at the end of the service. "It was brave of you to come all by yourself."

"You've all made me feel right at home. Clearly, this is my Father's house."

Driving back to Lorna, I pass the sign again: "Riverstone." I know it from somewhere . . . from . . . Oh! I've seen it on a letter to Ari. It's the little town where Stephen lives, somewhere in the countryside of upstate New York. *It's here!*

Three years earlier, I had found the letters from Alba. That was when God started His work of forgiveness in my heart toward Stephen. Now I find myself in the town where he lives. Curiosity impels me to find his street address in a telephone directory and to drive around looking for it. *There!* It's not a street, really, just a lane. Do I dare turn in and try to see the house? Oh! I jam on the brakes and stare.

It's a lovely old house. Two cars (not new) in front, children's toys and bikes, swings, a dog . . . my heart sinks. It looks like a real home. For a real family. *The Ilaynias*, the mailbox says. Impossible. *We* are the Ilaynias, Ariel and me. What is this house with our name on it that I cannot even enter? It is a painful, bewildering moment.

I drive past, dazed, then turn around, stop, and look again. I can see past the house to the meadows in back, purple with flowers, and rolling hills. A baby goat is in the yard, and a little child. Bending over the child is a man. Oh, God, it's him! The one who had been my husband.

I can't catch my breath. I put the car in gear and slowly start to drive away. I stop. I'm so close to him, in that field with the boy. He has no idea. He thinks—if he thinks of me at all—that I am 3,000 miles away in California. There is something cosmically dishonest about this. I leave the car and walk slowly, on shaking knees, toward the yard, past the goat, to the back porch. He's gone. Had I been hallucinating?

"Stephen?" My voice is timid, quaking. Once more: "Stephen!"

An upstairs window opens. He glances through and, mistaking me for his neighbor, calls out: "Be right down. Derrick cut his hand . . . be right there."

There are frogs in the pond on the meadow. Am I completely crazy to be here? Is there still time to get away? How can I stop shaking?

The door opens. "Hi!" The greeting freezes on Stephen's face. "Oh, my gosh!" he whispers. "B-Barbara?" His smile melts in bewilderment, astonishment, then (this really *is* crazy) his arms open wide. "Barbara! I don't believe it!" He reaches to embrace me. "What are you . . .? Come in, come in!"

"Perhaps I shouldn't have . . . another time . . ." But his arm is on my shoulder, leading me into the house. "Michelle and the kids are here. Her family is visiting."

"Please, I'd rather not intrude."

"Nonsense, c'mon in!" He yells for his wife. "Michelle! Come downstairs, quick! Guess who's here!"

From upstairs comes a puzzled "Who . . .?" Then they are all there: Michelle, the three boys, her brother and his wife. Stephen, his arm around my shoulder, presents me with elation: "Everybody, this is Barbara—my first wife. This is Ariel's *mother*!"

Mine is not the only flustered soul in that room. If Stephen had received me with tension, anger, suspicion, we'd have all understood. But he is radiant. He is protecting me, paying homage to me, and making it clear this is a special moment. Never did I expect to be received this way.

Stephen makes introductions, and the three little boys line up to say hello.

"I know all about you from Ari's stories," I say, "but I had no idea you'd all grown so big!" Michelle and I exchange pleasant greetings and news about Ari's current activities. All this time, Stephen's arm doesn't leave my shoulder. The shaking is gone now; in its place is a strong, centered sense of my highest self, a knowledge that I am in the right place at the right time.

Michelle excuses herself. She has to drive her relatives to the bus depot, but she'll return shortly. "I can't stay long," I murmur. "I have to get back to the city for my flight . . ."

"Sit down," Stephen insists, ushering me into the living room. "I have so much to tell you. I can't believe you're here; it's a miracle! Do you realize . . .? Guess what I was doing in my studio this very morning!"

"Working on a new piece of art?"

"No. I was writing a list." Stephen sits on the edge of the sofa, his face alive with the boyish exuberance so characteristic of him. "A long list of all the things I have to clean up with you."

"Clean up?"

"Things for which I must ask your forgiveness. And this very day you show up, 3,000 miles and 19 years later, on my doorstep!"

Lord, I breathe, *You knew the whole time. This was all prepared!*

Stephen leads me out into the green-and-purple field behind the house. His dog follows, leaping happily after frogs in the pond. Stephen is talking rapidly; he can't stop the outpouring words. "I failed you," he says. "I failed completely in my responsibility to Ariel. I won't make excuses; I failed both of you. As a husband and a father. You were a good wife to me, and I was horrible to you."

"You—"

"I know," he cuts me off. "I betrayed a love you trusted. I think I understand how deeply that betrayal cut, its implications and its consequences. I'm truly sorry. I feel that I ruined your life. You haven't remarried, never had the fullness of love and family again . . ."

The worst of it—I can't tell him, of course—but the worst was when he had said he didn't love me, that he had *never* loved me. *Never?* Then I must have been crazy. If he had never loved me, then all the loving years, the happy madness we had shared was all my imagination. It meant I had no idea what love was. It meant my whole life had never happened.

Tears fall. I can't stop them. I turn away, embarrassed. "That was long ago," I say. "Much has happened since then. But I did forgive you . . . and I'm glad you've been happy. You have a nice family."

"You mean that? You forgive me?"

"I'm a Christian now," I continue. "Today I can understand things that frightened and bewildered me back then."

"Tell me."

"At the time, it seemed the person I loved was disintegrating, disappearing. The person you became was a stranger. Your eyes—" Recalling how hard his eyes had become, I couldn't go on.

"Say it."

"There was a burning evil in your eyes. It wasn't you. It wasn't the man I had loved and married. Others saw it too. It was terrifying." I shuddered, remembering. "I had come face to face with the demonic, with a frightening force that transformed my husband, my lover, into a monster. I was frightened—for me and for the baby."

He slows his steps and looks down past his boots to the soft, green grass and purple flowers underfoot. "I know. It took years to rid myself of the demons inside."

I'm surprised. I hadn't expected him to understand. Looking directly into his eyes, I tell him, "There are no demons there now. Your soul is restored. I wonder, if I had then the spiritual weapons I have today, maybe I'd have been able to combat the horror of what I was facing. I was fighting for our marriage with reason and psychotherapy. I didn't know anything back then about spiritual warfare. Maybe, if I could have called upon the Lord to fight for you, to stay . . . but I was so afraid. Forgive me. I was just too afraid."

My breath catches in my throat when I realize what I have just said: "Forgive me." *I asked Stephen to forgive me!*

Stephen holds me tight. For a long time. "The divorce never should have happened," he says, his lips in my hair. "I loved you. I always loved you. I still do."

The Lord is doing His work in the field of purple flowers. I have asked Stephen for his forgiveness, the very thing I thought I'd die before doing. And Stephen has uttered the magic words, the healing balm of my eternal wound. He *had* loved me. I had not been crazy. He just validated that what we had back then was real.

We circle the field and walk past the horses. The hand of God is visible. I am Lazarus, returning from the dead. I don't mean that as a figure of speech; it's true. I've been dead these many years. Now I breathe the fresh air of a lilac garden and I am alive. He *had* loved me. It had all been real. *I* was real. My life, ripped so brutally from me 19 years before, is restored. Perhaps now I can even dare to live it?

I wipe tear-smeared mascara from my face as Stephen tells me about his life, his happiness with his family, his goals, his work. He asks about Ari's life and mine. His arm still on my shoulder, he leads me toward his studio, a separate little building on the property. "Come see my new work."

Inside, he pulls out etchings and engravings from the bins and offers them. "Which ones do you like?"

Even in my bitterest moments, I had always loved his work. His sculptures and engravings still enrich our home. "No," I hold up my hand, "you make your living from these."

"Please! I want you to have them." I demur, but he insists, and I choose two magnificent pieces. One for me. One for Ari. "Let me wrap these for you." He begins to sign each piece.

"Put the date on, too," I say. "This is an important date."

"I would like to sign it 'with love.' Can you accept that?"

"Yes."

He whips out the packing crates, nails, tape—it all comes together easily. He was always "handy," as my mom calls it. Stephen has been taking care of broken, leaking things for another family these many years. For *The Ilaynias.* For a woman who is his "wife" and three little boys. I'm still trying to absorb the reality of it.

Outside the studio, Stephen cuts a bouquet of mint to take back to the house for a pot of tea. Michelle has returned from the bus depot; she is setting a tea table on the back porch. She doesn't appear surprised by my unannounced arrival. Perhaps Stephen had told her about the list—the list of grievances for which he wanted to ask my pardon.

Chatting like old friends, it feels like a surrealistic haze to me. We speak casually, naturally, about things we don't usually trust each other to hear. Michelle mentions, for example, their recent vacation in the Caribbean. But then, afraid I'll think they have money, she adds quickly, "the first vacation we've had in years." They ask about my job, and I tell them about a jealous colleague who is trying to force me out. I inquire about Michelle's parents and their boys . . .

It is time to leave. The three boys line up at the car to say good-bye, extending their innocent little arms for a hug. Ari has told me about them after his occasional visits to their home, but I didn't imagine the sweetness of their faces. My heart lunges toward them, these dear sons that I would never have. They look wide-eyed back at me, curious, puzzled about where I fit in. Stephen's joy at having me there, his pride when he announced, "This is Ariel's mother!" made its mark with them.

The eldest asks that I give his love to Ari. I assure him I will. The second looks me squarely in the eye. I wink at him and he giggles. The littlest one pulls back when I reach to hug him. "Ari didn't take photos of me," he says, feeling left out.

"Ah, but I heard stories about you," I say. "I even have a picture your daddy drew when you were born." He smiles then and releases the hug.

I have no memory of the drive back. I am drained. I don't know where I'm going from this point on, but I know for sure my life will never be the same. Isaiah 54: *Redemption. Restoration.*

"Wow!" Lorna wipes tears from her face as I recount the morning's events. "You realize what happened there, don't you? Your honor was restored today! Stephen *honored* you when you arrived. The degradation of the abandonment, the shame of rejection . . . today he restored the truth of his love that was rightfully yours. He affirmed it had been real. Your marriage had been real." I still cannot speak; I am absorbing it all.

"Barbara, I am so glad this happened. I'm convinced you've never remarried all these years because of this unfinished business. This will clear space in your life for a new husband."

"You really think so?"

"I know it. You wanna bet you meet Mr. Right in less than 12 months?"

Back in New York City, on my bed in the Marriott Hotel, I let go and cry. Hot, flowing tears swell into great, uncontrollable sobs. I don't realize how loud they are until a chambermaid knocks on my door to see if I'm all right. I cry until I am empty and full of light. Then, about 2:30 in the morning, I go to the desk and write a letter to my son.

I'm not sure I understand all that has happened, but it was good. I may never see them again, this family called "The Ilaynias," but it is finished. The hatred, the rejection, the shame, the searing loneliness that knew no anaesthetic—it is finished. I complete my letter to Ari.

We accept God's grace and are free now—maybe—free to love again. Walk in peace, my son. I could imagine you playing in the purple flowers. I could see images of you in Stephen's studio. I saw the wholeness, the unity of our family. I love you more than life. Mom.

To Stephen I send another note:

Bye for now. I leave you with Malachi 2:14-16: " . . . the Lord is acting as the witness between you and the wife of your youth, because you have broken faith with her, though she is your partner, the wife of your marriage covenant. Has not the Lord made them one? In flesh and spirit they are his. And why one? Because He was seeking godly offspring. So guard yourself in your spirit, and do not break faith with the wife of your youth. 'I hate divorce,' says the Lord God of Israel . . . So guard yourself in your spirit, and do not break faith."

For me, there's Isaiah 54:6-7:

The Lord will call you back as if you were a wife deserted and distressed in spirit—a wife who married young, only to be rejected, says your God. For a brief moment I abandoned you, but with deep compassion I will bring you back.

Kinsman Redeemer

"The LORD bless him!" Naomi said to her daughter-in-law . . . . "That man is our close relative; he is one of our kinsman-redeemers."

RUTH 2:20

My daughter, should I not try to find a home for you, where you will be well provided for? Is not [he] a kinsman of ours?

RUTH 3:1-2

Since my encounter with Stephen, I am at peace. I don't feel a need to date anymore. I'm content to be with friends, work with my church, and live my life. If God wants me with a man, He will arrange it. "Lord," I tell Him, "choosing a mate is clearly not what I do best; I'm giving it up to You. If You want me single, fine. If You want me married, then You go find the right person and point him out with a neon sign. Like . . . for example . . . let's see . . . Okay, Lord. Let it be a sign between us that I'll know it's Mr. Right, sent by You, if after our first meeting he asks me for *three dates*." Good. That's unlikely enough to make it clear, don't you think?

Everything is far away: my work, church, and friends form a big triangle that has me traveling about 75 miles a day. Typically I leave for the office at 7:00 and, when I go to church meetings in the evening, I get home at 11:00 at night. Then I listen to phone messages, open mail, and do laundry. All the little things that face us after work face me late at night. I'm wearing out. I love my townhouse, my community, and my neighbors, but I'm never home. I pray, *Please, Lord, bring my activities closer to my home.*

"Be careful what you pray for," Patti warns, "you might get it."

At work the honeymoon is over. The first few years were glorious. I was the Golden Girl who initiated new marketing and PR programs, who sits on the national marketing steering committee. I love my role in this prestigious international organization. I'm proud of my contribution. But now it is becoming a political nightmare. A woman from the tax department, Arlene, has been maneuvering to get my job. She is a master political manipulator. What's worse, she's engaged to marry a partner.

I have no skill with internal politics. My focus is on being good at what I do. It's naive, maybe, thinking if I just do an outstanding job, I'll be appreciated and rewarded, right? Wrong. It is going from bad to worse. Anxiety twists my stomach day and night. I've prayed and asked my Bible study group to pray about it, for almost two years now, but it's on a downhill course. Today the managing partner tells me it is over; he asks me to resign.

I can barely breathe. I am devastated. My God, my God, have You forgotten me? I grasp my Bible, flip the pages randomly and they open to Isaiah 48:20-22.

Leave Babylon, flee from the Babylonians! Announce this with shouts of joy and proclaim it. Send it out to the ends of the earth; say, "The LORD has redeemed his servant Jacob." They did not thirst when he led them through the deserts; he made water flow for them from the rock; he split the rock and water gushed out. "There is no peace," says the LORD, "for the wicked."

Flee Babylon and be joyful? Is the firm "Babylon," as Lorna has always asserted? Then why do I feel devastated instead of joyful? God is saving me, the Bible says, and I won't thirst in the desert of unemployment. The wicked will be punished. It's hard to believe all that right now. But if He is with me, if He has designed this situation for my well-being, let Him show me. Right now, I have a tough time trusting.

Jason's partner in his law firm is Brian, an attorney who specializes in corporate terminations. Brian spends considerable time helping me negotiate a separation.

"You are asking for too much, Barbara," says the managing partner. "Even departing partners don't get more."

"I don't know what partners get," I reply. "I know what *I'm* getting is the shaft."

With Brian's help, I walk away with a sizable settlement, but I know a good part of it will go to attorneys' fees. Several weeks pass, and Brian's invoice has not arrived. I call and ask Brian to send it. "There is no invoice, Barbara," Brian says. "Good luck on your job search. I'll cover you in prayer." His generosity humbles me before the Lord.

"Thank You, Father. Forgive me that I doubted You. You are in this with me, Lord. I'm not alone, and I'm so grateful. You are my true employer, and You will use me well. I am ready for my next assignment!"

Patti grins. "Weren't you complaining that you had to travel too far to work?"

"I know, I know. You warned me to be careful what I pray for. I might get it."

Today, as part of my new job pursuit, I'm networking at the Chamber of Commerce.

"Hello, Barbara. How are you?"

"Fine, Nate, and yourself?"

Nate is an executive recruiter. He gave me good advice seven or eight years ago when I left the computer company. Whenever I run into him our conversation is always the same. "How are you?" "Fine. And you?" Tonight Nate adds, "And how is the firm treating you?"

"Funny you should ask. Actually, I'm leaving the firm. Got any brilliant leads for me?"

He hands me his card. "Come on up to my office. We can talk about your options."

Nate is professional, a good counselor. He makes some suggestions and gives me a few leads. "You have an impressive résumé. There's no doubt you'll find a good position." He leans back in his chair. "And when you do, you won't have the free time you have now. Don't spend it worrying. It's natural to be concerned, but try to enjoy. Unwind, relax, do things you don't have time to do when you work." This leads to talk about the things we enjoy, what we consider important—family, recreation, hobbies. Two hours pass. Got to go.

Nate sees me to the door. "You say you hike on Saturdays with your friends? I enjoy hiking. Would you mind one more in your group?"

"Not at all; join us. I leave at 9:00."

After a five-mile walk, spectacular scenery, and a hearty brunch at the patio restaurant near the trail's beginning, my friends say good-bye and head for their cars. Nate asks if I'd care to walk some more. Why not? I'm not working; I've got time to smell the roses. We wander, unhurried, into the late-spring canyon.

"So you come from a Jewish New York family too! Where did you live?" Both of us, coincidentally, grew up in the same part of the city and later moved to New Jersey. I ask about his consulting work and his teaching at the local college. "I teach business courses at night—been doing it for 18 years. It's what I love more than anything." As he talks about himself and his family, it is obvious that Judaism is central to Nate's life. I wonder what he'll say when he finds out this nice Jewish girl is a born-again Christian.

"For me, our Jewish heritage is important, too, Nate, but I've journeyed on to the next chapter."

"What do you mean?"

"The Bible has two parts: the Old Testament and the New—like a play in two acts. For me, both testaments are holy, God-inspired Scripture."

"Both?"

"Yes. The Old Testament foretells the New, and the New fulfills the prophecies of the Old. It's extraordinary."

"The New Testament is about . . ." he can hardly pronounce the name, "Jesus."

"About the promised Messiah, yes."

"Barbara, I don't understand."

"I believe in Jesus, Nate, as the living God incarnate. I believe that, through the Holy Spirit, He is alive in me. I'm a Christian."

"So you're *not* Jewish?"

"Yes, I am. Every bit as much as you."

"Jews don't believe in Jesus."

"Some do. Jesus revealed Himself to me, Nate. That doesn't change my blood or my heritage. I still laugh at the same Yiddish jokes you do. I respect the Sabbath, and I love my people, Israel." Nate shakes his head, confused. "Imagine if Hitler were to come to California," I continue. "You can bet I'd be in the concentration camp the same as you."

Nate is quiet on the way home. I expected that. I've met other interesting Jewish men these past years. The minute they hear I'm converted, they drop me like a hot potato. Probably Nate will too, and that's fine. Best to get it clear from the start.

We pass a garage sale on the way home. Nate can't resist. In the pile of rubble, he finds a small ceramic sculpture of a teacher with his blackboard, buys it, and hands it to me. "Here. So you won't forget today."

How interesting that the style is identical to a ceramic sculpture Jason and Patti had given me some years ago, the one of Jesus surrounded by wooly white sheep, carrying a black lamb in His arms. "That's you," Patti had said, "the black one." That ceramic, like the one Nate gives me now, was made by monks at a monastery in the San Bernardino Mountains.

Arriving at my house, Nate holds the car door open. "There's an Agatha Christie play at the playhouse tomorrow night. Want to go?"

"Tomorrow? Well, okay."

I tug and pull at my key because it is stuck in the door.

"Here, let me try." Nate works the key until it turns.

"Thanks."

"And next Saturday night is the annual ball to inaugurate the new Chamber president. I'd love to have you go with me."

"Oh, well, I—"

"Do you like jazz? I have a box at the Hollywood Bowl, and there's a great concert in August . . . if you care to . . .?"

"Nate! I don't plan that far ahead. Let's talk about it later." He opens the gate and waves good-bye.

I pick up my list of errands and set out. At the shoemaker's shop it hits me. *Three dates in a row.* I rush out to my car where I can talk privately to God. "What are You doing? Have You gotten our signals crossed? I mean, Nate is very nice and all; I can tell he'll be a good, trustworthy friend, but . . . c'mon, Lord, don't You think there's too big a gap in our ages? And he's not even Christian." I mentally check the items on my Perfect-Mr.-Right list. No, this is not it. God has made a mistake.

Agatha Christie at the playhouse is fun. We get home late though; it's almost one o'clock. I have to get up in the morning for church.

"Why don't you sleep in tomorrow? You can use the rest," Nate suggests.

"Nate," I hold his gaze, "church is a priority in my life. When I start missing church because I get in too late on Saturdays, I'll stop dating." He raises his two hands in front of him as if to retreat from his suggestion.

The Chamber Inauguration Ball is fun too. I like being around Nate, but I'm uncomfortable when he says how much he likes me. I have to speak plainly before someone gets hurt. "Nate, I'm glad we met. We are going to be really good friends. But please, don't misunderstand. 'Friends' is all it will ever be."

"Fine." He is undaunted. "Friends is fine."

Now I can relax and have a good time.

The alarm goes off and I stretch. We're going to see The Festival of Arts' Pageant of the Masters show in Laguna Beach. But there's still time to read luxuriously in bed on plumped-up pillows. I pad into the kitchen, put on the coffee pot, and step out to my sunny brick patio. Purple bougainvillea and yellow roses climb white stucco walls. Red azaleas in terra-cotta pots, white jasmine and camellias. Fragrant. Maybe I'll read out here. The garden? Or plumped pillows? I fill a delicate china cup. It's been a long time since I've been properly courted by a gentleman. Such an old-fashioned word, "courted." But that's what Nate's been doing. Courting me. And darn, it feels good! Too bad he isn't my type. Frankly, I'm a little uneasy about spending the whole day together. What if we run out of things to say?

Coffee, camellias, and a book—this is about as good as it gets. Why complicate my life with a man? After 22 years of developing a career and raising Ari by myself—such a good kid, I wonder what I did to deserve him—the hard part is over. He'll graduate in two years and I'll be able to take life a little easier.

I step out of the shower and slip into a red tank top, a red floral cotton skirt, and sandals. The doorbell rings. I whisper a prayer and hurry downstairs into his car.

Moving leisurely from one display to the next, enjoying the beauty of artistic forms, I steal a glance at Nate when I think he won't notice. A pleasant-looking man. Not tall or gorgeous, certainly older than I'm used to, but energetic, active. He has a slim, wiry frame. Thinning hair, mostly gray. Smiling eyes. He seems happy. I've always been attracted to artistic, complicated men full of existential *angst*. But with Nate, I'm comfortable. Very comfortable. He makes me feel that my every word, every gesture, is perfect. I feel whimsical, spontaneous. Free.

After absorbing the art exhibit, we follow a path along the ocean that meanders past a little beach through floral gardens, twisted trees, and rising cliffs. We're awed by the lush, tropical abundance of color and the sounds of the sea. These are moments shared like a sacrament. Down along the cliffs, we find an inlet, a hidden cove on a rocky shore. Waves crash with a roar and fall, meek and submissive, in foaming streams upon the sand. I shake off my sandals and run barefoot to embrace the sea, inhaling the briny fragrance, the soft, cool foam around my legs. Nate laughs behind me. "You have to touch and feel everything—like a child!"

I never saw it coming. An unexpected wave rises quickly on the rock alongside me, crashes and covers me head to toe. It is an all-enveloping, brutal cold. Now a pitiful, drowning rat, I cling to the rock until the wave subsides and return meekly to where Nate sits on a grassy slope. "Uh oh, you really got a soaking! Are you okay?" He averts his eyes from my clinging wet clothes.

"I'm fine. It'll dry quickly in the sun." Nate leans toward me and I see the kiss coming. Not just a friendly kiss, a real kiss, lingering . . . I like it.

A wooden staircase covered with bougainvillea leads to the road back to the center of town. We wander past enticing shops and choose one of the more intimate restaurants.

Dinner is quiet. Fresh flowers on a white tablecloth.

"This looks like an elegant English pub."

"I've never seen an English pub," Nate replies, his eyes holding mine over the rim of his glass. "But I'd like to see one with you. In fact—" He looks away.

"What?"

Nate shakes his head. "Just a thought that flashed through my mind."

"Tell me."

"Not tonight."

"When?"

"When you're ready."

I look down, aware I might be flirting with fragile sensitivities. "I may never be ready," I say, hoping to let him know delicately.

"Never is a long time. But I'm a patient man."

"After a while, patience might be foolishness."

He leans across the table, serious. "It would be most regrettable if you were to journey all the way to the conclusion of your life and pass right by, without stopping, what may prove to be its finest chapter."

I look away.

Nate's father, almost 90 years old, and recently widowed, lives with him. Nate cares devotedly for him. When we plan to be out for the evening, Nate first rushes home from work to prepare dinner and stays with his father while he eats. "Dad's home alone all day, and I'm out a lot," he explains. "It breaks up his loneliness."

His father is delighted that we're seeing one another. "He thinks I'm a nice Jewish girl," I tell Nate. "I don't want to deceive him. You ought to tell your father I'm a Christian."

"There's no point," Nate says. "At his age, it could be quite a shock."

"You're right. Since there's nothing serious between us, there's no reason to upset him."

Nate calls me in the morning. "Dad took it very well."

"You told him? Why?"

"Just in case something 'serious' develops."

Mom, by the way, is not the mother I knew growing up. Today she bubbles with gratitude for life's blessings. She is warm and hospitable, endearing herself to strangers. A sparkling personality has emerged. Exiting a concert of New Orleans jazz, she walks with bouncing steps and snaps her fingers. "Oh, your father would have loved that! It was his kind of music." In her seventh decade, Mom is opening to laughter as a flower opens to light. She is another of God's miraculous gifts to me. And I delight in the discovery of her.

Nate and his brother, Jon, are planning to celebrate their father's ninetieth birthday in New York, where Jon and most of their family live. "Come with me," Nate urges. "I want you to meet *der ganze mishproche*—family, friends, old college buddies. We'll make a vacation of it and play tourist. It'll be fun." Fun? This is serious business. Nate's family is close. More than a hundred relatives from seven states will gather to honor the family patriarch. How can I slip quietly into this party unnoticed?

In the rented hall, Nate takes the microphone. "It's great to be home. After living in California for 30-plus years, New York—where all of you are—is still 'home.' By the way, let me introduce Barbara—the love of my life." He extends his hand toward where I sit.

My mouth falls open. How *could* he do that? We've made no commitments! I want to escape and hide my reddened face while Nate continues the speech he has prepared to honor his father. Next to me, one of Nate's cousins observes my discomfort. He leans toward me and asks, "Are you in love with him?"

Startled at such a personal question from a stranger, I stutter, "Nate is . . . very special."

Numerous family members take turns at the microphone, sharing cherished anecdotes and memories of Nate's dad. Nate leans closer to me, with his arm over the back of my chair. "I want Dad to hear all this while he is still alive. What good does it do at a funeral?"

At the end of the evening, Sol thanks everyone profusely. "I was born, so they tell me, a long, long time ago. I am an old fossil, and my ears are worn out, so I couldn't hear a lot of what was said. But I am deeply touched that you all have gone to such trouble for me. I will read your written remarks over and over again."

It's a beautiful party. It means so much to Nate and Sol to be in New York with their family again.

We return to Jon and Tina's house close to 1:00 in the morning. Ready to fall into bed, we are startled when the phone rings. "Probably one of the kids," Jon says, picking it up. "Hello? Yes, she is." He hands the phone to me. "It's your mother."

Mom? Calling from California?

"How was the party, dear?"

"Great, Mom, but you're usually asleep hours and hours ago. What's up?"

"Barbara, honey . . . I don't know how to tell you . . ."

A bomb goes off in my brain. Her words don't make any sense. "You're wrong, Mom, I spoke to Dad yesterday, just before we got on the plane . . . he promised that the two of you would be at Ari's bicycle race this morning."

Mom and Dad have been divorced for more than 20 years. By God's grace, since they started attending our Bible study group two years ago, they have become friends again. Dad is there to help if Mom's television breaks down or if she needs to evaluate a new insurance policy. He drives her into the city to see her brother when her brother has surgery, and they are both at all our family gatherings.

"I know, dear, that was the plan. Dad was to pick me up at 7:00 this morning. When he didn't come, I called his house several times and kept getting the answering machine. Finally, I drove over there with your sister." Her voice drops. "That's when we found him. I wanted to wait until after Sol's party to tell you. I'm so sorry."

It has to be a mistake; Dad wasn't even sick. He rides his bike and walks daily, works on home improvement projects, has an active social life and jams with his musician friends. No, Daddy is very much alive.

Patiently, Mom repeats he has died until I believe her. My heart freezes inside my chest and my entire body goes rigid. I hang up the phone quietly. No hysterics. No tears. Nothing.

"What is it, sweetheart?" Nate is concerned.

"Daddy . . . my dad . . ." I hear my voice, mechanical, separated from my heart. "I have to catch the first plane back. They need me to help plan the funeral."

Nate is incredulous. "How? This is so unexpected . . . did she say how?"

"No. She found him in bed. Fully dressed. In his jeans."

Nate puts his arm around me. "I'm so sorry, sweetheart. I'll call the airline and we'll go together."

"Oh, no! No, Nate. You haven't had a vacation in 11 years. This week with your family means so much to you. And tomorrow is Passover, the first Passover with your brother and Tina since you moved to California. Stay, please. You deserve it."

"No way. I'm not letting you go home to face this alone."

Funny, I face everything in my life alone. How strange to have someone at my side. Ivan once said, "I want to take care of you," and for those words, I'd have followed him to the end of the earth. Nate never says it; he just *does* it. When Nate encircles me within his arms and holds my head against his chest, I know—as I knew living in the Clark family cottage—that this is a safe spot, a treasured refuge in a frightening, violent, deceptive world.

Mom and Julia are waiting when Nate and I arrive in Los Angeles. "He looked so good last month at your surprise birthday dinner," Mom keeps murmuring. "Who'd have guessed . . . so soon?"

Mom and Julia saw Daddy after he died, so for them it is real. But I cannot imagine him still, inactive, sleeping. He hardly ever sleeps. "A waste of time," he always said, "so many interesting things to do."

We make numerous phone calls, but none of us belong to a Temple, so it's hard to find a rabbi or mortuary available on Passover. What to do? Nate suggests, "What about Paul, your pastor?" A pastor! I almost smile, imagining how the family would react.

"Who cares?" my sister says. "Pastor Paul and Daddy loved each other. Isn't that more important than having a stranger, just because he's a rabbi?"

Mom shrugs. "It's fine with me. I feel the same way."

I dial my pastor's number. "Paul, will you do a Jewish funeral?"

"Well . . ." Paul clears his throat. "It's an unusual request. But you know how I felt about Jordan; we were friends. Let me pray about it. Erica will be home in a few minutes. We'll talk and pray about it. Then I'll call you back."

It's a beautiful service. Paul reads verses from the Old Testament and talks about the wonderfully complex and interesting person Daddy was. I love his memories of my dad; he understands the essence of the man. Then he asks if anyone else would like to share his or her thoughts. I am startled to see Mom—my shy mom who never speaks in a group—stand in front of everyone.

"Jordan was my first and last love," she says. "Oh, maybe I couldn't live with him, but he was an extraordinary man, a genius . . ." Mom delivers an amazing eulogy about Dad's rare gifts and talents. After Mom, there is a spontaneous outpouring from people in his environmental group, from fellow musicians, and from friends in my church who share wonderful memories. How sad that Dad isn't here to enjoy them.

For the next six weeks, Julia and I meet at Dad's house almost every day, cleaning out his files and preparing the property for sale. "It must be hard for you going there every day," Nate sympathizes.

"Actually, I rather like it. In Daddy's house, I feel close to him. He is in the piano, in his books, in the beautiful letters he has written, even in the mess of his files. I feel his presence right there with us, like he isn't dead at all, just away on a trip. I tell myself Julia and I are straightening things up while he's gone. Like a favor. He'll be back soon."

While we work at Dad's house, the phone rings frequently. Julia and I take turns explaining to callers that Jordan has died, and receive their condolences. This time when it rings again, it's Julia's turn. "Oh, I'm sorry," she says. Then, "Oh dear, oh, I'm so sorry. Is there anything I can do?"

"What's going on?" I ask her. "That's what *they're* supposed to say to *you*!"

She cups the receiver with her hand and whispers, "You want to talk to her? This woman is hysterical."

I take the phone. "Forgive me," the woman says between deep, rasping sobs. "But I loved him so much. I had no idea. I knew something was wrong . . . he usually calls me a couple of times a day, and when I didn't hear from him . . . I've been trying to reach him for days."

Dad had mentioned a lady friend he'd met several months ago. In fact, Nate and I once ran into them out on a hiking trail. Dad had been delighted that this woman shared his interests and funny little phobias. "She may be a keeper," he'd said. Julia and I didn't know her name and had no way to notify her of the funeral. "Oh, God," she weeps, "in all these years, I never lived until he came along. My life just died with him."

"I'm so sorry," I hear myself say, and my tears flow. I can cry for her pain; I cannot cry for my own.

It's a torment not knowing if Dad had become a Christian before he died. He'd said he couldn't accept Jesus. On the other hand, while cleaning his kitchen counter, I find questions scribbled on scraps of paper next to his radio. Little notes written to himself were evidence he'd been listening to Christian teaching.

Joy, Dad's next-door pianist friend, is a Christian. She assures me Dad had become one too. Is it true? Or is she saying that to make me feel better? I pray the Lord will let me know for sure.

God's blessings go far beyond what we can imagine. Eight years ago, I'd had my first opportunity to buy a home, the townhouse Ari and I loved so much. Shortly after, when I lost my job and could not make the payments, I gave the townhouse up to God and was resigned (not easily, but with many tears) to sell before it foreclosed. But, as God held the hand of Abraham who was about to slay his son, he held mine before I called a realtor. He told me, in prayer, that the house would be His gift to me. And somehow, throughout those unemployed months, even when sometimes we couldn't buy food, we made the payments. Eventually, He led me to the great job at the international firm, and I was easily able to maintain the house.

I had assumed that, by giving me the job, the Lord had fulfilled His promise of "giving me" the house. Not so. Today, when Julia and I complete the sale of Daddy's house, my half of the proceeds is the exact amount—to the dollar—required to pay off my mortgage! God knows this is *not* the way I wanted it to happen, but the townhouse is now, just as God had promised, fully mine. When God told me, "The house is My gift to you," I now discover He meant it literally.

I don't pretend anymore that Nate and I are "just friends." Nate grieves with me for the dead and nurtures relationships with the living—our families and our friends. We seek wisdom in one another's counsel, and he walks with me through the wretchedness of my job search. We do everything together. And "together" transforms my life.

"What made you ask for three dates, that first time we hiked?" I love to ask.

"I liked your résumé," he says. "Very impressive."

Had I met Nate a few years earlier, before I'd met Jesus, I wouldn't have given it a chance. Back then I only admired artistic creation, sexual passion, and adventure. God's love, and the love of His people, taught me what counts.

And what counts is *being there* when you're needed, not just when it's convenient. I'm learning to recognize the real thing. Nate is real.

Daddy's gone, and Ari is away at school. Thank God for Nate to fill the emptiness. "Want to drive up the coast to see Ari?" he often suggests. We travel well together, moving at the same rhythm, exploring every corner of the area, marveling at the beauty around us. Six or seven times we've made the trip, discovering more of California and one another.

It is not ideal between Nate and Ari, however. They both work hard at it, but there's a subtle undercurrent of tension. "Don't worry about it, Mom," Ari assures me. "We'll work it out. It takes time."

"For years, Ari, you've been the only man in my life. Are you feeling a bit displaced?"

"Sort of, but it's a relief too. It's kind of heavy being responsible for your happiness. I'm really glad Nate is taking charge of that."

"You always wanted me to remarry, to give you a father."

"I'm a little old for that now, but don't worry, it'll be fine. Nate's a good guy. We just communicate differently. I like to talk and delve into people. He prefers to do things, like sports. But I'll give Nate one thing," Ari laughs, "he's not intimidated by you!"

"What? Why would anyone be?"

"You're a strong woman, Mom. You're tough and bright. A survivor. A lot of men want a pretty puffball on their arm to admire them. You always have ideas and opinions about better ways to do things. Some men are scared to death of that."

"You're kidding. I don't scare *you*."

"Nope. You taught me to be tough too."

"Well, Nate seems to like it."

"Nate likes *you*, Mom. He puts up with the rest. It's a struggle to keep you from running the show, but he stands his ground. Try to cool it. Give the guy a break."

Darn that kid. How'd he get to be so smart? He says I'm strong. Well, I've had to be. I had to make decisions alone while I raised a child and built a career, and make them fast. I'm not used to consulting with someone else.

There's a lot I'm not used to. When my car breaks down and I'm stranded, there is someone to call. "I'll be right there," Nate says. When an appliance breaks and I panic about what it'll cost to fix it, Nate says, "I'll be right there." Every time I hear those words, "I'll be right there," something inside me melts a little. I am imperfect, sometimes unlovely, and still he cherishes me. In the shelter of his unconditional love, I am shedding fear.

"He makes me feel beautiful," I tell my mom.

"But you are beautiful," Mom says.

She's never said that before; she'd always found me ugly. "Never mind what I said, I was a darned fool. You were a beautiful girl and now you are a beautiful woman. Nate sees your beauty; I just hope one day you will too." My mother looks at me in a way she never has before, her eyes soft and loving. I have longed all my life for her to look at me this way, but I'm not used to it; I'm uncomfortable.

"Can you imagine marrying a man you can't pray with?" a woman at church asks my friend Deborah. "Not being able to pray together, I think she'd be lonely."

"It would be hard for you or me," Deborah replies, "because our husbands are our prayer partners, but Barbara has always prayed alone."

My sister shakes her head. "I don't get it; Nate's not her type."

"What's her 'type'?" Deborah asks.

"You know . . . a showstopping looker. The kind women die for."

"She's much smarter now," Deborah retorts. "She's got someone who makes *her* feel like a showstopper. And wouldn't any of us die for that!"

Several people from church caution me about dating a man who isn't Christian. "You are defying the Word and God Himself." Surprisingly, though, my Bible study group supports the union. They feel God's blessing upon us. Three women with whom I pray weekly, and whose spiritual maturity I admire, also feel at peace about it.

Still, I struggle in the spirit about God's will. "Does my peace about Nate come from You, Lord? Or is it merely my heart's desire? Do You want me to give him up, Father? If so, I'm willing, but I need Your help. Do what You must to keep me in Your will."

I feel Him asking, *Do you really desire to submit to My will?*

"Yes, Lord." (If it's not too painful.)

Seek My counsel.

I know what that means. I've avoided talking about this with Pastor Paul, because I know the Lord will speak to me through him. Paul and Erica like Nate. But we avoid talking about where the relationship is going. Now, with trepidation, I promise God I will accept my pastor's counsel as God's own guidance for me. I just don't want to hear what He has to say.

Trembling, I reach for the phone. "Hello, Paul. I think I have to talk to you."

"Yes, Barbara. I've been expecting this call for some time."

"I've put it off for months."

"Me too," he sighs. "Erica says come over for dinner tomorrow night and we'll talk."

So soon? Is this lovely chapter of my life with Nate to end so quickly? I'm a nervous wreck, and I try to concentrate on prayer. Drifting off to sleep, exhausted, I am awakened by . . . is it a dream? A message? A spoken word?

Ruth.

I am washed in the warmth of calm. Ruth, of course. I love the story of Ruth and her kinsman redeemer. Didn't the son of Naomi marry outside of Israel? And did the Lord not make something wonderful of this union with a pagan Moabite woman? Having embraced her husband's faith and the God of the Hebrews, she was privileged to become a direct-line ancestor of Jesus Himself! Ruth. Not all marriages outside the faith are cursed.

Erica clears the dinner table while Pastor Paul and I settle into comfortable armchairs near the fire. The coffee cup in my hand is shaking. "I should have come sooner, but—"

"Yes, I understand. Erica and I have prayed for years that the Lord would send a good man to you, and you know how fond of Nate we are. But he is not a Christian, and we've been concerned. You've been heavy on my mind. I've been praying for the right words, for wisdom. We love you—we love Nate, too—and we didn't want to see you hurt."

"You 'didn't' want . . . why the past tense?"

Paul glances over at Erica stacking dishes in the sink. She casts him a sly, knowing glance and turns back to her work. Paul settles back into the blue plaid chair. "The Lord's timing is always a wonder to me," he begins. "Had you come just days earlier, I could not have said what I am about to say to you." He takes a deep breath. "The Lord has answered my prayers with a series of . . . I don't know if they are dreams or visions or visitations, but with a message. Of that I'm sure."

I lean forward. "What's the message?"

"We find it in numerous verses, as in Deuteronomy 7:2-4, also in 2 Corinthians 6. God commands his people to have nothing to do with their neighbors outside of Israel." Paul lifts his Bible from a small table next to his chair and reads.

Make no treaty with them . . . Do not intermarry with them. Do not give your daughters to their sons or take their daughters for your sons, for they will turn your sons away from following Me to serve other gods . . .

"It appears that the primary concern is that intermarriage would cause the believer to turn away from serving God, the Holy One of Israel. Also, the word 'unbeliever' in the Old Testament refers to heathens, the enemies of the God of Israel, the children of darkness. You, Barbara, are a Jew, a daughter of Israel. The Jewish faith, as you know, is the foundation of Christianity. Nate believes in the same God you do and, technically, for you to marry him would not be to marry outside of Israel. Most importantly, Nate is supportive of your worship. I do not fear he would lead you astray or cause you to compromise the integrity and character of your Christian life."

Paul puts his hands together, his fingers forming a tent. "In my 'vision,' just last night," he says, "I saw myself walking on the shore with Jesus. He pointed at a man in the distance and said, 'Behold a true Israelite, in whom there is no guile.' In the Bible, the man of whom He spoke was Nathaniel who became Jesus' disciple. In my vision, the man at whom Jesus pointed was Nate."

My voice trembles. "Paul, do you mean—?"

"I'm truly not sure what it means, but there is something else. I can be a softy, sometimes. After all, I do love you, and I long to see you happy. I was concerned about the possibility of receiving what I *wanted* to hear, you understand? So I shared these dreams and readings with Erica, to get her reaction. Erica usually takes a hard line when it comes to putting the Lord's Word first."

"Yes? What did she say?"

"I said . . ." Erica walks into the den, drying her hands on a dish towel, "this is a strange 'coincidence.' Paul and I had both been concerned these past months, watching you and Nate become closer and more involved. I kept urging Paul to talk with you about it. 'The sooner the better,' I told him. 'Painful as it is, it gets worse if you wait.'" Erica sits in the chair next to Paul and takes his hand. "But God's timing isn't ours. While Paul was doing his study of intermarriage in Scripture, the Lord was working on me in my prayer times too. So when Paul asked what I thought, I had to admit that in these last couple of days I also had been seeing it in a different light."

"You too? In just the last couple of days? That is so strange, because something kept me all these months from talking with you about it. I hadn't felt I could call until yesterday, when God had given me an extraordinary peace by putting Ruth on my heart."

Paul and Erica listen with a hint of a smile on their faces.

"So . . .?" I hardly dare to hope. "You'll give us your blessing?"

Paul lifts his hand, palm out, as if to slow me down. "I know you understand the difference between the perfect will of God and the permissive will of God—"

"And this comes under the category of permissive will?"

"Yes. And you must clearly understand that *you* are making the choice here. I cannot do that for you."

"So, if I choose to marry Nate, and it's God's 'permissive will' . . . ?" I leave the question hanging uneasily.

"Obviously, that isn't Plan A," Paul replies, "but God has been known to bless, and bless richly, many a Plan B."

"Will you do our premarital counseling?"

Paul nods. "We know the dynamics between the two of you pretty well, but there are some things I'd like to discuss with Nate. Ask if he'll come back here with you. Is Thursday good?"

Nate is not pleased when I tell him. "Are you serious? If they had counseled you to break this off, you would have done it?"

"I made a deal with God, Nate. He knows better than anyone how hard that would be for me, but yes, I said I would give you up to remain in His will. And I prayed that He would, through Paul, reveal His will to me."

"This is crazy. Don't you have a mind of your own? Don't you know if this is right or it isn't?"

"All the problems we have on Earth started a long time ago in a garden when a guy turned away from God's guidance to decide for himself what is right and wrong. We're not as wise as God, Nate. All my life I depended on my own wisdom, and look where it got me. I've given that up to follow Him. Whatever the cost."

"The cost might have been me! How do you think that makes me feel?"

"I'm sorry if it offends you. I can't love you if it isn't blessed by God. It's that simple."

"I give up. You Christians are really weird."

Thursday evening, settled comfortably near the fire with hot coffee, Nate is deep in conversation with "Rabbi Paul," as he always calls him.

"It's no big deal to me if we don't share the same faith," he tells Paul. "My mother was an orthodox Jew and my father was an atheist. It worked fine, all those years, because they respected each other's differences. I can appreciate Barbara's faith, but I expect that she, in turn, will respect mine."

"You may find there's more involved than mutual respect and tolerating her absence on Sunday mornings," Paul warns. "It invades every aspect of her life. Have you any idea what it means to live with a born-again Christian who has Jesus in her heart?"

"I think so." Nate rubs his chin. "It's a little like sharing her with a lover—and knowing he gets top priority every time."

"Boy, you hit it on the nail! That's exactly right. Now, seriously, Nate, can you live with that?"

Nate shrugs. "If I want her, I guess I'll have to."

We are preparing to pick up Nate's dad for Rosh Hashanah services at the Temple when abruptly Nate encircles me in his arms and kisses me. With his lips close on mine, he whispers, "Marry me."

"What? Was that a proposal?" He smiles. "Well, then," I tease, "do it properly."

Nate slides to the floor on one knee and takes my hand. "Marry me, Barbara; it's the right thing to do."

I am overcome with the magic of the moment but cannot answer just yet.

Seated at his side in the Temple, listening to the recitation of the prayers and the readings from the psalms, Nate's dignity and goodness touch me deeply. This is the kind of man I should have married years ago. And through Nate, God ensures that the ties to my Judaic heritage and my people remain strong. It's fine with Nate that I celebrate Christmas and Easter, but we must observe the High Holy Days and Passover too. I take Nate's arm. He looks down affectionately, and I nod yes.

"Yes?"

"Yes."

Announcing our engagement, extending our private love to family and friends, is exciting. "He is a good man," Mom assures me. "He enjoys life. He'll be good for you."

Sol is beaming. "Once I see you two married, I can die in peace. I only regret Nate's mother isn't here to know you and see his happiness." He places a small velvet box in my hand. "This was her wedding ring. I'd be honored if you choose to wear it."

Nate and I hug him. "You'll come to live with us, Dad."

Sol raises his hand to cut us off. "No!"

"But we want you, Dad."

"Listen to me." Sol's gravelly voice is authoritative. "When I married Nate's mother, she brought her father to live with us. It was a nightmare. We never had privacy. Never had our own life. Our schedule revolved around his needs. No. I will not do that to you. Your love needs intimacy and spontaneity. Be happy. Find me a retirement home and visit regularly. Then I'll be happy too." Nate's dad is shy. To give up living with his son to live with strangers is a sacrifice of considerable magnitude. I am humbled.

Nate calls "Rabbi Paul" to ask if he'll marry us. "It will be my pleasure," Paul responds, "to marry Barbara to the Israelite in whom there is no guile."

All the years since Lewis and I sat on the doorstep of their cottage, his words have burned on my heart. *Someone should take care of you. When it's right, you get married and get on with your life.* I can't let another day go by without telling them—well, telling her. I don't know how much we can tell Lewis anymore.

Lewis's initial stroke had led to another. Zada worked with him, day and night, for weeks, months, to get him functioning again. Then there was another. And another. Now, with Lewis needing her, Zada quit the job she'd taken after their kids were grown and gone.

"You were doing so well at the bank, getting all those promotions. You miss it?"

"Oh, it was fun, sure it was. But this is my job now."

She looks at Lewis. The tall body, propped up in a wheel chair, is devoid of sight, speech, movement or capacity to respond. At least that's how most people perceive him. Zada sees something else. She talks constantly to him, to the man she'd built a life with. No one comes into Zada's house and walks past Lewis without a greeting. She stops them in front of his wheelchair. "Say hi to Lewis," she says. Leaning down to look Lewis squarely in his unseeing eyes, she lets him know, "Lewis, Barbara's come to visit."

I take his hand and stroke it, remembering the man I had admired so much. "Hi, Lewis. It's Barbara. I'm so glad to see you." Turning to Zada, I ask, "Does he hear us? Does he know what's going on?"

"It's intermittent, dear. He goes in and out. But yes, generally speaking, he knows what's going on. I make sure he knows." She makes him part of every conversation, every decision, every holiday and occasion. For his children and his grandchildren, Lewis is the center of attention, loved, caressed, and cared for by every last one of them. Zada will accept no less.

She tends every moment to his physical needs. She sees that his limbs are in a comfortable position, feeds him, bathes him, brushes his teeth, gets him into his bed next to her for sleep, and gets him up and dressed in the morning. She comforts him, rubs his hands so he knows she's there, speaks soothing words, and loves him tenderly. She scolds him when he's uncooperative about eating or getting dressed or when she perceives he's in a bad mood. How can she tell? She knows. It's a two-way communication and she lives and breathes it every moment of her life.

"He's impossible when I try to get him dressed to go out" she says. "Resists in every way he can. It's odd. The only time he cooperates is when I'm dressing him for church. He gets upset if we miss church."

Zada has sold the big white house and had a smaller house built to accommodate a wheelchair throughout, even in the shower. The open space allows her to work in the kitchen and still keep Lewis under her watchful eye. She won't leave him for a minute, even to shop or go to the post office. Sometimes one or the other of her grandchildren comes during vacation time to help out. That gives some relief. Eventually there have to be helpers who come regularly. Lewis is a big man, heavy for her to lift and move.

"People tell me to put him in an institution," she complains. "They think it's too much for me to handle."

"Is it?" I ask.

"He took care of *me* all these years; it's the least I can do for him. You know how they treat people in places like that?" She leans forward, takes his hands in hers, and rubs warmth into them. "Who would love him? Who would care what he feels and hears, or if he's cold or needs to go to the bathroom? He can't speak up, and they'd ignore him. No. It would be too horrible." She grips Lewis's hand tighter. "I'll never let that happen to you, darlin'."

People mean well; they're concerned for Zada when they make the suggestion. But I see that it only wounds her, because they aren't seeing and loving Lewis, the whole Lewis, as she does.

She goes into the kitchen, and I follow. "I pray for him," she says softly. "Day and night, all day, I pray for him. First I prayed he'd get well. And for a while I thought he would. Then, more strokes came, each one worse than the last. And I knew he wouldn't." She pauses to sip her water.

"Now I pray the Lord to take him home. This is torturing him. Lewis can't stand to be helpless and dependent. If he can't function like a man, he wants to go home. But it's been three years now, and the Lord still keeps him here with me. So He's not through with Lewis yet. And I guess it's my job to keep him well so God's purpose can be fulfilled."

Sometimes she laughs at the irony of how God deals with us. Growing up in a small rural town in Utah, she and Lewis had never known a nonwhite person until they came to California as adults. Lewis hadn't shaken his mistrust of people who seemed "different"; he was uncomfortable with cultures unfamiliar to him. "Wouldn't you know," she confides, "of all the caretakers we've had, there were two who stayed the longest and were the most devoted to his every need. One was a young black man, the other a Hispanic. Lewis came to love them both very much. I told him, I said, 'Lewis, the Lord still has lessons for you to learn.'"

Once in a while, when there's a caretaker at the house, I try to get Zada out, to give her a change of scene. But when she's away, even for just a few minutes, she starts fidgeting. "I forgot to tell Tom to heat the potatoes; Lewis hates his potatoes lukewarm. And he's got to shift his position or he'll get sores . . ."

"Zada, Tom knows all that, doesn't he?"

"I've got to get back, dear, do you mind?"

Three years have turned to six, seven, eight. In addition to her unceasing care for Lewis, Zada dedicates a lot of time to their church, she tends her garden, and stays close to her growing family. These days she's engrossed in creating an album of memories of the man that Lewis was. "Some of his grandkids are too young to remember much about him. I think it's important."

She has survived the death of her eldest child and the loss of a little granddaughter. When two of her children suffered the agonies of divorce, she kept hope alive in them until they rediscovered healthy new marriages. Now tragedy hits another granddaughter (one of Patty's). Returning to Zada's house after choir practice, beautiful 17-year-old Rachel was hit by a drunk driver and is in a comatose state (perhaps forever). Her parents care for her at home as devotedly as Zada tends to Lewis.

"Does Lewis know all this?" I ask, "Does he understand?"

"Oh, he knows all right. You bet he knows."

"Hi, Zada! Hi, Lewis," I call, entering the house with Nate. I bend down to kiss Lewis's cheek before settling on the sofa. I am bursting to share our good news. "Nate's asked me to marry him!"

"Oh, that's wonderful!" Zada beams. "You're a good man, Nate. I knew it the first time we met." She embraces him warmly. "If Barbara cares for you, you're part of this family. Whether you want us or not, you're stuck with us."

"We'll be married as soon as Nate can sell his house. But—"

"But what, dear? No 'buts' I hope."

"It's just, I know how hard it is for you to transport Lewis, but we wouldn't feel the wedding was right unless you two were there."

"Well, let's just see what Lewis has to say about this." Zada pushes herself off the sofa to face the wheelchair. She takes Lewis's hands and gazes into his unseeing eyes. "Listen carefully, darlin'. You remember Nate? He's come here with Barbara before. They're gettin' married, Lewis. Barbara's gettin' married!"

A flicker crosses his eyes and, for a brief moment, we know they are in focus. The formless sounds he sometimes makes come forth. But there is effort here. His lips move with difficulty, trying to shape words. They come, coarse and slow, but they come.

"Th-a-a-a . . . is-z-z-z . . . Tha-a-z . . .ver-r-r-yee . . . go-o-o-d."

The three of us look at one another astounded.

"Did I hear that right?" I ask. "Did he really say it?"

"Oh yes, he sure did. Lewis has always wanted to see you married, dear. Seems he still does. So! I guess that settles it. We'll be there, both of us."

We hold each other in a happy embrace, happy for my marriage and happy because we'd had Lewis back with us for a moment.

Our wedding will be beautiful. Except that Dad won't be there. Nor, to my disappointment, will Lorna. She's busy and the trip is costly. Instead, we talk a long time on the phone. "I send my blessings," she says. "With Nate's love, hopefully, you'll break the cycle of aloneness and heal your wounds."

"He's so good to me. Still, I'm scared to death. How do I know it will last 'until death do us part'?"

"You don't. But give it all you've got."

"I did that once, long ago, remember? And then what?"

"You got kicked in the gut. Left in the cold. But, Barbara, your fear is building walls. And walls create separateness. They are a false sense of protection; they don't work. You can only protect with love. And there is no love without vulnerability."

"Risk getting hurt, you mean."

"Exactly. Hiding behind walls, you have no power. Expose your vulnerability, that's real strength." She's trying to shake me loose. "This is your *marriage*, Barbara. Hold nothing back. In order to live fully with him, be prepared to accept pain."

Truth cloaked in paradox. Doesn't the Bible say we must die to self in order to be born anew, fresh and pure? Didn't Jesus say it too?

> *For whoever wants to save his life will lose it, but whoever loses his life for me will save it* (Luke 9:24).

Lorna is speaking truth: my defenses keep me from true union. Only in vulnerability will I find power. God's strength—just like a man's—is manifested in our weakness! When a woman is helpless before a man, he melts and will do anything for her. With God it's no different.

I've forgotten how to reveal my softness. All these years I've been exerting energy to cover and protect my wound. I've surrounded myself with a wall of self-sufficiency. Nate's love is breaking through, but there's a long way to go.

Lorna leaves me with a last thought. "Spend time with your inner child. Connect again with the six-year-old who envisioned dancing to the moon. *This is where your power lies*. You have lost the vision. Recapture it."

Weather forecasters have been predicting rain all week. "Pray for sun," I beg my Bible study friends.

"We're all praying. It won't rain."

"Oh? Did you tell that to the weathermen?"

"Don't have to. We're going right to the source!"

Nate tells my mom, "Pray for sun."

I laugh. "You're asking Mom to pray? Mom doesn't pray!"

"I know," he admits. "But just in case the sun does shine, I don't want you Christians getting all the credit."

The bride is 49 years old, the groom almost 61. Old enough, hopefully, to know what they're doing this time. Our wedding takes place outdoors in the holy sanctuary of God's creation. Helping me dress are three women with whom I've prayed every Thursday night for several years (my "prayer maidens," Nate calls them).

"You nervous?" Deborah asks.

"No, why? It's only my life."

"Would you like to pray with us before you walk to the altar?" We reach for one another's hands and bow our heads. "We pray, Lord, for Your blessing on this union," Deborah begins, "and Your headship over this household. Sanctify this marriage and keep devotion alive between Nate and Barbara and between them and You. Dear God, let their love be a blessing upon their household, their families, and their community."

Ari, looking very sharp in a tuxedo, arrives. "Ready, Mom? It's time."

More than a hundred guests, some from the east coast, from London and Israel, sit on white lawn chairs facing the flower-decked gazebo in an oak grove, where Nate's rabbi and my pastor wait. Mom looks happy. My uncle (who was afraid when I became a Christian that he'd not attend my wedding) is beaming. My cousin's little girl carries a basket of flowers down the gravel lane through the gardens and the oaks, scattering rose petals on my path. Behind her, Nate's tall, dark-haired niece and nephew, followed by redheaded Ari, with Cass's blonde daughter, Rebecca, looking just like Cass when I first knew her.

Nate, wearing a yarmulka and tallis around the neck of his tuxedo, waits for me. The music changes abruptly to the "Wedding March." My cue. *Please, God, let Daddy be here at my side; he won't want to miss this. And little baby Michael, the son I didn't have, may he forgive me and be here too.*

My eyes search for Lewis and Zada as I walk down the aisle. My cousins said they'd watch for their car and get Lewis into a wheelchair. True to their word, there they are, Lewis in a suit, no less, dress shirt, and tie. I give Zada a "thumbs-up" as I walk by.

"No trouble dressing him today," she whispers with a smile, "no trouble at all."

I approach the gazebo (also serving as a chuppah). Nate radiates a frank and open happiness. Ari steps forward to read aloud the poem that I wrote for my groom:

When first we met I did believe
You'd be a friend to me.
A caring friend, a special friend—no more could I conceive.
You waited, knowing wisely the losses I had grieved
And with a gentle whisper, upon my heart you breathed.
You healed my fears with laughter and truth that can't deceive
Patiently, and knowing how, your love with mine was weaved.

"Do you, Nathan, take this woman . . . ?" Nate winks at me when I take his arm and we face our guests as man and wife.

Celebration begins on the patio at the fountain. Allan (who discipled me when I first became a Christian) speaks out a blessing and leads the guests in prayer. "Marriage, the formation of a new family, is a root to the vines in Israel's fields . . ."

Nate's brother and sister-in-law, our best man and matron of honor, make a loving toast and precipitate an avalanche of good wishes from others. Dinner is served in the rose arbor, and conversation sparkles in the evening air.

God shines a brilliant sun upon our nuptials, in full defiance of the weather forecasters. Thank You, Lord! We eat, laugh, and dance . . . and dance . . . and laugh . . . and dance until we wave good-bye and evening falls, bringing in a shower of the promised rain, a fresh, clear cleansing of the night.

It is not good for the man to be alone. I will make a helper suitable for him (Genesis 2:18).

We drive off in a downpour toward the rolling green hills of Carmel Valley. For 10 blissful days, we stroll, holding hands, down country lanes, petting horses and dogs. We talk with local artists at a small village café where they serve hot, homemade rolls for breakfast. Five miles away, the picture-book town of Carmel-by-the-Sea delights us with elegant art, restaurants and beaches full of cypress trees and sculpted driftwood. One aimless drive along an early-spring road brings us unexpectedly to the town of Salinas. "Salinas! Where John Steinbeck lived, where he wrote *East of Eden*!" The old Victorian house that had been his home is now a small museum and library. We buy several of his books, eager to rediscover the power of Steinbeck's mighty gift.

It is a sweet, idyllic honeymoon, the perfect beginning.

Living together is easier for me, I'm sure, than for Nate. I'm more rigid, more exacting. Nate is gentle, easygoing. "Who else would put up with my kitty sleeping in our bed?"

He shrugs. "Part of the package, I guess. Just keep her on your side, okay?"

In our home, nothing is hidden. My notebooks and photo albums, which caused Ivan such torment when he saw them, are displayed on open shelves. Stephen's art hangs on our walls. Nate isn't threatened by any of that; he sees my past as part of me. In his acceptance, I am now at home, sheltered in the love of my husband and my God.

Our marriage has blessed us with two years of peace and tenderness. Embraced by Nate's affection and generosity, I discover that love is more, much more, than mere passion. It's what makes you feel secure and safe; it creates a world where you belong. A strange but lovely feeling floats down and covers me like a soft, invisible, gossamer veil.

Pastor Paul and Erica have moved to the east coast and I am looking for a church closer to home. I am drawn to an unpretentious, A-frame structure that houses a small congregation of Christ-centered people. The service is beautiful in its simplicity. I feel the presence of the Holy Spirit, the Spirit that brought me to my knees at the intolerable name of Jesus, the One that precipitated uncontrollable tears my first day in a church. In this unassuming little place, the Spirit lifts me outside of myself into the grandeur of humility, the glory of submission.

But in a new church, I lose the closeness I shared with people. We were family. We were free to be outrageous and funny, free to share weakness and fear, free to call for help. In my old church, every face represented a story, a life, an individual. Here, the faces are anonymous. Dear God, if this is where I'm to be, open these people to me. Lead me to someone with special gifts or experiences, someone interesting I can learn from.

I sit often next to a blonde, blue-eyed woman named Carol. She is plump and warm and gentle, and she talks a lot about her four kids and many grandchildren. That isn't my area of specialty, but I like her.

"I'm surprised the Spirit led me to this missions-oriented church," I tell her, "because frankly, I'm not missions-oriented."

"Oh? Why's that?"

"I'm Jewish. Jews live and let live. We don't have missionaries and I'm not comfortable intruding on other cultures. Except . . ."

She looks interested. "Except what?"

"Ever hear of a book called *Peace Child* by Don Richardson? It takes place in Dutch New Guinea among Stone Age cannibals. They're headhunters who use their victims' skulls as pillows. It's an exciting adventure and beautifully written, sometimes poetic, and it reveals a different kind of humanity."

"Oh?" Carol encourages me to continue.

"Yes. The story is told from the natives' point of view. You get into their homes and families and intrigues and trials; you see how they experience the arrival of the missionary and his wife into their jungles—" I break off, wondering if I'm boring her, but Carol is listening intently. I continue. "The missionary's wife is a nurse. She works alone, even performing surgeries in these very primitive conditions, and helps cure their diseases. Her husband works with the cannibals to transform their social values from treachery and violence to caring for one another.

"Well, I don't want to ramble on, but read it—and his other book, *Lords of the Earth*. For me they were eye-openers. I hadn't understood before how missionaries can change lives for the better without destroying cultures."

Carol smiles. "My husband will be glad you liked the books," she says. "He wrote them."

"Your husband?" I shake my head, stunned. "What do you mean? What's your last name?"

"Richardson," she laughs. "And my husband is Don."

"I can't believe it! *You're* the nurse who pulled arrows out of warriors in the jungle?" I feel silly. It is *her* life I've been telling her about! This quiet woman dwelt with headhunting cannibals for almost 20 years. "How did you stand it, living in the jungle? No heat or running water or even chairs! Scorpions, vipers, jungle beasts—weren't you scared?"

"Actually, we loved it," Carol says. "Don and I both knew, all our lives, that's what we were destined to do. It felt natural being there. Productive and useful. Frankly, I miss it."

"You sure had guts."

"I don't know. Being a single mother takes guts too."

"I had no choice. I didn't sign up for it."

"And 20 years in the corporate world! As far as I'm concerned, *that's* scary."

"You're just saying that. Besides, you speak the tribal language and Indonesian!"

"So? You speak French and Spanish and German. No, I do mean it. God equips each of us differently, Barbara, and assigns us to different mission fields.

Headhunting cannibals are easier for me than corporate politics. Your field is just as dangerous. Your poisonous insects are hidden, but they sting, too, don't they?"

As we get to know them better, Don and Carol tell remarkable stories that aren't in Don's books. "When Don first got out of school preparing for the mission field," Carol recalls, "his burning desire was to go to Java, Indonesia. On that crowded island there were *60 million* souls to reach, and he longed to get to every one of them. But the Mission had other ideas. They sent him to a small, unknown Sawi tribe in the swamps of Dutch New Guinea. Was he disappointed? Maybe, just at first. But he gave himself completely to the work and to these people. Over the next 15 years, he became a part of them, and together they saw the evolution of God's plan in that shadowy part of the world.

"When we returned to the States, Don wrote *Peace Child*. Imagine! It was translated into 26 languages and went out to 120 million people around the world in the *Readers Digest* magazine condensed book section. So Don reached twice the 60 million he'd originally hoped to reach. And if that weren't enough to show that God answers prayer, all three of our sons grew up to become missionaries. One is serving in—you guessed it—Indonesia!

"Remember that, Barbara. When you think your prayers are being ignored, God may be in the process of answering them in ways richer than you ever thought to ask."

Wow. I'd prayed to meet someone interesting, someone I could learn from. Thank You, Lord! And Carol is right. I had prayed to bring my life closer to home; that forced me out of the firm in downtown Los Angeles and brought me, as communications director, to a company three miles from home. Then Nate, who lives in my town, came into my life and, lastly, I am planted in a local church. My work, my love and my church are all within my own community. The pieces are creating a whole.

How we celebrate when Ariel graduates from the university! Nate and I, together with Mom, my uncle and cousins, Cass and Rebecca, gathered in San Luis Obispo to mark the milestone with laughter and great hopes.

Now Ari is seeking a job to launch his career. It's a bad time. The economy has hit bottom and competition is fierce. A lot of the graduates are not finding jobs. He interviews for more than eight hours at a first-rate, high-tech company, and they pass him on from one manager to another. There are many strong candidates for this position, and Ari wants it badly. Days later, the call comes: the job is his. But he may have to give up a dream to get it.

Ari has always wanted to do missions work. He couldn't while in school; he had to have a job. But he looked forward eagerly to it the summer after graduation, and he is all set to go. "Unfortunately, the company wants me right away. I'll lose this job if they have to wait three months."

"You might," Nate agrees. "How important is the missions work?"

"Very important. I really believe the Lord wants me to do it."

"Then do it. You may never get the chance again, and you'll always regret it."

"What if I lose the job? It's a tough market out there."

"Then you'll lose it. And you'll keep looking for another. Worst case, you'll pump gas for a year until you find the right thing."

"Pray about it," I advise. "If it really is God's will, He won't let you down."

Ari prays, then calls George, his boss-to-be, and explains he has plans for the summer.

"What kind of plans?" George knows graduates often want to spend the summer at the beach.

Ari hesitates to say, knowing a lot of people are turned off by Christianity and missions. "I volunteered with IV, an organization at Cal Poly, to help build a school and reservoir in Mexico."

"IV? You mean Inter-Varsity? Is this a missions project?"

"Yes! You know about IV?"

"I'm a Christian too," says George. "Tell you what. If you're willing to compromise the amount of time you spend down there, I'll speak to the search committee. They won't understand the missions stuff, but they might be sympathetic to the community-aid aspect of it. Maybe I can get a month's delay on your start date."

"Praise the Lord!" Ari is so excited. "I report to a Christian! Can you beat that?"

I hug him. "You don't mind that it's just one month instead of three?"

"It seems to be the Lord's leading, Mom. I'm fine with it. I'm just grateful to be getting this job *and* still go to Mexico. You were right. God doesn't let us down."

December 1992. Lewis Clark lived his last eight years helpless, immobile, blind and voiceless, communicating, in a way known only to them, with a woman whose love for him is boundless. Now, Zada says, "He has gone home, eager to meet his Lord. At last he can embrace the daughter and granddaughters who'd gone ahead and are waiting." Her eyes twinkle and she shakes a fist. "And he better be waiting with open arms for *me* when the time comes, or I'll give him what for."

God gave these two people to me and used them to prepare a transformation of my heart for Him. Lewis changed the masculine paradigm for me. Zada, the Proverbs 31 woman, is my inspiration for the feminine spirit whose grief cannot touch the power of her faith or tarnish her ebullience. In their home, love created a sanctuary of healing, a marriage of life-giving strength. As for them and their household, they are surely the beloved ones of God.

Lewis's children and grandchildren orchestrate the funeral. They make the music, sing the songs, and pray the benedictions. The program lists each one by name: 5 children, their spouses, 28 living grandchildren and . . . "Lewis's sweetheart, Zada."

Nate's office is losing money. If we close it down and let the staff go, Nate can work from home on the more lucrative consulting and keep what he earns, instead of paying all the rent, salaries and equipment. We'd be able to recover. But Nate hesitates. "It's not so simple," he wipes his forehead. "My staff has been with me for more than 10 years; they need their jobs. And I have a tenant subleasing. I can't just walk away."

Torn between our own financial needs and the needs of others, I ask Nate, "Pray with me about it. Let God be the CEO and show us what to do." Nate is skeptical. He is not used to turning over control.

We don't have a cloud by day and a pillar of fire by night, but God is clearly leading. Within just a few months, one employee leaves for a new job. Another quits because her husband is retiring. The third becomes ill and cannot work anymore. And the tenant announces, apologetically, that he found an office better suited to his needs. He is moving out.

Nate throws up his hands. "Seems like we've run out of reasons to stay."

Nate's niece, Cameron, is visiting tonight with her new boyfriend. Nate winks at me, and I nod; they look good together. Suddenly, Nate folds over with pain.

"What is it, honey?" I rush to him.

"Don't know. It hurts so much I can't breathe." Nate isn't one who admits to pain or illness. He figures if he ignores it long enough it will go away. He's not ignoring this, so I know it is bad. With Cameron and her friend to help, I rush Nate to the hospital. They determine it's his gallbladder, and schedule surgery to remove it.

I call the church to get this on the prayer chain. Our pastor comes quickly to the hospital and prays at Nate's bedside. Nate isn't used to people praying over him, but he accepts it graciously.

"We checked your blood type," Pastor tells him. "I've got the same, so if you need any transfusions, call me." He pats a beeper on his belt. "Any time, day or night, you hear?"

"Hey, thanks." Nate's voice is weak, but he reaches his hand to Pastor. "Thanks. I appreciate that."

A couple from my prayer group arrives. "How is Nate doing?" They lay hands on him and pray. Nate shoots a helpless glance at me. "Guess it can't hurt, huh? Like chicken soup?"

I put a cool towel on his forehead. "Better. They're praying to the One who invented chicken soup."

"It's nice of you guys to come, especially so late," he tells them. "Thanks."

"Oh, we're not leaving. We'll pray with Barbara through the surgery and we'll stay until we know you're all right."

"Hey, Nate!" Ari and his girlfriend bounce into the room carrying the cool fresh air of outdoors with them. "What's this about you getting cut up tonight?"

Nate smiles, but it's an effort to talk. I answer for him. "Yes, doctor says Nate is going to be down for a few weeks."

Ari puts a hand on his arm. "We'll be here with Mom through the surgery. Would you like us to pray for you?"

Hurting as he is, Nate can't suppress a sardonic chuckle. "Are you sure you can't bring chicken soup instead?"

An attendant comes to wheel Nate out. I hold his hand, following as far down the corridor as they allow, and blow a kiss as they push his stretcher through the double doors to the operating room. "We'll be here when you wake up, honey," I call after him. "We'll be—"

"I know, I know . . ." he closes weary eyes, " . . . praying."

We remain in the waiting room until 3:00 in the morning, when the surgery is over and we know Nate will be fine. Later that same morning, Nate is out of bed, trying to stand and walk. I beg him to lie down. "Rest, please, darling, can't you rest just for a day?"

"I'm fine. It hurts, but I'm fine." He falls back on his pillow. "You look tired, sweetheart. You been here all night? Go home. Get some sleep."

I lay my head on his chest, careful to stay clear of his sliced abdomen. "I'll be back this afternoon."

In the stillness of our empty house, I catch my breath. If anything had happened to Nate, my life would be a colorless void. I shudder, sinking to my knees. Thank You, Jesus, that he's okay. Thank You, thank You, thank You.

Nate is healing faster than anyone could have imagined. The doctor shakes his head. "Never seen anything like it, more power to him."

Um-hmm. Prayer power. And I do wish more of it for him.

Nate's dad is adjusting well to the retirement home. He's particularly close to a woman there who is "coincidentally" a born-again Christian. She talks to Sol about God, but he says it's nonsense. "Isn't it odd," I observe to Nate, "three generations of Jewish men attached to Christian women. You married one, your nephew is engaged to another, and your dad's best friend is born-again. Is there a message here?"

"I guess it just means we're broad-minded. Ha ha!"

Sol and I are in a seafood restaurant. His hearing is pretty bad, so talking is difficult. I write notes but he gets impatient reading them, so I end up shouting. My father-in-law enjoys our discussions about God and creation, but he likes to goad me. "An intelligent girl like you, can you really believe such stuff?"

"Does it matter whether we believe it or not, if it's true?"

"Bah."

"Okay, Sol, if there's no God, you tell me how the world was created. Maybe a bunch of haphazard molecules bashed around in just the right way and made it all come together?" He shrugs, noncommittal. "You don't think it requires supreme intelligence to conceive of and make animals and flowers and the extraordinary complexity of human anatomy and the ecosystem of the forest? Well, you need a lot more faith than *I* have to buy that!" I have to talk loudly so he can hear. All around the restaurant, heads turn to stare at us.

Sol brings his hands, palm down, onto the table, "There are some things we just don't know. When the time comes, we'll find out."

"You're nearing the end of your days on earth, Sol. Don't you want to prepare for the journey before you? Don't you wonder who God is and what He wants from you?"

"Sure, I wonder," Sol agrees in his slow, raspy voice, "just haven't met anyone who can tell me. And that, my lovable dear, includes you."

"You're right, Sol, I can't tell you. But here's a book that can." I hold up my Bible.

"Bah!" He changes the subject. "Darling girl, would you possibly have time to drive me to the doctor tomorrow? I have an appointment at 2:30."

"No problem, my Bible study doesn't start until 7:00."

"Bible study? You still go to Bible study? So when do you graduate already?"

I laugh. "*Your* graduation may be coming up before mine, Sol. Are you ready?"

"Darling," he kisses my cheek, "I appreciate your concern."

Sometimes trusting God takes faith that surpasses mine. It never, however, surpasses Ari's. Six years ago, my son had put himself in God's hand when he risked his job to do missions work. Now he's ready to give up an outstanding career for full-time ministry. "It'll be about two years before I leave, but that's the plan," he announces.

"It's wonderful to live your passion, but you'll be giving up your financial security. You know that, don't you?"

"My security is in God."

"Well, when it's time, you'll give fair notice, two to four weeks; but as long as you're here, give your all to the job, earn your promotions, and perform 'as unto the Lord.'"

"Mom . . ." He's exasperated. His mom always says the obvious. "I'm giving them my 'all,' but I've also given them notice that I'll be leaving."

"You what?! Two years in advance? Isn't that a bit foolish? Why, you've probably locked yourself out of any promotions that might come along. They'll be grooming someone else for your spot, and you'll be lucky if you can stay until you're ready to go."

He rolls his eyes in one of those here-we-go-again, she's-hung-up-on-security looks. "I did what I thought was right. I felt led to do it, and I did it. Okay?"

He's trusting in Jesus. God is his security. And I'm worrying. What kind of example is that?

> Trust in the LORD with all your heart and lean not on your own understanding; in all your ways acknowledge him and he will make your paths straight (Proverbs 3:5-6).

Six months later, Ari calls, all excited. "I have to talk to Nate. Two departments in my company are vying to give me a promotion. I have to choose which one I want."

A lesson in humility. Again.

Nate wishes his former wife were not so consumed with bitterness. "We should be friends. After all, we shared a home and a life for 27 years. Now when I see her at the Temple and say hello, she turns her back."

"I'll pray about it for you." His sceptical look says, *Yeah right, honey; you do that.* "Don't forget, I'm praying to the God who parted the Red Sea."

"Those were just practice warm-ups for melting Cynthia."

Ari meets Cynthia for the first time when they drive up for the wedding of Nate's niece. Cynthia is helping her elderly mother out of the car, but she has a dilemma: She can't leave her mother alone while she parks the car. At that moment, "coincidentally," Ari walks by.

"Excuse me, young man! Can you help get my mother up to the reception room?"

"Certainly. Be glad to." Ari takes the old lady's arm while Cynthia parks. She catches up with them in the hall. "Thank you, you're very kind. By the way, I'm Cynthia, the bride's aunt. And you?"

"I'm Ariel Ilaynia." She doesn't recognize the name. "The bride's cousin. Or step-cousin, I guess." Her foot pauses midair a few seconds before she recovers her balance and continues up.

During the festivities she keeps her distance from Nate. But after the dinner, when people are mingling and dancing, I approach and touch her arm. "Cameron and her new husband look very happy. Isn't it great to be so young, just starting out?" Startled, she returns my smile.

Nate reaches over and gives his ex-wife an impulsive hug. "And we're happy for them, aren't we, Cynthia?" Stunned into immobility, she doesn't push him away.

Can it be a crack in the ice?

We are brought together with Cynthia again, some months later, when the newly wed Cameron is diagnosed with throat cancer. Nate is badly shaken. "Call your pastor," he says. "Ask him to pray for her."

I try—successfully, I hope—to hide my surprise. "Cameron is on our prayer chain, darling; many people are praying for her recovery."

"But your pastor—ask *him* to pray." That evening, I'm astonished to hear him ask again, "Did you call? Did you talk to your pastor?"

Cynthia arrives at the hospital while Cameron is in surgery; she finds Nate and me in the visitors waiting lounge. Together, as the hours pass, we wait. We chat. We invite Cynthia to join us for lunch in the hospital cafeteria.

Cameron's recovery is not easy, but we keep her faithfully on the prayer list at church. By year's end, we are thrilled to learn she is well again. And there is healing of another kind too. Having spent all those hours with us at the hospital, Cynthia now feels comfortable enough to call when she feels a need to talk. She's lonely, I imagine.

The following year, their nephew, Cameron's brother, is accepted into his university honor society. After the ceremony, Cynthia joins us when the family celebrates at a nearby restaurant.

Nate offers to take Cynthia home because she lives close to us. The drive provides an opportunity for the two of them to talk, like they used to, about people they love and are concerned about. "Mom is failing," Cynthia tells him. "She's deteriorated drastically these last weeks. I don't work anymore; I'm with her day and night." She can't keep back the tears. "It's heartbreaking to see her mind crumbling like dust." Cynthia has dark circles under her eyes now. Her skin has a sickly pallor and hangs loosely. Obviously, the emotional strain, together with the physical effort, is taking a toll on her. Overwhelmed by intensive caregiving, and struggling alone, she turns to the man who said he'd be her friend. He proves he is.

Her mother's suffering eventually ends. Cynthia invites us to the funeral and the reception afterward, at her home. We wash our hands with the pitcher of water at the front door and enter the house.

I lay my hand on Cynthia's arm. "I didn't know your mother, Cynthia, so I can't honestly grieve for her. But I know how I'd feel if *my* mother died. So I grieve for you."

She grasps me in a warm, impulsive hug. Heads turn toward us, startled. "Cynthia, this is a tough time for you. You might consider . . . there's a Bible study at your neighbor's house, she's a mutual friend of ours, and I'm there every week. They are a lovely group of women who know what hard times are. Would you care to join us?"

Cynthia shakes her head "Thanks, I appreciate the thought, but that isn't my sort of thing. I'm Jewish, you know."

"Of course. I just thought . . . my mom's Jewish, too, but she comes. She says she's found peace and strength in this circle. If you change your mind, don't hesitate to call."

Cynthia's bitterness yields to friendship. A year later, when Nate's dad is very ill, she offers her sympathy and assistance. "I've been through this; I can help you find the right facilities for his care."

The walls come tumbling down. As they did for the faithful in Jericho, they do for those who seek God's intervention today.

Sometimes you pray for something over and over, year after year, and you begin to wonder if God is paying any attention. For six long years I've been praying that He'd reveal my true life's work. Marketing is my bread and butter, but for sure it isn't my life's work. I want desperately to connect with that. Moses was 80 before he was called to lead the people out of Egypt. Corrie ten Boom was past 50 when her quiet life in the watchmaker's shop was shattered and she started sheltering Nazi-hunted Jews. She was close to 60 when she preached around the world. I'm getting on, too, Lord; what's it to be for me?

"God has gifted you as a communicator in the business world," a Christian friend tells me. "Maybe the corporate world is meant to be your mission field." Yes, for years it was, but it is time for something else. The restlessness, the disparity between what I must do and what I love to do gnaws at me.

Fritzi and Finnegan, cousins of Nate, are visiting from London to conduct workshops for psychotherapists, introducing their innovative approach to psychology and psychic transformation. They are staying with us, and I enjoy their dynamic, warm and super-energetic presence.

They get in late one night and Fritzi heats up a pot of tea. "I sense tension in you, frustration. Anything we can do to help?"

"Not really." The tea is soothing. "But I'd like to feel the kind of joy in my work that you and Finn do in yours. Your work and your passion are one and the same. I don't have that."

"What would you do if you didn't need to work?"

I mumble about working with abused children, leading study groups for college kids, helping at church.

"I don't hear conviction. C'mere." Fritzi pats the sofa opposite her chair. "Settle down. Take a deep breath and close your eyes. I'm going to ask a few questions." I feel myself relax. "Take a good look. Who is there inside you?"

"My guardian angels, Big Louie and Tinkerbell."

"Tell me about them."

"Big Louie is tough and street-smart. He protects me. Tinkerbell is small and delicate and beautiful, with angel dust all around her. She creates beautiful things. She's an artist."

"Does she protect you too?"

"No."

Fritzi leans forward and speaks softly. "Hold Big Louie and Tinkerbell in your hands." I stretch my hands out, palms up. "Hmmm, that's interesting, your hands are far apart. Are Big Lou and Tink talking to one another?"

"No, they turn their backs."

"Why?"

"They don't trust one another."

"Oh?"

"Tinkerbell says Big Louie will destroy her. Louie says Tinkerbell will destroy *me*, and he's not about to let her."

"Thank him for that. Now ask if they will turn around to face each another."

"They say no."

"Ask them, please, just for a moment."

I struggle for a long while to get these two, my survival and my creativity, to recognize one another. Hands folded across her chest, Tinkerbell steals a petulant look at Big Louie. He glances at her with a contemptuous sneer. "That's as far as they can go."

"Okay," Fritzi says, "you're doing fine. You poor thing, your wonderful resources are so fragmented; they are fighting within and tearing you apart. We want to see your survival skills and your creative abilities working together, strengthening and encouraging one another. Can you imagine that?" I squint, unsure. "Understand, Barbara. This is the secret to finding your life's work. This is your homework until we return and can work with you some more: try to get Big Lou and Tink talking. Will you do that?"

Please, God, show me how. Fritzi hit upon a deep truth, and it hurts.

January 14, 1994, 4:31 A.M. In the black of night, Nate and I are almost thrown out of bed by the jackhammer of a roaring California earthquake. The brutal, jarring thrusts go on and on. Will they never stop? Clutching one another in the jolting terror, the roar in our ears is punctuated by the sounds of breaking windows, crashing furniture, a city collapsing upon itself.

Then stillness. The utter silence of death in dying embers. It is completely dark, within and without. When we dare to loose our hold on one another, I reach for the lamp on the night table next to our bed. Can't find it. There's no lamp. No table. Just the emptiness of air.

"Don't get out of bed, the floor will be full of glass," Nate says. Feeling his way in the dark, Nate bumps into things that shouldn't be there, stumbles over huge pieces of furniture and is bruised by corners where floor space is supposed to be.

It takes a long time to find a flashlight. In the weak, narrow beam is a mountainous pile of rubble. Nate climbs over the rubble toward the stairs, attempting to reach his father in the guest room downstairs. Sol is staying with us this week because he's ill. "Don't move, Dad, don't try to get out of bed!" But Dad can't hear; he removes his hearing aid when he sleeps. It seems to take forever to get past the wreckage in the library to reach his room.

Something definitive has happened. We are surrounded by a city of death and injury, and our home has crumbled around us. There is dread in my heart, a knowing that part of my life has come to an end. I sit on the steps, rocking back and forth, and moan.

"It's okay, sweetheart, everything's fine. We aren't hurt. We can deal with the rest."

"It's not okay, it's not okay. People are dying. Animals are crushed. The city is crippled."

"Honey, we don't know that. I'm sure it's fine."

"I know. I know." Amidst the cold broken glass on the steps, I sit and rock, sit and rock, sit and rock.

Daylight reveals what is left of our broken, splintered home. There is no gas. No water. No electricity. No phones. In the kitchen, we work our way through six inches of broken glass embedded in hardened sauce and syrup on the floor to reach the battery-operated radio on the far side. What we hear confirms my worst fears. Freeways collapsed in the night. Apartment houses tumbled, crushing residents like ants. Shopping centers folded upon themselves. On college campuses, buildings disappeared into mounds of brick, stone and concrete. Our town looks like Beirut after the bombing.

With our water cut off, we haul buckets from the common-area swimming pool to flush toilets. We need supplies. We drive out in a major city on streets without traffic lights. You can only make right turns. Stores are shattered and empty and desperate; they can provide nothing.

Thank God, Mom is all right. She is shaken, but her house is whole. She says we should stay with her; she has gas, water and electricity. Mom is a trouper. She prepares breakfast and dinner for all of us every day and takes care of Nate's dad while we work to restore our house.

The pastor of my church phones every parishioner to see how each one is doing. He calls back those who are doing well and sends them out to help those who aren't. His teenage daughter comes to our house, rolls up her sleeves, and dives into the muck. Ari has been here every day, too, tackling the tough stuff, and we use all the daylight hours to clean the mess. We come out mostly unhurt, except for Ari. Rusted debris flew into his eye while he was cleaning our kitchen and he has to have it surgically removed. Twice.

Nate's brother and sister-in-law from New York are scheduled to visit this weekend. "Don't come," we tell them, "we can't host anyone now."

"Don't worry about it, we're coming to help."

Six of us, working for 11 days, finally restore order. Most everything is smashed, and cracks (some half an inch wide) make abstract patterns crisscrossing the walls, but we can function. Inspectors come to determine the extent of damage. "There are broken tiles in the bathroom," I point out, as the head inspector goes upstairs.

"Don't worry about the tiles, lady, the whole wall is coming down."

"Oh." I swallow. "Anything else?"

"Floors, ceilings, walls, and some broken pipe. That's about it."

We could, like most of our neighbors, move to a small apartment for a year or two while the townhouse is rebuilt, then move back, but it means disrupting our lives twice. Besides, ever since we married, Nate has wanted a house that belongs to both of us. "The townhouse is yours," he says, "and I know you love it.

Nothing less than an earthquake could shake you loose."

It's more than that, I confide to Deborah. "The townhouse was a special gift from God, a provision. Don't you think if we were to move it would seem unappreciative?"

"This house was perfect for a single woman and her son. Maybe the Lord intended you to have it for a certain time. Maybe—just maybe—now that you're married, it's no longer appropriate."

I prepare my heart to leave, and pray—hard—that God will bring us to the right house at the right time at the right price. It has to be beautiful and bright and cheery. And—oh, yes—affordable.

Our real estate broker, Roger, has shown me almost 40 houses now, some more interesting than others, but none that feels like home. Every time we go into a house, I scribble notes and make concentrated calculations. "Let's see, maybe supplies can go here—no, the copy machine won't fit."

"I found it," Roger says today. "You've got to see this house!"

The neighborhood, heavy with mature trees on hilly streets, is beautiful. In front of the two-story house, the lawn rises on a richly landscaped hill. Roger opens the front door and I catch my breath. From the entrance hall, I see a spacious living room, flooded with sunlight, surrounded by large picture windows that bring the lush outdoor greenery inside. New, near-white carpet. Fresh paint. Nothing to tear down and redo. Looking around at the open airy space, I'm filled with joy. If I could, I'd put my arms around this house and hug it. "This is it!" I say. "Call Nate!"

Roger laughs. "You're still in the entry hall. Don't you want to see the rest?" We wander through the tiled, sunlit kitchen and the family room. There are endless closets and shelves for office supplies. Oh, look, a magical garden off the brick patio with a full-size pool, and five airy bedrooms. Five? We were looking for four.

"We should never have come here, Roger. This is perfect, and I love it. But you promised not to show anything outside our price range."

Roger flips through the computer printout. "It is at the top of your range, but it's a bank foreclosure. Maybe we can get it within budget." I send a skeptical look his way. He looks around. "Something I don't understand. The house is in perfect condition. Impeccable. But it's been on the market close to a year and there have been no lookers. No one's been here!"

"Close to a year? That's when I started praying about finding the right house. I think He's had His finger on *this* one for *us*."

Roger snaps his fingers. "Bingo! I knew there was an explanation."

We submit an offer far below the listed price. Suddenly, after having sat unseen for almost 12 months, the house becomes a beehive of brokers and prospective buyers. Other offers come in, all much higher than ours, and the bank tries to force us off the deal. For 10 days, I hold my breath. Thank God, the other buyers don't qualify quickly enough. Good. We're still in. The bank has to accept our offer, and they counter. Back and forth for two, almost three weeks of hard negotiation, they come down a wee bit, we go up. There remains a huge gap. The bank demands a final "go" or "no go" offer. Hearts in our throats, we come up just a little higher than we planned. It's still a far cry from what they're asking. No answer for several days; we've lost it for sure. *Please, please, please* . . . then . . . it's a go!

"Whew!" Roger lets out a sigh. "I was afraid they wouldn't accept such a low bid. Maybe, since it's the end of the year, they have to get it off their books."

"And maybe . . .?"

"Okay, okay! Maybe the Lord had His hand on it for *you*."

The earthquake wrought mass destruction in our valley. But for us, from the tragic destruction came unexpected blessings: first the beautiful new house, and then, at last, the answer to a years-long prayer asking that the Lord reveal the work He has for me.

The answer comes while cleaning up after the earthquake, picking up the contents of our closets and almost a thousand books thrown violently from our floor-to-ceiling bookshelves. Sorting through to reorganize this mountain of madness, I discover dozens of manuscripts—novels, literary studies, a screenplay coauthored with Karl—things I've written all my life. Collected, side by side, my writings cover a four-foot shelf. (And this does not include closets full of articles, brochures, and marketing materials produced in more than 20 years of work.) I sit cross-legged on the floor, dazed before this unpublished, unknown, nameless body of work.

This is it! God made me a writer; He would have me write. Recalling my mother's poems hidden in her attic, I realize I am to bring to light what my parents dreamed in dark shadows. Lorna's been saying it for years, over and over: I should be writing. Not the business stuff I write to help grow companies, she says, but the stuff of truth that grows people.

But *how*? How do I get it off the shelf to where it can do some good? *What* do I write? For whom? And where do I go with it? I know nothing about publishing. *Show me, Lord, show me.*

Susan calls (the same Susan who hiked the canyon with me and saw the goatherd with his flock). "If you need anything for your new house, stop by and see my friend Joan. She's having a huge garage sale. Check it out."

Joan's small house and garden are maintained with love and good taste. "Your house, like mine, is full of books. What do you do?"

"I teach and coach writers. When I see talent, I try to connect them with agents and help them through the publishing process."

My heart stops. *What led me to cross her path at just this time?* "Really! How can *I* get to work with you?"

"You'd have to enroll in a course I teach. After that, when I've seen your work, we'll see."

Joan's course is a fountain of information about publishing and an inspiration to write again. When her six-week course ends, I dread being without her. Her writers' workshops are limited to five in a group, and the waiting list is long. Could be a couple of years.

Ten days later, my telephone rings. "There's an unexpected opening in my Thursday workshop. It's a good group of strong writers. Would you like to join?"

"Would I! But what about people on your waiting list?"

"I like your work. I'd like to have *you* in there. But if you come, you make a commitment to be there every week and to bring work. Doesn't matter whether it's an article, story, novel, poem, screenplay—just bring something. We read one another's work and provide a running critique."

Yes! Yes! Oh, thank You, Lord—an open door! And now the pressure is on to produce pages. One can't come empty-handed on Thursday. Over and over I ask, *What am I to write, Lord, for whom and why?*

Nate's nephew asks, "How does someone like *you* become a Christian?" I hear this question all the time. I hear it from Christians who wonder how it happened to a Jew, and from people who ask how it can happen to a thinking person. So many ask, and I've never told. I pull up a fresh page on the computer screen and center a title:

Twelve Stones: The Journey of a Jew to Jesus

Or maybe . . .

Twelve Stones: An Altar of Remembrance

No, let's make it:

Twelve Stones: Notes on a Miraculous Journey

The earthquake opened a way for me to write this book and tell you what God did with a strong-willed child who drew from her own strength, unwilling to give up control. To tell how, with His exquisite sense of irony, He brought me, in my fortieth year, to something truly different: He brought me to helplessness. God says:

My power is made perfect in your weakness (2 Corinthians 12:9).

My life proves the truth of that verse. My strength, the strength of which I was so proud, was, in fact, my ultimate weakness, because it kept me from calling out, "Help me, Lord!" It kept me from His mighty power. Not until I was in over my head, when I knew I had exhausted all my resources, did He step in to take over. I was at the bottom of a hellish pit, and He made of it the highest, most glorious point of my journey, the place where He could touch me with new life.

God can use anyone and anything to bring us to Him. In my life, He used a Jewish father, Catholic playmates, a shamanic medicine woman, gurus of Eastern religions, and a herd of goats as stepping-stones to His love and salvation. I am grateful and humbled and awed. But I forget. Each time new trials come, I forget, and I am afraid. I remember only that generations of Israelites lived in slavery under the whip of Pharaoh and in Hitler's death camps, and anxiety bubbles up to possess me again.

God knows my nature; He knows yours too. He knows our memory of His love is short. That's why He had a member from each of the 12 tribes of Israel carry a stone to build an altar of remembrance. They were to remember the miracles the Lord had done for them, how He parted the Red Sea and held back the Jordan River. Each time they looked upon that altar, they were to remember.

This book is my altar of 12 stones for the God who protects His people time and time again. He does no less for me. I write to remember the miracles that remind me that He works in ways contrary to the ways of the world. I write to remember, and to honor what God has done.

About the Author

A Fulbright scholar with an M.A. in Comparative Literature from the University of Wisconsin, Barbara lived in Paris for several years as a translator and assistant editor of the *Paris Review* before returning to the USA to teach French and French literature at the University of California-Los Angeles (UCLA).

Subsequently, as a writer and researcher for her "hero," undersea explorer Jacques Cousteau, Barbara worked in Los Angeles, California, and in Monaco, France, providing research to guide the undersea expeditions seen on his television series, and "ghost-writing" two of Cousteau's books.

Her other publications include a short story in *The Paris Magazine*, literary reviews for *The French Review* and *FM Magazine*, reviews of books and dance concerts for the *Los Angeles Times*, and feature articles for the *Los Angeles Times* and other Western newspapers.

Barbara then developed a career of 20-plus years in marketing. Beginning at a large Los Angeles advertising agency as a copywriter on national accounts, she was later recruited by multinational companies as a corporate communications executive to develop and write national and international advertising/public relations programs.

Barbara left the corporate world to do what she loves best: writing. She now lives near her children and grandchildren with her husband and pets on a forested mountain in the Pacific Northwest, where she continues writing books to come.

"I write," she says, "that we may share facets of living, severe and sweet. That is the hope of the written word, that in the sharing, we are bound to love."

Acknowledgments

God always has a "Plan A" for our lives, a great plan for our welfare, not for our destruction. In our own strength, however, we make poor decisions that take Plan A off track and that threaten calamity. But God can take our off-track lives and create something beautiful from them. It's Plan B, but it's still beautiful. He did that for me, and He can do that for you, too.

My love and gratitude to the following people without whom this story could not be told:

Most of all, my incomparable son, who gave me a reason, when I needed it most, to live out the rest of the story.

My courageous and caring mom, who put her own feelings aside, urging me not to compromise on writing the truth, even when it was not pretty.

My brilliant and fabulous dad (now deceased), who, with his insatiable curiosity and wonderment at life, lovingly taught me to "shoot for the moon."

My wonderful husband, whose generous and faithful love gave me a new lease on life.

Joan Jones, a mentor whose encouragement made this book possible, and who made such a difference in the lives of writers before cancer took her in her prime.

Brian Williams, Megan Garman, Ann Johnston and Anita Manthe for their critique, encouragement and love throughout the process.

Marian Fagan, whose astute comments and observations helped smooth a rough first draft.

Pastor Bob and his wife, Gloria, for their spiritual counsel and friendship over the years that nourished and strengthened my spiritual life. They believed in my book and gave me the encouragement I needed to pursue writing it.

Ahna Philips and John Eames, my insightful, supportive agents who believed the book was worthy and whose efforts made it happen.

Alex Field, my publisher, because he had faith and he made this book come to life.

Tamara Rice, for her loving spirit, enthusiastic encouragement and efforts to help me realize my dream.

Also Available
from Regal Books

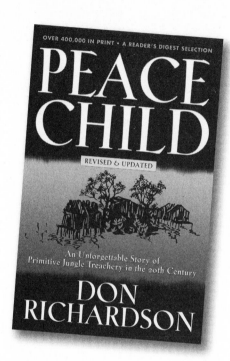
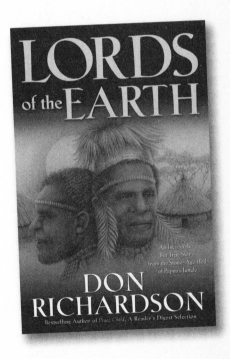